THE RECORD COLLECTOR'S HANDBOOK

THE
RECORD COLLECTOR'S HANDBOOK

Alan Leibowitz

Publishers   EVEREST HOUSE   New York

Library of Congress Cataloging in Publication Data

Leibowitz, Alan.
   The record collector's handbook.

   1. Music, Popular (Songs, etc.) —Discography. 2. Sound recordings—Collectors and collecting. 3. Sound recordings—Prices. I. Title.
ML156.4.P6L42   016.7899'12   78-72181
ISBN 0-89696-015-3

Copyright © 1980 by Alan Leibowitz
All Rights Reserved
Published simultaneously in Canada by
Beaverbrooks, Pickering, Ontario
Manufactured in the United States of America
Designed by Joyce Cameron Weston
First Edition   FG 980

This book is dedicated to the memory of Bob Roth

ACKNOWLEDGEMENTS

I would like to express my thanks to the dealers and collectors who patiently submitted to the often painstaking interview process. Without their expertise this book would not have been possible, and their opinions have been duly factored into the ratings.

They include: Norman Feinberg, Joel Bernstein (Rock and Roll); Richard C. Norton (Cast Recordings); Fred Stack (Personalities and Vocalists); Leon Leavitt, Jack Woker (Jazz).

I would also like to thank Richard Seidel and Steve Schwartz for providing me with essential research material, as well as Danny Riccio and all the people at Zoundz Records and Jack Woker at Cheapo Records for allowing me to conduct my research on their premises.

CONTENTS

PREFACE	9
INTRODUCTION	13
ABOUT THE LISTINGS	35

PART I: ROCK AND ROLL

1. Collecting Rock and Roll Records	43
2. The Rock and Roll Recordings	45
3. Anthologies, Various Artists	78

PART II: SHOW BUSINESS

4. Collecting Cast Recordings	83
5. American Cast Recordings	85
6. English Cast Recordings	91
7. Collecting Movie Soundtracks	95
8. Movie Soundtrack Recordings	97
9. Personalities and Vocalists	104
10. Composers and Lyricists	120
11. Anthologies, Various Artists	123

PART III: JAZZ

12. Collecting Jazz Records	127
13. Jazz Recordings	130
14. Anthologies, Various Artists	180

PREFACE

SAY WHAT YOU WILL about the obsessive nature of the hardcore record collector; perhaps you've seen him at flea markets or yard sales sifting through other people's "junk" with the fervor of an archaeologist on a dig. At heart, he is not only a music lover but also an archivist of the first order. For unlike those who are satisfied with a few favorite albums or who rely on the radio or tapes to fulfill their musical needs, he is literally a *keeper* of records. Sometimes, in fact, his collection may number more records than he could possibly listen to and digest in a lifetime. The notion, however, of possessing a particular piece of music that is unique to or significant within one's special field of interest (jazz, rock, shows, etc.) provides another kind of satisfaction.

But a great many treasured recordings, you might point out, have been reissued and are currently available in new, attractive packaging and acoustically superior pressings. What, then, is the appeal of collecting original issues of such material? As in trying to define any passion, there is no easy answer. For we are now discussing extramusical considerations, or the record as art object. One could, however, make the following observations: that it is only human to want to own that which is acknowledged to be worth owning; and that the original issue, its cover art and liner notes resonant with an historical appeal no reissue can match, represents the closest the collector can get to the actual recording experience.

THE
RECORD COLLECTOR'S
HANDBOOK

INTRODUCTION

THE PURPOSE OF THIS BOOK is to shed a bit of light on a large body of information that is common knowledge in the most rarefied circles but remains largely unknown to the uninitiated—to identify, as a point of interest, which records are most coveted by collectors and dealers. The records listed herein are the long-playing, 33⅓ rpm variety (both 10″ and 12″), an accepted musical standard since the LP's introduction in 1948. But to gain some perspective on the record industry and the emergence of the LP, and to at least acknowledge a few rarities from the past, a bit of history is in order.

Incunabula

In the beginning was the cylinder. And a man named Gianni Bettini had acquired an Edison phonograph in 1888, ten years after Edison was granted a patent on his "favorite invention" and three years before the phonograph was made available to the public at large as a medium of home entertainment.

Edison and his competitors had originally envisioned the phonograph as a business implement, specifically as an office dictating machine. Territorial agencies were set up to lease the machines, but with the exception of the Columbia Phonograph Company, whose territory included the government offices of the District of Columbia, they all lost money. Mechanical kinks and outright hostility from stenographers faced with the prospect of losing their jobs conspired to suppress the demand for phonographs.

In the west, a man named Louis Glass, convinced that his franchise, the Pacific Phonograph Company, would certainly go under, developed the coin-in-the-slot phonograph and installed one such machine in the Palais Royal Saloon in San Francisco. By 1890, hundreds of these prototypical jukeboxes were placed in drugstores, ice-cream parlors, amusement parks, and other public places. While few could afford to own a phonograph in 1891, when they first went on sale to the public for $150, the demand for recorded entertainment was by now a proven commodity.

One who could afford to own a phonograph is the aforementioned Bettini—son of a wealthy Italian landowner, married to an American socialite, opera lover, and inveterate tinkerer. His principal objection to the current state of the art was the poor quality of sound reproduction, which required the listener to don cumbersome, stethoscopic ear tubes in order to raise the volume to an adequate hearing level. The alternative was the metal horn, but this device was acoustically inferior to the ear tubes. So Bettini set out to improve upon Edison's phonograph.

In the end, he invented a so-called "spider" stylus that attached itself to the diaphragm (where sound waves are produced) at various points rather than at just one. He reasoned that if more sound vibrations are gathered, more force is brought to bear on the recording stylus, which would, in turn, cut deeper into the blank wax cylinder. When played back, Bettini had achieved the desired effects: greater clarity of timbre and increased volume. He patented his new stylus in 1889 and dubbed his modified Edison machine the Micro-Phonograph.

More important, though, than his acoustic improvements were Bettini's contributions to the recorded repertoire. At last, here was a man interested in preserving for posterity the great voices of the age. But in this regard, Signor Bettini stood apart. For throughout the 1890s, the first decade of commercial recording, both Edison's National Phonograph Company and Columbia, the industry's first giant, catered to a nondiscriminating public seemingly entranced by any sounds emanating from the new "talking machine." There were favorites, to be sure—John Philip Sousa, whistling virtuoso John Y. Atlee, and actor Russell Hunting, with his popular "Casey" stories, were three early recording stars—but more often than not, cylinders were issued as Sentimental, Negro, Comic, Irish, etc. with the performers remaining anonymous.

The record companies should not be overly chastised, however, for ignoring the serious music of the day. Once the price of phonographs reached an affordable level (the Edison Standard Phonograph, the industry's most popular model, sold for twenty dollars in 1897), the demand for cylinders increased dramatically, and new ideas about *what* to record were sacrificed in order to maintain the prosperous status quo. There was also the problem of duplicating cylinders, a laborious procedure often requiring performers to repeat their renditions over and over before as many strategically placed recording horns as could accommodate the sound (usually three for singers, ten for brass bands). Needless to say, it would have been difficult, even if the record companies were so inclined, to convince financially secure, often temperamental artists to participate in such a barbaric process.

Bettini traveled in such circles. In 1892 he went into the business of manufacturing his spider stylus, which could be easily adapted to existing machines, and his offices in the Judge Building at 110 Fifth Avenue became a meeting place for artists and cognoscenti of the music and theater worlds. As more and more recordings of such legendary figures as Yvette Guilbert, Nellie Melba, Sigrid Arnoldson, Sarah Bernhardt and Mark Twain were made, Bettini's private collection of celebrity cylinders grew to enviable proportions.

Sometime in the mid-1890s, when a method of duplication became feasible, Bettini began offering cylinders for sale at prices ranging from two dollars to six dollars per cylinder (at a time when the going rate was fifty cents). Ever the aesthete, he duplicated cylinders to order only, with no intention of expanding his mail-order business beyond that which fortune dictated. According to Roland Gelatt in *The Fabulous Phonograph:* "Considering Bettini's prices and the small scale on which he operated, it is doubtful whether he sold more than a few hundred copies of any one recording. In no other way can the fact be explained that today Bettini cylinders are even rarer than Gutenberg Bibles or Shakespeare quartos." Only a small number of Bettini cylinders are known to exist, including a group of fifteen by lesser-known singers discovered in Mexico City in 1945 and twenty-two cylinders by more established artists which turned up in a barn near Syracuse, New York in 1952.

But what of Bettini himself and his magnificent collection of "originals"? After selling his patents to Edison, he moved to Paris in 1902 and continued to make recordings until 1908 when the flat disc was rapidly rendering the cylinder obsolete. Eventually, he abandoned the phonograph business entirely, serving as a war correspondent in 1914 and later as an emissary of the Italian government, in whose employ he returned to the United States where he died in 1938. His personal collection was stored in a French warehouse and destroyed during World War I.

As dashing a figure as he was, surrounded by talented personalities and privy to the birth of an exciting industry, for the purposes of this book Bettini interests us as the first record collector of note and as a dealer in ultradesirable merchandise. For the principle of a small company, usually short-lived, issuing records by artists of generally acknowledged interest within a particular genre persists as a basis for determining some of the most valuable LPs extant.

The Disc

The first *gramophone* records appeared on the market in 1894. They were single-sided, seven-inch discs pressed in hard rubber with a playing time of approximately two minutes. The man behind the gramophone was Emile Berliner, a self-educated German immigrant who, although not the first to conceive of the idea of recording onto disc (Edison had considered this approach early on but found that the sound deteriorated badly as the stylus neared the center of the disc), he was the first to achieve its practical application.

As mentioned earlier, the method of duplicating cylinders was far from satisfactory. It involved attaching, by means of a metal rod, the recording stylus of a so-called "slave" machine

INTRODUCTION

to the playback stylus of another machine; as the latter reproduced the sounds of the master cylinder, those vibrations were passed through the metal rod and inscribed on a wax blank. However, since there was a limited number of master cylinders and each could only withstand about twenty-five playings, it was impossible to satisfy the demand for a particularly fast-selling cylinder. By contrast, an almost limitless supply of duplicates could be made from one master disc by fashioning a reverse, or negative matrix of the original and then stamping positive discs in some suitable material. This also meant that recording artists no longer had to repeat their performances ad nauseam to ensure the desired supply, surely an attractive selling point to those who had heretofore resisted the industry's appeal.

But the early gramophones posed little threat to the established phonograph business. For one thing, the rubber discs, though infinitely sturdier than the delicate wax cylinders, tended to warp. Another drawback was the fact that the gramophone's turntable was rotated manually, as opposed to the phonograph's, which was driven by a spring motor. The desired velocity was seventy revolutions per minute, but if cranked at more or less than the prescribed speed, the pitch would waver accordingly.[1]

Both of these problems were eventually solved by a man named Eldridge Johnson. Actually, Berliner himself switched from rubber to a shellac composition in 1897, but in 1899 it was Johnson who developed a method of recording onto wax, which was acoustically superior, and a means of converting the original into a reverse metal stamper. Originally the operator of a small machine shop in Camden, New Jersey where as a sideline he built experimental models for inventors, Johnson also developed an inexpensive spring motor whose handle would unwind itself as the machine played. Thus, by 1899 the Improved Gramophone, as it was called, could compete with the phonograph for the public's attention.

[1] For many years the speed of gramophone records fluctuated between 70 and 82 rpm. It became stabilized at 78 rpm in 1925 with the introduction of electronically powered turntables.

These developments, of course, hardly went unnoticed by those in the business of selling phonographs, and to protect their interests they went to court. Seizing upon an apparent technical overlap in Berliner's original patent specifications, Columbia obtained a temporary restraining order prohibiting the sale of gramophones. Two months later, the preliminary injunction was set aside to permit further investigation of the matter, and business was allowed to continue as usual. The ensuing legal maneuvers, however, provided drastic changes within the industry.

To better understand what followed, it is necessary to examine Berliner's operation. His gramophone business was divided into three separate, interdependent enterprises: the manufacturing and assembling of machines was tended to by Johnson in Camden; the critical procedure of converting an original master disc into a negative matrix stamper was supervised personally by Berliner at the home office in Washington, DC (the stamper was then sent to a company in New Jersey where the discs were pressed); and the advertising and selling of the products was entrusted to a man named Frank Seaman, who operated out of New York City. And it was Seaman's National Gramophone Company that Columbia actually named in the suit, figuring that without a sales agency, Berliner's manufacturing facilities would come to a halt.

A shrewd businessman long dissatisfied with his financial arrangement with Berliner, Seaman saw in the legal skirmishes an opportunity to strike out on his own. In March of 1899 he surreptitiously erected his own plant to manufacture a thinly disguised copy of the Improved Gramophone, which he called the Zonophone. In October of 1899 the orders from Seaman suddenly stopped. Johnson, with a factory full of unplaced merchandise, had no choice but also to break with Berliner. He formed the Consolidated Talking Machine Company, and with the help of an ambitious advertising campaign, eventually translated his huge inventory into cash.

Further complications abounded. Since Columbia's suit, although directed at Seaman, involved the validity of Berliner's patents, and since Seaman was no longer beholden to Berliner for his merchandise, there was no reason for Seaman to contest the suit. He admitted that the gramophone patents were, indeed, an infringement on the phonograph patents and asked the court to issue an injunction against the Berliner Gramophone Company forbidding the sale of gramophone merchandise. In June of 1900 the court ruled in Seaman's favor. Thus, Frank Seaman not only deserted Berliner to manufacture a competing instrument, he also made it legally impossible for the inventor of the gramophone to sell his own merchandise.

Seaman's turncoat behavior may be explained by a secret alliance he had formed with Columbia, which was looking for a way to enter the disc market and viewed an association with Seaman as at least a foot in the door. With such support, Seaman then brought suit against Eldridge Johnson's growing Consolidated company, charging that, in reality, it was a subsidiary of the Berliner Gramophone Company. But in March of 1901 the court ruled in favor of Johnson, except in one curious particular: he could no longer use the word *gramophone* in marketing his product. Although even that decision was overturned in the Court of Appeals some two months later, Johnson did not press the advantage. Now unencumbered by legal constraints, he chose to start afresh, and he named his gramophone the Victor Talking Machine. From that point on, the word *gramophone* was dropped from the American vocabulary (though retained in England), and the word *phonograph* served to describe all types of talking machines.

As for Berliner, his lawyers were finally able to overturn Seaman's injunction, thereby ending a year of enforced idleness. But his tripartite empire had been destroyed. He could once again call his patent his own, but by now the unquestioned leader in disc merchandise was Johnson. Ironically, Johnson did not aspire to the position of industrial tycoon. He had broken with Berliner not out of hostility or ambition, but as an act of self-preservation. In fact, by October 1901, Johnson was willing to sell his entire business to Berliner and retire on the proceeds, but Berliner could not raise the capital to buy him out. Further negotiations resulted in the formation of a new corporation, with Berliner receiving 40 percent of the common stock and Johnson the remainder. For his share in the company, Berliner contributed the original gramophone patents; for his share Johnson contributed a flourishing, well-organized business.

Unable to shut down Victor's operations by legal means, Columbia dissolved its agreement with Seaman's Zonophone Company. Noting Victor's rising sales and the concurrent decline of cylinders in the public's esteem, Columbia was desparate to manufacture a competing disc machine. But there was still the patent problem.

Columbia's deliverance came from an unexpected source. Berliner had originally chosen rubber, then shellac, over wax recordings, fearing that the use of wax encroached upon the cylinder's domain. Johnson, with his Improved Records, realized that wax was the best possible material on which to record, but on the advice of his lawyers he decided not to apply for a patent on his own wax recording process for fear of similar legal reprisals. Meanwhile, Joseph W. Jones, a young clerk in Berliner's Washington laboratory in the early days of the gramophone, observed that wax was indeed the proper medium and blithely filed a patent claim for inscribing sounds on a blank wax disc. In 1901 the patent was granted, and Columbia bought it from Jones for twenty-five thousand dollars. Now each camp was armed with suitable patents on which infringement could be claimed. Rather than face long and costly litigation, Victor and Columbia decided to pool their patents, and by January of 1902 the Columbia Disc Graphophone appeared on the market, with seven-inch records selling for fifty cents and ten-inchers for a dollar. Controlling as they did every important patent relating to the manufacture of disc machines and records, Victor and Columbia established a supremacy in the American record industry which would last for more than half a century.

While the disc continued to challenge the cylinder both in and out of court in America, it made even more remarkable strides in Europe where the cylinder's roots were not so deep. True, the Pathé brothers opened the highly successful Salon du Phonographe in Paris, a sort of musical automat in which customers sat in luxurious surroundings, deposited a fifteen-centime token, and heard the latest cylinder recordings. And in Milan the Anglo-Italian Commerce Company recorded many of that city's leading opera stars, including a youthful Enrico Caruso. But by 1900 the disc had proven its preeminence throughout Europe, thanks largely to the enterprising William Barry Owen, who had been granted the exclusive right to sell gramophone merchandise abroad. Owen had observed Seaman's aggressive promotional tactics in America, and after forming the Gramophone Company in London in 1898, he subjected Great Britain to a similar advertising blitz. It was so successful that the importation of machines and records could not meet the demand, and a separate record pressing plant was built in Hanover, Germany. Soon another branch, Deutsche Grammophon, opened in Berlin, and similar projects were launched in Russia, Austria, Spain, and France.

Finally, by 1901 a method of molding cylinders for mass duplication was perfected, but the war had already been lost. While cylinder sales increased at a modest pace, the disc business boomed.

Boom, Ruin, and Recovery

With the introduction of the Victrola in 1906 the phonograph and record industry entered a period of great prosperity. Just as the onerous ear tubes were replaced by the metal horn for the sake of convenience, for the phonograph to be universally accepted as a fixture in the American parlor, the obtrusive horn had to be concealed. The Victrola, with its internal horn and record-storage space, was an immediate hit.

To the early enthusiasts, the new design was deemed inferior in tone to the open-horn instruments, and for that reason Victor continued to manufacture open-horn machines as late as 1925. But to a new, style-conscious public—many of whom had never owned a phonograph and had no basis for comparison—the Victrola, be it console or table model, became a desired piece of furniture and somewhat of a status symbol. *Victrola* became nearly synonymous with *phonograph,* and when Victor's competitors introduced their *ola* machines (Columbia's was called the Grafonola, Edison's the Amberola) Eldridge Johnson felt compelled to advertise his as the Victor Victrola.

Victor's superiority was even more evident in their roster of recording artists. Much like today's rock stars, the opera stars of the early twentieth century were idolized for their glamorous and flamboyant way of life. Though, inevitably, popular trifles with true mass appeal accounted for most of Victor's sales, Victor's policy of signing the leading lights of the Metropolitan Opera Company to exclusive, long-term contracts represented a virtual monopoly of important talent. Johnson was not interested simply in making money; his vigorous advertising campaigns tended to inflate both the artists' reputations and Victor's sagacity for having signed them.

Victor's greatest star and most effective salesman was Enrico Caruso. Before long-term contracts and royalty arrangements became commonplace, Caruso recorded for the Anglo-Italian Commerce Company in Milan, for Zonophone, and for the Red Label series inaugurated by the Gramophone Company in London. Actually, the idea of deluxe, high-priced records originated in St. Petersburg, where a local record merchant suggested recording members of the Russian Imperial Opera and affixing their records with red labels to distinguish them from ordinary fare. Based on the commercial success of their Russian venture, the Gramophone Company went to Milan in 1902 to record Caruso, who, at thirty, was on the threshold of international fame.

Johnson had worked out an exchange agreement with the Gramophone Company, and his first batch of imported Red Seals (as he preferred to call them) included seven of the ten songs recorded by Caruso. In January of 1904, just two months after his New York Metropolitan debut, Caruso signed his first contract with Victor. Ten new recordings followed and five more in 1905—all with piano accompaniment. In 1906 Caruso made his first records with orchestral backing, no mean feat considering the limited recording techniques of the time. An unqualified success, Caruso's 1906 recordings became a staple of the Victor catalog, and they serve as a demarcation line for collectors, who prize the earlier issues for their rarity.

Commercially, artistically, and technologically Columbia ran a distant second to Victor. Typical of the company's ill timing and shortsightedness was their Grand Opera series, launched in 1903. Although such luminaries as Edouard de Reszke, Marcella Sembrich, and Ernestine Schumann-Heink graced the Columbia catalog, the discs were inferior tonally to Victor's and met with little success. The series was soon discontinued, thereby relinquishing to Victor the entire celebrity field.[2] When the Red Seal records eventually caught the public's fancy, Columbia tried to reenter the celebrity market, but Victor had already signed all the important artists. Not until 1908 did Columbia offer any real competition, via affiliations with the European companies Fonotipia and Odean, but these imported discs featured artists who where not yet well known in America. The initial market for operatic recordings in America had been created by Caruso and perpetuated by Victor's astute advertising approach.

At the same time, Columbia was also in competition with Edison for the diminishing cylinder trade, and it was faring little better. In 1909 Columbia stopped producing cylinder machines and records but made a deal with the Indestructible Record Company to market cylinders with the Columbia label. In 1912 Columbia abandoned the cylinder business entirely.

As for Edison, he had always maintained the superiority of the cylinder over the disc as a means of reproducing sound, and he had developed a loyal clientele, especially in poorer, rural areas where the Edison name had almost magical connotations. But Victor's overwhelming success was irrefutable evidence of public preference, and in 1913 Edison introduced the Diamond Disc Phonograph. He continued to produce cylinders to the end (leaving the phonograph business in 1929), but more as an act of faith than as a profitable venture. How doubly ironic, then, that many consider the Diamond Disc the finest phonograph of the acoustic era and, given its creator, that it virtually sounded the final death knell for the cylinder.

Despite Victor's dominance, profits were plentiful for all

[2] Not unexpectedly, the thirty-two records issued by Columbia now command high prices among collectors.

three companies. From 1914 to 1916 many of the basic patents expired, and such newcomers as Brunswick, Sonora, Vocalion, and dozens of others entered the arena. The war in Europe further stimulated the economy. In London, Louis Sterling of English Columbia struck upon the idea of recording songs by cast members from such successful revues as *Business As Usual,* Irving Berlin's *Watch Your Step,* and *Cheep,* starring Beatrice Lillie. The records were fast sellers, especially among soldiers on leave, and so began the illustrious history of original cast recordings. America was in the throes of a national dance craze, and record companies kept in step by issuing an abundance of turkey trots, tangos, one-steps, and the like. In 1917 Victor released "Livery Stable Blues" by the Original Dixieland Jazz Band, and a new, indigenous art form began to be documented. Although its members were white, the ODJB played in an exuberant style derived from the Negro music of New Orleans. The group took New York and then London by storm, and "Livery Stable Blues" sold over a million records.

With such unprecedented sales, the executives of the phonograph industry paid little heed to the impact created by a new form of home entertainment: the radio. Perhaps they thought there was little cause for alarm, given the amateurish level of early broadcasting (for which the record companies were partially responsible since they forbade artists under contract to perform in the new medium). But within a year after station KDKA in Pittsburgh began broadcasting in 1919, stations popped up all over the United States and Canada, and nightly audiences increased from thousands to millions. Just as the idea of capturing sound to be reproduced at will seemed miraculous in the early days of the "talking machine," the notion of hearing performers "live" from long distance was novel and exciting. And, best of all, it was free! By 1924 radio had captivated the public, and phonograph sales were on the decline. Ample evidence could be found in warehouses and showrooms throughout the country, where unwanted phonographs and elaborate cabinets, the results of overproduction based on previous sales figures, remained unsold despite intensive advertising.[3]

[3] In 1924 Victor was the largest advertiser of any American corporation.

Capitulation came first in the form of combination radio-phonographs. The most popular was the Radiola produced by the Radio Corporation of America, which had gained virtual control of the radio industry by the mid-1920s through patent acquisitions. Now housed together, it became even more evident that the radio receiver, not the phonograph, was the superior sound reproducer. Clearly, it was only a matter of time before the electrical methods of radio would be used for recording purposes, thereby making all records then in circulation obsolete.

The advantages of recording by means of the new process developed by Western Electric were numerous. For one, the tonal spectrum was greatly extended. Bass frequencies previously unheard added body to the music; treble frequencies allowed sibilants to be heard distinctly for the first time. And the new records were louder, yet free of distortion. Recording techniques were also vastly improved. The recording horn was replaced by the microphone, which provided unlimited amplification of sound, and through proper microphone placement, great numbers of musicians could perform in spacious surroundings with uniform fidelity assured. For example, "Adeste Fideles," recorded at the Metropolitan Opera House in 1925, featured fifteen glee clubs and the entire audience, over 4000 voices. The record was dramatic proof of the power of the new process, and it was extremely popular with the buying public.

At first, however, the new records were introduced with no publicity whatsoever, the result of a secret agreement between Victor and Columbia to remain silent about such revolutionary developments until a backlog of electrically recorded material could be made available on a large scale. An improved phonograph suitable for playing the new discs would also have to be developed. The idea of planned obsolescence, instituted by Henry Ford with new models every year, had not gone unnoticed by those in charge of the phonograph industry, and the new records, shipped to dealers without warning, sounded unbearably raucous when played on the old-style machines.

Late in 1925, with much fanfare, the Orthophonic Victrola and the Columbia Viva-tonal Phonograph were unveiled. Subsequent sales did not reach the heights of preradio days, but consumer interest had been successfullly reactivated, and record factories were once again operating at capacity. The revitalization of the phonograph industry, however, would be short-lived, as the stock market crash in October, 1929 brought all retail business to a halt.

By now, in addition to live programming, one could hear most popular records on the radio. In such dire financial times, records became eminently dispensable. Record sales in the United States dropped from 104 million in 1927 to 6 million in 1932, and phonograph production declined from close to a million to a mere forty thousand. Those companies that did not go completely under were either sold for a pittance or forced to merge with more promising, related industries.

Actually, the merger of RCA and Victor[4] (in January, 1929) took place well before the crash, but eventually the plant in Camden was given over almost exclusively to the production of radios, and recording activity was drastically reduced. Columbia continued on its checkered path,[5] first being sold to the Grigsby-Grunow Company, manufacturers of Majestic radios and refrigerators, and then when that company went bankrupt, to the American Record Company, specialists in bargain discs for the chain store trade, for seventy thousand dollars. Brunswick became a subsidiary of Warner Bros., pioneers in the talking picture field (*The Jazz Singer,* 1927), which saw the record affiliate as a potential, promotional tool for its musical stars. And in Europe the two majors, English Columbia and HMV, formed Electric & Musical Industries (E.M.I.) in order to survive.

It must be noted that the demand for serious music persisted among the affluent, and specialty shops in urban centers continued to furnish imported records from Europe, where radio had not yet made such massive inroads. But, in general, records

---

[4] Eldridge Johnson, mechanic turned businessman, had sold his controlling stock in Victor to a group of New York bankers in 1927 for $30 million.
[5] Columbia had actually gone bankrupt in 1923 due to overproduction and some shady stock market maneuvers, only to be reorganized by Louis Sterling, head of English Columbia, solely for the purpose of acquiring the rights to the Western Electric recording process.

were considered a luxury of the past, and the industry appeared to be on the brink of extinction.

As America emerged from its economic doldrums, an old ally, with the aid of an act of Congress, would start the record industry on the road to recovery. From the coin-in-the-slot days of the 1890s, the fortunes of the automatic phonograph, or jukebox, have been entwined with those of the record industry. With the repeal of Prohibition on December 5, 1933 thousands of new locations became available, and jukeboxes proliferated in bars and restaurants throughout the country. The jukebox not only provided low-cost entertainment for patrons and additional revenue for owners, but it also became a reliable way to determine which records would be most popular with the buying public. Soon, *Variety* and *Billboard* began to report such record trends, giving rise to the popular "Hit Parade" radio program. All of which, of course, encouraged record sales.

Two record men in particular were instrumental in reversing the downward trend in record sales. Jack Kapp, formerly of Brunswick, formed the American branch of Decca Records in 1934 and introduced a line of inexpensive, popular recordings aimed at the jukebox trade. At this time, the standard price for a ten-inch popular record (as opposed to the higher priced celebrity records) was seventy-five cents; the new Decca records sold for thirty-five cents. Victor (Bluebird) and Columbia (Okeh) had previously introduced budget lines, but they featured relatively unknown performers. When Kapp left Brunswick, he brought with him such name artists as the immensely popular Bing Crosby, the Dorsey Brothers, and Fletcher Henderson among others. The "rightness" of Kapp's marketing approach, given the still-unclear financial picture, soon became apparent, and by 1939 Decca rivalled RCA Victor as the number-one record seller. Meanwhile, at RCA, Edward Wallerstein, also formerly of Brunswick, had developed an inexpensive record player whose speakers and amplifier could be provided by existing radio sets. At $16.50 the Duo Jr., as it was called, converted many to the hobby of record collecting. Wallerstein was later recruited by William S. Paley, president of CBS, to reorganize the lackluster Columbia Record Company (purchased as part of the American Record Company in 1938 for seven hundred thousand dollars). With big money behind him, Wallerstein set out at once to improve the Columbia catalog, signing not only the popular bands of Duke Ellington and Benny Goodman, but many prestigious symphony orchestras as well. By 1941 competition among the majors was intense and sales figures were healthy.

A period of retrenchment, however, would follow. The war cut off the supply of shellac (the basic record ingredient; processed from the lac plant of India). And a strike by the American Federation of Musicians, led by James Caesar Petrillo, brought all recording to a stop and, eventually, the record companies to their knees (despite President Roosevelt's intercession in their behalf). Petrillo, recalling the days when dance halls and restaurants featured live music instead of jukeboxes and broadcasting networks had their own studio orchestras, demanded a royalty payment on every record produced, for the purpose of setting up a trust fund to benefit unemployed musicians. When the record companies refused, he called for a 100 percent ban on all recording activity, which took effect August 1, 1942.[6]

The record companies were determined to tough it out; after all, they considered themselves employers of musicians. And, indeed, the effect of the ban was not immediately noticeable, since record dates were planned months in advance and large stockpiles of unreleased material lay ready in the vaults. But for every hit song introduced on Broadway or in films and heard on the radio, there was no accompanying record to meet the glaring demand. Decca, which relied almost exclusively on the pop market, surrendered first, in September of 1943 (they couldn't wait to record the original cast of the smash *Oklahoma!*). Columbia and Victor held out until November, 1944. By then the situation was perilous; their stockpiles had dwindled to next to nothing, artists were defecting to Decca, and

[6] Singers were not subject to the strike, but with no professional accompaniment few efforts were made. Curiously, a few records were made by the Harmonicats and other such groups, since for some reason Petrillo did not consider the harmonica to be a musical instrument.

when restrictions on the nonmilitary use of shellac were relaxed, the potential for huge profits could not be ignored. Although certainly justified—technological advances in the entertainment industries had obviously usurped the role of live music in many ways—the AFM strike left an unfortunate gap in recorded history.[7]

At the close of World War II, business was once again booming. General prosperity and pent-up demand translated into enormous sales. The figures for 1947 showed that approximately four hundred million records had been sold, nearly four times the prewar high. But another war, an internal struggle over the size of the disc and the speed at which it turned, followed. As a puzzled public looked on, Columbia and RCA Victor engaged in what came to be known as the War of the Speeds.

The LP

A few abortive attempts had been made to lengthen the record's playing time before Edward Wallerstein unveiled Columbia's new Microgroove, long-playing record at a press conference in 1948. Going back to 1906, the Neophone Company of London issued mammoth twenty-inch platters (made of plastic with a cardboard base) with a playing time of eight to ten minutes. They were expensive, excessively noisy, and quickly fell into oblivion. A more legitimate attempt was made by RCA in 1931. By increasing the number of grooves and by slowing down the speed to 33⅓ rpm,[8] they were able to produce a 12″ (also 10″) record of flexible plastic that contained about fourteen minutes of music on each side. But 1931 was not the year to introduce a new record. That, along with RCA's failure to produce an inexpensive, slow-speed turntable and the fact that the records tended to wear out after a few playings under the

---

[7] Jazz lovers in particular bemoan the lack of documentation of this critical transitional period, when the big swing bands were breaking down in favor of smaller combos and the bebop of Charlie Parker and Dizzy Gillespie was in the air.

[8] The 33⅓ speed had previously been used for the Vitaphone, a sound synchronization process of the early talkies, and for radio broadcast transcriptions.

heavy tone arm of the 30s, brought to project to a swift conclusion.

Wallerstein had been with RCA at the time and was careful not to make those same mistakes. While Columbia's research team (under the direction of Peter Goldmark) applied the final touches, the Philco Company of Philadelphia was hired to produce a record player made to Columbia's specifications (Columbia had long ceased making phonographs). The result was a record with 224 to 300 groves per inch instead of 96 to 120 for the conventional 78 rpm disc; and by once again reducing the speed to 33⅓ rpm (the lowest speed at which inexpensive electrical motors could operate efficiently) playing time was increased to about twenty-three minutes per side. The records were pressed in vinylite, a nonbreakable plastic, and Philco had developed a lightweight pickup (about seven grams of pressure) to minimize wear.

The advantages of the LP were obvious: Longer works could be heard without interruption; more music could be offered at a cheaper price; the vinylite surface was less prone to scratches and relatively noise free; and it took up considerably less storage space. The latter was graphically demonstrated at that press conference in June, 1948. As members of the press entered the Waldorf-Astoria Hotel suite they saw a stack of 78s nearly eight-feet high next to a stack of 101 LPs, containing the same amount of music, measuring only fifteen inches. Wallerstein went on to explain that, in an effort to convert the public to the new speed, Columbia would hand over its research data and manufacturing specifications to all interested companies. Furthermore, Columbia would make no attempt to collect patent fees or royalties.

Wallerstein had made the same offer two months earlier to David Sarnoff, president of RCA, who reportedly spoke highly of Columbia's new project. However, with no reply forthcoming, Columbia decided to launch the LP. Initial sales were not overwhelming, but they were brisk enough to circulate over a million LPs by the end of 1948.

By now, several smaller companies had expressed their intention to produce LPs, but rumors were rampant that RCA was about to retaliate with an entirely new disc and record player whose turntable would revolve at more than 40 revolutions per minute. Condemned in advance as not being in the best public interest, the 45 appeared in early 1949. It was widely assumed at the time that an order had been given to develop any kind of new-speed record and player, as long as it was not interchangeable with the LP. Responding to such criticism, an RCA executive argued in the February, 1949 issue of *Saturday Review* that standardization of speed is vital, but that other viewpoints should be considered. RCA's "other viewpoint" was seven inches in diameter with a large center hole and a playing time comparable to the conventional 78 rpm disc. Also made of vinylite, its only apparent advantage over the LP was that it could be more easily stored. Even the rapid-action, drop-style record changer could not mask the fact that it played only three to five minutes of music.

Nevertheless, resorting to tactics tried and true, RCA advertised the 45 with a vengeance. And the record players were sold at close to cost in an effort to offset Columbia's head start. Clearly the 78 belonged to the past, but what would replace it? Decca, Mercury, and of course the smaller, classical labels opted for the LP; Capitol hedged by making records in all three speeds. All that was clear was that the public wasn't buying. For the first time in many years, record sales were on the decline.

In February, 1950, after spending millions to promote the 45, RCA adopted the LP for its classical repertoire. In February, 1951 (the same year Edward Wallerstein retired) Columbia issued its first 45s. For jukeboxes, which relied on frequent change of selection, the small, durable 45 was ideal, and it soon displaced the 78 in the pop market. Obviously, the 45 and the LP were destined to coexist.

The full flowering of the 45 and its identification with an emerging musical revolution was yet to come. With the advent of television, radio was forced to rely more and more on recorded entertainment. Radio stars were wooed away by the new medium, and sponsors realigned their advertising budgets accordingly. But as the pop stylings of Perry Como, Doris Day, Eddie Fisher, et al. gave way to Bill Haley and the Comets, Elvis Presley, and the like, a new, potent buying force—the white, middle-class teenager—resuscitated the airways, giving rise to the disc jockey, the top-forty programming format, and, as hundreds of smaller record companies entered the get-rich-quick singles sweepstakes, the payola scandal of 1959. Today the sale of 45s constitutes a tiny percentage of the record market (the success of the "concept" album, ushered in by the Beatles' *Sgt. Pepper's Lonely Hearts Club Band,* and the rise in popularity of FM programming signalled a new approach), but the 45 epitomizes the heyday of rock and roll, and the collecting of singles remains a major field.

A more potent threat to the supremacy of the LP is tape. The theory of electromagnetic tape recording had been known since the turn of the century, but (for reasons outside the scope of this rather boiled-down overview) its commercial possibilities were not realized until after World War II.

In the wake of the Allied invasion, American engineers were surprised to find a number of German radio stations equipped with Magnetophone tape recorders (the Magnetophone, like the early phonographs, was first marketed in 1935 as a dictating machine). An awkward, noisy instrument with fourteen-inch reels and a tape speed of 30 ips (inches per second), the Magnetophone nevertheless produced a sound quality equal to the best recordings available. By 1948, thanks to successful efforts by the Minnesota Mining and Manufacturing Company to reduce the speed to 15 ips and even to 7½ ips (thereby doubling and quadrupling the amount of recorded material stored on the tape), every major record and radio studio had installed a 15 ips machine.

For radio, tape eliminated telltale surface noise, making it virtually impossible to distinguish between taped broadcasts and live broadcasts; better yet, mistakes could be edited out and corrections inserted. In the recording studio, tape was more efficient and economical. As techniques became more sophisticated, for example, overdubbing allowed the accompaniment and vocals to be recorded separately, thereby obviating the necessity of keeping the musicians on hand while the singer struggled to make the right "take." Or, the best segments of various takes could be spliced together to secure the desired results. Nowadays, in fact, the giant multichannelled console, with an unlimited range of electronic possibilities, has so revolutionized recording techniques that the producer often usurps the role of the artist as a creative force.

But will tape replace the LP as a source of recorded home entertainment? It might have seemed so to some in 1955, for tape recording was then the only way to hear a striking, new development—stereophonic sound. However, stereo tapes were very costly, and it would be only a matter of time (1958) before less expensive binaural disc recordings would be made available. Eight-track cartridges and cassettes, as opposed to open-reel tape, established a mass market for prerecorded tapes and, as befits the age, have made the automobile a potential listening room. If record technology continues to keep pace, however, there is no reason to believe the LP will fall out of favor. The tape industry has shown enormous growth in the last few years, but the sale of records has increased at virtually the same rate.

ABOUT THE LISTINGS

THE RECORDS LISTED are American releases, with the exception of English cast recordings. In those categories listed by artist (Rock, Jazz, Composer and Lyricists, Personalities and Vocalists) the records are arranged alphabetically by label, and by record number within each label.

Ratings vs Prices

I chose a five-star rating system over specific prices because of the exceptional fluidity of the collectors' market. Many factors affect supply and demand and, therefore, a record's price. Domestic reissues (especially with original cover art), exact replicas of American LPs imported primarily from Japan, and faithfully duplicated bootlegs all contribute to the constant state of flux.[1] There are also regional factors. A record like the Baysiders' *Over the Rainbow* (p. 47), for instance, commands a much higher price in New York where the group originated than, say, California. Or, perhaps a large supply of a particular rare record is unearthed in some warehouse, thereby causing the price to drop in that area; yet elsewhere the record remains unavailable. What is its value? A rating system has its drawbacks, especially in the five-star range where a fifty-dollar record and a hundred-dollar record would be rated equally; but fixed prices strikes me as both presumptuous, given the rare record market's capricious nature, and potentially misleading, in that it ignores the individual needs of the buyer and seller. My inten-

[1] A prime example is *Introducing the Beatles* (Vee Jay 1062). There have been so many issues with slight variations of this obviously important and desirable record, including a very convincing bootleg, that fear and confusion have devalued the price of the original (even when positively identified).

tion was to indicate what a record is likely to fetch (*at the professional dealer's level*) and let the buyer and seller fend for themselves.

A price key is provided at the beginning of each category. They may vary slightly from genre to genre, since certain kinds of records are more actively traded than others. A three-star jazz record ($12–$20), for example, would probably sell for less than a three-star rock record ($15–$25), depending, again, on the individual needs of both buyer and seller.

Condition

The importance of condition with respect to the value of a rare record cannot be overemphasized. Obviously a copy of *The Caine Mutiny* (the most valuable LP) (see p. 98) will bring big bucks no matter how scratched. But for less fabulous, though hard-to-find items, scratches (even if inaudible, since grading is visual as well as aural), writing on the cover, split covers, water stains, etc.—all spell a drop in value.

With the used record network expanding at an astonishing rate, the fussiness of the collector has become legendary. I've heard many dealers complain of not being able to sell a truly rare record in vg+ condition (very good plus implies minimal marks, very little surface noise) for close to what they expected, whereas the same record in new or excellent condition brought much more than they anticipated. Some collectors, in fact, maintain two collections—one of mint, unplayed records and one for everyday listening. A tip: to determine if a record has been played, look first to the center hole for any signs of wear or for spindle marks around the hole from placing the record on the turntable. Factory-sealed records are most desired, but there is always the risk of there being a defective, or wrong record inside.

All records listed herein are rated as if they are in new or excellent (very few playings, no defects whatsoever) condition.

Mono/Stereo Price Fluctuations

Stereo issues appear in boldface and generally bring five to ten dollars more (for a legitimate item) than their monophonic counterparts. Notable exceptions are those records issued around 1967–68 when the mono record was being phased out entirely and relatively few were pressed (see Elvis Presley —*Speedway* p. 69). The situation is analogous to the introduction of stereo in 1958. Accounting as they did for only about 10 percent of total sales, stereo issues of records in demand from the late fifties and early sixties are particularly scarce (see *Sodom and Gomorrah* p. 102). Fake stereo—electronically "enhanced" or rechannelled versions of material originally recorded in mono—is universally scorned.

How to Determine the Original Issue[2]

Cover changes, original label colors, and other such information is given where pertinent, but I'm afraid this is mostly a learn-as-you-go process; a discussion of the evolution of hundreds of record companies and their label idiosyncracies would constitute another book. Suffice it to say that most of the records listed are originals, and reissues are identified as such wherever possible. Be sure to match record title with catalog number (reissues are often assigned different, usually higher catalog numbers).

Older records often have a more substantial look and feel to them than later pressings, but for records issued within the last twenty years, this is not likely to be the case. One convenient, though general way to date a record is to find the company's address on the cover or label (if available); the five-digit zip code was instituted in July, 1963, and earlier addresses may read, for example, "New York 23, NY."

The Used Record Store

In the mid-1970s a different kind of record store appeared in some of the larger cities and university towns. Its basic stock is the overflow from a multibillion dollar industry: cutouts (records deleted from a company's catalog and remaindered at a bargain price; usually a corner of the cover is cut off or notched or has a hole punched through it),[3] promotional copies of new

---

[2] See also p. 127 for a brief discussion of major jazz labels regarding this topic.
[3] This is the last stage of a record's commercial life through normal merchandising channels. Once this final supply is depleted it may, in time, command a high price depending on the artist or musical content.

records unwanted by reviewers and disc jockeys, and used records (or to be more precise, previously owned records, since some are unused). You might not find the latest Joni Mitchell album, but if you do it will cost you considerably less than it would at one of the chain store record marts. And since the flow of used records invariably yields a number of out-of-print titles, you may find records that are unobtainable elsewhere. However, not all out-of-print records are rare, since rarity is a function of demand as well as supply, and less desirable titles are priced accordingly (or should be). It must be noted that many used record stores also sell new products at prices comparable to the larger record emporiums, but the emphasis tends to be on smaller labels with limited distribution.

Many used record stores also encourage trading, roughly on a two-for-one basis; that is, two of your records (by marketable artists and in good condition) for one of theirs. In this way, the store owner avoids a cash outlay while building up his stock and insuring a turnover of merchandise. Records may also be traded for credit toward more expensive rare items.

In short, the used record store is an alternative shop, catering not so much to the average consumer as to the aficionado. It represents a mainstream approach to a business that has heretofore existed mainly through subterranean channels. In the Boston-Cambridge area, for example, before the proliferation of used record stores, records were sold on the streets of Harvard Square and at other campuses. Now there are at least ten used record stores (and no street vendors) dotting the area, and similar operations are flourishing in just about every major United States city.

Stalking the Rare Record

The most obvious place to find rare records is in a store that sells used records or through a mail-order dealer. Dealers advertise in a variety of hobby or music-oriented magazines (*High Fidelity, Downbeat,* etc.) and publish lists in such intermediaries as *Record Exchanger* (Box 2144, Anaheim, California 92804), *Goldmine* (PO Box 61-J, Fraser, Michigan 48026), and *Kastlemusick Exchange* (170 Broadway, Suite 201, New

ABOUT THE LISTINGS

York, New York 10038). Many dealers favor auctions, while others prefer set sale (specific prices).

Used record stores and mail-order dealers represent the top of the record chain, but field work can be rewarding for those with the time and energy. Everybody has records, if only a few. They're all around you—in your aunt's attic, the neighbor's basement, the local thrift shop, church bazaars, yard sales, flea markets. There always seems to be a box of records at the feet of someone who couldn't care less about them. Of course 95 percent of the records are worthless, but among the Mitch Miller sing-alongs and the "special TV offer" records and the Al Hirt records (*Cotton Candy* recently popped up in one of my nightmares; I put a match to it but the damn thing wouldn't melt) and Iron Butterfly, Tom Jones, *The Sound of Music,* polka records, kiddie records, Christmas records—somewhere among the ubiquitous dreck is the record you've been looking for for the last five years.

Could this really be happening? Excitedly, you remove the record from its jacket to check condition—it's mint! "I'll pay up to five dollars," you tell yourself. "After all, this is only a garage sale." Mentally composing yourself, you approach the owner. "Does fifty cents sound okay?" he says. "Is Paris a city?" you want to scream, fishing in your pockets for the required change.

Or, instead of a record you want, you stumble across a record of value in which you have no interest. It can always be traded or sold to a used record store. Don't expect even half the cash value for it (although some stores will offer more in trade), but considering your investment, a nice profit can be realized. Scoring an entire collection at the right price, or any kind of quantity buying, presents other welcome complications. However, unless you're a dealer or have ready outlets, your bargaining power lies solely in the quality of your merchandise.

Collecting LP's is an interesting game. I hope this book provides some basic information for those who wish to play and a measure of amusement for those who already participate.

PART I
ROCK AND ROLL

1. COLLECTING ROCK AND ROLL RECORDS

THE RICH MIX OF BLACK AND WHITE musical elements that fostered rock and roll accounts for the many different kinds of records to be found here. Rhythm and blues, rockabilly (itself a hybridization of country songs and blues delivered with a backbeat typical of urban black music), the so-called British Invasion (Beatles, Yardbirds, etc.), surf music, soul music, acid rock, folk rock, punk, and new wave—all have their champions among collectors. In addition, records by selected artists in such seemingly unrelated minor genres as blues, gospel music, and boogie-woogie have become collectible as forerunners of the rhythm and blues movement of the Fifties.

Because of the enormous popularity of rock and roll—the popular music of the age—there are more dealers and collectors here than in any other category. Consequently, the lines of communication have been well established and, unlike the other categories, there are many specialty magazines and regularly held record conventions concerned specifically with the buying and selling of rock and roll records. The market is not limited to just records either; memorabilia, including toys, games, buttons, posters, and promotional literature are also actively sought and traded. (I've even heard tell of a collector who has a Beach Boys gold record hanging on his living room wall.) Special interview records, foreign issues of American LPs, records on colored plastic, picture records—basically anything unique by a marketable artist—are similarly prized.

Given such rabid activity and the fact that rock and roll is a relatively recent development, extreme price fluctuations from dealer to dealer are not uncommon. Many records from the late sixties and early seventies, for example, are eminently col-

43

lectible, but they are too "new" for a fair price to be established with any certainty. In such transactions, it is simply a matter of the dealer's opinion and how much the buyer is willing to spend.

Price Key: 1 = $5 to $10; 2 = $10 to $15; 3 = $15 to $25; 4 = $25 to $40; 5 = over $40.

2. THE ROCK AND ROLL RECORDINGS

Johnny Ace
4 Johnny Ace, Duke 70 (10")
4 Johnny Ace Memorial Album, Duke 71 (orange cover; yellow and purple label)
1 Johnny Ace Memorial Album, Duke 71 (red cover; orange label)

Faye Adams
3 Shake a Hand, Warwick 2031, *2031*

Adrian and the Sunsets
1 Breakthrough, Sunset 63-601

The Adventurers
2 Can't Stop Twistin', Columbia 1747, *8547*

APO Executives
3 A Compendium (w/Tami Lynn), AFO 0002

Jewel Akens
1 The Birds and the Bees, Era 110, *100*

Arthur Alexander
2 You Better Move On, Dot 3434, *25434*

Davie Allan and the Arrows
1 Apache '65, Tower 5002, *5002*
1 Blues Theme, Tower 5078, *5078*
1 The Cycle-delic Sounds of Dave Allan and the Arrows, Tower 5094, *5094*

Bernie Allen and his Stereo Mad Men
2 Musically Mad, RCA *1929*

Dave Allen
4 Color Blind, International Artists 11

Lee Allen
5 Walkin' With Mr. Lee, Ember 200 (red label)
3 Walkin' With Mr. Lee, Ember 200 (black label)

Ray Allen and the Upbeats
3 Tribute to 6, Blast 6804

Richie Allen and the Pacific Surfers
1 Stranger From Durango, Imperial 9212, *12212*
1 The Rising Surf, Imperial 9229, *12229*
1 Surfer's Slide, Imperial 9243, *12243*

Tony Allen and the Night Owls
3 Rock and Roll With Tony Allen and the Night Owls, Crown 5231

Gene Allison
2 Gene Allison, Vee Jay 1009

Keith Allison
1 In Action, Columbia 2641, *9441*

The Allman Brothers
1 The Allman Brothers, Atco 308
1 Idlewild South, Atco 342

Sheldon Allman
2 Sing Along With Drac, Del Fi *1213*

Tommy Allsup
3 The Buddy Holly Songbook, Reprise 6182, *6182*

Amboy Dukes
1 Amboy Dukes, Mainstream 56104, *6104*
1 Journey to the Center of the Mind, Mainstream *6112*
1 Migration, Mainstream *6118*

Amen Corner
1 Round, Deram *18014*

Lee Andrews and the Hearts
1 Biggest Hits, Lost Nite 101
1 Dean Tyler Presents Lee Andrews and the Hearts, Lost Nite 113

The Angels
1 The Angels Sing, Ascot 13009, *16009*
3 And the Angels Sing, Caprice 1001, *1001*
2 My Boyfriend's Back, Smash 27039, *67039*
2 A Halo to You, Smash 27048, *67048*

Paul Anka
2 Paul Anka, ABC-Paramount 240, *240*
1 My Heart Sings, ABC-Paramount 296, *296*
1 Paul Anka Sings His Big 15, ABC-Paramount 323, *323*
1 Paul Anka Swings For Young Lovers, ABC-Paramount 347, *347*
1 Anka at the Copa, ABC-Paramount 353, *353*
2 It's Christmas Everywhere, ABC-Paramount 360, *360*
1 Strictly Instrumental, ABC-Paramount 371, *371*
1 Paul Anka Sings His Big 15, Vol. 2, ABC-Paramount 390, *390*
1 Paul Anka Sings His Big 15, Vol. 3, ABC-Paramount 409, *409*
2 Diana, ABC-Paramount 420, *420*
3 Fabulous Paul Anka and Others, Riviera 0047

Annette (Funicello)
1 Annette, Buena Vista 3301
1 Annette Sings Anka, Buena Vista 3302
1 Hawaiiannette, Buena Vista 3303
1 Italiannette, Buena Vista 3304
1 Dance Annette, Buena Vista 3305
2 The Story of My Teens, Buena Vista 3312
1 Teen Street, Buena Vista 3313
2 Muscle Beach Party (movie soundtrack), Buena Vista 3314, *3314*
2 Beach Party (movie soundtrack), Buena Vista 3316, *3316*
1 Annette on Campus, Buena Vista 3320
2 Bikini Beach (movie soundtrack), Buena Vista 3324, *3324*
2 Pajama Party (movie soundtrack), Buena Vista 3325, *3325*
2 Annette Sings Golden Surfin' Hits, Buena Vista 3327
1 Something Borrowed, Something Blue, Buena Vista 3328
1 Annette Funicello, Buena Vista 4037

Aquatones
5 The Aquatones Sing, Fargo 3001

Area Code 615
1 Area Code 615, Polydor *4002*
1 Trip in the Country, Polydor *4025*

Aristocrats
1 Boogie and Blues, HiFi 610

Ginny Arnell
1 Meet Ginny Arnell, MGM 4228, *4228*

Jane Asher
1 Alice in Wonderland, London 1206

The Astronauts
1 Surfin' With The Astronauts, RCA 2760, *2760*
1 Everything is A-OK, RCA 2782, *2782*
1 Competition Coupe, RCA 2858, *2858*
1 The Astronauts Orbit Campus, RCA 2903, *2903*
1 Go Go Go, RCA 3307, *3307*
1 Favorites For You, Our Fans, From Us, RCA 3359, *3359*
1 Down the Line, RCA 3454, *3454*
1 Travelin' Men, RCA 3733, *3733*

Au Go-Go Singers
3 They Call Us Au Go-Go Singers, Roulette 25280, *25280*

Sil Austin
2 Slow Walk Rock, Mercury 20237
1 Everything's Shakin', Mercury 20320 or Wing 12227
2 Battle Royal (w/R. Prysock), Mercury 20434, *60106*
1 Slow Walk Rock, Wing 12168 (reissue of Mercury 20237)

Frankie Avalon
2 Frankie Avalon, Chancellor 5001
1 Young Frankie Avalon, Chancellor 5002
1 Swingin' On a Rainbow, Chancellor 5004
2 The Hit Makers (w/Fabian), Chancellor 5009
1 Summer Scene, Chancellor 5011
2 A Whole Lotta Frankie, Chancellor 5018
1 And Now About Mr. Avalon, Chancellor 5022, *5022*
1 Italiano, Chancellor 5025, *5025*
1 You Are Mine, Chancellor 5027, *5027*
1 Frankie Avalon's Christmas Album, Chancellor 5031, *5031*
1 Frankie Avalon Sings Cleopatra Plus 13 Other Great Hits, Chancellor 5032, *5032*

2 Facade (Young And In Love), Chancellor 69801 (deluxe box w/portrait)

The Avons
5 The Avons, Hull 1000

Badfinger
1 Straight Up, Apple *3387*

Joan Baez
3 Folksingers Around Harvard Square (w/others), Veritas 1

Ross Bagdasarian
1 Mixed Up, Liberty 3451, *7451*

La Vern Baker
2 La Vern Baker Sings Bessie Smith, Atlantic 1281, *1281*
3 La Vern, Atlantic 8002
3 La Vern Baker, Atlantic 8007
2 Blues Ballads, Atlantic 8030
2 Precious Memories, Atlantic 8036, *8036*
2 Saved, Atlantic 8050, *8050*
2 See See Rider, Atlantic 8071, *8071*
3 The Best of La Vern Baker, Atlantic 8078, *8078*

Mickey Baker[1]
2 Wildest Guitar, Atlantic 8035, *8035*

Balladeers
1 Alive-O, Del Fi 1204

Frank Ballard
4 Rhythm and Blues Party, Philips 1985

Hank Ballard and the Midnighters
5 Their Greatest Hits, Federal 295-90 (10")
5 The Midnighters, Federal 541
3 Their Greatest Juke Box Hits, King 541
4 Hank Ballard and the Midnighters Vol. II, King 581
2 Singin' and Swingin', King 618
2 The One and Only Hank Ballard, King 674
3 Mr. Rhythm and Blues, King 700
2 Spotlight on Hank Ballard, King 740
2 Let's Go Again, King 748
2 Dance Along, King 759
2 The Twistin' Fools, King 781
2 Jumpin' Hank Ballard and the Midnighters, King 793
2 1963 Sound of Hank Ballard and the Midnighters, King 815
1 Biggest Hits, King 867
1 A Star in Your Eyes, King 896
1 Those Lazy, Lazy Days, King 913
1 Glad Songs, Sad Songs, King 927
1 24 Hit Tunes, King 950
1 Hank Ballard Sings 24 Great Songs, King 981
1 You Can't Keep a Good Man Down, King *1052*

The Barbarians
3 The Barbarians, Laurie 2033, *2033*

Gene Barge
1 Dance With Daddy G, Checker 2994

Barracudas
2 A Plane View, Justice 143

[1] See also *Mickey and Sylvia.*

THE ROCK AND ROLL RECORDINGS 47

Barry and the Tamerlanes
2 I Wonder What She's Doing Tonight, Valiant 406

Dave Bartholomew
2 Fats Domino Presents Dave Bartholomew, Imperial 9162, *12076*
2 New Orleans House Party, Imperial 9217, *12217*

Baskerville Hounds
1 The Baskerville Hounds, Featuring Space Rock, Part 2, Dot 3823, *25823*

Battered Ornaments
1 Battered Ornaments, Harvest *422*

Baysiders
4 Over the Rainbow, Everest 5124, *1124*

Beach Boys
1 Smiley Smile, Brother *9001*
2 20/20, Capitol *133*
2 Close-Up, Capitol *253* (2 LPs)
4 Good Vibrations, Capitol *422*
2 Surfin' Safari, Capitol 1808, *1808*
2 Surfin' U.S.A., Capitol 1890, *1890*
2 Surfer Girl, Capitol 1981, *1981*
2 Little Deuce Coupe, Capitol 1998, *1998*
1 Shut Down, Vol. 2, Capitol 2027, *2027*
1 All Summer Long, Capitol 2110, *2110*
2 Beach Boys Christmas Album, Capitol 2164, *2164*
2 Beach Boys Concert, Capitol 2198, *2198*
2 Beach Boys Today, Capitol 2269, *2269*
1 Summer Days (and Summer Nights), Capitol 2354, *2354*
2 Beach Boys Party, Capitol 2398, *2398*
1 Pet Sounds, Capitol 2458, *2458*
5 Beach Boys Deluxe Set, Capitol 2813, *2813* (3 LP boxed set)
1 Wild Honey, Capitol 2859, *2859*
5 Smiley Smile, Capitol *2891*
4 Stack-O-Tracks, Capitol *2893*
2 Friends, Capitol *2895*

Jimmy Beasley
2 The Fabulous Jimmy Beasley, Crown 5014
1 Twist With Jimmy Beasley, Crown 5247

Beatles
5 Beatles Christmas Album, Apple *100* (available to Beatles fan club members only) [2]
5 Ain't She Sweet (w/others), Atco 169, *169*
1 Meet the Beatles, Capitol 2047, *2047*
1 Beatles Second Album, Capitol 2080, *2080*
3 Chartbusters, Vol. IV (2 songs by the Beatles), Capitol 2094, *2094*
1 Something New, Capitol 2108, *2108*
3 Big Hits From England and the U.S.A. (2 songs by the Beatles), Capitol 2125, *2125*
2 Beatles Story, Capitol 2222, *2222* (2 LPs)
1 Beatles '65, Capitol 2228, *2228*
1 Early Beatles, Capitol 2309, *2309*
1 Beatles VI, Capitol 2358, *2358*
1 Help! (movie soundtrack), Capitol 2386, *2386*
1 Rubber Soul, Capitol 2442, *2442*

5 Yesterday and Today, Capitol 2553, *2553* (butcher cover) [3]
1 Yesterday and Today, Capitol 2553, *2553* (trunk cover) [4]
1 Revolver, Capitol 2576, *2576*
1 Sgt. Pepper's Lonely Hearts Club Band, Capitol 2653, *2653*
3 Magical Mystery Tour, Capitol 2835
1 Magical Mystery Tour, Capitol *2835*
4 The Amazing Beatles (w/others), Clarion 601, *601* (reissue of Atco 169)
3 Discotheque in Astrosound (2 songs by the Beatles), Clarion 609, *609*
3 Great American Tour, INS Radio News 1001/1002
2 This is Where It Started (w/others), Metro 563, *563* (reissue of MGM 4215)
3 The Beatles (with Tony Sheridan and Guests), MGM 4215
4 The Beatles (with Tony Sheridan and Guests), MGM *4215*
3 American Tour with Ed Rudy, Radio Pulsebeat #2 (interviews)
3 American Tour With Ed Rudy, Radio Pulsebeat #3 (interviews)
2 Savage Young Beatles, Savage 69 (mono only) [5]
2 (Peter) Best of Beatles, Savage 71 (mono only) [6]
5 The Beatles vs. the Four Seasons, Vee Jay 30, *30* (2 LP repackage of Vee Jay 1062 and a Four Seasons LP; very rare in stereo)
3 Hear the Beatles Tell All, Vee Jay 202 (noncommercial, promotional LP; interviews)
3 Introducing the Beatles, Vee Jay 1062, *1062* (w/"Love Me Do" and "P.S. I Love You")
2 Introducing the Beatles—Vee Jay 1062, *1062* (w/Ask Me Why" and "Please, Please Me")
5 The Beatles & Frank Ifield, Vee Jay 1085, *1085* (original cover with drawing of the four Beatles)
3 Jolly What! (Beatles and Frank Ifield), Vee Jay 1085, *1085* (second cover with drawing of old man)
3 Songs, Pictures, and Stories of the Fabulous Beatles, Vee Jay 1092 (reissue of Vee Jay 1062 with different, fold-out cover)
5 Songs, Pictures, and Stories of the Fabulous Beatles, Vee Jay *1092* (stereo issue of above)

Beau Brummels
1 Introducing the Beau Brummels, Autumn 103
3 Introducing the Beau Brummels, Autumn *103*
1 Beau Brummels, Vol. 2, Autumn 104, *104*
1 Best of the Beau Brummels, Vault 114, *114*
1 Beau Brummels, Vol. 44, Vault *121*
2 Beau Brummels '66, Warner Bros. 1644, *1644*
1 Triangle, Warner Bros. 1692, *1692*
1 Bradley's Barn, Warner Bros. *1760*

Bee Gees
2 Odessa, Atco 2-702 (2 LPs; felt cover)
1 Bee Gees' 1st, Atco 223, *223*

---

[2] The most reliable way to distinguish an original copy from the nearly identical bootleg is to check the color of the apple core on the record label; the original's is white, while the bootleg's is smeared, or off colored.

[3] and [4] The original butcher cover shows the Beatles in butcher smocks holding pieces of meat and various parts of disembodied dolls; public outcry forced Capitol to recall its initial shipments, and a second cover, the so-called trunk cover (a relatively innocuous photo of the four perched in and around a large overseas trunk), was pasted over the original "butcher" cover. To determine if the butcher cover is underneath, hold the record jacket up to a light and look to the center and far right of the jacket for Ringo's black sweater to show faintly through.

[5] and [6] Since Savage is itself an early bootleg label, I hesitate to use the word original in discussing these two records, but it is necessary to point out that they have been bootlegged with stereo covers; the originals are mono only.

ROCK AND ROLL

1 Horizontal, Atco 233, *233*
1 Idea, Atco *253*
1 Rare, Precious, and Beautiful, Atco *264*

Freddie Bell and the Bellboys
3 Rock and Roll—All Flavors, Mercury 20289

Tony Bellus
4 Robbin' the Cradle, NRC 8

The Belmonts[7]
2 Carnival of Hits, Sabina 5001

Jesse Belvin
1 Brook Benton and Jesse Belvin, Crown *350*
1 The Casual Jesse Belvin, Crown 5145
1 The Unforgettable Jesse Belvin, Crown 5187
1 But Not Forgotten, Custom 1058
2 Just Jesse Belvin, RCA 2089, *2089*
2 Mr. Easy, RCA 2105, *2105*
1 Jesse Belvin's Best, RCA Camden 960, *960*

Boyd Bennett
5 Boyd Bennett, King 594

Brook Benton
1 Brook Benton and Jesse Belvin, Crown *350*
1 Brook Benton at his Best!, Epic 3573
1 It's Just a Matter of Time, Mercury 20421

Rod Bernard
1 Rod Bernard, Jin 4007

Chuck Berry[8]
2 Two Great Guitars (w/Bo Diddley), Checker 2991
2 After School Session, Chess 1426
2 One Dozen Berrys, Chess 1432
2 Chuck Berry Is On Top, Chess 1435
2 Rockin' at the Hops, Chess 1448
2 New Juke Box Hits, Chess 1456
2 More Chuck Berry, Chess 1465
2 On Stage, Chess 1480
2 Chuck Berry's Greatest Hits, Chess 1485
2 St. Louis to Liverpool, Chess 1488
2 Chuck Berry in London, Chess 1495
2 Fresh Berry's, Chess 1498
2 Golden Decade, Chess 1514 (2 LPs)
2 Pop Origins (w/Howlin Wolf), Chess 1544

Richard Berry
2 Richard Berry and the Dreamers, Crown 5371

Peter Best, see Beatles.

Big Bopper
5 Chantilly Lace, Mercury 20402

Big Brother and the Holding Company
1 Big Brother and the Holding Company, Mainstream 56099, *6099*

Big Daddy
3 Big Daddy's Blues, Gee 704, *704*
1 Twist Party, Regent 6106

[7] See also *Dion and the Belmonts.*
[8] All Chess LPs original black label, mono only.

Big Maybelle
2 Big Maybelle Sings the Blues, Epic 22011
2 Big Maybelle Sings, Savoy 14005
2 Blues, Candy and Big Maybelle, Savoy 14011

The Big Three
1 The Big Three, FM 307, *307*
1 Live at the Recording Studio, FM 311, *311*

Acker Bilk
1 Stranger on the Shore, Atco 129, *129*

Bill Black
1 Smokie, Hi 12001
1 Saxy Jazz, Hi 12002
1 Solid and Raunchy, Hi 12003
1 That Wonderful Feeling, Hi 12004, *32004*
1 Movin', Hi 12005, *32005*
1 Bill Black's Record Hop, Hi 12006, *32006*
1 Let's Twist Her, Hi 12006, *32006* (reissue of above)

Cilla Black
1 Is It Love?, Capitol 2308, *2308*

Otis Blackwell
4 Singin' the Blues, Davis 109

Bobby Blue Bland
1 2 in Blues (w/Johnny Guitar Watson), Crown 5358
1 Two Steps from the Blues, Duke 74
1 Here's the Man, Duke 75
1 Call On Me, Duke 77
1 Ain't Nothing You Can Do, Duke 78
1 The Soul of the Man, Duke 79
1 The Best of Bobby Blue Bland, Duke 84
1 The Best of Bobby Blue Bland, Vol. 2, Duke 86
1 Touch of the Blues, Duke 88
1 Spotlighting the Man, Duke 89

The Blasters
1 Sounds of the Drags, Crown 392

Blue Cheer
1 Vincebus Eruptum, Philips 200-264, *600-264*
1 Outsideinside, Philips *600-278*
1 New! Improved!, Philips *600-305*
1 Blue Cheer, Philips *600-333*
1 The Original Human Being, Philips *600-347*
1 Oh Pleasant Hope, Philips *600-350*

Blues Magoos
1 Psychedelic Lollipop, Mercury 21096, *61096*
1 Electric Comic Book, Mercury 21104, *61104*

Gary U.S. Bonds
2 Dance Till Quarter to Three, Legrand 3001
2 Twist Up Calypso, Legrand 3002
2 Greatest Hits of Gary U.S. Bonds, Legrand 3003

Bonnevilles
1 Meet the Bonnevilles, Drum Boy 1001

Bonniwell Music Machine
2 Bonniwell Music Machine, Warner Bros. 1732, *1732*

THE ROCK AND ROLL RECORDINGS 49

Bonzo Dog Band
1 Gorilla, Imperial *12370*
1 Urban Space Man, Imperial *12432*
1 Tadpoles, Imperial *12445*
1 Keynsham, Imperial *12457*

Pat Boone
1 Pat Boone Sings Guess Who? (Tribute to Elvis), Dot 3501, *25501*

Earl Bostic
1 Best of Bostic, King 500
1 Bostic For You, King 503
1 Alto-tude, King 515
1 Dance Time, King 525
1 Let's Dance With Earl Bostic, King 529
1 Bostic Rocks, King 571

Jimmy Bowen
4 Jimmy Bowen, Roulette 25004
3 Buddy Knox and Jimmy Bowen, Roulette 25048

David Bowie
5 David Bowie, Deram 16003, *18003*
5 Man of Words/Man of Music, Mercury *61246*

Will Bradley[9]
3 Boogie-Woogie, Epic 3115

Tiny Bradshaw
4 Tiny Bradshaw, King 295-74 (10")
5 Tiny Bradshaw, King 501
3 Great Composer (A Tribute to Tiny Bradshaw), King 653
1 24 Great Songs, King 953

Brainbox
1 Brainbox, Capitol *596*

Donnie Brooks
2 The Happiest, Era 105

Hadda Brooks
3 Femme Fatale, Crown 5010
3 Swings the Boogie (w/Pete Johnson), Crown 5058
2 Sings and Swings, Crown 5374, *374*

Boots Brown, see p. 135.

Buster Brown
4 The New King of the Blues, Fire 102

Charles Brown
5 Mood Music, Aladdin 702 (10")
5 Mood Music, Aladdin 809
3 Million Sellers, Imperial 9178
3 Best of the Blues (6 titles by Brown), Imperial 9257
2 Charles Brown Sings His Christmas Songs, King 775
1 The Great Charles Brown, King 878
1 Ballads My Way, Mainstream 56035, *6035*
5 Drifting Blues, Score 4011

James Brown
2 Please Please Please, King 610
2 Try Me, King 635
2 Think, King 683

2 The Amazing James Brown and His Famous Flames, King 743
1 Jump Around, King 771
1 James Brown and His Famous Flames Tour the U.S.A., King 804
1 The James Brown Show, King 826
1 Prisoner of Love, King 851
1 Pure Dynamite, King 883

Nappy Brown
2 Nappy Brown Sings, Savoy 14002

Roy Brown
5 Battle of the Blues (Roy Brown vs. Wynonie Harris), King 607
1 Roy Brown Sings 24 Hits, King 956

Ruth Brown
2 Late Date With Ruth Brown, Atlantic 1308, *1308*
4 Ruth Brown, Atlantic 8004
3 Miss Rhythm, Atlantic 8026
3 Best of Ruth Brown, Atlantic 8080
1 Ruth Brown '65, Mainstream 56034, *6034*
1 Along Comes Ruth, Philips 200-028, *600-028*

Lenny Bruce
5 Lenny Bruce is Out Again, Philles 4010

Ray Bryant, see p. 135.

Bubble Puppy
3 A Gathering of Promises, International Artists 10

Buckinghams
1 Kind of a Drag, USA 107

Tim Buckley
1 Goodbye and Hello, Elektra 318, *7318*
1 Happy/Sad, Elektra 74045

Buddies
1 The Buddies and the Compacts, Wing 12293, *16293*
1 Go Go With the Buddies, Wing 12306, *16306*

Buffalo Springfield
3 Buffalo Springfield, Atco *200* (includes "Go and Say Goodbye" instead of "For What It's Worth")

Dorsey Burnette
1 Dorsey Burnette, Dot 3456, *25456*
1 Tall Oak Tree, Era 102, *700*
1 Greatest Hits, Era 800

Johnny Burnette
5 Johnny Burnette and the Rock 'n Roll Trio, Coral 57080[10]
3 Dreamin', Liberty 3179, *7179*
3 Johnny Burnette, Liberty 3183, *7183*
3 Johnny Burnette Sings, Liberty 3190, *7190*
3 Hits and Other Favorites, Liberty 3206, *7206*
3 Roses Are Red, Liberty 3255, *7255*
3 Johnny Burnette Story, Liberty 3389, *7389*
1 Dreamin', Sunset 1179, *5179*

[9] See also p. 134.

[10] The words "Printed in the U.S.A." appear on the lower right-hand corner of the back cover of the original issue, but not on the near identical bootleg.

Jerry Butler
1 Jerry Butler Esquire, Abner 2001

Edd "Kookie" Byrnes
1 Edd "Kookie" Byrnes, Warner Bros. 1309, *1309*

Cadets
3 Cadets, Crown 370
4 Rockin' n' Reelin', Crown 5015

Cadillacs
5 The Fabulous Cadillacs, Jubilee 1045 (blue label)
3 The Fabulous Cadillacs, Jubilee 1045 (black label)
3 The Crazy Cadillacs, Jubilee 1089
4 Cadillacs Meet the Orioles, Jubilee 1117
3 Twistin' With the Cadillacs, Jubilee 5009

Cake
1 Cake, Decca 4927, *74927*
1 A Slice of the Cake, Decca *75039*

Louise Harrison Caldwell
3 All About the Beatles, Recar 2012

John Cale
1 Academy in Peril, Reprise 2079
1 Paris 1919, Reprise *2131*

Randy California
1 Kapt. Kopter and the Twirly Birds, Epic *31755*

Cab Calloway
3 Cotton Club Revue, Gone 101

Jo Ann Campbell
4 Twistin' and Listenin', ABC-Paramount 393, *393*
3 All the Hits by Jo Ann Campbell, Cameo 1026, *1026*
1 Starring Jo Ann Campbell, Coronet 199
3 I'm Nobody's Baby, End 306

Cannibal and the Headhunters
1 Land of 1000 Dances, Date 3001, *3001*, or Rampart 3302, *3302*

Freddy Cannon
2 The Explosive Freddy Cannon, Swan 502
2 Freddy Cannon Sings Happy Shades of Blue, Swan 504
3 Solid Gold Hits!, Swan 505
2 Palisades Park, Swan 507
2 Freddy Cannon Steps Out, Swan 511, *511*
1 Action!, Warner Bros. 1612, *1612*
2 Greatest Hits, Warner Bros. 1628, *1628*

Capital City Rockets
1 Capital City Rockets, Elektra *75059*

Captain Beefheart
2 Safe As Milk, Buddah *5001* (w/bumper sticker)

Caravan
1 Caravan, Verve/Forecast 3066

Caravelles
1 You Don't Have to Be a Baby to Cry, Smash 27044, *67044*

Cathy Carr
1 Ivory Tower, Dot 3674, *25674*
1 Ivory Tower, Fraternity 1005
1 Shy, Roulette 25077, *25077*

Leroy Carr
2 Blues Before Sunrise, Columbia 1799

Mel Carter
2 When a Boy Falls in Love, Derby 702
1 Hold Me, Thrill Me, Kiss Me, Imperial 9289, *12289*
1 My Heart Sings, Imperial 9300, *12300*
1 Easy Listening, Imperial 9319, *12319*

Cascades
2 Rhythm of the Rain, Valiant 405
3 Rhythm of the Rain, Valiant *405*

Casinos
1 Then You Can Tell Me Goodbye, Fraternity 1019

Castells
2 So This Is Love, Era 109, *109*

Catalinas
1 Fun, Fun, Fun, RIC 1006

Cathy Jean and the Roommates
5 At the Hop, Valmor 789

Centurians
2 Surfer's Pajama Party, Del Fi 1228, *1228*

Chad and Jeremy
1 The Best of Chad and Jeremy, Capitol 2470, *2470*
1 More Chad and Jeremy, Capitol 2546, *2546*
1 Before and After, Columbia 2374, *9174*
1 I Don't Want to Lose You, Columbia 2398, *9198*
1 Distant Shores, Columbia 2564, *9364*
1 Of Cabbages and Kings, Columbia 2671, *9471*
1 The Ark, Columbia *9699*
1 5 Plus 10 Equals 15 Fabulous Hits, Fidu 101

Challengers
3 The Challengers Go Sidewalk Surfing, Triumph 100

Chamaeleon Church[11]
1 Chamaeleon Church, MGM *4574*

Champs
3 Go Champs, Go, Challenge 601
2 Everybody's Rockin' With the Champs, Challenge 605
3 Everybody's Rockin' With the Champs, Challenge *605*
1 Great Dance Hits, Challenge 613, *613*
1 All-American, Challenge 614, *614*
1 Champs and the Famous Cyclones, International Award 223

Gene Chandler
1 The Duke of Earl, Vee Jay 1040, *1040*

Bruce Channel
2 Hey Baby, Smash 27008, *67008*

[11] With Chevy Chase.

THE ROCK AND ROLL RECORDINGS

Chantays
  2 Pipeline, Dot 3516, *25516*
  2 Two Sides of the Chantays, Dot 3771, *25771*

Chantels
  3 The Chantels on Tour, Carlton 144, *144*
  5 We Are the Chantels, End 301 (group photo cover)
  1 We Are the Chantels, End 301 (jukebox cover)
  3 There's Our Song Again, End 312
  1 The Chantels Sing Their Favorites, Forum 9104

Charioteers
  2 Sweet and Low, Columbia 6014 (10")
  1 Charioteers (w/Billy Williams), Harmony 7089

Charlatans
  3 High Coin, Philips *600–039*

Ray Charles[12]
  2 Ray Charles, Atlantic 8006
  2 Yes Indeed!, Atlantic 8025
  2 What'd I Say, Atlantic 8029
  2 Ray Charles In Person, Atlantic 8039 (black label)
  2 The Genius Sings the Blues, Atlantic 8052
  1 Do the Twist!, Atlantic 8054
  1 The Ray Charles Story, Vol. 1, Atlantic 8063
  1 The Ray Charles Story, Vol. 2, Atlantic 8064
  1 The Ray Charles Story, Vol. 3, Atlantic 8083
  1 The Ray Charles Story, Vol. 4, Atlantic 8094
  2 The Ray Charles Story, Atlantic 2–900 (2 LPs; includes Atlantic 8063 and 8064)
  3 The Original, Hollywood 504
  3 Fabulous Ray Charles, Hollywood 505

Charms—see Otis Williams and the Charms

Charts
  5 Our Best to You (w/others), Everlast 201

Lincoln Chase
  1 The Explosive Lincoln Chase, Liberty 3076

Chicken Shack
  1 Accept Chicken Shack, Blue Horizon *4809*
  1 O.K. Ken?, Blue Horizon *7705*
  1 100 Ton Chicken, Blue Horizon *7706*
  2 Forty Blue Fingers, Freshly Packed and Ready to Serve, Epic *26414*

Chiffons
  4 My Secret Love, BT Puppy *1011*
  3 He's So Fine, Laurie 2018
  3 One Fine Day, Laurie 2020
  2 Sweet Talkin' Guy, Laurie 2036, *2036*

Children of the Night
  1 Dinner With Drac, Pip 6822

Chipmunks (w/David Seville)
  1 Let's All Sing With the Chipmunks, Liberty 3132
  2 Let's All Sing With the Chipmunks, Liberty 3132, *7132* (red plastic)
  1 Sing Along With the Chipmunks, Liberty 3159, *7159*
  1 The Alvin Show, Liberty 3209, *7209*
  1 Chipmunk Songbook, Liberty 3229, *7229*

[12] See also p. 137.

  1 Christmas With the Chipmunks, Liberty 3256, *7256*
  1 Christmas With the Chipmunks, Liberty 3334, *7334*
  1 The Chipmunks Sing the Beatles Hits, Liberty 3388, *7388*
  1 Chipmunks Sing With Children, Liberty 3405, *7405*
  1 Chipmunks A-Go-Go, Liberty 3424, *7424*

Chocolate Watch Band
  1 Riot on Sunset Strip (movie soundtrack; w/others), Tower 5065, *5065*
  5 No Way Out, Tower 5096, *5096*
  5 The Inner Mystique, Tower *5106*
  5 One Step Beyond, Tower *5153*

Chordettes
  2 Chordettes, Cadence 30001
  1 The Chordettes Sing Never on Sunday, Cadence 3056, *25056*

Chosen Few
  1 Takin' All the Love I Can, Maple 6000

Lou Christie
  1 Lightning Strikes, MGM 4360, *4360*
  1 Painter of Hits, MGM 4394, *4394*
  2 Lou Christie, Roulette 25208, *25208*

Circus Maximus
  1 Circus Maximus, Vanguard *79260*
  1 Never Land Revisited, Vanguard *79274*

City
  3 Now That Everything's Been Said, Ode 244012[13]

Jimmy Clanton
  3 Jimmy's Happy/Jimmy's Blue, Ace 100 (2 LPs)
  2 Just a Dream, Ace 1001
  2 Jimmy's Happy, Ace 1007
  2 Jimmy's Blue, Ace 1008
  2 My Best to You, Ace 1011
  2 Teenage Millionaire, Ace 1014
  2 Venus in Blue Jeans, Ace 1026
  1 Best of Jimmy Clanton, Philips 200–154, *600–154*

Claudine Clark
  2 Party Lights, Chancellor 5029

Dave Clark Five
  2 It's Here Luv, INS Radio News 1006 (interview LP)

Dee Clark
  2 Dee Clark, Abner 2000
  2 How About That, Abner 2002
  1 You're Looking Good, Vee Jay 1019
  1 Dee Clark, Vee Jay 1028
  1 Hold On, It's Dee Clark, Vee Jay 1037
  1 The Best of Dee Clark, Vee Jay 1047

Gene Clark
  2 Gene Clark With the Gosdin Brothers, Columbia 2618, *9418*

Petula Clark, see p. 106.

[13] Bootleg has black and white cover rather than color; group includes Carole King.

ROCK AND ROLL

Cleftones
- 3 Heart and Soul, Gee 705
- 4 Heart and Soul, Gee 705
- 3 For Sentimental Reasons, Clef 707
- 4 For Sentimental Reasons, Clef 707

Buzz Clifford
- 3 Baby Sittin' with Buzz, Columbia 1616, *8416*

Claude Cloud
- 5 Let's Get Cat-Static (w/S. Taylor), MGM 281 (10")
- 4 Designed for Dancing (Rock 'n Roll), MGM 3466

The Clovers
- 5 The Clovers, Atlantic 1248
- 4 The Clovers, Atlantic 8009
- 4 The Clovers Dance Party, Atlantic 8034
- 1 The Original Love Potion Number Nine, Grand Prix 428
- 4 In Clover, Poplar 1001
- 3 In Clover, United Artists 3033, *6033*
- 3 Love Potion Number Nine, United Artists 3099, *6099*

The Coasters
- 3 The Coasters, Atco 101 (yellow label)
- 2 The Coasters' Greatest Hits, Atco 111
- 2 One By One, Atco 123, *123*
- 2 Coast Along With the Coasters, Atco 135, *135*
- 1 That's Rock and Roll, Clarion 605

Eddie Cochran
- 5 Singin' to My Baby, Liberty 3061
- 4 Eddie Cochran, Liberty 3172
- 5 Eddie Cochran, Liberty 7172
- 2 Never to Be Forgotten, Liberty 3220
- 1 Summertime Blues, Sunset 1123, *5123*

Cozy Cole[14]
- 2 Cozy Cole, King 673
- 2 Cozy Cole's Hits, Love 500

Jerry Cole and His Spacemen
- 1 Outer Limits, Capitol 2044, *2044*
- 1 Hot Rod Dance Party, Capitol 2061, *2061*
- 1 Surf Age, Capitol 2112, *2112*

Collegians
- 4 Sing Along With the Collegians, Winley 6004

Bobby Comstock and the Counts
- 1 Out of Sight, Ascot 13026, *16026*

Contours
- 2 Do You Love Me, Gordy 901

Sam Cooke
- 2 Sam Cooke, Keen 2001
- 2 Encore, Keen 2003
- 2 Tribute to the Lady, Keen 2004, *2004*
- 2 Hit Kit, Keen 86101
- 2 I Thank God, Keen 86103
- 2 The Wonderful World of Sam Cooke, Keen 86106
- 1 Cooke's Tour, RCA 2221, *2221*
- 1 Hits of the 50's, RCA 2236, *2236*
- 1 Sam Cooke, RCA 2293, *2293*
- 1 My Kind of Blues, RCA 2392, *2392*

- 1 Twistin' the Night Away, RCA 2555, *2555*
- 1 Best of Sam Cooke, RCA 2625, *2625*
- 1 Mr. Soul, RCA 2673, *2673*
- 1 Night Beat, RCA 2709, *2709*
- 1 Ain't That Good News, RCA 2899, *2899*
- 1 Sam Cooke at the Copa, RCA 2970, *2970*
- 1 Shake, RCA 3367, *3367*
- 1 Try a Little Love, RCA 3435, *3435*

Les Cooper
- 3 Wiggle Wobble, Everlast 202

Copperhead
- 1 Copperhead, Columbia 32250

Dave "Baby" Cortez
- 1 Dave "Baby" Cortez, Clock 331

Count Five
- 2 Psychotic Reaction, Double Shot 1001, *5001*

Johnny Crawford
- 1 Captivating Johnny Crawford, Del Fi 1220
- 1 A Young Man's Fancy, Del Fi 1223, *1223*
- 1 Rumors, Del Fi 1224, *1224*
- 1 His Greatest Hits, Del Fi 1229, *1229*
- 1 Greatest Hits, Vol 2, Del Fi 1248, *1248*
- 1 Johnny Crawford, Guest Star 1470
- 1 Johnny Crawford Sings Songs From *The Restless Ones* (movie soundtrack), Supreme 110, *210*

Pee Wee Crayton
- 2 Pee Wee Crayton, Crown 5175

Crescendos
- 2 Oh Julie, Guest Star 1453

Crests
- 4 The Crests Sing All Biggies, Coed 901
- 3 The Best of the Crests, Coed 904
- 5 The Best of the Crests, Coed *904*

Crew Cuts
- 1 Rock and Roll Bash, Mercury 20144

Bob Crewe
- 2 Kicks, Warwick 2009, *2009*
- 2 Crazy in the Heart, Warwick 2034, *2034*

Crickets[15]
- 5 The "Chirping" Crickets (w/B. Holly), Brunswick 54038
- 2 In Style With the Crickets, Coral 57320
- 4 In Style With the Crickets, Coral *757320*
- 2 Something Old, Something New, Something Blue, Something Else, Liberty 3272, *7272*
- 1 California Sun, Liberty 3351, *7351*

Jim and Ingrid Croce
- 3 Croce, Capitol *315*

Arthur "Big Boy" Crudup
- 5 Mean Ol' Frisco, Fire 103

Cryan Shames
- 1 Sugar and Spice, Columbia 2589, *9389*

[14] See also p. 138.
[15] See also *Buddy Holly*.

THE ROCK AND ROLL RECORDINGS

1 A Scratch in the Sky, Columbia 2786, *9586*
1 Synthesis, Columbia *9719*

Crystals
5 Twist Uptown, Philles 4000, *4000*
4 He's A Rebel, Philles 4001
5 Crystals Sing the Greatest Hits, Vol. 1, Philles 4003

Frank "Floorshow" Culley
2 Rock 'n Roll Instrumentals for Dancing (w/B. Tate; one side each), Baton 1201

Sonny Curtis
1 Beatle Hits, Imperial 9276, *12276*
1 1st of Sonny Curtis, Viva 36012
1 The Sonny Curtis Style, Viva 36021

Johnny Cymbal
2 Mr. Bass Man, Kapp 1324, *3324*

Cyrkle
1 Red Rubber Ball, Columbia 2544, *9344*
1 Neon, Columbia 2632, *9432*

Wes Dakus
2 The Wes Dakus Album, Capitol 6120
1 Wes Dakus' Rebels, Kapp 1356, *3536*

Dick Dale and His Deltones
2 Dick Dale and His Deltones, Capitol 1886, *1886*
2 King of the Surf Guitar, Capitol 1930, *1930*
2 Checkered Flag, Capitol 2002, *2002*
2 Mr. Eliminator, Capitol 2053, *2053*
2 Summer Surf, Capitol 2111, *2111*
3 Rock Out (Live at Ciro's), Capitol 2293, *2293*
2 Surfers' Choice, Deltone 1001
1 Wild Hot Rod (w/Bo Troy and his Hot Rods), Diplomat 2304
1 Surf Family (w/Hollywood Surfers), Dubtone 1246
1 Surfing (w/Surfaris, Surf Boys, Surf Kings), Guest Star 1433

Dale and Grace
1 I'm Leaving It Up to You, Montel-Michelle 100

Jimmy Daley and the Ding-a-Lings
2 Rock Pretty Baby, Decca 8429 (movie soundtrack)

Damita Jo
1 Damita Jo With Steve Gibson and the Red Caps, ABC-Paramount 378

Dante and the Evergreens
4 Dante and the Evergreens, Madison 1002

Bobby Darin
2 Bobby Darin, Atco 102
2 That's All, Atco 104, *104*
2 This is Darin, Atco 115, *115*
2 Darin at the Copa, Atco 122, *122*
2 It's You Or No One, Atco 124, *124*
2 25th Day of December With Bobby Darin, Atco 125, *125*
1 Two of a Kind (w/J. Mercer), Atco 126, *126*
2 The Bobby Darin Story, Atco 131, *131* (white cover)
2 Love Swings, Atco 134, *134*
2 Twist With Bobby Darin, Atco 138, *138*

2 Bobby Darin Sings Ray Charles, Atco 140, *140*
2 Things and Other Things, Atco 146, *146*
2 For Teenagers Only, Atco 1001
1 The Shadow of Your Smile, Atlantic 8121, *8121*
1 In a Broadway Bag, Atlantic 8126, *8126*
1 If I Were a Carpenter, Atlantic 8135, *8135*
1 Inside Out, Atlantic 8142, *8142*
1 Bobby Darin Sings Dr. Doolittle, Atlantic 8154, *8154*
2 Oh! Look at Me Now, Capitol 1791, *1791*
2 Earthy, Capitol 1826, *1826*
2 You're the Reason I'm Living, Capitol 1866, *1866*
2 18 Yellow Roses, Capitol 1942, *1942*
2 Golden Folk Hits, Capitol 2007, *2007*
2 From Hello Dolly to Goodbye Charlie, Capitol 2194, *2194*
2 Venice Blue, Capitol 2322, *2322*
2 Best of Bobby Darin, Capitol 2571, *2571*

James Darren
1 Album No. 1, Colpix 406
1 Gidget Goes Hawaiian, Colpix 418, *418*
1 James Darren Sings For All Sizes, Colpix 424, *424*
1 Love Among the Young, Colpix 428, *428*

Dartells
1 Hot Pastrami, Dot 3522, 25522

Darts
1 Hollywood Drag, Del Fi *1244*

Dave, Dee, Dozy, Beaky, Mick and Tich
1 Greatest Hits, Fontana 27567, *67567*
1 Time to Take Off, Imperial *12402*

Maxwell Davis
4 Maxwell Davis and his Tenor Sax, Aladdin 709 (10")
4 Maxwell Davis, Aladdin 804 (includes 2 titles from Aladdin 709)
3 Blue Tango, Score 4016 (reissue of Aladdin 804)

Spencer Davis
1 Gimme Some Lovin', United Artists 3578, *6578*
1 I'm a Man, United Artists 3589, *6589*

Bobby Day
5 Rockin' With Robin, Class 5002

Deep River Boys
3 Presenting the Deep River Boys, RCA Camden 303
2 Spirituals and Jubilees, Waldorf Music Hall 108 (10")
4 Deep River Boys, "X" 1019

De-Fenders
1 Drag Beat, Del Fi *1242*
1 The De-Fenders Play the Big Ones, World Pacific 1810, *1810*

Dells
5 Oh What a Nite, Vee Jay 1010 (brown label)
3 Oh What a Nite, Vee Jay 1010 (black label)

Del Satins
4 Out to Lunch, BT Puppy *1019*

Delta Rhythm Boys
1 Swingin' Spirituals, Coral 57358, *757358*
2 Delta Rhythm Boys in Sweden, Jubilee 1022

2 Delta Rhythm Boys, Mercury 25153 (10")
2 Dry Bones, RCA 3085 (10")
2 Delta Rhythm Boys, RCA Camden 313 (includes RCA 3085)

Del Vikings
1 Del Vikings and the Sonnets, Crown 5368
4 Come Go With Me, Dot 3695
5 Come Go With the Del Vikings, Luniverse 1000
4 They Sing . . . They Swing, Mercury 20314
4 The Swinging, Singing Del Vikings Record Session, Mercury 20353

Demensions
3 My Foolish Heart, Coral 57430
4 My Foolish Heart, Coral 757430

Detergents
1 The Many Faces of the Detergents, Roulette 25308, *25308*

Deuce Coupes
1 The Shut Downs, Crown *393*
1 Hot Rodder's Choice, Del Fi *1243*

Deviants
2 Ptooee, Sire *97001*
2 Disposable, Sire *97005*
2 33, Sire *97016*

Devil's Anvil
1 Hard Rock From the Middle East, Columbia 2664, *9464*

Billy Devroe and the Devilaires
1 Censored, Tampa 31
1 Billy Devroe and the Devilaires, Vol. 2, Tampa 39

Diablos—See Nolan Strong and the Diablos

Dials
2 It's Monkey Time, Time 52100, *2100*

Diamonds
2 The Diamonds, Mercury 20309
1 The Diamonds Meet Pete Rugolo, Mercury 20368, *60076*

Dickey Doo and the Don'ts
2 Madison, United Artists 3094, *6094*
2 Teen Scene, United Artists 3097, *6097*

Bo Diddley[16]
2 Bo Diddley, Checker 1431
2 Go Bo Diddley, Checker 1436
2 Have Guitar Will Travel, Checker 2974
2 In the Spotlight, Checker 2976
2 Bo Diddley is a Gun Slinger, Checker 2977
2 Bo Diddley is a Lover, Checker 2980
2 Bo Diddley's a Twister, Checker 2982
2 Bo Diddley, Checker 2984
2 Bo Diddley and Company, Checker 2985
2 Surfin' With Bo Diddley, Checker 2987
2 Bo Diddley's Beach Party, Checker 2988
2 16 All Time Greatest Hits, Checker 2989
2 Two Great Guitars (w/Chuck Berry), Checker 2991
2 Hey Good Lookin', Checker 2992
2 500% More Man, Checker 2996
2 The Originator, Checker 3001

16 All Checker LPs black label, mono only.

Mark Dinning
2 Teen Angel, MGM 3828, *3828*
1 Wanderin', MGM 3855, *3855*

Dion (DiMuci)
2 Ruby Baby, Columbia 2010, *8810*
1 Donna the Prima Donna, Columbia 2107, *8907*
1 Wonder Where I'm Bound, Columbia *9773*
2 Alone With Dion, Laurie 2004
2 Runaround Sue, Laurie 2009
4 Runaround Sue, Laurie 2009 (green plastic)
2 Lovers Who Wander, Laurie 2012
2 Dion (DiMuci) Sings His Greatest Hits, Laurie 2013
2 Love Came to Me, Laurie 2015
2 Dion (DiMuci) Sings to Sandy, Laurie 2017
2 Dion (DiMuci) Sings the 15 Million Sellers, Laurie 2019
2 More of Dion's (DiMuci) Greatest Hits, Laurie 2022
1 Dion (DiMuci), Laurie *2047*

Dion and the Belmonts
2 Presenting Dion and the Belmonts, Laurie 2002
2 Wish Upon a Star With Dion and the Belmonts, Laurie 2006
2 By Special Request, Laurie 2016

Dixie Cups
1 Riding High, ABC-Paramount 525, *525*
2 Chapel of Love, Red Bird 100, *100*
2 Iko Iko, Red Bird 103, *103*

Carl Dobkins Jr.
4 Carl Dobkins, Jr., Decca 8938, *78938*

Dick Dodd
1 First Evolution of Dick Dodd, Tower 5142, *5142*

Fats Domino
2 Here Comes Fats Domino, ABC-Paramount 455, *455*
2 Fats on Fire, ABC-Paramount 479, *479*
2 Getaway With Fats Domino, ABC-Paramount 510, *510*
3 Fats Domino, Everest 280
1 Fats Domino, Grand Award 267, *267*
3 Rock and Roll, Imperial 9004
3 Rockin' and Rollin', Imperial 9009
3 This is Fats Domino, Imperial 9028
3 Here Stands Fats Domino, Imperial 9038
3 This is Fats, Imperial 9040
3 The Fabulous Mr. D, Imperial 9055
3 Fats Domino Swings, Imperial 9062
3 Let's Play Fats Domino, Imperial 9065
3 Fats Domino Sings Million Record Hits, Imperial 9103
3 A Lot of Dominos!, Imperial 9127, *12066*
3 I Miss You So, Imperial 9138
3 Let the Four Winds Blow, Imperial 9153, *12073*
4 What a Party, Imperial 9164
4 Twistin' the Stomp, Imperial 9170
3 Million Sellers by Fats, Imperial 9195
3 Just Domino, Imperial 9208
3 Walking to New Orleans, Imperial 9227
3 Let's Dance With Domino, Imperial 9239
3 Here He Comes Again, Imperial 9248
1 Fats Domino '65, Mercury 21039, *61039*
1 Southland U.S.A., Mercury 21065, *61065*
1 Fats is Back, Reprise *6304*

THE ROCK AND ROLL RECORDINGS

Don and the Goodtimes
1 Greatest Hits, Burdette 300
1 So Good, Epic 24311, *26311*
1 Where the Action Is, Wand 679

Lonnie Donegan
3 Skiffle Folk Music, Atlantic 8038, *8038*
1 Lonnie Donegan, Dot 3394
1 An Englishman Sings American Folk Songs, Mercury 20229

Ral Donner
1 Ral Donner, Ray Smith and Bobby Dale, Crown 5335
5 Takin' Care of Business, Gone 5012

Doors
1 L.A. Woman, Elektra *75001* (window cover)

Lee Dorsey
1 Ride Your Pony, Amy 8010, *8010*
1 Working in the Coal Mine, Amy 8011, *8011*
4 Ya Ya, Fury 1002
2 Ya Ya, Sphere Sound 7003 (reissue of Fury 1002)

Steve Douglas and the Rebel Rousers
1 Twist, Crown 5254

Dovells
1 Bristol Stomp, Parkway 7006
1 All the Hits of the Teen Groups, Parkway 7010
1 For Your Hully Gully Party, Parkway 7021
1 You Can't Sit Down, Parkway 7025

Dreamlovers
3 The Bird, Columbia 2020, *8820*

Drifters
5 Clyde McPhatter and the Drifters, Atlantic 8003
4 Rockin' and Driftin', Atlantic 8022
3 The Drifters' Greatest Hits, Atlantic 8041
2 Save the Last Dance for Me, Atlantic 8059, *8059*
2 Up On the Roof, Atlantic 8073, *8073*
2 Our Biggest Hits, Atlantic 8093, *8093*
2 Under the Boardwalk, Atlantic 8099, *8099*
2 Good Life With the Drifters, Atlantic 8103, *8103*
2 I'll Take You Where the Music's Playing, Atlantic 8113, *8113*
2 Drifters' Golden Hits, Atlantic 8153, *8153*

Duals
2 Stick Shift, Sue 2002 (2 covers)

Dubs
3 Dubs Meet the Shells, Josie 4001
5 Dubs Meet the Shells, Josie *4001*

Du Droppers
3 Du Droppers, Groove 0104

Patty Duke
1 TV's Teen Star, Unart 20005, *21005*
1 Don't Just Stand There, United Artists 3452, *6452*
1 Patty, United Artists 3492, *6492*
1 Greatest Hits, United Artists 3535, *6535*
1 Patty Duke Sings Songs From Valley of the Dolls and Other Selections, United Artists 3623, *6623*

Champion Jack Dupree
3 Blues From the Gutter, Atlantic 8019, *8019*
2 Champion Jack's Natural and Soulful Blues, Atlantic 8045, *8045*
2 Champion of the Blues, Atlantic 8056
2 Two Shades of Blues (w/ Jimmy Rushing; one side each), Audio Lab 1512
2 Low Down Blues (w/L. Johnson; one side each), Continental 16002
3 Champion Jack Dupree Sings the Blues, King 735

Duprees
3 You Belong to Me, Coed 905
3 Have You Heard, Coed 906

Dust
2 Dust, Kama Sutra *2041*
2 Hard Attack, Kama Sutra *2059*

Bob Dylan[17]
1 Broadside Ballads, Vol. 1, Broadside 301
1 Blonde on Blonde, Columbia C2L-41 (2 LPs)
1 Bob Dylan, Columbia 1779
5 Freewheelin', Columbia 1986 (w/"Let Me Die in My Footsteps")
1 Freewheelin', Columbia 1986 (w/out "Let Me Die in My Footsteps")
1 The Times They Are A-Changin', Columbia 2105
1 Another Side of Bob Dylan, Columbia 2193
1 Bringing It All Back Home, Columbia 2328
1 Highway 61 Revisited, Columbia 2389
5 Highway 61 Revisited, Columbia 2389 (w/alternate version of "From a Buick"; identifiable by 1A matrix number on both sidse)
1 Bob Dylan's Greatest Hits, Columbia 2663
1 John Wesley Harding, Columbia 2804

Earls
4 Remember Me Baby, Old Town 104

Easybeats
1 Friday On My Mind, United Artists 3588, *6588*
1 Falling Off the Edge of the World, United Artists 6667

Duane Eddy
2 Have Twangy Guitar Will Travel, Jamie 3000, *3000* (green cover)
1 Have Twangy Guitar Will Travel, Jamie 3000, *3000* (red cover)
1 Especially For You, Jamie 3006, *3006*
1 Twangs the Thang, Jamie 3009, *3009*
1 Songs of Our Heritage, Jamie 3011, *3011*
1 $1,000,000 Worth of Twang, Jamie 3014, *3014*
1 Girls, Girls, Girls, Jamie 3019, *3019*
1 $1,000,000 Worth of Twang, Vol. 2, Jamie 3021, *3021*
1 Twistin' With Duane Eddy, Jamie 3022, *3022*
1 Surfin', Jamie 3024, *3024*
1 In Person, Jamie 3025, *3025*
1 16 Greatest Hits, Jamie 3026, *3026*

Tommy Edwards
1 It's All in the Game, MGM 3732, *3732*

---

[17] See also *Harry Belafonte* (p. 105), *Carolyn Hester*.

ROCK AND ROLL

Donnie Elbert
- 3 Have I Sinned, Deluxe 12003
- 3 The Sensational Donnie Elbert Sings, King 629

Eldorados
- 5 Crazy Little Mama, Vee Jay 1001 (brown label)
- 3 Crazy Little Mama, Vee Jay 1001 (black label)

Electric Prunes
- 1 I Had Too Much to Dream, Reprise 6248, *6248*

Elgins
- 1 Darling Baby, VIP 400

Eliminators
- 1 Liverpool, Dragsters, Cycles and Surfing, Liberty 3365, 7365

Shirley Ellis
- 1 Name Game, Congress 3003
- 1 Sugar, Let's Shing-a-Ling, Columbia 2679, *9479*

The End
- 1 Introspection, London 560

Endle St. Cloud
- 3 Thank You All Very Much, International Artists 12

Scott Engel
- 1 I Only Came to Dance With You, Tower 5026, *5026*

Preston Epps
- 3 Bongola, Top Rank 349

Esquerita
- 5 Esquerita, Capitol 1186

Essex
- 1 Easier Said Than Done, Roulette 25234, *25234*
- 1 A Walkin' Miracle, Roulette 25235, *25235*
- 1 Young and Lively (w/A. Humes), Roulette 25246, *25246*

Eternity's Children
- 2 Eternity's Children, Tower *5123*

Paul Evans
- 1 Hear Paul Evans in Your Home Tonight, Carlton 129, *129*
- 1 Folk Songs of Many Lands, Carlton 130, *130*
- 2 The Fabulous Teens, Guaranteed 1000, *1000*

Even Dozen Jug Band
- 2 Even Dozen Jug Band, Elektra 246, *7246*

Everly Brothers
- 3 Everly Brothers, Cadence 3003
- 3 Songs Our Daddy Taught Us, Cadence 3016
- 3 Everly Brothers Best, Cadence 3025
- 3 Fabulous Style of the Everly Brothers, Cadence 3040
- 4 Fabulous Style of the Everly Brothers, Cadence *25040*
- 3 Folk Songs, Cadence 3059, *25059*
- 3 15 Everly Hits, Cadence 3062, *25062*
- 1 It's Everly Time, Warner Bros. 1381, *1381*
- 3 A Date With the Everly Brothers, Warner Bros. 1395, *1395* (fold-out cover)
- 2 A Date With the Everly Brothers, Warner Bros. 1395, *1395*
- 1 The Everly Brothers, Warner Bros. 1418, *1418*
- 1 Instant Party, Warner Bros. 1430, *1430*
- 1 Golden Hits of the Everly Brothers, Warner Bros. 1471, *1471*
- 2 Christmas With the Everly Brothers, Warner Bros. 1483, *1483*
- 1 Everly Brothers Sing Great Country Hits, Warner Bros. 1513, *1513*
- 1 Very Best of the Everly Brothers, Warner Bros. 1554, *1554*
- 1 Rock 'n Soul, Warner Bros. 1578, *1578*
- 1 Gone, Gone, Gone, Warner Bros. 1585, *1585*
- 1 Beat 'n Soul, Warner Bros. 1605, *1605*
- 1 In Our Image, Warner Bros. 1620, *1620*
- 1 Two Yanks in London, Warner Bros. 1646, *1646*
- 1 Hit Sound, Warner Bros. 1676, *1676*
- 1 Everly Brothers Sing, Warner Bros. 1708, *1708*
- 1 Roots, Warner Bros. *1752*
- 1 Everly Brothers Show, Warner Bros. *1858*

Shelley Fabares
- 1 Shelley, Colpix 426, *426*
- 1 The Things We Did Last Summer, Colpix 431, *431*

Fabian
- 2 Hold That Tiger, Chancellor 5003, *5003*
- 1 Fabulous Fabian, Chancellor 5005, *5005*
- 2 The Hit Makers (w/Frankie Avalon), Chancellor 5009
- 2 Good Old Summertime, Chancellor 5012, *5012*
- 3 Rockin' Hot, Chancellor 5019
- 2 Fabian's 16 Fabulous Hits, Chancellor 5024, *5024*
- 2 Facade (Young and Wonderful), Chancellor 69802 (deluxe box w/portrait)

Adam Faith
- 1 Adam Faith, Amy 8005
- 1 England's Top Singer, MGM 3951, *3951*

Marianne Faithfull
- 1 Greatest Hits, London *547*
- 1 Marianne Faithfull, London 3423, *423*
- 1 Go Away From My World, London 3452, *452*
- 1 Faithfull Forever, London 3482, *482*

Fantastic Baggys
- 4 Tell 'Em I'm Surfin', Imperial 9270
- 5 Tell 'Em I'm Surfin', Imperial *12270*

Chris Farlowe
- 1 Fabulous Chris Farlowe and the Thunderbirds, Columbia 2593, *9393*
- 1 Paint it Farlowe, Immediate *152010*

Fendermen
- 5 Mule Skinner Blues, Soma 1240

Ernie Fields
- 2 In the Mood, Rendezvous 1309, *1309*

Fifty Foot Hose
- 1 Cauldron, Limelight *86062*

Fireballs (w/Jimmy Gilmer)
- 2 Torquay, Dot 3512, *25512*
- 1 Sugar Shack, Dot 3545, *25545*
- 1 Lucky 'Leven, Dot 3643, *25643*

THE ROCK AND ROLL RECORDINGS

1 Campusology, Dot 3709, *25709*
1 Firewater, Dot 3856, *25856*
4 Fireballs, Top Rank 324, *624*
4 Vaquero, Top Rank 343, *643*
3 Here Are the Fireballs, Warwick 2042

Fire Escape
1 Psychotic Reaction, GNP-Crescendo *2034*

Fireflies
5 The Swingin' Fireflies, Taurus *1002*

Toni Fisher
2 The Big Hurt, Signet 509

Five Emprees
2 Five Emprees, Freeport 3001, *4001*
1 Little Miss Sad, Freeport 3001, *4001* (reissue)

Five Keys[18]
5 Best of the Five Keys, Aladdin 806
4 Five Keys On Stage, Capitol 828
4 Fantastic Five Keys, Capitol 1769
4 Five Keys, King 688
3 Rhythm and Blues Hits Past and Present, King 692
4 On the Town, Score 4003

5 Royales
5 Rockin' 5 Royales, Apollo 488
4 Dedicated to You, King 580
4 The 5 Royales Sing For You, King 616
4 5 Royales, King 678
3 All Time Hits, King 955

Five Satins
5 Five Satins Sing, Ember 100 (red cover, red label)
3 Five Satins Sing, Ember 100 (red cover, black label)
2 Five Satins Sing, Ember 100 (black cover, black label)
3 Five Satins Encore, Ember 401
1 Five Satins Sing, Mt. Vernon 108

Flairs
3 The Flairs, Crown 5356

Flamingos
2 Flamingos, Checker 1433
2 Collector's Showcase, Vol. 3, Courtellation 3
2 Flamingo Serenade, End 304
2 Flamingo Favorites, End 307
2 Requestfully Yours, End 308
2 Sound of the Flamingos, End 316
1 Their Hits, Then and Now, Philips 200-206, *600-206*
3 The Flamingos Meet the Moonglows, Vee Jay 1052

Flamin Groovies
2 Supersnazz, Epic 26487
2 Flamingo, Kama Sutra 2021
1 Teenage Head, Kama Sutra *2031*

Fleetwoods
1 Mr. Blue, Dolton 2001, *8001*
1 Fleetwoods, Dolton 2002, *8002*
1 Softly, Dolton 2005, *8005*
1 Deep in a Dream, Dolton 2007, *8007*
1 Fleetwoods Sing the Best of the Oldies, Dolton 2011, *8011*
1 Fleetwoods' Greatest Hits, Dolton 2018, *8018*

1 Fleetwoods Sing For Lovers By Night, Dolton 2020, *8020*
1 Goodnight My Love, Dolton 2025, *8025*
1 Before and After, Dolton 2030, *8030*
1 Folk Rock, Dolton 2039, *8039*

Wade Flemons
1 Wade Flemons, Vee Jay 1011

Phil Flowers
1 I Am the Greatest, Guest Star 1456
1 Phil Flowers Sings a Tribute, Guest Star 1457

Wayne Fontana and the Mindbenders
1 Game of Love, Fontana 27542, *67542*

Frankie Ford
3 On a Sea Cruise With Frankie Ford, Ace 1005

Neal Ford and the Fanatics
1 Neal Ford and the Fanatics, Hickory 141, *141*

Four Knights
4 Spotlight Songs, Capitol 346
3 Four Knights, Coral 52221
2 Million Dollar Baby, Coral 57309, *757309*

Four Lovers (Later became Four Seasons)
5 Joyride, RCA 1317[19]

Four Seasons
1 Dawn (Go Away), Philips 200-124, *600-124*
1 Born to Wander, Philips 200-129, *600-129*
1 Rag Doll, Philips 200-146, *600-146*
1 All the Song Hits of the Four Seasons, Philips 200-150, *600-150*
1 Four Seasons Entertain You, Philips 200-164, *600-164*
1 Four Seasons Sing Big Hits by Burt Bacharach, Hal David, Bob Dylan, Philips 200-193, *600-193*
1 Gold Vault of Hits, Philips 200-196, *600-196*
1 Working My Way Back to You, Philips 200-201, *600-201*
1 2nd Gold Vault of Hits, Philips 200-221, *600-221*
1 Lookin' Back, Philips 200-222, *600-222*
1 Four Seasons Christmas Album, Philips 200-223, *600-223*
1 New Gold Hits, Philips 200-243, *600-243*
5 Beatles vs. Four Seasons, Vee Jay 30, *30* (2LPs; very rare in stereo)
2 Sherry and 11 Others, Vee Jay 1053, *1053*
2 Four Seasons Greetings, Vee Jay 1055, *1055*
2 Big Girls Don't Cry, Vee Jay 1056, *1056*
1 Ain't That a Shame, Vee Jay 1059, *1059*
2 Golden Hits, Vee Jay 1065, *1065*
2 Stay and Other Great Hits, Vee Jay 1082, *1082*
2 Folk-Nanny, Vee Jay 1082, *1082*
2 More Golden Hits by the Four Seasons, Vee Jay 1088, *1088*
2 We Love Girls, Vee Jay 1121, *1121*
1 Recorded Live On Stage, Vee Jay 1154, *1154*

Four Tops
3 Jazz Impressions, Workshop 217

Four Tunes
3 12 X 4, Jubilee 1039

---
[18] See also *Jack Teagarden*, p. 173.
[19] Bootleg version says "collector's edition" on back cover.

ROCK AND ROLL

Kim Fowley
1 Born to Be Wild, Imperial *12413*
1 Outrageous, Imperial *12423*
1 Good Clean Fun, Imperial *12443*
1 Love is Alive and Well, Tower 5080, *5080*

Inez Foxx
1 Mockingbird, Sue 1027 (reissue of Symbol 4400)
1 Inez and Charlie Foxx, Sue 1037
2 Mockingbird, Symbol 4400

Connie Francis
1 Who's Sorry Now, MGM 3686

Aretha Franklin
1 Songs of Faith, Checker 10009
1 Aretha, Columbia 1612, *8412*

Alan Freed
4 Alan Freed Rock 'N Roll Show, Brunswick 54043
4 Rock 'N Roll Dance Party, Vol. 1, Coral 57063
4 Rock 'N Roll Dance Party, Vol. 2, Coral 57115
3 Go Go Go (Alan Freed's TV Record Hop), Coral 57177
3 Rock Around the Block, Coral 57213
4 Alan Freed Presents the Kings Henchmen, Coral 57216

Bobby Freeman
1 C'mon and Swim, Autumn 102
1 Get in the Swim With Bobby Freeman, Josie 4007, *4007*
3 Do You Wanna Dance, Jubilee 1086, *1086*
2 Twist with Bobby Freeman, Jubilee 5010
2 The Lovable Side of Bobby Freeman, King 930

Frank Frost
5 Hey Boss Man!, Phillips, 1975

Max Frost and the Troopers
1 The Shape of Things to Come, Tower *5147*

Frumious Bandersnatch
2 Frumious Bandersnatch, Muggles Gramaphone Works

Fugitives
4 The Fugitives at Dave's Hideout, Hideout 1001

The Bobby Fuller Four
3 KRLA King of the Wheels, Mustang 900
4 KRLA King of the Wheels, Mustang *900*
3 I Fought the Law, Mustang 901, *901*

Jerry Fuller
2 Teenage Love, Lin 100

Cecil Gant
3 Cecil Gant, King 671
5 The Incomparable Cecil Gant, Sound 601

Jerry Garcia and Howard Wales
1 Hooteroll, Douglas *30859*

Don Gardner and Dee Dee Ford
2 I Need Your Lovin', Fire 105

Hen Gates and his Gaters
1 Let's Go Dancing to Rock and Roll, Masterseal 700

Marvin Gaye
1 The Soulful Moods of Marvin Gaye, Tamla 221
2 "That Stubborn Kinda' Fellow," Tamla 229

Gentle Soul
1 Gentle Soul, Epic *26374*

Barbara George
2 I Know, AFO 5001

Gerry and the Pacemakers
1 Don't Let the Sun Catch You Crying, Laurie 2024
1 Gerry and the Pacemakers' Second Album, Laurie 2027, *2027*
1 I'll Be There, Laurie 2030, *2030*
1 Greatest Hits, Laurie 2031, *2031*
1 Girl On A Swing, Laurie 2037, *2037*
1 Ferry 'Cross the Mersey, United Artists 3387, *6387* (movie soundtrack)

Ghouls
1 Dracula's Deuce, Capitol 2215, *2215*

Robin Gibb
1 Robin's Reign, Atco *323*

Steve Gibson and the Red Caps[20]
5 You're Driving Me Crazy, Mercury 25115 (10")
5 Blueberry Hill, Mercury 25116 (10")

Mickey Gilley
2 Lonely Wine, Astro 101
1 Down the Line, Paula 2195

Jimmy Gilmer[21]
4 Buddy's Buddy, Dot 3577, *25577*

Lloyd Glenn
4 Chica—Boo, Aladdin 808
3 Piano Stylings, Score 4006
3 After Hours, Score 4020
5 Lloyd Glenn, Swingtime 1901 (10"?)

Golden Earring
1 Miracle Mirror, Capitol *164*
1 Winter Harvest, Capitol 2823, *2823*
1 Golden Earring, Capitol *11315*
1 Golden Earring, Dwarf 2000
1 Moontan, Track 396 (nude cover)

Golden Gate Quartet
1 The Golden Gate Quartet Sings Favorite Spirituals, RCA Camden 308

Good Rats
1 Good Rats, Kapp *3580*

Dickie Goodman
3 The Many Heads of Dickie Goodman, Rori 3301

Lesley Gore
2 I'll Cry If I Want To, Mercury 20805, *60805*
1 Lesley Gore Sings of Mixed Up Hearts, Mercury 20849, *60849*

[20] See also *Damita Jo*.
[21] See also *Fireballs*.

1 Boys, Boys, Boys, Mercury 20901, *60901*
1 Girl Talk, Mercury 20943, *60943*
1 Golden Hits of Lesley Gore, Mercury 21024, *61024*
1 My Town, My Guy and Me, Mercury 21042, *61042*
1 All About Love, Mercury 21066, *61066*
1 California Nights, Mercury 21120, *61120*
1 Golden Hits, Vol. 2, Mercury *61185*

Graham Gouldman
2 Graham Gouldman Thing, RCA 3945, *3945*

Gogi Grant, see p. 110.

Grass Roots
1 Where Were You When I Needed You?, Dunhill 50011, *50011*

Grin
1 Grin, Spindizzy *30321*
1 1 Plus 1, Spindizzy *31038*
1 All Out, Spindizzy *31701*

G.T.O.'s
1 Permanent Damage, Straight *1059*

Buddy Guy (w/Junior Wells)
2 Buddy and the Juniors, Blue Thumb 20 (marble colored plastic)

Bill Haley and the Comets
4 Shake, Rattle and Roll, Decca 5560 (10")
2 Rock Around the Clock, Decca 8225
1 Rock Around the Clock, Decca *78225*
2 Music for the Boy Friend (He Digs Rock 'N Roll), Decca 8315
1 Music for the Boy Friend (He Digs Rock 'N Roll), Decca *78315*
2 Rock 'N Roll Stage Show, Decca 8345
1 Rock 'N Roll Stage Show, Decca *78345*
2 Rockin' the Oldies!, Decca 8569
1 Rockin' the Oldies!, Decca *78569*
2 Rockin' Around the World, Decca 8692, *78692*
2 Rockin' the Joint, Decca 8775, *78775*
2 Bill Haley's Chicks, Decca 8821, *78821*
2 Strictly Instrumental, Decca 8964, *78964*
5 Rock with Bill Haley and the Comets, Essex 202
1 Twistin' Knights at the Roundtable, Roulette 25174, *25174*
3 Rock and Roll Dance Party, Somerset 4600
3 Rock With Bill Haley and the Comets, Trans World 202
1 Bill Haley with His Comets, Vocalion 3696
1 Bill Haley and His Comets, Warner Bros. 1378, *1378*
1 Haley's Juke Box, Warner Bros. 1391, *1391*

Larry Hall
4 "Sandy" and Other Larry Hall Hits, Strand 1005
5 "Sandy" and Other Larry Hall Hits, Strand *1005*

Ha'Pennys
2 Love Is Not the Same, Fersch 1110

Happenings
1 Happenings, B. T. Puppy 1001, *1001*
1 Back to Back (w/the Tokens), B. T. Puppy 1002, *1002*
1 Psychle, B. T. Puppy 1003, *1003*
1 Happenings Golden Hits, B. T. Puppy *1004*

Slim Harpo
1 Raining in My Heart, Excello 8003
2 Baby Scratch My Back, Excello 8005
1 Tip On In, Excello 8008
1 The Best of Slim Harpo, Excello 8010
1 Slim Harpo Knew the Blues, Excello 8013

Harptones, see Paragons.

Emmy Lou Harris
3 Gliding Bird, Jubilee 8031[22]

Wynonie Harris
5 Party After Hours (w/others), Aladdin 703 (10")
5 Battle of the Blues (Roy Brown vs. Wynonie Harris), King 607

George Harrison[23]
1 Electronic Sound, Zapple *3358*

Wilbert Harrison
2 Kansas City, Sphere Sound 7000

Dale Hawkins
5 Suzie-Q, Chess 1429
2 Let's All Twist (at the Miami Beach Peppermint Lounge), Roulette 25175, *25175*

Ronnie Hawkins
4 Ronnie Hawkins, Roulette 25078, *25078*
4 Mr. Dynamo, Roulette 25102, *25102*
3 The Folk Ballads of Ronnie Hawkins, Roulette 25120, *25120*
3 Ronnie Hawkins Sings the Songs of Hank Williams, Roulette 25137, *25137*
2 Best of Ronnie Hawkins, Roulette 25255, *25255*

Screamin' Jay Hawkins
3 At Home With Screamin' Jay Hawkins, Epic 3448
2 I Put a Spell On You, Epic 3457
1 What That Is, Philips 600–319
1 Screamin' Jay Hawkins, Philips 600–336

Willie Hayden
2 Blame It On the Blues, Dooto 293

Roy Head
1 Treat Me Right, Scepter 532, *532*
3 Roy Head and the Traits, TNT 101

Heartbeats
4 Thousand Miles Away, Roulette 25107 (white label)
2 Thousand Miles Away, Roulette 25107, *25107* (orange label)

Hearts and Flowers
1 Now Is the Time For Hearts and Flowers, Capitol 2762, *2762*
1 Of Horses, Kings and Forgotten Women, Capitol *2868*

Jimi Hendrix
1 Jimi Hendrix Experience, Reprise 6261
1 Axis—Bold As Love, Reprise *6281*

[22] Bootleg cover is black and white rather than color.
[23] See also Silkie.

Clarence "Frogman" Henry
    3 You Always Hurt the One You Love, Argo 4009
    1 Clarence "Frogman" Henry, Roulette *42039*

Herd
    2 Lookin' Thru You, Fontana *67579*

Carolyn Hester
    2 Carolyn Hester, Columbia 1796, *3596*[24]

Chuck Higgins
    4 Pachuko Hop, Combo 300

Hi Lites
    3 For Your Precious Love, Dandee 206

Hillmen
    1 The Hillmen, Together *1012*

Ron Holden
    3 I Love You So, Donna 2111

Eddie Holland
    1 Eddie Holland, Motown 604

Hollies
    1 Evolution, Epic 24315, *26315*
    1 Dear Eloise/King Midas in Reverse, Epic 24344, *26344*
    3 Here I Go Again, Imperial 9265, *12265*
    2 Hear! Here!, Imperial 9299, *12299*
    2 The Hollies, Imperial 9312, *12312*
    2 Bus Stop, Imperial 9330, *12330*
    2 Stop! Stop! Stop!, Imperial 9339, *12339*

Buddy Holly[25]
    3 Best of Buddy Holly, Coral 8, *78* (2 LPs)
    4 Buddy Holly, Coral 57210
    3 Buddy Holly Story, Coral 57279, *757279*
    3 Buddy Holly Story, Vol 2, Coral 57326, *757326*
    3 Buddy Holly and the Crickets, Coral 57405, *757405*
    3 Reminiscing, Coral 57426, *757426*
    3 Showcase, Coral 57450, *757450*
    3 Holly in the Hills, Coral 57463, *757463*
    2 Buddy Holly's Greatest Hits, Coral 57492, *757492*
    2 Giant, Coral 57504, *757504*
    5 That'll Be the Day, Decca 8707 (black or pink label)
    4 That'll Be the Day, Decca 8707 (multi-colored label)
    2 The Great Buddy Holly, Vocalion 73928

Hollywood Argyles
    5 Alley Oop, Lute 9001

Hondells
    2 Go Little Honda, Mercury 20940, *60940*
    2 The Hondells, Mercury 20982, *60982*

Honeycombs
    2 Here Are the Honeycombs, Interphon 88001, *88001*

Lynn Hope
    4 Lynn Hope and his Tenor Sax, Aladdin 707 (10")
    4 Lynn Hope, Aladdin 805
    2 The Maharaja of the Saxophone, King 717
    3 Tenderly, Score 4015

[24] With Bob Dylan on harmonica.
[25] See also *Crickets*.

Lightnin' Hopkins
    2 Blues Underground, "D" 8000
    3 Mojo Hand, Fire 104
    2 Lightnin' Hopkins, Herald 1012
    3 Free Form Patterns, International Artists 6
    3 Lightnin' Hopkins Strums the Blues, Score 4022
    1 Last of the Great Blues Singers, Time 70004

Johnny Horton
    1 Spectacular Johnny Horton, Columbia 1362, *8167*
    1 Johnny Horton Makes History, Columbia 1478, *8269*
    2 Honky Tonk Man, Columbia 1721, *8779*

Shakey Horton
    1 The Soul of Blues Harmonica, Argo 4037, *4037*

Hot Doggers
    1 Surfin' U.S.A., Epic 24054, *26054*

Hour Glass
    1 Hour Glass, Liberty 3536, *7536*
    1 Power of Love, Liberty 3555, *7555*

Joe Houston
    2 Surf Rockin', Crown *313*
    2 Rocks and Rolls All Night, Crown 5006
    2 Blows All Night Long, Modern 1206
    2 Rock and Roll With Joe Houston and His Rockers, Tops 1518

Howlin' Wolf
    2 Moanin' in the Moonlight, Chess 1434
    2 Howlin' Wolf, Chess 1469
    1 The Real Folk Blues, Chess 1502
    1 More Real Folk Blues, Chess 1512
    2 Pop Origins (w/C. Berry), Chess 1544

Hullaballoos
    1 England's Newest Singing Sensations, Roulette 25297, *25297*
    1 Hullaballoos On Hullaballoo, Roulette 25310, *25310*

Human Beinz
    1 Nobody But Me, Capitol *2906*
    1 Evolutions, Capitol *2926*
    1 Nobody But Me, Gateway *3012*

Humble Pie
    1 As Safe as Yesterday, Immediate *101*

Ivory Joe Hunter
    4 Ivory Joe Hunter, Atlantic 8008
    3 The Old and the New, Atlantic 8015
    2 This is Ivory Joe Hunter, Dot 3569, *25569*
    1 The Fabulous Ivory Joe Hunter, Goldisc 403
    4 16 of His Greatest Hits, King 605
    2 I Need You So, Lion 70068
    3 I Get That Lonesome Feeling, MGM 3488
    2 Golden Hits, Smash 27037, *67037*
    2 The Artistry of Ivory Joe Hunter (w/Memphis Slim), Strand 1123

Tab Hunter, see p. 111.

THE ROCK AND ROLL RECORDINGS

Brian Hyland
1 Let Me Belong to You, ABC-Paramount 400, *400*
1 Sealed With a Kiss, ABC-Paramount 431, *431*
1 The Bashful Blonde, Kapp 1202, *3202*

Ian and the Zodiacs
1 Ian and the Zodiacs, Philips 200-176, *600-176*

Idle Race
1 Birthday Party, Liberty *7603*

Frank Ifield, see Beatles.

Iggy and the Stooges[26]
1 Raw Power, Columbia *32111*

Illinois Speed Press
1 Illinois Speed Press, Columbia *9792*
1 Duet, Columbia *9976*

Impacs
1 Impact!, King 886

Impacts
1 Wipe Out, Del Fi 1234, *1234*

Impalas
4 Sorry (I Ran All the Way Home), Cub 8003, *8003*

Impressions
1 For Your Precious Love, Vee Jay 1075, *1075*

Jorgen Ingmann
1 Apache, Atco 130

Ink Spots
4 Something Old, Something New, King 535
4 Ink Spots, King 642
1 Ink Spots, Tops 1561

Innocents
2 Innocently Yours, Indigo 503

In-Sect
2 Introducing the In-Sect, RCA Camden 909

Insect Trust
1 Hoboken Saturday Night, Atco 313
1 The Insect Trust, Capitol *109*

International Submarine Band
3 Safe At Home, LHI 12,001 (Bootleg has shiny black and white label; original label is dull and in color.)

Isley Brothers
2 Shout!, RCA 2156, *2156*
1 Twist and Shout, Wand 653

It's a Beautiful Day
1 Marrying Maiden, Columbia *1058*
2 It's a Beautiful Day, Columbia *9768*

Ivy League
1 Tossing and Turning, Cameo 2000, *2000*

[26] See also *Stooges.*

Jacks
3 The Jacks, Crown *372*
4 Jumpin' With the Jacks, Crown 5021
5 Jumpin' With the Jacks, RPM 3006

Bull Moose Jackson
3 Bull Moose Jackson Sings His All Time Hits, Audio Lab 1524

Chuck Jackson
2 Chuck Jackson and Young Jesse, Crown 5354
1 Dedicated to the King (Tribute to Elvis), Wand 680, *680*

Lil' Son Jackson
3 Rockin' and Rollin', Imperial 9142

Wanda Jackson
5 Wanda Jackson, Capitol 1041
5 Rockin' With Wanda!, Capitol 1384
5 There's a Party Goin' On, Capitol 1511, *1511*
3 Right Or Wrong, Capitol 1596, *1596*
2 Love Me Forever, Capitol 1911, *1911*

Illinois Jacquet, see p. 153.

Mick Jagger
2 Performance, Warner Bros. 2554 (movie soundtrack)

Elmore James
1 Elmore James, Crown 5168
1 The Sky is Crying, Sphere Sound 7002
1 I Need You, Sphere Sound 7008

Etta James
1 At Last, Argo 4003, *4003*
1 The Second Time Around, Argo 4011, *4011*
1 Etta James, Argo 4013, *4013*
1 Etta James Sings For Lovers, Argo 4018, *4018*
1 Etta James Top Ten, Argo 4025, *4025*
1 Etta James Rocks the House, Argo 4032, *4032*
1 Queen of Soul, Argo 4040, *4040*, Crown 5209
1 Etta James, Crown 5209
1 The Best of Etta James, Crown 5234
1 Twist With Etta James, Crown 5250
1 Etta James, Crown 5360

Jan and Dean
5 Jan and Dean, Dore 101
5 Save For a Rainy Day, J and D 101
1 Jan and Dean's Golden Hits, Liberty 3248, *7248*
1 Jan and Dean Take Linda Surfing, Liberty 3294, *7294*
1 Surf City, Liberty 3314, *7314*
1 Drag City, Liberty 3339, *7339*
1 Dead Man's Curve, Liberty 3361, *7361*
1 Ride the Wild Surf, Liberty 3368, *7368*
1 The Little Old Lady From Pasadena, Liberty 3377, *7377*
1 Command Performance, Liberty 3403, *7403*
1 Pop Symphony Number 1, Liberty 3414, *7414*
1 Jan and Dean's Golden Hits, Vol. 2, Liberty 3417, *7417*
1 Folk 'n Roll, Liberty 3431, *7431*
1 Filet of Soul, Liberty 3441, *7441*
1 Jan and Dean Meet Batman, Liberty 3444, *7444*
1 Popsicle, Liberty 3458, *7458*
1 Golden Hits, Vol. 3, Liberty 3460, *7460*

ROCK AND ROLL

Jaynettes
2 Sally Go Round the Roses, Tuff 13

Bill Jennings, see p. 154.

Kris Jensen
2 Torture, Hickory 110

Jesters, see Paragons.

Jive Five
1 United Artists 3455, *6455*

Johnny and the Hurricanes
5 Live at the Star Club (Hamburg, Germany), Atila 1030
3 The Big Sound of Johnny and the Hurricanes, Big Top 1302
3 Johnny and the Hurricanes, Warwick 2007
3 Stormsville, Warwick 2010, *2010*

John's Children
3 Orgasm, White Whale *7128*

Bubber Johnson
2 Come Home, King 569
2 Bubber Johnson Sings Sweet Love Songs, King 624

Buddy Johnson
2 Rock and Roll Stage Show, Mercury 20209
1 Buddy Johnson Wails, Mercury 20330, *60072*
1 Rock and Roll Stage Show, Wing 12111 (reissue of Mercury 20209)

Lonnie Johnson
2 Low Down Blues (w/ J. Dupree; one side each), Continental 16002
2 Lonesome Road, King 520

Marv Johnson
2 Marvelous, United Artists 3081, *6081*
1 More, United Artists 3118, *6118*
1 I Believe, United Artists 3187, *6187*

Pete Johnson[27]
3 Swings the Boogie (w/H. Brooks), Crown 5058

Plas Johnson
2 Bop Me Daddy, Tampa 24

Robert Johnson
1 King of the Delta Blues Singers, Columbia 1654
1 King of the Delta Blues Singers, Vol. 2, Columbia 30034

Bruce Johnston
3 Surfin' 'Round the World, Columbia 2057, *8857*
2 Surfers Pajama Party, Del Fi 1228, *1228*

Brian Jones
1 Brian Jones Presents the Pipes of Pan at Joujouka, Rolling Stones *49100*

David Jones
1 Davy Jones, Bell 6067
1 David Jones, Colpix 493, *493*

[27] See also p. 154.

Jimmy Jones
3 Good Timin', MGM 3847, *3847*

Joe Jones
2 You Talk Too Much, Roulette 25143, *25143*

Paul Jones
1 Paul Jones Sings Songs From the Film Privilege and Others, Capitol 2795, *2795*

Louis Jordan
3 Louis Jordan's Greatest Hits, Decca 5035, *75035*
4 Let the Good Times Roll, Decca 8551
2 Somebody Up There Digs Me, Mercury 20242
1 Man We're Wailin', Mercury 20331
5 Come Blow Your Horn, Score 4007

Judas Jump
1 Scorch, Pride *0003*

Don Julian (w/the Meadowlarks)
3 Greatest Oldies, Amazon 1009

Bill Justis
2 Solid & Raunchy, Phillips 1950

Kak
2 Kak, Epic *26429*

Kaleidoscope
2 Side Trips, Epic 24304, *26304*
2 A Beacon From Mars, Epic 24333, *26333*
1 Incredible Kaleidoscope, Epic *26467*
1 Bernice, Epic *26508*

Kalin Twins
3 Kalin Twins, Decca 8812, *78812*

Ernie K-Doe
2 Mother-In-Law, Minit 0002

Kenny and the Kasuals
5 Impact, Mark 5000

Jack Kerouac, see p. 112.

Killing Floor
1 Killing Floor, Sire *97019*

B.B. King
1 Singin' the Blues, Crown 5020
1 B. B. King Wails, Crown 5115
1 King of the Blues, Crown 5167
1 My Kind of Blues, Crown 5188
1 Twist With B. B. King, Crown 5248
1 Easy Listening Blues, Crown 5286

Ben E. King
2 Spanish Harlem, Atco 133, *133*
2 Ben E. King Sings For Soulful Lovers, Atco 137, *137*
2 Don't Play That Song, Atco 142, *142*
1 Greatest Hits, Atco 165, *165*
1 Seven Letters, Atco 174, *174*
1 Young Boy Blues, Clarion 606, *606*

Freddie King
- 4 Freddie King Sings, King 762
- 2 Freddie King Goes Surfin', King 856
- 1 Freddie King Gives You a Bonanza of Instrumentals, King 928

Kinks
- 2 You Really Got Me, Reprise 6143
- 2 Kinks Size, Reprise 6158
- 2 Kinda Kinks, Reprise 6173
- 1 Kinda Kinks, Reprise *6173*
- 1 Kinks Kinkdom, Reprise *6184*
- 1 Kinkdom, Reprise *6184*
- 2 The Kink Kontroversy, Reprise 6197
- 1 The Kink Kontroversy, Reprise *6197*
- 1 Face to Face, Reprise 6228, *6228*
- 1 Live Kinks, Reprise 6260, *6260*

Kit Kats
- 1 It's Just a Matter of Time, Jamie 3029, *3029*
- 1 Kit Kats Do Their Thing Live, Jamie 3032, *3032*

Knickerbockers
- 1 Jerk and Twine Time, Challenge 621, *621*
- 1 Lies, Challenge 622, *622*
- 3 Lloyd Thaxton Presents the Knickerbockers, Challenge 12664

Gladys Knight and the Pips
- 3 Letter Full of Tears, Fury 1003
- 1 Gladys Knight and the Pips, Maxa 3000
- 1 Gladys Knight and the Pips, Sphere Sound 7006

Terry Knight and the Pack
- 1 Reflections, Cameo 2007, *2007*
- 2 Terry Knight and the Pack, Lucky Eleven 8000

Knights
- 2 Across the Board, Ace 200854
- 2 1967, Ace 201303
- 1 Hot Rod High, Capitol 2189, *2189*

Knockouts
- 2 Go Ape With the Knockouts, Tribute 1202

Buddy Knox
- 1 Golden Hits, Liberty 3251, *7251*
- 4 Buddy Knox, Roulette 25003
- 3 Buddy Knox and Jimmy Bowen, Roulette 25048
- 1 Gypsy Man, United Artists 6689

Kodaks and the Starlites
- 3 Kodaks Versus the Starlites, Sphere Sound 7005

Jerry Kole and the Strokers[28]
- 1 Hot Rod Alley, Crown 9309

Billy J. Kramer and the Dakotas
- 2 Little Children, Imperial 9267, *12267*
- 2 I'll Keep You Satisfied, Imperial 9273, *12273*
- 2 Trains, Boats and Planes, Imperial 9291, *12291*

Krazy Kats
- 2 Movin' Out, Damon 12478

[28] See also *Ritchie Valens*.

Kustom Kings
- 1 Kustom City U.S.A., Smash 27051, *67051*

Patti LaBelle and the Bluebelles
- 1 Over the Rainbow, Atlantic 8119, *8119*
- 2 The Apollo Presents the Bluebelles (Sweethearts of the Apollo), Newtown 631
- 2 Sleigh Bells, Jingle Bells and Blue Belles, Newtown 632
- 1 On Stage, Parkway 7043

Major Lance
- 1 Monkey Time, Okeh 12105, *14105*
- 1 Um, Um, Um, Um, Um, Um, Okeh 12106, *14106*
- 1 Major's Greatest Hits, Okeh 12110, *14110*

Larks
- 1 The Jerk, Money 1102

Rod Lauren
- 2 I'm Rod Lauren, RCA 2176, *2176*

Annie Laurie
- 2 It Hurts to Be In Love, Audio Lab 1510

Lazy Lester
- 1 True Blues, Excello 8006

Dr. Timothy Leary
- 1 You Can Be Anyone This Time Around, Douglas 1
- 1 Turn On, Tune In, Drop Out, Mercury *61131* (movie soundtrack)

Leaves
- 2 All the Good That's Happening, Capitol 2638, *2638*
- 2 Hey Joe, Mira 3005, *3005*

Brenda Lee
- 2 Brenda Lee, Decca, 4039, *74039*
- 1 This is Brenda, Decca 4082, *74082*
- 1 Emotions, Decca 4104, *74104*
- 1 Brenda Lee, All the Way, Decca 4176, *74176*
- 1 Sincerely, Brenda Lee, Decca 4216, *74216*
- 1 Brenda, That's All, Decca 4326, *74326*
- 1 All Alone Am I, Decca 4370, *74370*
- 1 Let Me Sing, Decca 4439, *74439*
- 1 Top Teen Hits, Decca 4626, *74626*
- 1 Bye Bye Blues, Decca 4755, *74755*
- 1 Coming On Strong, Decca 4825, *74825*

Dickey Lee
- 1 Tale of Patches, Smash 27020, *67020*
- 1 Dickey Lee Sings Laura and the Girl from Peyton Place, TCF Hall 8001, *8001*

Jackie Lee
- 1 The Duck, Mirwood 7000, *7000*

Left Banke
- 2 Walk Away Renee, Smash 27088, *67088*
- 2 Left Banke Too, Smash *67113*

Legends
- 1 Legends Let Loose, Capitol 1925, *1925*
- 1 Dynamic Sounds of the Legends, Columbia 1707, *8507*
- 2 Legends Let Loose, Ermine 101

Leiber-Stoller Big Band
2 Yakety Yak, Atlantic 8047, *8047*

John Lennon
3 John Lennon Sings the Great Rock and Roll Hits (Roots), Adam VIII *8018*

John Lennon and Yoko Ono
3 Wedding Album, Apple *3361*
2 Live Peace in Toronto, Apple *3362* (w/calendar)
2 Unfinished Music No. 1 (Two Virgins), Apple *5001*
2 Unfinished Music No. 2 (Life With the Lions), Zapple *3357*

Bobby Lester, see the Moonglows.

Barbara Lewis
1 Hello Stranger, Atlantic 8086, *8086*
1 Snap Your Fingers, Atlantic 8090, *8090*
1 Baby, I'm Yours, Atlantic 8110, *8110*
1 It's Magic, Atlantic 8118, *8118*

Bobby Lewis
2 Tossin' and Turnin', Beltone 4000

Jerry Lee Lewis
4 Jerry Lee Lewis, Sun 1230
3 Jerry Lee's Greatest, Sun 1265

Smiley Lewis
5 I Hear You Knocking, Imperial 9141

Lightnin' Slim
1 Rooster Blues, Excello 8000
1 Bell Ringer, Excello 8004
1 High and Low Down, Excello 8018

Little Anthony and the Imperials
2 We Are the Imperials, End 303
2 Shades of the 40's, End 311

Little Caesar and the Romans
3 Memories of Those Oldies But Goodies, Vol. 1, Del Fi 1218

Little Esther, see Esther Phillips

Little Eva
3 Loco-Motion, Dimension 6000, *6000*

Little Milton
1 We're Gonna Make It, Checker 2995
1 Little Milton Sings Big Blues, Checker 3002

Little Richard
2 Little Richard, RCA Camden 420
2 Here's Little Richard, Specialty 100
1 Here's Little Richard, Specialty 2100 (reissue of Specialty 100)
1 Little Richard, Specialty 2103
1 The Fabulous Little Richard, Specialty 2104
1 Biggest Hits, Specialty 2111

Little Walter
1 Little Walter's Best, Checker 3004
2 Best of Little Walter, Chess 1428

Little Willie John
3 Fever, King 564 (brown cover)
2 Fever, King 564 (blue cover)
1 Talk to Me—King 596
1 Mister Little Willie John, King 603
1 Action, King 691
1 Sure Things, King 734
1 At a Record Session, King 802
1 These Are My Favorite Songs, King 895
1 Little Willie John Sings All Originals, King 949

Lively Ones
1 Surf-Rider, Del Fi 1226, *1226*
1 Surf Drums, Del Fi 1231, *1231*
1 This is Surf City, Del Fi 1237, *1237*
1 Great Surf Hits, Del Fi 1238, *1238*
1 Surfin' South of the Border, Del Fi 1240, *1240*

Liverpool Beats
1 The Liverpool Beats!, Rondo 2026

Liverpool Five
1 Liverpool Five Arrive, RCA 3583, *3583*
1 Out of Sight, RCA 3682, *3682*

Nils Lofgren
2 Authorized Bootleg, A & M *8362*

Lord Sitar
3 Lord Sitar, Capitol *2916*

Los Bravos
1 Bring a Little Lovin', Parrott 71021
1 Black is Black, Press 73003, *83003*

Lost and Found
2 Forever Lasting Plastic Words, International Artists 3

Lothar and the Hand People
3 Space Hymn, Capitol *247*
2 Presenting Lothar and the Hand People, Capitol *2997*

John D. Loudermilk
1 Language of Love, RCA 2434, *2434*
1 Twelve Sides of Loudermilk, RCA 2539, *2539*
1 John D. Loudermilk, RCA 3497, *3497*

Louisiana Red
1 Louisiana Red Sings the Blues, Atco 389, *389*
1 The Low Down Back Porch Blues, Roulette 25200

H.P. Lovecraft
1 We Love You (Whoever You Are), Mercury *1031*
1 H. P. Lovecraft, Philips 200-252, 600-252
1 Lovecraft, Philips *600-279*
1 Valley of the Moon, Reprise *6419*

Love Sculpture
1 Forms and Feelings, Parrott *71035*
2 Blues Helping, Rare Earth 505 (rounded cover)

Jim Lowe
1 Songs They Sang Behind the Green Door, Dot 3051
1 Door of Fame, Mercury 20246

THE ROCK AND ROLL RECORDINGS

Frankie Lymon[29]
 2 Frankie Lymon at the London Palladium, Roulette 25013
 3 Rock 'n' Roll, Roulette 25036
 2 Jerry Blavat Presents Frankie Lymon's Greatest Hits, Roulette 25250

Willie Mabon
 2 Willie Mabon, Chess 1439

Lonnie Mack
 1 What of That Memphis Man, Fraternity 1014

Mad River
 2 Paradise Bar & Grill, Capitol *185*
 2 Mad River, Capitol *2985*

Majors
 1 Meet the Majors, Imperial 9222, *12222*

Mando and the Chile Peppers
 2 On the Road With Rock and Roll, Golden Crest 3023

Manfred Mann
 1 The Manfred Mann Album, Ascot 13015, *16015*
 1 My Little Red Book of Winners, Ascot 13021, *16021*
 1 Up the Junction, Mercury *61159* (movie soundtrack)

Manhattans
 1 Dedicated to You, Carnival 201, *201*
 1 For You and Yours, Carnival 202, *202*
 1 With These Hands, Deluxe 12000
 1 Million to One, Deluxe 12004

Barry Mann
 2 Who Put the Bomp in the Bomp, Bomp, Bomp, ABC-Paramount 399
 3 Who Put the Bomp in the Bomp, Bomp, Bomp, ABC-Paramount *399*

Carl Mann
 5 Like, Mann, Philips 1960

Charles Manson
 2 Lie, Awareness 22145

Marathons
 2 Peanut Butter, Arvee 428

Marcels
 2 Blue Moon, Colpix 416

Bobby Marchan
 2 There's Something on Your Mind, Sphere Sound 7004

Ernie Maresca
 1 Shout Shout (Knock Yourself Out), Seville 77001, *87001*

Mar-Keys
 1 Last Night, Atlantic 8055
 1 Do the Popeye With the Mar-Keys, Atlantic 8062

Martha and the Vandellas
 2 Come and Get These Memories, Gordy 902
 1 Heat Wave, Gordy 907

George Martin
 1 Off the Beatle Track, United Artists 3377, *6377*
 1 Hard Day's Night, United Artists 3383, *6383*
 1 George Martin, United Artists 3420, *6420*
 1 Help!, United Artists 3448, *6448*
 1 Beatle Girls, United Artists 3539, *6539*

Marvelettes
 2 Please Mr. Postman, Tamla 228
 1 The Marvelettes Sing, Tamla 229
 1 Marvelous Marvelettes, Tamla 237

Marvin and Johnny
 3 Marvin and Johnny, Crown 5381

Dave Mason
 2 Alone Together, Blue Thumb, *8819* (marble-colored plastic)

Nathaniel Mayer
 2 Going Back to the Village of Love, Fortune 8014

Paul McCartney
 3 The Family Way, London 76007, *82007* (movie soundtrack)

McClevertys
 1 The Fabulous McClevertys, Verve 2034[30]

McCoys
 1 Hang On Sloopy, Bang 212

Jimmy McCracklin
 1 Jimmy McCracklin Sings, Chess 1464
 1 I Just Gotta Know, Imperial 9219
 1 Every Night, Every Day, Imperial 9285, *12285*
 1 Think, Imperial 9297, *12297*
 1 My Answer, Imperial 9306, *12306*
 1 New Soul of Jimmy McCracklin, Imperial 9316, *12316*

MC5
 1 Back in the U.S.A., Atlantic *8247*
 1 High Time, Atlantic *8285*
 2 Kick Out the Jams, Elektra *74042* (liner notes by John Sinclair)

Mike McGear[31]
 1 McGear, Warner Bros. *2825*

Big Jay McNeely
 4 Big Jay McNeely, Federal 295-96 (10")
 3 Big Jay McNeely, King 295-96 (10") (reissue of Federal 295-96)
 3 Big Jay in 3-D, King 530
 2 Big Jay in 3-D, King 650
 3 A Rhythm and Blues Session, Savoy 15045 (10")

Clyde McPhatter
 5 Clyde McPhatter and the Drifters, Atlantic 8003 (black label)
 3 Clyde McPhatter and the Drifters, Atlantic 8003 (multicolored label)
 4 Love Ballads, Atlantic 8024 (black label)

---
[29] See also *Teenagers*.
[30] Includes "Don't Blame it on Elvis."
[31] Paul McCartney's brother.

2 Love Ballads, Atlantic 8024 (multicolored label)
3 Clyde, Atlantic 8031 (black label)
2 Clyde, Atlantic 8031 (multicolored label)
3 Best of Clyde McPhatter, Atlantic 8077
1 Welcome Home, Decca, 75231
5 Clyde McPhatter With Billy Ward and His Dominoes, King 559
2 Ta Ta, Mercury 20597, *60252*
2 Golden Blues Hits, Mercury 20655, *60655*
2 Lover Please, Mercury 20711, *60711*
2 Rhythm and Soul, Mercury 20750, *60750*
2 Greatest Hits, Mercury 20783, *60783*
2 Songs of the Big City, Mercury 20902, *60902*
2 Live at the Apollo, Mercury 20915, *60915*
2 Let's Start Over Again, MGM 3775, *3775*
2 Greatest Hits, MGM 3866, *3866*
1 May I Sing For You, Wing 12224, *16224*

Mellokings
4 Tonight Tonight, Herald 1013

Memphis Slim[32]
1 Memphis Slim, Candid 8024, *9024*
1 Memphis Slim, Chess 1455
1 Memphis Slim, King 885
1 The World's Foremost Blues Singer, Strand 1046, *1046*
1 Memphis Slim at the Gate of Horn, Vee Jay 1012

Jim Messina and His Jesters
2 The Dragsters, Audio Fidelity 3037, *7037*

Metrotones
2 Tops in Rock and Roll, Columbia 6341 (10")

Mickey and Sylvia[33]
2 Love is Strange, RCA Camden 863, *863*
4 New Sounds, Vik 1102

The Midnighters, see Hank Ballard and the Midnighters.

Amos Milburn
5 Party After Hours (w/others), Aladdin 703 (10")
5 Rockin' the Boogie, Aladdin 704 (10")
5 Rockin' the Boogie, Aladdin 810
4 Million Sellers, Imperial 9176
2 "The" Blues Boss, Motown 608
5 Let's Have a Party, Score 4012

Millennium
1 Begin, Columbia *9663*

Chuck Miller
1 Songs After Hours with Chuck Miller, Mercury 20195

Hayley Mills
1 Let's Get Together, Buena Vista 3311

Roy Milton
3 Rock 'n Roll vs. Rhythm and Blues, Dooto 223

Garnet Mimms and the Enchanters
1 Cry Baby, United Artists 3305, *6305*

[32] See also *Ivory Joe Hunter.*
[33] See also *Mickey Baker.*

Mindbenders
1 A Groovy Kind of Love, Fontana 27554, *67554*

Sal Mineo, see p. 114.

Miracles (w/Smokey Robinson)
3 Hi, We're the Miracles, Tamla 220
2 Cookin' With the Miracles, Tamla 223
2 Shop Around (w/others), Tamla 224
2 I'll Try Something New, Tamla 230
2 Christmas With the Miracles, Tamla 236
2 The Fabulous Miracles, Tamla, 238
1 Miracles On Stage, Tamla 241
3 Doin' Mickey's Monkey, Tamla 245

Mr. Gasser and the Weirdos
1 Hot Rod Hootenanny, Capitol 2010, *2010*
1 Rods 'n Ratfinks, Capitol 2057, *2057*
1 Surfin', Capitol 2114, *2114*

Freddie Mitchell
2 Freddie Mitchell, Vik 1030

Mom's Apple Pie
1 Mom's Apple Pie, Brown Bag *14200* (vagina cover)

Monkees
1 The Monkees, Colgems 101, *101*
1 More of the Monkees, Colgems 102, *102*
2 Headquarters, Colgems 103, *103*
1 Pisces, Aquarius, Capricorn and Jones, Ltd., Colgems 104, *104*
1 The Birds, the Bees and the Monkees, Colgems 109, *109*
2 Instant Replay, Colgems *113*
1 Monkees' Greatest Hits, Colgems *115*
2 The Monkees Present, Colgems *117*
3 Changes, Colgems *119*
2 Barrel Full of Monkees, Colgems *1001*
3 Head, Colgems *5008* (movie soundtrack)

Montage
1 Montage, Laurie *2049*

Chris Montez
1 Let's Dance, Monogram 100

Moody Blues
1 Go Now (The Moody Blues #1), London 3428, *428*

Moonglows
2 Look It's the Moonglows, Chess 1430
2 Best of Bobby Lester and the Moonglows, Chess 1471
2 Collector's Showcase, Vol. 2, Constellation 2
3 The Flamingos Meet the Moonglows, Vee Jay 1052

Bobby Moore and the Rhythm Aces
1 Searching For My Love, Checker 3000, *3000*

Gatemouth Moore
3 I'm a Fool to Care, King 684

Scotty Moore
3 The Guitar That Changed the World, Epic 24103, *26103*

Van Morrison
1 Blowin' Your Mind, Bang 218, *218*

Mothers of Invention (w/ Frank Zappa)
1 Freak Out, Verve 5005-2, 65005-2 (2 LPs)
1 Absolutely Free, Verve 5013, 65013
1 We're Only In It For the Money, Verve 5045, 65045
1 Ruben and the Jets, Verve 65055

Move
1 Shazam, A & M 4259
1 Looking On, Capitol 658
1 Message From the Country, Capitol 811

Moving Sidewalks
2 Flash, Tantara 6919

Moon Mullican
1 Instrumentals, Audio Lab 1568
5 Moon Over Mullican, Coral 57235
2 Moon Mullican Sings His All-Time Greatest Hits, King 555
2 Moon Mullican Sings and Plays 16 of His Favorite Tunes, King 628
2 The Many Moods of Moon Mullican, King 681

Music Machine
1 Turn On the Music Machine, Original Sound 5015, 8875

Mustangs
1 Dartell Stomp, Providence 001

Dave Myers and the Surftones
1 Greatest Racing Themes, Carole 8002
1 Hangin' Twenty, Del Fi 1239, 1239

Napoleon XIV
1 They're Coming to Take Me Away, Ha-Haaa!, Warner Bros. 1661

Nashville Teens
1 Tobacco Road, London 3407, 407

Nazz
3 Nazz, SGC 5001
3 Nazz Nazz, SGC 5002
3 Nazz 3, SGC 5004

Neighborhood Children
1 Neighborhood Children, Acta 38005

Ricky Nelson
1 For Your Sweet Love, Decca 4419, 74419
1 Rick Nelson Sings For You, Decca 4179, 74179
1 The Very Thought of You, Decca 4559, 74559
1 Spotlight on Rick, Decca 4608, 74608
2 Ricky, Imperial 9048
2 Ricky, Imperial 9050
2 Ricky Sings Again, Imperial 9061, 12090
2 Songs by Ricky, Imperial 9082, 12030
2 More Songs by Ricky, Imperial 9122, 12059
2 Rick is 21, Imperial 9152, 12071
2 Album Seven By Rick, Imperial 9167, 12082
2 Best Sellers, Imperial 9218
2 It's Up to You, Imperial 9223
1 Million Sellers, Imperial 9232, 12232
2 A Long Vacation, Imperial 9244
1 A Long Vacation, Imperial 12244
1 Ricky Nelson Sings For You, Imperial 9251, 12251
4 Teen Time, Verve 2083

Sandy Nelson
1 Teen Beat, Imperial 9105, 12044

Willie Nelson
1 And Then I Wrote, Liberty 3239, 7239
1 Here's Willie Nelson, Liberty 3308, 7308

Aaron Neville
1 Like it 'Tis, Minit 40007, 24007
1 Tell It Like It Is, Parlo 1

Newbeats
1 Bread and Butter, Hickory 120
1 Big Beat Sounds, Hickory 122, 122
1 Run Baby Run, Hickory 128, 128

New Colony Six
1 Breakthrough, Sentar 101
1 Colonization, Sentar 3001, 3001

New York Dolls
1 New York Dolls, Mercury 1-675
1 Too Much, Too Soon, Mercury 1-1001

Nico
1 The Marble Index, Electra 74029
1 Desert Shore, Reprise 6242
2 Chelsea Girl, Verve 5032, 65032

Nightcaps
3 Wine, Wine, Wine, Vandan 8124

Nightcrawlers
2 The Little Black Egg, Kapp 1520, 3520

Night Owls
1 Twisting the Oldies, Valmor 79

Jack Nitzsche
2 The Lonely Surfer, Reprise 6101, 6101
2 Dance to the Hits of the Beatles, Reprise 6115, 6115
2 Chopin '66, Reprise 6200, 6200

Terry Noland
5 Terry Noland, Brunswick 54041

Steve Noonan
1 Steve Noonan, Elektra 74017

NRBQ
2 NRBQ, Columbia 9858
1 Boppin' the Blues, Columbia 9981

Andrew Oldham Orchestra
1 The Rolling Stones Songbook, London 3457, 457
1 East Meets West, Parrot 61003, 71003

Johnny Olenn
3 Just Rollin' With Johnny Olenn, Liberty 3029

Olympics
1 Doin' the Hully Gully, Arvee 423
1 Dance By the Light of the Moon, Arvee 424
1 Party Time, Arvee 429

ROCK AND ROLL

The Ones
2 The Ones, Ashwood House 1105

Yoko Ono, see John Lennon and Yoko Ono.

Roy Orbison
3 Lonely and Blue, Monument 4002
4 Lonely and Blue, Monument *14002*
1 Crying, Monument 4007
2 Crying, Monument *14007*
1 Greatest Hits, Monument 4009
2 Greatest Hits, Monument *14009*
1 In Dreams, Monument 8003
2 In Dreams, Monument *18003*
4 Roy Orbison at the Rock House, Sun 1260

Original Soundtrack[34]
3 You Gotta Walk It Like You Talk It, Spark 02

Orioles
2 Greatest All Time Hits, Big A Records 2001
1 Modern Sounds of the Orioles, Charlie Parker 816, *816*
4 Cadillacs Meet the Orioles, Jubilee 1117

Tony Orlando
3 Bless You, Epic 3808, *611*

Orlons
1 Watusi, Cameo 1020
1 All the Hits, Cameo 1033
1 South Street, Cameo 1041
1 Not Me, Cameo 1054
1 Biggest Hits, Cameo 1061
1 Golden Hits, Cameo 1067
1 Down Memory Lane, Cameo 1073

Other Half
1 The Other Half, Acta *38004*

Johnny Otis
4 The Johnny Otis Show, Capitol 940
5 Rock and Roll Hit Parade, Dig 104

Outsiders
1 Time Won't Let Me, Capitol 2501, *2501*
1 Album #2, Capitol 2568, *2568*
1 In, Capitol 2636, *2636*
1 Happening Live, Capitol 2745, *2745*

Paisleys
1 Cosmic Mind at Play, Audio City 70

Paragons
2 Paragons Meet the Jesters, Jubilee 1098
2 Paragons vs. the Harptones, Musicnote 8001
2 Simply the Paragons, Rare Bird 8002
3 War: Jesters vs. the Paragons, Winley 6003

Peanut Butter Conspiracy
1 For Children of All Ages, Challenge 2000

David Peel
1 The Pope Smokes Dope, Apple *3391*

[34] Early *Steely Dan*.

Penguins
2 The Cool, Cool Penguins, Dooto 242

Jim Pepper
3 Pepper's Pow Wow, Embryo *731*

Carl Perkins
4 Whole Lotta Shakin', Columbia 1234
3 Country Boy's Dream, Dallie 4001
5 Dance Album, Sun 1225
4 Teen Beat (The Best of Carl Perkins), Sun 1225 (reissue of Dance Album)

Pep Perrine
2 Live and In Person, Hideout 1003

Peter and Gordon
1 A World Without Love, Capitol 2115, *2115*
1 I Don't Want to See You Again, Capitol 2220, *2220*
1 I Go to Pieces, Capitol 2324, *2324*
1 True Love Ways, Capitol 2368, *2368*
1 Peter and Gordon Sing and Play the Hits of Nashville, Tennessee, Capitol 2430, *2430*
1 Woman, Capitol 2477, *2477*
1 The Best of Peter and Gordon, Capitol 2549, *2549*
1 Lady Godiva, Capitol 2664, *2664*

Paul Peterson
1 Lollipops and Roses, Colpix 429, *429*
1 My Dad, Colpix 442, *442*

Ray Peterson
2 Tell Laura I Love Her, RCA 2297, *2297*

Phantom
1 Divine Comedy, Capitol *11313*

Esther Phillips (aka Little Esther)
5 Memory Lane, King 622
1 Release Me, Lenox 227

Gene Phillips
2 Gene Phillips and the Rockers, Crown 5375

Warren Phillips and the Rockets
1 Rocked Out, Parrott *71044*

Piano Red (aka Dr. Feelgood)
3 Jump Man Jump, Groove 1001
3 Piano Red in Concert, Groove 1002
1 Happiness is Piano Red, King 1117

Bobby Pickett and the Crypt Kickers
2 Monster Mash, Garpax 57001, *67001*

Pixies Three
1 Party With the Pixies Three, Mercury 20912, *60912*

Plastic Ono Band, see John Lennon and Yoko Ono.

Platters
5 The Platters, Federal 549
5 The Platters, King 549 (reissue of Federal 549)
5 The Platters, King 651
2 The Platters, Mercury 20146
2 The Platters, Volume Two, Mercury 20216

THE ROCK AND ROLL RECORDINGS

2 The Flying Platters, Mercury 20298
1 Flying Platters Around the World, Mercury 20366, *60043*
1 Remember When, Mercury 20410, *60087*
1 Encore of Golden Hits, Mercury 20472, *60243*
1 Reflections, Mercury 20481, *60160*
1 Life is Just a Bowl of Cherries, Mercury 20589, *60245*
1 More Encore of Golden Hits, Mercury 20591, *60252*

Playmates
1 At Play With the Playmates, Roulette 25403

Power Plant
2 The Golden Dawn, International Artists 4

Elvis Presley
3 Singer Presents Elvis Singing Flaming Star and Others, RCA *279* (sold only in Singer Sewing Machine centers in conjunction with 1968 TV special)
5 Elvis' Christmas Album, RCA (LOC) 1035 (original issue w/fold-out cover; includes 10 pages of photos)
3 Elvis Presley, RCA 1254
1 Elvis Presley, RCA *1254* ("fake" stereo; black label)
3 Elvis, RCA 1382
1 Elvis, RCA *1382* ("fake" stereo; black label)
3 Loving You, RCA 1515
1 Loving You, RCA *1515* ("fake" stereo; black label)
3 Elvis' Golden Records, RCA 1707
1 Elvis' Golden Records, RCA *1707* ("fake" stereo; black label)
2 King Creole, RCA 1884 (movie soundtrack)
1 King Creole, RCA *1884* ("fake" stereo; black label)
3 Elvis' Christmas Album, RCA 1951 (reissue of RCA 1035)
1 Elvis' Christmas Album, RCA *1951* ("fake" stereo; black label)
3 For LP Fans Only, RCA 1990
1 For LP Fans Only, RCA *1990* ("fake" stereo; black label)
4 A Date With Elvis, RCA 2011 (double-pocket issue)
3 A Date With Elvis, RCA 2011 (single-pocket issue)
1 A Date With Elvis, RCA *2011* ("fake" stereo; black label)
5 50,000,000 Elvis Fans Can't Be Wrong (Elvis' Gold Records, Vol. 2), RCA 2075 (black cover)
3 50,000,000 Elvis Fans Can't Be Wrong (Elvis' Gold Records, Vol. 2), RCA 2075 (white cover)
1 50,000,000 Elvis Fans Can't Be Wrong (Elvis' Gold Records, Vol. 2), RCA *2075* ("fake" stereo; black label)
2 Elvis is Back, RCA 2231, *2231*
2 GI Blues, RCA 2256, *2256* (movie soundtrack)
2 His Hand in Mine, RCA 2328, *2328*
2 Something For Everybody, RCA 2370, *2370*
2 Blue Hawaii, RCA 2426, *2426* (movie soundtrack)
2 Pot Luck, RCA 2523, *2523*
2 Girls, Girls, Girls, RCA 2621, *2621* (movie soundtrack)
3 It Happened at the World's Fair, RCA 2697, *2697* (movie soundtrack)
2 Fun in Acapulco, RCA 2756, *2756* (movie soundtrack)
2 Elvis' Golden Records, Vol. 3, RCA 2765, *2765*
2 Kissin' Cousins, RCA 2894, *2894* (movie soundtrack)
2 Roustabout, RCA 2999, *2999* (movie soundtrack)
2 Girl Happy, RCA 3338, *3338* (movie soundtrack)
2 Elvis For Everyone, RCA 3450, *3450*
3 Harum Scarum, RCA 3468, *3468* (movie soundtrack)
4 Frankie and Johnny, RCA 3553, *3553* (movie soundtrack)
2 Paradise Hawaiian Style, RCA 3643, *3643* (movie soundtrack)
3 Spinout, RCA 3702, *3702* (movie soundtrack)
2 How Great Thou Art, RCA 3758, *3758*

3 Double Trouble, RCA 3787, *3787* (movie soundtrack)
4 Clambake, RCA 3893 (movie soundtrack)
2 Clambake, RCA *3893* (movie soundtrack)
5 Elvis' Golden Records, Vol. 4, RCA 3921
2 Elvis' Golden Records, Vol. 4, RCA *3921*
5 Speedway, RCA 3989 (movie soundtrack)
2 Speedway, RCA *3989*

Johnny Preston
2 Running Bear, Mercury 20592, *60250*
4 Come Rock With Me, Mercury 20609, *60609*
1 Running Bear, Wing 12246, *16246*

Pretty Things
2 The Pretty Things, Fontana 27544, *67544*
2 S.F. Sorrow, Rare Earth 506 (rounded cover)
1 Parachute, Rare Earth 515

Lloyd Price
1 The Exciting Lloyd Price, ABC-Paramount 277, *277*
1 Mr. Personality, ABC-Paramount 297, *297*
1 Lloyd Price ("Mr. Personality" Sings the Blues), ABC-Paramount 315, *315*
1 "Mr. Personality's" 15 Hits, ABC-Paramount 324
1 The Fantastic Lloyd Price, ABC-Paramount 346, *346*
1 Lloyd Price Sings the Million Sellers, ABC-Paramount 366, *366*
1 Cookin', ABC-Paramount 382, *382*
2 Lloyd Price, Specialty 2105

Red Prysock
2 Rock 'n Roll, Mercury 20088
2 Fruit Boots, Mercury 20211
2 The Beat, Mercury 20307
2 Battle Royal (w/S. Austin), Mercury 20434, *60106*

Pyramids
1 Penetration, Best 1001

Suzi Quatro
1 Suzi Quatro, Bell *1302*
1 Quatro, Bell *1313*

Question Mark and the Mysterians
1 96 Tears, Cameo 2004, *2004*
1 Action, Cameo 2006, *2006*

Raindrops
1 The Raindrops, Jubilee 5023, *5023*

Marvin Rainwater
3 Songs By Marvin Rainwater, MGM 3534
3 Marvin Rainwater Sings With a Heart, With a Beat, MGM 3721
3 Gonna Find Me a Bluebird, MGM 4046

Teddy Randazzo
1 Journey to Love, ABC-Paramount 352, *352*
1 T.N.T., ABC-Paramount 421, *421*
1 Big Wide World, Colpix 445, *445*
2 I'm Confessin' Vik 1121

Rattles
1 Searchers Meet the Rattles, Mercury 20994, *60994*
1 Greatest Hits, Mercury 21127, *61127*

ROCK AND ROLL

Ravens
3 Write Me a Letter, Regent 6062 (green label)
1 Write Me a Letter, Regent 6062 (red label)

Raw Holly
1 Raw Holly, Coral 757515

Red Krayola
3 The Parable of Arable Land, International Artists 2
3 God Bless the Red Krayola and All Who Sail With It, International Artists 7

Eivets Rednow, see Stevie Wonder.

Otis Redding
2 Pain in My Heart, Atco 161, *161*
1 King and Queen (w/C. Thomas), Stax 716, *716*
1 Otis Redding Sings Soul Ballads, Volt 411, *411*
1 Otis Blue, Volt 412, *412*
1 Soul Album, Volt 413, *413*

Jimmy Reed
1 I'm Jimmy Reed, Vee Jay 1004
1 Rockin' With Reed, Vee Jay 1008

Lula Reed
2 Blue and Moody, King 604

Jim Reeves
2 Jim Reeves Sings, Abbott 5001

Reflections
1 Just Like Romeo and Juliet, Golden World 300

Regents
1 Discotheque, Capitol 2153, *2153*
2 Barbara Ann, Gee 706, *706*

Remains
3 The Remains, Epic 24214
4 The Remains, Epic *26214*

Diane Renay
1 Navy Blue, 20th Century Fox 3133, *4133*

Reparrata and the Delrons
1 Whenever a Teenager Cries, World Artists 2006

Johnny Restivo
2 Oh Johnny, RCA 2149, *2149*

Revels
2 Revels On a Rampage, Impact 1

Paul Revere and the Raiders
4 Like Long Hair, Gardena 1000
1 In the Beginning, Jerden 7004, *7004*
5 Paul Revere and the Raiders, Sande 1001

Todd Rhodes
2 Todd Rhodes Plays His Hits, King 295-88 (10")
2 Dance Music That Hits the Spot, King 658

Rhythm Rockers
1 Soul Surfin', Challenge 617

Charlie Rich
4 Lonely Weekends, Phillips 1970

Cliff Richard (and the Shadows)
1 Cliff Sings, ABC-Paramount 321, *321*
1 Listen to Cliff, ABC-Paramount 391, *391*
2 Wonderful to Be Young, Dot 3474, *25474* (movie soundtrack)
1 Hits From the Original Sound Track of Summer Holiday, Epic 24063, *26063*
1 It's All In the Game, Epic 24089, *26089*
1 Cliff Richard in Spain With the Shadows, Epic 24115, *26115*
1 Swinger's Paradise, Epic 24145, *26145* (movie soundtrack)

Billy Lee Riley
1 Harmonica and the Blues, Crown 5277
1 Southern Soul, Majo 1933
1 Harmonica Beatlemania, Mercury 20974, *60974*

Rip Chords
1 Hey Little Cobra, Columbia 2151, *8951*
1 Three Window Coupe, Columbia 2216, *9016*

Johnny Rivers
1 The Sensational Johnny Rivers, Capitol 2161, *2161*

Rivieras
2 Campus Party, Riviera 701
1 Let's Have a Party, USA 102

Rivingtons
1 Doin' the Bird, Liberty 3282, *7282*

Road Runners
1 The New Mustang, London 3381, *381*

Marty Robbins
5 Rock and Roll 'n Robbins, Columbia 2601 (10")

Robins
5 Rock 'n Roll, Whippet 703

Sugar Chile Robinson
2 Boogie Woogie, Capitol 589

Rock-A-Teens
5 Woo-Hoo, Roulette 25109, *25109*

Rockets
1 The Rockets, White Whale *7116*

Rockin' Rebels
3 Wild Weekend, Swan 509

Rocky Fellers
1 Killer Joe, Scepter 512

Rod and the Cobras
1 Rod and the Cobras at a Drag Race at Surf City, Somerset 20500, *20500*

Tommy Roe
1 Sheila, ABC-Paramount 432, *432*
1 Something For Everybody, ABC-Paramount 467, *467*

Rokes
3 Che Mondo Strano, RCA International 185

Rolling Stones
4 It's Here Luv!, INS Radio 1003 (interview LP)
1 Big Hits, London NP-1
2 Satanic Majesties Request, London NPS-2 (3-D cover)
1 The Rolling Stones, London 3375
1 12 × 5, London 3402
1 The Rolling Stones, Now!, London 3420
1 Out of Our Heads, London 3429
1 England's Greatest Hitmakers, London 3430
1 December's Children, London 3451
1 Aftermath, London 3476
1 Got Live If You Want It, London 3493
1 Between the Buttons, London 3499

Ronettes
2 Ronettes Featuring Veronica, Colpix 486, *486*
4 Presenting the Fabulous Ronettes Featuring Veronica, Philles 4006
5 Presenting the Fabulous Ronettes Featuring Veronica, Philles *4006*

Ronnie and the Daytonas
2 GTO, Mala 4001
2 Sandy, Mala 4002

Rumblers
2 Boss, Downey 1001, *1001*
1 Boss, Dot 3509, *25509*

Todd Rundgren
1 Runt, Ampex *10105*
3 Runt: The Ballad of Todd Rundgren, Ampex *10116*

Jimmy Rushing, see p. 169.

Charlie Ryan
2 Hot Rod Lincoln Drags Again, Hilltop 6006
3 Hot Rod, King 751

Bobby Rydell
1 We Got Love, Cameo 1006
1 Bobby Sings, Bobby Swings, Cameo 1007
1 Bobby's Biggest Hits, Cameo 1009
1 Bobby Rydell Salutes the Great Ones, Cameo 1010, *1010*
1 Bobby Rydell Sings, Strand 1120, *1120*

Sacred Mushroom
1 The Sacred Mushroom, Parallax 4001

Sagittarius
1 Present Tense, Columbia 9644
1 The Blue Marble, Together *1002*

Tommy Sands
1 Steady Date, Capitol 848
2 Sing Boy Sing, Capitol 929 (movie soundtrack)
1 Teenage Rock, Capitol 1009
2 Sands Storm, Capitol 1081
1 When I'm Thinking of You, Capitol 1239, *1239*
1 Sands at the Sands, Capitol 1364, *1364*

Santo and Johnny
1 Santo and Johnny, Canadian-American 1001, *1001*
1 Beatles Greatest Hits, Canadian-American 1017, *1017*

Sapphires
1 Who Do You Love, Swan 513

Peter Sarstedt
1 Every Word You Say Is Written Down, United Artists 5558
1 Where Do You Go To My Lovely, World Pacific 21895
1 As Though It Were a Movie, World Pacific *21899*

Scaffold
2 Thank U Very Much, Bell *6018*

Jack Scott
3 Burning Bridges, Capitol 2035, *2035*
5 Jack Scott, Carlton 107, *107*
5 What Am I Living For, Carlton 122
4 I Remember Hank Williams, Top Rank 319, *619*
5 What In the World's Come Over You, Top Rank 326, *626*
5 The Spirit Moves Me, Top Rank 348, *648*

Little Jimmy Scott, see p. 116.

Linda Scott
2 Starlight, Starbright, Canadian-American 1005, *1005*
2 Great Scott, Canadian-American 1007
3 Great Scott, Canadian-American *1007*
2 Linda, Congress 3001
1 Hey, Look At Me Now, Kapp 1424, *3424*

Searchers
1 Meet the Searchers, Kapp 1363, *3363*
1 This Is Us, Kapp 1409, *3409*
1 New Searchers LP, Kapp 1412, *3412*
1 Searchers No. 4, Kapp 1449, *3449*
1 Take Me For What I'm Worth, Kapp 1477, *3477*
1 Hear! Hear!, Mercury 20914, *60914*
1 Searchers Meet the Rattles, Mercury 20994, *60994*

Neil Sedaka
3 Neil Sedaka, RCA 2035, *2035*
1 Circulate, RCA 2317, *2317*
1 Little Devil, RCA 2421, *2421*
1 Neil Sedaka Sings His Greatest Hits, RCA 2627, *2627*
1 Italiano, RCA *1040*
1 Smile, RCA *1081*
1 Breaking Up Is Hard to Do, RCA Camden 7006

Seeds
1 The Seeds, GNP-Crescendo 2023, *2023*
1 A Web of Sound, GNP-Crescendo 2033, *2033*
1 Future, GNP-Crescendo 2038, *2038*
1 Sky Saxon Blues Band, GNP-Crescendo 2040, *2040*
1 Raw and Alive, GNP Crescendo *2043*

Seekers
1 The Seekers, Marvel 2060, *3060*

Sensations
2 Let Me In, Argo 4022

Sentinels
1 Big Surf, Del Fi 1232, *1232*
1 Surfer Girl, Del Fi 1241, *1241*

Serpent Power
2 Serpent Power, Vanguard 79252

ROCK AND ROLL

David Seville[35]
- 1 Music of David Seville, Liberty 3073
- 1 Witch Doctor, Liberty 3092

Shades of Blue
- 1 Happiness Is the Shades of Blue, Impact 101

Shadows[36]
- 1 Surfing With the Shadows, Atlantic 8089, *8089*
- 1 The Shadows Know, Atlantic 8097, *8097*

Shadows of Knight
- 1 Gloria, Dunwich 666, *666*
- 1 Back Door Men, Dunwich 667, *667*

Shangri-las
- 2 Leader of the Pack, Red Bird 101
- 2 Shangri-las '65, Red Bird 104
- 1 I Can Never Go Home Anymore, Red Bird 10 (reissue of Shangri-las '65)

Del Shannon
- 2 Handy Man, Amy 8003, *8003*
- 1 Del Shannon Sings Hank Williams, Amy 8004, *8004*
- 1 One Thousand Six Hundred Sixty-One Seconds, Amy 8006, *8006*
- 3 Runaway, Big Top 1303
- 2 Little Town Flirt, Big Top 1308
- 1 Best of Del Shannon, Dot 3824, *25824*
- 1 This is My Bag, Liberty 3453, *7453*
- 1 Total Commitment, Liberty 3479, *7479*
- 1 The Further Adventures of Charles Westover, Liberty 7539

Helen Shapiro
- 1 A Teenager in Love, Epic 24075, *26075*

Shells, see Dubs.

Shep and the Limelites
- 2 More Oldies, Roulette 25350

Sheppards
- 3 The Sheppards, Constellation 4

Sherry's
- 1 At the Hop With the Sherry's, Guyden 503

Shiloh
- 1 Shiloh, Amos 7015

Shirelles
- 1 Tonight's the Night, Scepter 501
- 1 The Shirelles Sing to Trumpets and Strings, Scepter 502
- 1 Baby It's You, Scepter 504
- 1 Shirelles and King Curtis Give a Twist Party, Scepter 505

Shirley and Lee
- 5 Let the Good Times Roll, Aladdin 807
- 4 Let the Good Times Roll, Imperial 9179
- 4 Let the Good Times Roll, Score 4023
- 2 Let the Good Times Roll, Warwick 2028

Troy Shondell
- 1 The Many Sides of Troy Shondell, Everest 5206, *1206*

Shondells
- 2 Shondells at the Saturday Hop, La Louisianne 109

Silhouettes
- 3 Get a Job, Goodway 100

Silkie
- 2 You've Got to Hide Your Love Away, Fontana 27548, *67548*[37]

Silly Surfers
- 1 Sounds of Silly Surfers, Mercury 20977, *60977*

Gene Simmons
- 1 Jumpin' Gene Simmons, Hi 12018, *32018*

Simon and Garfunkel
- 3 Hit Sounds of Simon and Garfunkel, Pickwick 3059
- 2 Simon and Garfunkel, Sears 435

Simon Sisters (Carly and Lucy)
- 2 Simon Sisters, Kapp 1359
- 2 Cuddle Bug, Kapp 1398

Sir Douglas Quintet
- 1 Best of Sir Douglas Quintet, Tribe 37001, *47001*

Skyliners
- 3 Skyliners, Calico 3000

Slade
- 1 Play It Loud, Cotillion *9035*
- 2 Ballzy, Fontana *67598*

Millie Small
- 1 My Boy Lollipop, Smash 27055, *67055*

Small Faces
- 1 There Are But Four Small Faces, Immediate *125200*2[38]
- 1 Ogden's Nut Gone Flake, Immediate *125200*8 (round cover)

Huey "Piano" Smith
- 4 Having a Good Time, Ace 1004
- 4 For Dancing, Ace 1015
- 2 'Twas the Night before Christmas, Ace 1027
- 1 Huey "Piano" Smith, Grand Prix *418*

Ray Smith
- 1 Ray Smith and Patt Cupp, Crown 5364
- 5 Travelin' With Ray, Judd 701

Sonics
- 2 Merry Christmas From the Wailers, the Sonics, and the Galaxies, Etiquette 2
- 1 Here Are the Sonics, Etiquette 024
- 1 The Sonics Boom, Etiquette 027
- 1 Introducing the Sonics, Jerden 7007, *7007*

---

[35] See also *Chipmunks*.
[36] See also *Cliff Richard*.
[37] With George Harrison on sitar.
[38] Bootleg cover in black and white.

THE ROCK AND ROLL RECORDINGS

Sophomores
  4 The Sophomores, Seeco 451

Bob B. Soxx and the Blue Jeans
  2 Zip-A-Dee-Doo-Dah, Philles 4002

Spaniels
  5 Goodnite, It's Time to Go, Vee Jay 1002 (brown label)
  3 Goodnite, It's Time to Go, Vee Jay 1002 (black label)
  3 The Spaniels, Vee Jay 1024

Alexander Spence
  2 Oar, Columbia *9831*

Spiders
  5 I Didn't Want To Do It, Imperial 9140

Spring
  1 Spring, United Artists 5571

Dusty Springfield
  1 Dusty in Memphis, Atlantic *8214*
  1 Stay Awhile/I Only Want to Be With You, Philips 200–133, *600–133*
  1 Dusty, Philips 200–156, *600–156*
  1 Oooooooweeee!!!!, Philips 200–174, *600–174*
  1 You Don't Have to Say You Love Me, Philips 200–210, *600–210*

SRC
  2 Milestones, Capitol *134*
  2 Traveler's Tale, Capitol *273*
  2 SRC, Capitol *2991*

Terry Stafford
  2 Suspicion, Crusader 1001, *1001*

Standells
  2 Standells In Person at P.J.'s, Liberty 3384, *7384*
  1 Live and Out of Sight, Sunset 1186, *5136*
  1 Dirty Water, Tower 5027, *5027*
  1 Why Pick On Me, Tower 5044, *5044*
  1 Hot Ones, Tower 5049, *5049*
  1 Try It, Tower 5098, *5098*

Tommy Steele
  2 Rock Around the World, London 1770

Steely Dan, see Original Soundtrack.

Dodie Stevens
  1 Dodie Stevens, Dot 3212, *25212*
  1 Over the Rainbow, Dot 3323, *25323*
  1 Pink Shoelaces, Dot 3371, *25371*

Al Stewart
  2 Love Chronicles, Epic *26564*

John Stewart and Scott Engel
  1 I Only Came to Dance With You, Tower 5026

Gary Stites
  1 Lonely For You, Carlton 120, *120*

Stone Poneys
  2 The Stone Poneys, Capitol 2666, *2666*

  1 Evergreen, Vol. 2, Capitol 2763, *2763*
  1 Stone Poneys, Vol. 3, Capitol *2863*

Roland Stone
  2 Just a Moment of Your Time, Ace 1018

Stooges[39]
  2 The Stooges, Elektra *74051*
  2 Fun House, Elektra *74071*

Billy Storm
  1 Billy Storm, Buena Vista 3315
  1 This is the Night (w/the Valiants), Famous 504

Strangeloves
  1 I Want Candy, Bang 211

String-a-longs
  1 Matilda, Dot 3463, *25463*
  1 Pick-a-Hit, Warwick 2036, *2036*

Nolan Strong and the Diablos
  2 Fortune of Hits, Fortune 8010
  1 Fortune of Hits, Vol. 2, Fortune 8012
  1 Mind Over Matter, Fortune 8015

Sunny and the Sunliners
  1 Talk to Me, Teardrop 2000

Sunrays
  2 Andrea, Tower 5017, *5017*

Super Stocks
  1 Thunder Road, Capitol 2060, *2060*
  1 Surf Route 101, Capitol 2113, *2113*
  1 School is a Drag, Capitol 2190, *2190*

Supremes
  4 Meet the Supremes, Motown 606 (original cover w/group on stools)
  1 A Bit of Liverpool, Motown 623, *623*

Surf Stompers
  1 Original Surfer Stomp, Del Fi 1236, *1236*

Surfaris
  1 The Surfaris Play, Decca 4470, *74470*
  1 Hit City '64, Decca 4487, *74487*
  1 Fun City U.S.A., Decca 4560, *74560*
  1 Hit City '65, Decca 4614, *74614*
  1 It Ain't Me, Babe, Decca 4683, *74683*
  1 Wipe Out, Dot 3535, *25535*

Sweet Thursday
  1 Sweet Thursday, Tetragrammaton *112*

Swinging Blue Jeans
  1 Hippy Hippy Shake, Imperial 9261, *12261*

James Taylor
  2 James Taylor, Apple *3352*

Kingsize Taylor and the Dominos
  1 Real Gonk Man, Midnight 2101, *2101*

---
[39] See also *Iggy and the Stooges.*

Sam "The Man" Taylor[40]
1 Rockin' at the Hop, Lion 70054 (reissue of MGM 3473)
5 The Big Beat, MGM 293 (10")
4 Music With the Big Beat, MGM 3473

Teddy Bears
5 Teddy Bears Sing!, Imperial 9067, *12010*

Teddy and the Pandas
1 Basic Magnetism, Tower *5125*

Teenagers (w/Frankie Lymon)
4 Teenagers, Gee 701 (red label)
1 Teenagers, Gee 701 (gray label)

Teen Queens
1 Teen Queens, Crown *373*
2 Eddie My Love, Crown 5022

Temptations
1 Meet the Temptations, Gordy 911

Them
1 Them, Parrot 61005, *71005*
1 Them Again, Parrot 61008, *71008*

Third Rail
1 Id Music, Epic 24327, *26327*

13th Floor Elevators
4 Psychedelic Sounds, International Artists 1
4 Easter Everywhere, International Artists 5
3 Live, International Artists 8
3 Bull of the Woods, International Artists 9

Carla Thomas
1 Gee Whiz, Atlantic 8057, *8057*
1 King and Queen (w/O. Redding), Stax 716, *716*

Sonny Thompson
2 Moody Blues, King 568
2 Mellow Blues For the Late Hours, King 655

Big Mama Thornton
1 She's Back, Back Beat 68

The Three Chuckles
3 The Three Chuckles, Vik 1067

Johnny Thunder
1 Loop De Loop, Diamond 5001, *5001*

Thunderbirds
2 Meet the Fabulous Thunderbirds, Red Feather 1

Johnny Tillotson
2 Johnny Tillotson's Best, Cadence 3052, *25052*
1 It Keeps Right On A-Hurtin', Cadence 3058, *25058*
1 You Can Never Stop Loving Me, Cadence 3067, *25067*

Tokens
1 Intercourse, B. T. Puppy 1027 (unreleased LP)
1 The Lion Sleeps Tonight, RCA 2514, *2514*
1 We Sing Folk, RCA 2631, *2631*

[40] See also *Claude Cloud* and p. 173.

1 Wheels, RCA 2886, *2886*
1 The Tokens Again, RCA 3685, *3685*

Tomorrow
1 Tomorrow, Sire *97012*

Tonto's Expanding Head Band
1 Zero Time, Embryo *732*

Tornadoes
2 Bustin' Surfboards, Josie 4005, *4005*
1 Telstar, London 3279

Mitchell Torok
2 Caribbean, Guyden 502, *502*

Al Tousan
3 The Wild Sounds of New Orleans, RCA 1767

Bobby Lee Trammell
3 Arkansas Twist, Atlanta 1503

Trashmen
3 Surfin' Bird, Garrett 200, *200*

Tremeloes
1 Here Are the Tremeloes (w/Brian Poole), Audio Fidelity 2177, *6177*
1 Here Comes My Baby, Epic 24310, *26310*
1 Even the Bad Times Are Good, Epic 24326, *26326*
1 Suddenly You Love Me, Epic 24363, *26363*
1 World Explosion, Epic *26388*

Treniers
1 Souvenir Album, Dot 3257
2 Go, Go, Go, Epic 3125

Troggs
1 Wild Thing, Atco 193, *193*
1 Wild Thing, Fontana 27556, *67556*
1 Love Is All Around, Fontana *67576*

Doris Troy
1 Doris Troy, Apple *3371*

Trumpeteers
4 Milky White Way, Score 4021

Ike Turner
1 Ike Turner Rocks the Blues, Crown 5367, *367*

Ike and Tina Turner
5 River Deep, Mountain High, Philles 4011
2 The Sound of Ike and Tina Turner, Sue 2001
2 Dance, Sue 2003
2 Dynamite, Sue 2004
2 Don't Play Us Cheap, Sue 2005
2 It's Gonna Work Out Fine, Sue 2007

Joe Turner
2 Boss of the Blues, Atlantic 1234, *1234*
3 Big Joe Rides Again, Atlantic 1332, *1332*
3 Joe Turner, Atlantic 8005
3 Rockin' the Blues, Atlantic 8023
3 Big Joe Is Here, Atlantic 8033
1 Best of Joe Turner, Atlantic 8081

THE ROCK AND ROLL RECORDINGS

2 Joe Turner and Pete Johnson, EmArcy 36014
1 And the Blues Will Make You Happy Too, Savoy 14012
1 Careless Love, Savoy 14016

Sammy Turner
3 Lavender Blue Moods, Big Top 1301, *1301*

Titus Turner
1 Sound Off, Jamie 3018

Turtles
1 You Baby, White Whale 112, *7112*
1 Happy Together, White Whale 114, *7114*
1 Golden Hits, White Whale, 115, *7115*
1 Turtles Present the Battle of the Bands, White Whale *7118*
1 Turtle Soup, White Whale *7124*
1 More Golden Hits, White Whale *7127*
1 Wooden Head, White Whale *7133*

Twins
2 Teenagers Love the Twins, RCA 1708

Twistin' Kings
1 Twistin' the World Around, Motown 601

Conway Twitty
1 It's Only Make Believe, Metro 512, *512*
3 Conway Twitty Sings, MGM 3744, *3744*
3 Saturday Night With Conway Twitty, MGM, 3786, *3786*
3 Lonely Boy Blue, MGM 3818, *3818*
1 Conway Twitty's Greatest Hits, MGM 3849, *3849*
2 Rock and Roll Story, MGM 3907, *3907*
2 Conway Twitty Touch, MGM 3943, *3943*
2 Portrait of a Fool, MGM 4019, *4019*
2 R & B '63, MGM 4089, *4089*
2 Hit the Road!, MGM 4217, *4217*

Red Tyler and the Gyros
2 Rockin' and Rollin', Ace 1006
1 Twistin' with Mr. Sax, Ace 1021 (reissue of Ace 1006)

Tymes
1 So Much in Love, Parkway 7032
1 Sound of the Wonderful Tymes, Parkway 7038, *7038*
1 Somewhere, Parkway 7039, *7039*

Unbeetables
2 Live at Palisades Park, Dawn 5050

Ricky Vale
2 Everybody's Surfin', Strand 1104, *1104*

Ritchie Valens
1 Ritchie Valens and Jerry Kole, Crown 5996, *556*
4 Ritchie Valens, Del Fi 1201
4 Ritchie, Del Fi 1206
5 In Concert at Pacoima Jr. High, Del Fi 1214
4 His Greatest Hits, Del Fi 1225
4 Greatest Hits, Vol. 2, Del Fi 1247

Larry Verne
2 Mr. Larry Verne, Era 104

Versatones
2 The Versatones, RCA 1538

Vettes
1 Rev-Up, MGM 4193, *4193*

Vibrations
1 Watusi, Checker 2978

Viceroys
1 The Viceroys at Granny's Pad, Bolo 8000

Gene Vincent
5 Bluejean Bop, Capitol 764
5 Gene Vincent and the Blue Caps, Capitol 811
5 Gene Vincent Rocks and the Blue Caps Roll, Capitol 970
5 A Gene Vincent Record Date, Capitol 1059
5 Sounds Like Gene Vincent, Capitol 1207
5 Crazy Times, Capitol 1342, *1342*

Eddie "Cleanhead" Vinson, see p. 175.

Virtues
1 Guitar Boogie Shuffle, Strand 1061, *1061*

Viscounts
1 Harlem Nocturne, Amy 8008, *8008*
2 The Viscounts, Madison 1001

Wailers
2 Fabulous Wailers at the Castle, Etiquette 1
2 Merry Christmas From the Wailers, the Sonics, and the Galaxies, Etiquette 2
1 Wailers and Company, Etiquette 022
1 Wailers, Wailers Everywhere, Etiquette 023
1 Out of Our Tree, Etiquette 026
3 Fabulous Wailers, Golden Crest 3075 (original issue)
2 The Wailers Wail, Golden Crest 3075 (reissue)

Jerry Jeff Walker
2 Mr. Bojangles, Atco 259
1 5 Years Gone, Atco 297
1 Bein' Free, Atco 336
1 Driftin' Way of Life, Vanguard 6521

Junior Walker
1 Shotgun, Soul 701, *701*
1 Soul Session, Soul 702, *702*
1 Road Runner, Soul 703, *703*
1 "Live!", Soul 705, *705*

T-Bone Walker
2 T-Bone Blues, Atlantic 8020
2 Classics in Jazz, Capitol 370 (10")
2 The Great Blues Vocals and Guitar of T-Bone Walker Capitol 1958
2 T-Bone Walker Sings the Blues, Imperial 9098
2 Singing the Blues, Imperial 9116
2 I Get So Weary, Imperial 9146

Walker Brothers
1 Introducing the Walker Brothers, Smash 27076, *67076*
1 The Sun Ain't Gonna Shine Any More, Smash 27082, *67082*

Jerry Wallace
1 Just Jerry, Challenge 606
1 There She Goes, Challenge 612, *612*
1 Shutters and Boards, Challenge 616, *616*
1 In the Misty Moonlight, Challenge 619, *619*

Billy Ward and the Dominoes
  4 Billy Ward and the Dominoes, Decca 8621
  5 Billy Ward and His Dominoes, Federal 295-94 (10″)
  5 Billy Ward and His Dominoes, Federal 548
  5 Billy Ward and His Dominoes, King 548
  5 Clyde McPhatter With Billy Ward and His Dominoes, King 559
  4 Billy Ward and His Dominoes, King 733
  2 Sea of Glass, Liberty 3056
  2 Yours Forever, Liberty 3083
  2 Pagan Love Song, Liberty 3113, *7113*

Robin Ward
  2 Wonderful Summer, Dot 3555, 25555

Muddy Waters[41]
  1 Best of Muddy Waters, Chess 1427
  1 Muddy Waters Sings Big Bill Broonzy, Chess 1444
  1 Muddy Waters at Newport, Chess 1449
  1 Folk Singer, Chess 1483
  1 Real Folk Blues, Chess 1501
  1 Muddy, Brass and the Blues, Chess 1507
  1 More Real Folk Blues, Chess 1511
  1 Sail On, Chess 1539
  1 They Call Me Muddy Waters, Chess 1553
  1 Down on Stovall's Plantation, Testament 2210

Johnny Guitar Watson
  1 2 in Blues (w/B. Bland), Crown 5358
  1 Johnny Guitar Watson, King 857

Wee Willie Wayne
  3 Travelin' Mood, Imperial 9144

Mary Wells
  2 Bye Bye Baby, Motown 600
  2 The One Who Really Loves You, Motown 605
  1 Two Lovers, Motown 607
  1 Love Songs to the Beatles, 20th Century Fox 3178, *4178*

West Coast Pop Art Experimental Band
  1 Where's My Daddy, Amos 7004
  1 Part One, Reprise *6247*
  1 Vol. 2, Reprise 6270
  1 A Child's Guide to Good and Evil, Reprise *6298*

Ian Whitcomb
  1 You Turn Me On, Tower 5004, *5004*
  1 Ian Whitcomb's Mod, Mod Music Hall, Tower 5042, *5042*
  1 Yellow Underground, Tower 5071, *5071*
  1 Sock Me Some Rock, Tower *5100*

Who
  1 The Who Sing My Generation, Decca 4664
  1 Happy Jack, Decca 4892
  1 The Who Sell Out, Decca 4950

Marty Wilde
  1 Bad Boy, Epic 3686
  1 Wilde About Marty, Epic 3711
  2 Wilde About Marty, Epic 575

Cootie Williams, see p. 177.

[41] All Chess LPs, black label, mono.

Larry Williams
  1 Larry Williams' Greatest Hits, Okeh 12123
  3 Here's Larry Williams, Specialty 2109

Maurice Williams and the Zodiacs
  3 Stay, Herald 1014
  1 Stay, Sphere Sound 7007

Mel Williams
  5 All Through the Night, Dig 103

Otis Williams and His Charms
  5 Otis Williams and His Charms Sing Their All-Time Hits, Deluxe 570
  5 This is Otis Williams and His Charms, Deluxe 614
  4 Otis Williams and His Charms Sing Their All-Time Hits, King 570
  4 This is Otis Williams and His Charms, King 614

Paul Williams
  1 Paul Williams' Hucklebuckers, Savoy 15046 (10″)

Chuck Willis
  3 The King of the Stroll, Atlantic 8018
  2 I Remember Chuck Willis, Atlantic 8079, *8079*
  4 Chuck Willis Wails the Blues, Epic 3425
  4 Tribute to Chuck Willis, Epic 3728

J. Frank Wilson and the Cavaliers
  2 Last Kiss, Josie 4006, *4006*

Jackie Wilson
  3 He's So Fine, Brunswick 54042
  2 Lonely Teardrops, Brunswick 54045
  1 So Much, Brunswick 54050, *754050*
  1 Jackie Sings the Blues, Brunswick 54055, *754055*
  1 My Golden Favorites, Brunswick 54058
  1 A Woman, a Lover, a Friend, Brunswick 54059, *754059*

Jesse Winchester
  2 Jesse Winchester, Ampex *10104*

Wind in the Willows
  2 Wind in the Willows, Capitol *2956*

Jimmy Witherspoon, see p. 178.

Stevie Wonder
  1 Eivets Rednow, Gordy *932*
  2 Tribute to Uncle Ray, Tamla 232
  2 The Jazz Soul of Little Stevie, Tamla 233
  2 The 12 Year Old Genius, Tamla 240
  2 Workout Stevie Workout, Tamla 248
  2 With a Song In My Heart, Tamla 250
  2 Stevie at the Beach, Tamla 255
  1 Up-Tight, Tamla 268, *268*
  1 Down to Earth, Tamla 272, *272*
  1 I Was Made to Love Her, Tamla 279, *279*

Link Wray
  5 Link Wray and the Wraymen, Epic 3661
  3 Yesterday and Today, Record Factory 1929
  5 Jack the Ripper (w/the Wraymen), Swan 510
  3 Great Guitar Hits, Vermillion 1924
  3 Link Wray Sings and Plays Guitar, Vermillion 1925

THE ROCK AND ROLL RECORDINGS

Vernon Wray
2 Wasted, Vermillion 1927

Jimmy and Mama Yancey, see p. 178.

Zal Yanovsky
1 Alive and Well in Argentina, Buddah 5019

Yardbirds
3 For Your Love, Epic 24167, 26167
2 Having a Rave Up, Epic 24177, 26177
2 Over Under Sideways Down, Epic 24210, 26210
2 Little Games, Epic 24313, 26313
3 The Yardbirds, Epic 30135 (2 LPs)
3 Live Yardbirds Featuring Jimmy Page, Epic 30615
1 Sonny Boy Williamson and the Yardbirds, Mercury 21071, 61071
1 Blow-Up, MGM 4447, 4447 (movie soundtrack)

You Know Who Group
1 The You Know Who Group, International Allied 420

Kathy Young
1 The Sound of Kathy Young, Indigo 504

Steve Young
1 Rock Salt and Nails, A & M 4177

John Zacherley
1 Zacherley's Monster Gallery, Crestview 803, 803
1 Spook Along With Zacherley, Elektra 190, 7190
1 Monster Mash, Parkway 7018
1 Scary Tales, Parkway 7023

Frank Zappa[42]
2 200 Motels, United Artists 9956 (movie soundtrack)
1 Lumpy Gravy, Verve 8741, 68741

Zephyr
2 Zephyr, Command/Probe 4510
2 Going Back to Colorado, Warner Bros. 1897

Zodiacs
1 Zodiacs at the Beach, Snyder 5586

Zombies
1 Odessey & Oracle (Time of the Season), Date 4013
1 The Zombies, Parrot 61001, 71001

[42] See also *Mothers of Invention*.

3. ANTHOLOGIES, VARIOUS ARTISTS

ABC-Paramount
1 A Million or More Best Sellers, ABC-Paramount 216

Ace
2 Greatest 15 Hits on Ace, Ace 1012
2 Let's Have a Dance Party, Ace 1019
2 For Twisters Only, Ace 1020

Aladdin
5 Party After Hours, Aladdin 703 (10")
4 Rock 'n Roll With Rhythm and Blues, Aladdin 710 (10")

Apollo
2 Jackpot of Hits, Apollo 490

Argo
1 Remember the Oldies, Argo 649
1 Fanfare of Hits, Argo 656
1 The Blues, Vol. 1, Argo 4026
1 The Blues, Vol. 2, Argo 4027
1 Folk Festival of the Blues, Argo 4031
1 The Blues, Vol. 3, Argo 4034
1 The Blues, Vol. 4, Argo 4042

Arrawak
2 A Night Train of Oldies, Arrawak 101

Arvee
1 Golden Echoes, Arvee 433

Ascot
1 All-Girl Million Sellers, Ascot 13007, *16007*

Atco
1 Rockin' Together, Atco 103
1 Great Group Goodies, Atco 143
1 Apollo Saturday Night, Atco 159, *159*

Atlantic
2 Rock and Roll Forever, Atlantic 1239
1 Roots of the Blues, Atlantic 1348, *1348*
2 The Greatest Rock & Roll, Atlantic 8001
2 Rock & Roll Forever, Vol. 1, Atlantic 8010
2 Dance the Rock & Roll, Atlantic 8013
2 Rock & Roll Forever, Vol. II, Atlantic 8021
2 Rocking 50's, Atlantic 8037
1 The Greatest Twist Hits, Atlantic 8058
1 Solid Gold Groups, Atlantic 8065
1 Hound Dog's Old Gold, Atlantic 8068

Audio Lab
2 Two Shades of Blues, Audio Lab 1512
1 Highway of Blues, Audio Lab 1520

Authentic
1 Rhythm 'n Blues Groups, Authentic 501

Big Top
2 Mad Twists Rock and Roll, Big Top 1305
2 Fink Along With Mad, Big Top 1306

Cadence
2 Rock-a-Ballads, Cadence 3041
2 Rock-a-Hits, Cadence 3042
1 Golden Encores, Cadence 3043

Capitol
1 Arthur Murray Rock 'n Roll, Capitol 640
2 Teenage Rock, Capitol 1009
2 Everybody Rocks, Capitol 1025
1 Those Good Old Memories, Capitol 1414
1 My Son the Surf Nut, Capitol 1939, *1939*
1 Surfing's Greatest Hits, Capitol 1995, *1995*
1 Big Hot Rod Hits, Capitol 2024, *2024*
3 Chartbusters, Vol. IV, Capitol 2094, *2094*
3 Big Hits From England and the U.S.A., Capitol 2125, *2125*

Carlton
1 One Dozen Goldies, Carlton 121

Checker
1 Love Those Goodies, Checker 2973
1 Hits That Jumped, Checker 2975

Chess
3 Rock, Rock, Rock, Chess 1425[43] (movie soundtrack)
1 Oldies in Hi-Fi, Chess 1439
1 Bunch of Goodies, Chess 1441
1 Treasure Tunes From the Vault, Chess 1474
1 Group of Goodies, Chess 1478
1 Group of Goodies, Vol. 2, Chess 1491

Clarion
3 Discotheque in Astrosound, Clarion 609, *609*

Class
2 Gone But Not Forgotten, Class 5004

Colpix
1 Teenage Triangle, Colpix 444, *444*
1 More Teenage Triangle, Colpix 468, *468*

---

[43] Contains songs from the movie, as well as additional material by other Chess artists. There also exists an actual, complete soundtrack LP with songs by Frankie Lymon, The Three Chuckles, Johnny Burnette, and LaVern Baker; this is a disc jockey sample (no label or number) with red-ink drawing on a white cover; estimated value is $400.

ANTHOLOGIES, VARIOUS ARTISTS

Columbia
1 Exciting New Liverpool Sound, Columbia 2172
1 18 King Size Rhythm & Blues Hits, Columbia 2667, *9467*

Combo
5 Rockin' at the Drive-In, Combo 400

Constellation[44]
2 Collector's Showcase, Vol. 1, Constellation 1
2 Collector's Showcase, Vol. 5, Constellation 5
2 Collector's Showcase, Vol. 6, Constellation 6
2 Collector's Showcase, Vol. 7, Constellation 7

Coral
1 Hitsville, Coral 57269, *757269*
1 Teenage Goodies, Coral 57431, *757431*

Crown
2 Rock 'n Roll Dance Party, Crown 5001
2 Hollywood Rock 'n Roll Record Hop, Crown 5011
2 Gigantic Stars of Rock 'n Roll, Crown 5013
1 More of the Oldies and Goldies, Crown 5202
1 Oldies and Goldies, Crown 5241

Dawn
3 Rock and Roll Spectacular, Dawn 1119

Decca
1 Golden Oldies, Decca 4036
1 Out Came the Blues, Decca 4434

Del Fi
1 Campus Pajama Party, Del Fi 1218
1 Barrel of Oldies, Del Fi 1219
1 Very Best of the Oldies, Del Fi 1227
1 Battle of the Surfing Bands, Del Fi 1235, *1235*

Design
1 Out of Sight, Design 269

Dimension
4 The Dimension Dolls, Vol. 1 (The Cookies, Little Eva, Carol King), Dimension 6001

Dooto
2 The Best Vocal Groups (Earth Angel and Other Hits), Dooto 204
3 Rock 'n Roll vs Rhythm & Blues, Dooto 223
2 The Best Vocal Groups in Rock & Roll, Dooto 224
2 Hit Vocal Groups, Dooto 501
1 Great Groups, Dooto 855

Dot
1 Great Hits on Dot, Dot 3049
1 Young Love, Dot 3183

End
3 Rock & Roll Jamboree, End 302
2 Battle of the Groups, End 305
2 Battle of the Groups, Vol. 2, End 309
1 12 + 3 = 15 Hits, End 310
1 Alan Freed's Golden Pics, End 313
1 Alan Freed's Memory Lane, End 314
2 Alan Freed's Top 15, End 315

[44] For Vols. 2, 3, and 4, see the *Moonglows*, *The Flamingos* and *The Sheppards* respectively.

Epic
2 Cream of the Crop, Epic 3701
2 Please Say You Want Me, Epic 3702
1 Great Golden Grooves, Epic 24040

Etiquette
1 Northwest Collection, Vol. 1, Etiquette 1028

Everlast
5 Our Best to You, Everlast 201

Excello
2 Tunes to Be Remembered, Excello 8001

Famous
1 Rockin' Slumber Party, Famous 501

Fire
3 Here Are the Hits, Fire 100
3 Memory Lane, Fire 101

Flip
3 12 Flip Hits, Flip 1001
3 Original Recordings, Flip 1002

Fortune
1 Treasure Chest of Musty Dusties, Fortune 8011

Gateway
1 1964—The Year in Review, Gateway 9004

Gee
3 Teenage Party, Gee 702 (red label)
1 Teenage Party, Gee 702 (gray label)

GSP
1 Beach Party, GSP 6901

Guest Star
1 Rock & Roll Party, Guest Star 1406
1 Earth Angel, Guest Star 1432
1 On the Road, Guest Star 1449
1 10 Song Hits That Sold One Million Records, Guest Star 1474
1 Rhythm & Blues, Guest Star 1900
1 Shake a Hand, Guest Star 1904
1 Let the Good Times Roll, Guest Star 1905
1 Greatest R and B Stars, Guest Star 1906

Herald
3 Herald the Beat, Herald 1010
2 Pot of Golden Goodies, Herald 1015

Hideout
3 Best of the Hideouts, Hideout 1002

Hollywood
2 Merry Christmas Baby, Hollywood 501
3 R & B Hits, Hollywood 503

Hull
4 Your Favorite Singing Groups, Hull 1002

IGL
2 Roof Garden 2nd Annual Jamboree, IGL 103

Imperial
 2 Hitsville USA, Imperial 9084
 2 Hitsville, Vol. 2, Imperial 9099
 1 Solid Gold Hits, Imperial 9230
 2 Best of the Blues, Vol. 1, Imperial 9257
 2 Best of the Blues, Vol. 2, Imperial 9259
 2 New Orleans Our Home Town, Imperial 9260
 1 Giant Instrumental Rhythm & Blues Hits, Imperial 9271

Jamie
 1 Sounds of Success, Jamie 3017

Jerden
 1 Original Great Northwest Hits, Vol. 1, Jerden 7001, 7002
 1 Original Great Northwest Hits, Vol. 2, Jerden 7002, 7002
 1 Hitmakers, Jerden 7005, 7005

Jubilee
 3 Best of Rhythm & Blues, Jubilee 1014
 2 Rumble, Jubilee 1114
 2 Boppin', Jubilee 1118
 2 Whoppers, Jubilee 1119

KFM
 1 Murray the K Live From the Brooklyn Fox, KFM 1001

King
 3 All Star Rock and Roll Revue, King 513
 2 After Hours, King 528
 3 Rock and Roll Dance Party, King 536
 5 Battle of the Blues, King 607
 5 Battle of the Blues, Vol. 2, King 627
 3 Battle of the Blues, Vol. 3, King 634
 2 All Star Rock and Roll Revue, King 638
 2 Rock and Roll Revue, Vol. 2, King 654
 3 Battle of the Blues, Vol. 4, King 668
 1 25 Years of Rhythm and Blues Hits, King 725
 1 Hit Makers and Their Record Breakers, King 737
 1 25 Years of Rhythm and Blues Hits, Vol. 2, King 743
 1 Solo Spotlight, King 745
 1 Night Train, King 771
 1 Forgotten Million Sellers, King 792
 1 Carnival of Songs, King 819

Laurie
 1 Great Groups, Great Hits, Laurie 2010
 1 Greatest Golden Goodies, Laurie 2014

Minit
 1 New Orleans—Home of the Blues, Minit 0001
 1 We Sing the Blues, Minit 0003
 1 New Orleans—Home of the Blues, Vol. 2, Minit 0004

Modern
 2 Rock & Roll Dance Party, Modern 1210
 2 Hollywood Rock & Roll Record Hop, Modern 1211

Old Town
 2 Rock & Roll on the Old Town, Old Town 101

Philles
 3 Today's Hits, Philles 4004
 2 A Christmas Gift For You, Philles 4005

RCA
 2 Teenagers Dance, RCA 1540
 1 TV Record Hop, RCA 1800

Red Bird
 1 Red Bird Goldies, Red Bird 102

Regent
 1 Rock 'n' Roll, Regent 6015
 1 Rock & Roll Party #2, Regent 6042

Roulette
 2 Pajama Party, Roulette 25021
 2 Rock & Roll Record Hop, Roulette 25059
 2 Rock & Roll Bandstand, Roulette 25093

RPM
 2 Rock & Roll Dance Party, RPM 3001

Score
 5 I Dig Rock & Roll, Score 4002
 5 Rock & Roll Sock Hop, Score 4018

Somerset
 1 Rock & Roll Dance Party, Somerset 1300

Specialty
 1 Our Significant Hits, Specialty 2112

Sue
 1 The Sue Story, Sue 1021

Sun
 3 Sun's Gold Hits, Sun 1250

Swan
 2 Treasure Chest of Hits, Swan 501
 1 Twistin' All Night Long, Swan 506
 1 Hits I Forgot to Buy, Swan 512

Teem
 1 Guaranteed to Please, Teem 5002
 1 Greatest Teenage Hits of All Time, Teem 5003
 1 Approved by 10,000,000, Teem 5004
 1 Kings Sing the Blues, Teem 5005

United Artists
 1 Yesterday's Goodies, United Artists 3196, 6196

Vee Jay
 1 The Blues, Vee Jay 1020
 1 Teen Delights, Vee Jay 1021
 1 Unavailable, Vee Jay 1051

Veritas
 3 Folksingers Around Harvard Square, Veritas 1

PART II

SHOW BUSINESS

4· COLLECTING CAST RECORDINGS

D UE TO THE LIMITED NUMBER of records involved (this is the only field where one may actually entertain the notion of having everything), and the widespread interest among collectors in English cast recordings, this category differs from the others in that it includes non-American releases. In addition, I have chosen to include many private pressings of original cast productions. These are records of shows which would have otherwise gone unrecorded by commercial record companies. They are usually financed by someone involved in the production as a memento of the experience, or as gifts to cast members and friends, or for countless other reasons. Since, usually, very few records are pressed and distribution is next to nil, they are, in general, exceedingly scarce and highly desirable among serious collectors of original cast material.

The letters OC, TVC, and SC refer to the types of production. OC is an original cast production; TVC is a television cast production; and SC is a studio cast production (i.e., recorded specifically for record purposes and not as a by-product of an original theater or television production). The names following the type of production are those of the principal cast members.

Until recently, it seemed that every show collector was looking for the same twelve or so records. Within the last few years, however, many of these extremely rare items, including *Flahooley, Make a Wish, Top Banana, Hazel Flagg, By the Beautiful Sea, Of Thee I Sing, Seventeen,* and *Two's Company,* have been reissued. Each of these records previously sold for over seventy-five dollars, but the reissue (especially those with original cover art) have satisfied the immediate demand and greatly affected the current value of the original issues. In such cases, I have given the original issue a five-star rating, although the price may vary despite the LP's unquestioned rarity.

Price Key: 1 = $5 to $10; 2 = $10 to $15; 3 = $15 to $25; 4 = $25 to $40; 5 = over $40.

5. AMERICAN CAST RECORDINGS

2 The Adventures of Marco Polo, A. Drake, D. Morrow, Columbia 5111; TVC.
1 Ain't Supposed to Die a Natural Death, A. French, G. Edwards, M. Gentry, A&M 3510 (2LPs) ; OC.
3 Ali Baba and the 40 Thieves 40, B. Crosby, Golden 298:20; SC.
2 (The New) Alice in Wonderland, Or, What's a Nice Kid Like You Doing in a Place Like This?, D. Dana, S. Crothers, D. Drew, Hanna-Barbera 2051; TVC.
2 Alice Through the Looking Glass, J. Durante, N. Fabray, R. Montalban, A. Moorehead, RCA 1130, *1130;* TVC.
2 All About Life, Life magazine industrial show with G. Bleezarde, R. Whyte, others, Columbia 89424 (private pressing) ; OC.
2 All in Love, D. Atkinson, G. Byrne, D. DeLuise, Mercury 2204, *6204;* OC.
1 Allegro, J. Battles, L. Kirk, A. Dickey, RCA 1099, *1099;* OC.
3 The Andersonville Trial (nonmusical) , G. C. Scott, H. Berghof, 20th Century Fox 4000; OC.
2 Androcles and the Lion, N. Coward, E. Ames, N. Wisdom, RCA 1141, *1141;* TVC.
5 Angel, F. Gwynne, F. Sternhagen, no label, no # (private pressing) ; OC.
4 Ankles Aweigh, L. Parker, M. Dawson, Decca 9025; OC.
1 Annie Get Your Gun (California revival) , M. Martin, J. Raitt, Capitol 913; OC.
1 Anya, C. Towers, M. Kermoyan, L. Gish, I. Petina, United Artists 4133, *5133;* OC.
1 Anything Goes/Panama Hattie, E. Merman, F. Sinatra, B. Lahr, Larynx Disc 567 (private pressing) ; TVC.
3 Arabian Nights, L. Melchior, Decca 9013; OC.
5 Arms and the Girl, N. Fabray, G. Guetary, P. Bailey, Decca 5200 (10" LP) ; OC.
1 Around the World in 80 Days, L. Janney, C. Benson, Everest 1020; SC.
5 The Athenian Touch, M. Marlowe, B. McQueen, Broadway East 101, *101;* OC.

2 Babes in Toyland, K. Baker, K. Kemple, Decca 7004 (10" LP) ; SC
2 Babes in Toyland/The Red Mill (reissue of above) , W. Evans, E. Farrell, Decca 8458; SC
2 Bajour, C. Rivera, N. Dussault, H. Bernardi, Columbia 6300, *2700;* OC.
1 Baker Street, F. Weaver, I. Swenson, M. Gabel, MGM 7000, *7000;* OC.
2 Ballad For Bimshire, O. Davis, C. Spencer, J. Randolph, London 48002, *78002;* OC.
2 The Bandwagon/The Little Shows, H. Lang, E. Adams, C. Bruce, RCA 3155 (10") ; SC.
1 Bei Mir Bis Du Schoen, L. Fuchs, Decca 9115, *79115;* OC.

2 Ben Franklin in Paris, R. Preston, U. Sallent, S. Watson, Capitol 2191, *2191;* OC.
2 Best Foot Forward, L. Minnelli, P. Wayne, Cadence 4012, *24012;* OC.
4 Best of Burlesque, S. Britton, T. Poston, MGM 3644, *3644;* OC.
1 Billy Barnes L.A., K. Berry, J. Jameson, BB 1001; OC.
3 Billy Barnes Revue, B. Convy, K. Berry, J. Jameson, P. Regan, Decca 9076, *79076;* OC.
3 Billy No Name, D. Burks, U. Leonardos, A. Weeks, Roulette *11;* OC.
1 Black Nativity, M. Williams, A. Bradford, Vee Jay 5022, *5022;* OC.
1 Blackbirds of 1928/Shuffle Along, A. Long, T. Carpenter, RCA 3154 (10") ; OC.
1 Blackbirds of 1928, E. Waters, D. Ellington Orchestra, Sutton 270; SC.
5 Body in the Seine, A. Pearce, J. Symington, B. Ashley, G. S. Irving, Vitt Brown 1 (private pressing) ; SC.
2 The Boys From Syracuse, K. Morrow, R. Tronto, J. Marie, E. Hanley, Capitol 1933, *1933;* OC.
2 Bravo Giovanni, C. Siepi, M. Lee, G. S. Irving, Columbia 5800, *2200;* OC.
1 Breakfast at Tiffany's, M. T. Moore, R. Chamberlain, SPM 4788 (private pressing) ; OC.
1 Brecht on Brecht, L. Lenya, A. Johnson, V. Lindfors, Columbia 278, *203* (2 LPs) ; OC.
1 Brigadoon, R. Goulet, S. A. Howes, P. Falk, Columbia Special Products 385, *385;* TVC.
1 By Jupiter, B. Dishy, S. Sullivan, R. Kaye, RCA 1137, *1137;* OC.
5 By the Beautiful Sea, S. Booth, W. Evans, M. Barnes, Capitol 351; OC.

3 Cabin in the Sky (1964) , R. LeNoire, T. Middleton, K. Lester, Capitol 2073, *2073;* OC.
5 Call Me Madam, D. Shore, R. Nype, P. Lukas,[1] RCA 1000; OC.
5 Call Me Mister, B. Garrett, L. Winters, J. Munshin, Decca 7005 (10" LP) ; OC.
1 Canterbury Tales, G. Rose, H. Baddeley, M. Green, Capitol 229; OC.
1 Carmen Jones, G. Bumbry, Heliodor 25046, *25046;* SC.
1 Carousel, R. Goulet, M. Grover, Columbia Special Products 479, *479;* TVC.
1 Celebration, S. Watson, T. Thurston, K. Charles, Capitol *198;* OC.
2 Chee-Chee/Treasure Girl, B. Comden, Ava 26, *26;* SC.

[1] RCA had acquired the rights to the show, but its star, Ethel Merman, was under exclusive contract to Decca. Thus, this recording has Dinah Shore with the original cast.

85

1 The Chocolate Soldier/The Student Prince, N. Eddy, R. Stevens, Columbia 4060; SC.
2 The Chocolate Soldier, R. Merrill, R. Stevens, RCA 6005, *6005* (2 LPs) ; SC.
3 Christine, M. O'Hara, M. Meredith, N. Andrews, Columbia 5520, *2026;* OC.
2 Cinderella/Three to Make Music, M. Martin, RCA 2012, *2012;* TVC.
2 Cindy, J. Mayro, J. Masiell, T. Oliver, ABC-Paramount 2, *2;* OC.
3 Clara, B. Garrett, J. Komack, Commentary 02 (demo for the off Broadway production *"Beg, Borrow or Steal"*) ; SC.
5 Clown Around, cast unidentified, RCA *4741;* OC.
3 Cole Porter in Paris, P. Como, Bell 36508 (private pressing) ; TVC.
3 Colette, Z. Caldwell, R. Nelson, MIO International *3001;* OC.
1 Comedy From the Second City, A. Arkin, B. Harris, P. Sand, (Chicago) Mercury 2201, *6201;* OC.
• 1 The Committee, H. Camp, G. Goodrow, I. Riordan, Reprise 2023, *2023;* OC.
✓ 3 A Connecticut Yankee/Rio Rita, E. Wrightson, E. Malbin, RCA 1026; SC.
The Connection (OC), see *Freddie Redd*, p. 167.
The Connection (SC), see *Howard McGhee*, p. 158.
3 The Consul, M. Powers, P. Neway, G. Jongeyans, Decca 101 (2 LP boxed set) ; OC.
2 Conversation Piece, N. Coward, L. Pons, Columbia 163 (2 LP boxed set) ; SC.
3 Cotton Club Revue 1958, C. Calloway, Gone 101; OC.
3 The Cradle Will Rock, H. DaSilva, O. Stanton, M. Blitzstein, American Legacy 1001; OC.
1 The Cradle Will Rock, J. Orbach, L. Peters, MGM 4289, *4289* (2 LPs) ; OC.
✓ 2 Cricket on the Hearth, D. Thomas, M. Thomas, E. Ames, Norman Luboff Choir, RCA 1140, *1140;* TVC
✓ 1 Cry For Us All, H. Gallagher, J. Diener, R. Weede, Project 3 *1000;* OC.
5 The Crystal Heart, M. Dunnock, J. Stewart, V. Vestoff, no label, no # (private pressing) ; OC.

✓ 3 Dames at Sea, A. Margaret, Bell 1 (private pressing) ; TVC.
2 Damn Yankees, G. Verdon, S. Douglass, RCA 1021 (original issue, green cover only) ; OC.
2 The Dangerous Christmas of Red Riding Hood, L. Minnelli, C. Ritchard, ABC-Paramount 536, *536;* TVC.
✓ 2 Darling of the Day, V. Price, P. Routledge, RCA 1149, *1149;* OC.
2 Demi-Dozen, J. Connell, J. Fletcher, C. Cabot, Offbeat 4015; OC.
2 Der Jasager, J. Protschka, L. Bert, W. Vohla, MGM 3270; SC.
1 Der Jasager, reissue of above, Heliodor 25025, *25025.*
1 The Desert Song, W. Evans, K. Carlisle, Decca 7000 (10" LP) ; SC.
1 The Desert Song, G. Tozzi, K. Barr, RCA 1000, *1000;* SC.
✓ 1 The Desert Song/Roberta, G. MacRae, L. Norman, Capitol 384; SC.
✓ 2 Destry Rides Again, A. Griffith, D. Gray, Decca 9075, *79075;* OC.
2 Dime-a-Dozen, J. Fletcher, M. L. Wilson, R. Robbins, S. Browning, Cadence 30631, *25063* (2 LPs) ; OC.
✓ 2 Do Re Mi, P. Silvers, N. Walker, N. Dussault, J. Reardon, RCA 2002, *2002;* OC.
2 Do Re Mi, reissue of above, RCA 1105, *1105.*
2 Donnybrook, E. Foy, A. Lund, S. Johnson, Kapp 8500, *8500;* OC.

2 Down in the Valley, A. Drake, J. Wilson, Decca 4239, *74239;* SC.
1 Dressed to the Nines, C. Cabot, B. Minnart, M. L. Wilson, MGM 3914 ,*3914;* OC.
2 Earl of Ruston, Salvation Co., Capitol 465, *465;* SC.
4 Eileen/Polonaise, E. Wrightson, J. Carroll, F. Greer/ E. Wrightson, R. Inghram, RCA Camden 210; SC.
1 The Elephant Calf/Dear Old Democracy, B. Carroll, J. Antonio, Asch 9831; OC.
2 Ernest in Love, L. Martin, J. Irving, G. Raphael, L. Edmonds, Columbia 5530, *2027;* OC.
✓ 3 An Evening With Beatrice Lillie, London 1373 or 5212; OC.
1 An Evening With Mike Nichols and Elaine May, OC; Mercury 2200, *6200.*
2 Fade Out Fade In, C. Burnett, J. Cassidy, ABC 3, *3;* OC.
✓ 3 A Family Affair, S. Berman, E. Heckart, United Artists 4099, *5099;* OC.
4 Fanny, H. Rome, Heritage 0055 (10" LP) ; SC.
5 Feathertop, J. Powell, H. Conreid, H. O'Brian, no label, no # (private pressing) ; TVC.
2 The Firefly/Naughty Marietta, P. Britten Orchestra and vocalists, MGM 3080; SC.
1 The Firefly/Naughty Marietta, reissue of above, Lion 70090.
5 Flahooley, Y. Sumac, B. Cook, E. Truex, J. Courtland, Capitol 284; OC.
✓ 2 Flora the Red Menace, L. Minnelli, B. Dishy, C. Damon, RCA 1111, *1111;* OC.
2 The Flowering Peach/Is There Survival?, incidental music by Hovhaness from the play, MGM 3164.
3 Fly Blackbird, M. Grant, G. Price, R. Guillaume, Mercury 2206, *6206;* OC.
✓ 3 Ford 50th Anniversary Show, E. Merman, W. Martin, Decca 7027 (10" LP) ; TVC.
3 Four Below Strikes Back, N. Dussault, G. Furth, J. L. Law, Offbeat 4017; OC.
2 Four Saints in Three Acts, I. Matthews, A. Hines, A. Dorsey, RCA 2756; OC.
✓ 1 Foxy, L. Lahr, L. Blyden, J. Davidson, SPM 4636 (private pressing) ; OC.
3 Frankie and Johnny, D. Scholl, M. Mayo, MGM 3499; SC.
2 Freedomland U.S.A., J. Corey, J. Horton, E. Wrightson, Columbia 1484, *8275;* SC.
1 From the Second City, A. Arkin, S. Darden, B. Harris, P. Sand, Mercury 2203, *6203;* OC.
5 Gabriel Ghost, Powertree 5003; OC.
✓ 2 The Gay Life, W. Chiari, B. Cook, J. Munshin, E. Allen, Capitol 1560, *1560;* OC.
✓ 3 General Motors 50th Anniversary Show, D. Shore, C. Ritchard, D. Dailey, D. Morrow, RCA 1037; TVC.
1 Gertrude Stein's First Reader, S. Thornton, A. Sternberg, M. Anthony, F. Giordano, Polydor *24–7002;* OC.
4 Gift of the Magi, S. A. Howes, A. Case, B. Osterwald, United Artists 4013, *5013;* TVC.
✓ 3 The Girl in the Pink Tights, Jeanmaire, D. Atkinson, Columbia 4890; OC.
✓ 3 The Girl Who Came to Supper, J. Ferrer, F. Henderson, Columbia 6020, *2420;* OC.
✓ 4 Golden Apple, K. Ballard, S. Douglass, RCA 1014; OC.
2 Golden Apple, reissue of above, Elektra 5000.
2 Golden Rainbow, S. Lawrence, E. Gorme, Calendar *1001;* OC.
✓ 5 Good News, A. Faye, J. Payne, S. Kaye, no label, no # (private pressing, limited edition: 1000 copies) ; OC.

AMERICAN CAST RECORDINGS

1 The Great Waltz (California), G. Tozzi, J. Fenn, F. Poretta, A. Gillette, Capitol 2426, *2426;* OC.
3 Greenwich Village U.S.A., B. McHugh, P. Finley, J. Johnston, S. Cooper, 20th Century Fox 105-2 (2 LPs) ; OC.
2 Greenwich Village U.S.A., single record, abridged issue of above, 20th Century Fox 4005.
3 Greenwillow, A. Perkins, P. Kelton, E. McCown, RCA 2001, *2001;* OC.
2 Guys and Dolls/Famous George M. Cohan Songs, R. Charles, M. Amsterdam, A. Marsh, RCA Camden 167; SC.

✓1 Half a Sixpence, T. Steele, P. James, RCA 1110, *1110;* OC.
2 Half-Past Wednesday (Rumpelstiltskin), D. DeLuise, S. Garrison, R. Fitch, Columbia 1917, *8717;* OC.
2 Half-Past Wednesday (Rumpelstiltskin), reissue of above, Harmony 9560, *14560.*
1 Hallelujah Baby, L. Uggams, R. Hooks, A. Case, Columbia 6690, *3090;* OC.
1 A Hand is On the Gate, J. Premice, J. E. Jones, C. Tyson, M. Gunn, Verve 9040, *9040* (2 LPs) ; OC.
✓4 Hans Brinker or the Silver Skates, T. Hunter, P. King, Dot 9001; TVC.
3 Hansel and Gretel, J. Powell, Columbia 2055 (10" LP) ; SC.
3 Hansel and Gretel, B. Cook, R. Buttons, R. Vallee, S. Kaye, MGM 3690; TVC.
2 The Happiest Girl in the World, C. Ritchard, J. Rule, Columbia 5650, *2050;* OC.
✓3 Happy Hunting, E. Merman, F. Lamas, RCA 1026; OC.
2 The Happy Time, R. Goulet, D. Wayne, RCA *1144;* OC.
4 Hark!, D. Goggin, M. Solley, J. Blackton, no label, no # (private pressing, 2LPs) ; OC.
5 Hazel Flagg, H. Gallagher, B. Venuta, J. Whiting, RCA 1010; OC.
3 Hear! Hear!, F. Waring, Decca 9031; OC.
1 Heidi, M. Redgrave, J. Edwards, Capitol *2995;* TVC.
1 Hello Solly, M. Katz, L. Best, S. Porter, V. Lloyd, Capitol 2731, *2731;* OC.
2 Henry Sweet Henry, D. Ameche, R. Wilson, A. Playten, C. Bruce, ABC 4, *4;* OC.
1 Her First Roman, R. Kiley, L. Uggams, SPM no # (private pressing) ; OC.
✓2 Here's Love, J. Paige, C. Stevens, L. Naismith, F. Gwynne, Columbia 6000, *2400;* OC.
✓2 High Button Shoes, P. Silvers, N. Fabray, RCA Camden 457; OC.
✓2 High Button Shoes, reissue of above, RCA 1107, *1107.*
✓2 High Spirits, B. Lillie, T. Grimes, E. Woodward, ABC-Paramount 1, *1;* OC.
✓5 High Tor, B. Crosby, J. Andrews, Decca 8272; TVC.
1 House of Flowers, Y. Bavan, T. Oliver, H. Clarke, N. Nelson, United Artists 4180, *5180;* OC.
2 House of Leather, D. Libby, D. Menton, Fontana *67591;* OC (Minneapolis).
2 How Now Dow Jones, A. Roberts, M. Mason, B. Vaccaro, H. Sherman, RCA 1140, *1140;* OC.

✓1 I Had a Ball, B. Hackett, R. Kiley, K. Morrow, Mercury 2210, *6210;* OC.
✓1 Illya Darling, M. Mercouri, O. Bean, United Artists 8901, *9901;* OC.
2 In Circles, J. Kurnitz, A. Carmines, L. Guilliatt, Avant-Garde *108;* OC.
1 Inner City, L. Hopkins, L. Marshall, A. Nicholas, C. Hall, RCA *1171;* OC.
2 Irma la Douce, Z. Jeanmaire, Columbia 177; SC (French).

3 Jack and the Beanstalk, G. Kelly, Hanna-Barbera 8511, *8511;* TVC.
2 Jack and the Beanstalk, B. Graybo, L. Roberts, RKO-Unique 111; TVC.
2 Jamaica, L. Horne, R. Montalban, RCA 1036, *1036;* OC.
2 Jamaica, reissue of above with four additional songs but overture deleted, RCA 1103, *1103.*
3 Jayne Mansfield Busts Up Las Vegas, Las Vegas Revue, 20th Century Fox 3049.
✓3 Jennie, M. Martin, G. Wallace, R. Bailey, RCA 1083, *1083;* OC.
✓1 Jimmy, F. Gorshin, J. Wilson, A. Gillette, RCA *1162;* OC.
3 Joan, L. Guilliatt, E. Borden, J. Kurnitz, Judson 1001 (2 LPs) ; OC.
3 Johnny Johnson, L. Lenya, B. Meredith, MGM 3447; OC.
1 Johnny Johnson, reissue of above, Heliodor 25024, *25024.*
2 Juno, S. Booth, M. Douglas, Columbia 5380, *2013;* OC.
3 Just For Openers, M. Kahn, F. Flagg, R. Blair, R. G. Brown, UD 37W56, *37W56;* OC.

2 Kean, A. Drake, L. L. Venora, J. Weldon, Columbia 5720, *2120;* OC.
1 The King and I, T. Martin, D. Shore, RCA 1022; SC.
✓1 Kiss Me Kate, R. Goulet, C. Lawrence, J. Walter, M. Callan, Columbia Special Products 645, *645;* TVC.
1 Kiss Me Kate, G. Grant, H. Keel, A. Jeffreys, RCA 1984, *1984;* SC.
5 Kittiwake Island, K. Murray, G. Wood, L. Kazan, no label, no # (private pressing) ; OC.
3 The Kosher Widow, M. Picon, I. Jacobson, H. Jacobson, Golden Crest 4018; OC.
3 Kwamina, S. A. Howes, B. Peters, J. Carter, Capitol 1645, *1645;* OC.

5 Lady in the Dark, A. Southern, C. Carpenter, RCA 1882; TVC.
1 Lady in the Dark/Down in the Valley, G. Lawrence/B. Bell, RCA Vintage 503; OC/SC.
3 Leave it to Jane, K. Murray, J. Allen, A. Mango, Strand 1002, *1002;* OC.
2 Let it Ride, G. Gobel, S. Levene, B. Nichols, RCA 1064, *1064;* OC.
2 Let's Sing Yiddish, B. Bonus, M. Bern, Roulette *42022;* OC.
2 Li'l Abner Fo' Chillun, S. Applebaum, 20th Century Fox 3037; OC.
4 The Lieutenant, E. Mekka, no label, no # (private pressing, 2 LPs) ; OC.
✓4 Little Women, J. Carson, F. Henderson, R. Stevens, Kapp 1104, *1104;* TVC.
✓1 The Littlest Angel, C. Calloway, T. Randall, C. Stevens, Mercury *1-603;* TVC.
3 The Littlest Revue, T. Grimes, J. Grey, C. Rae, Epic 3275; OC.
1 Lonesome Train/Abraham Lincoln in Poetry and Prose, B. Ives, Decca 9065; SC.
✓5 Look Ma, I'm Dancin'!, N. Walker, H. Lang, Decca 5231 (10" LP) ; OC.
5 Love and Let Love, M. Rodd, V. Vestoff, M. O'Sullivan, Sam Fox 0371/0372 (private pressing) ; OC.
2 Lovers, R. Bean, M. Rivera, J. Engle, Goldust *723* (private pressing) ; OC.
✓3 Lute Song/On the Town, M. Martin, Decca 8030; OC/SC.

✓2 Mad Show, J. A. Worley, L. Lavin, Columbia 6530, *2930;* OC.
✓1 Maggie Flynn, S. Jones, J. Cassidy, RCA *2009;* OC.

5 Make a Wish, N. Fabray, S. Douglass, H. Gallagher, RCA 1002; OC.
3 The Man from Broadway, no label, no # (private pressing) ; OC (Detroit).
3 Man in the Moon, B. Baird, C. Baird, Golden 104; OC.
1 Man of La Mancha, J. Nabors, M. Horne, Columbia 31237; SC.
2 Man With a Load of Mischief, T. Noel, A. Cannon, R. Shelton, V. Vestoff, Kapp 4508, 5508; OC.
1 Mardi Gras!, M. Ayers Orchestra, Decca 4696, 74696; SC.
5 Maria Golovin, RCA 6142 (3 LP boxed set) ; TVC.
2 Me and Juliet, I. Bigley, B. Hayes, J. McCracken, R. Walston, RCA 1012; OC.
1 Me and Juliet, reissue of above, "fake" stereo, RCA 1098, 1098e.
3 The Medium and the Telephone, M. Powers, L. Coleman, Columbia 154 (2 LP boxed set) ; OC.
1 The Megilla of Itzik Manger, P. Burstein, L. Lux, M. Burstein, Columbia 3270; OC.
1 The Merry Widow, D. Kirsten, R. Rounseville, Columbia 4666; SC.
1 The Merry Widow, reissue of above, Columbia 838.
2 The Merry Widow, K. Carlisle, W. Evans, Decca 8004; SC.
1 The Merry Widow, reissue of above, Decca 8819.
1 The Merry Widow/The Student Prince, G. MacRae, L. Norman/G. MacRae, D. Warenskjold, Capitol 437; SC.
5 Mexican Hayride, B. Clank, W. Evans, J. Havoc, Decca 5232 (10" LP) ; OC.
3 Mickey Rooney Sings George M. Cohan, RCA 1520; TVC.
4 The Mikado, G. Marx, H. Traubel, D. King, Columbia 5480, 2022; TVC.
4 Mixed Doubles/Below the Belt, M. Kahn, J. Sell, L. Tomlin, UD 37W56, 37W56, Vol. 2; OC.
3 Mother Earth, P. Austin, D. Ervin, B. Callaway, Environmental 1001; OC (Los Angeles) .
5 Mr. Broadway, promo LP of TV show sponsored by Swift Meat Co., M. Rooney, G. DeHaven, J. Havoc, R. Sherwood, J. Dunn, E. Foy, Jr., no label 5315 (private pressing) ; TVC.
2 Mr. President, R. Ryan, N. Fabray, Columbia 5870, 2270; OC.
2 Mr. President, P. Como, K. Ballard, RCA 2630, 2630; SC.
3 Mr. Wonderful, S. Davis, Jr., O. James, C. Rivera, Will Mastin Trio, Decca 9032; OC.
4 Mrs. Patterson, E. Kitt, H. Dowdy, RCA 1017; OC.
2 Music from Shubert Alley, promo LP of TV show sponsored by Sinclair Refining Co., A. Williams, A. Drake, L. Kirk, Sinclair 2250 (private pressing) ; TVC.
4 Music in the Air, J. Pickens, RCA 1025; SC.
2 My Cousin Josefa, C. Alberghetti, J. Ritschel, L. Cozzens, Harlequin 3270; OC (San Diego) .
2 My Fairfax Lady, Kirby Stone Four, B. Gray, Jubilee 2030; OC.
1 My People, Duke Ellington Orchestra, J. Sherrill, Contact 1, 1; SC.
3 My Square Laddie, R. Gardner, Z. Pitts, N. Walker, Foremost 1; SC.

1 Naughty Marietta/The Red Mill, G. MacRae, M. Piazza/G. MacRae, L. Norman, Capitol 551; SC.
3 The Nervous Set, R. Hayes, T. Seitz, Columbia 5430, 2018; OC.
2 Never Be Afraid, B. Crosby (musical version of "The Emperor's New Clothes") , Golden 198:22; SC.
2 New Faces of 1952, E. Kitt, C. Lawrence, R. Clary, P. Lynde, R. Graham, RCA 1008; OC.
3 New Faces of 1956, A. Sani, I. Swenson, M. Smith, B. Hayes, T. Haynes, T. C. Jones, RCA 1025; OC.
2 New Faces of 1968, M. Kahn, R. Klein, B. Maggart, Warner Bros. 2551; OC.
3 New Girl in Town, G. Verdon, T. Ritter, G. Wallace, RCA 1027, 1027; OC.
2 New Girl in Town, reissue of above, RCA 1106, 1106.
2 The New Moon, F. George, P. Gregory, Decca 5378 (10" LP) ; SC.
1 The New Moon/Vagabond King, G. MacRae, L. Norman, Capitol 219; SC.
1 A Night in Venice, E. Stuarti, N. Fairbanks, L. Hurley, Everest 6028, 3028; OC.
4 No Man Can Tame Me, promo LP of original half-hour musical sponsored by General Electric Co., G. MacKenzie, J. Raitt, E. Foy, Jr., Empire 59–7487 (private pressing, one-sided LP with only three bands) ; TVC.
1 No Strings, C. Conner, B. Short, L. Baker, H. Mann, Atlantic 1383, 1383; SC.
3 Now is the Time For All Good Men, D. Cryer, S. Niven, Columbia 6730, 3130; OC.

5 O Say Can You See, J. Chaney, E. Wendel, N. Coster, Columbia 87195/87196 (private pressing) ; OC.
5 Of Thee I Sing, J. Carson, P. Hartman, B. Oakes, Capitol 350; OC.
1 Of Thee I Sing, C. O'Connor, C. Leachman, M. Lee, Columbia 31763; TVC.
3 Oh Captain, R. Clooney, J. Ferrer, MGM 3687; SC.
3 Oh Kay (revival cast) , D. Daniels, M. Stevens, B. West, M. Matheson, 20th Century Fox 4003, 4003; OC.
1 Olympus 7-0000, D. O'Conner, P. Newman, L. Blyden, Command 07, 07; TVC.
1 On the Flip Side, R. Nelson, J. Sommers, Decca 4836, 74836; TVC.
3 On Your Toes (revival cast) , V. Zorina, B. Van, E. Stritch, Decca 9015; OC.
2 110 in the Shade, R. Horton, I. Swenson, S. Douglass, RCA 1085, 1085; OC.
3 One Touch of Venus, M. Martin, Decca 9122, 79122; OC.
5 Pal Joey, H. Gallagher, E. Stritch, J. Froman, Capitol 310; OC.
5 Parade, D. Goodman, R. Tone, C. N. Reilly, Kapp 7005, 7005; OC.
5 Paris '90, C. O. Skinner, Columbia 4619; OC.
2 Paris By Night, Latin Quarter Revue, Pat 102.
2 A Party With Comden and Green, Capitol 1197, 1197; OC.
2 Peace, J. Kurnitz, G. McGrath, R. Bean, Metromedia 33001; OC.
2 La Perichole, C. Ritchard, P. Munsel, RCA 1029 (1 LP boxed set) ; OC.
1 Philomon, D. Latessa, H. Ross, Gallery 1; OC.
3 Pieces of Eight, J. Connell, E. Parsons, C. Cabot, Offbeat 4016; OC.
3 The Pied Piper of Hamlin, V. Johnson, RCA 1563; TVC.
3 Pinocchio, M. Rooney, M. Green, S. Kaye, Columbia 1055; TVC.
2 Pinocchio, P. Winchell, J. Mahoney, Decca 8463; SC.
3 Pipe Dream, H. Traubel, W. Johnson, J. Tyler, RCA 1023; OC.
2 Pipe Dream, reissue of above, "fake" stereo; RCA 1097, 1097e.
1 Plain and Fancy, R. Derr, B. Cook, S. Conway, N. Andrews, Capitol 603, 603; OC.
1 Playgirls, Las Vegas revue with K. Stevens, J. Wilson, C. Williams, C. Russell; Warner Bros. 1530, 1530.

AMERICAN CAST RECORDINGS

4 Polonaise/Eileen, E. Wrightson, R. Inghram/E. Wrightson, J. Carroll, F. Greer, RCA Camden 210; SC.
3 Pomegranada, A. Carmines, J. Kurnitz, M. Wright, Patsan 1101 (private pressing); OC.
1 Porgy and Bess, C. MacRae, S. Davis, Jr., Decca 8854, *78854;* SC.
1 Porgy and Bess, L. Winters, L. Lucas, Heliodor 25052, *25052;* SC.
1 Porgy and Bess, R. Stevens, R. Merrill, RCA 1124; SC.
3 Porgy and Bess, (recorded October 14, 1935, four days after the New York opening), L. Tibbett, H. Jepson, RCA Camden 500; OC.
2 Porgy and Bess, L. Armstrong, E. Fitzgerald, Verve 4011-2, *6040* (2 LPs); SC.
2 Les Poupees de Paris, P. Bailey, B. Crosby, G. Kelly, T. Martin, RCA 1090, *1090;* OC.
2 The Premise, G. Segal, T. J. Flicker, Vanguard 9092; OC.
1 The Prince and the Pauper, J. Davidson, C. Blodgett, J. Shepard, London 28001, *98001;* OC.
1 Promenade, M. Albert, S. Bolin, G. Price, A. Playten, RCA *1161;* OC.
1 Purlie, C. Little, M. Moore, Ampex *40101;* OC.

2 Rashomon, incidental music composed and conducted by L. Rosenthal for the original Broadway production, Carlton 5000, *5000;* OC.
1 The Real Ambassadors, L. Armstrong, C. MacRae, D. Brubeck, Lambert, Hendricks and Ross, Columbia 5850, *2250;* SC.
√1 Redhead, G. Verdon, R. Kiley, RCA 1048, *1048;* OC.
√2 Redhead, reissue of above with additional song; RCA 1104, *1104.*
2 The Red Mill/Up in Central Park, E. Farrell, W. Evans, Decca 8016; SC.
2 The Red Mill/Babes in Toyland, E. Farrell, W. Evans, Decca 8458; SC.
√3 Regina, N.Y. City Opera Co., Columbia 034-202, 035-202 (3 LP boxed set); OC.
√3 Rio Rita/A Connecticut Yankee, E. Wrightson, E. Malbin, RCA 1026; OC.
3 Riverwind, L. Brooks, E. Parrish, H. Blount, London 48001, *78001;* OC.
√2 Roberta, K. Carlisle, A. Drake, Decca 8007; SC.
2 Rockabye Hamlet, C. Dodd, L. Hartt, Irish Rovers, Rising *103;* SC.
√2 Rose Marie, J. Andrews, G. Tozzi, RCA 1001, *1001;* SC.
2 R.S.V.P. The Cole Porters, J. Jenkins, S. Jenkins, Respond *299;* OC.
1 Rugantino, N. Manfredi, O. Vanoni, A. Fabrizi, Warner Bros. 1528, *1528;* OC.
√4 Ruggles of Red Gap, J. Powell, D. Wayne, Verve 15000; TVC.
Rumplestiltskin (see "Half-Past Wednesday").

3 Saga of the Dinghat (industrial show sponsored by the New York Herald Tribune), H. Linden, Columbia 105811, *105845* (private pressing), OC.
√2 Sail Away, E. Stritch, J. Hurst, G. Dale, Capitol 1643, *1643;* OC.
5 St. Louis Woman, P. Bailey, H. Nicholas, R. Hill, Capitol 355 (10" LP); OC.
2 St. Louis Woman, reissue of above, "fake" stereo, Capital 2742, *2742.*
3 The Saint of Bleecker Street, D. Poleri, G. Lane, G. Ruggiero, RCA 6032 (2 LP boxed set); OC.
1 Salvation, P. Link, C. C. Courtney, Y. Bavan, C. Robert, Capital *337;* OC.

5 Sandhog, E. Robinson, W. Salt, Vanguard 9001; SC.
2 Santa Claus is Coming to Town, F. Astaire, M. Rooney, MGM *4732;* TVC.
5 The Sap of Life, K. Nelson, J. Dodge, no label, no # (private pressing); OC.
√3 Saratoga, H. Keel, C. Lawrence, C. Brice, RCA 1051, *1051;* OC.
4 Satins and Spurs, B. Hutton, Capitol 547 (10" LP); TVC.
3 Say Darling, D. Wayne, V. Blaine, J. Desmond, RCA 1045, *1045;* OC.
2 Second City: Cosa Nostra Story, D. Close, A. Schreiber, J. Brent, Mercury 27045, *67045;* OC.
1 The Second City Writhes Again, A. Arkin, B. Harris, S. Darden, Mercury *61224;* OC.
5 Seven Come Eleven, P. Bruns, C. Cabot, R. Robbins, M. L. Wilson, Columbia 5740 (private pressing); OC.
5 Seventeen, K. Nelson, A. Crowley, F. Albertson, RCA *1003;* OC.
5 Seventh Heaven, G. DeHaven, R. Montalban, C. Rivera, K. Kasnar, Decca 9001; OC.
√2 70 Girls 70, M. Natwick, H. Conried, L. Roth, Columbia *30589;* OC.
1 Shay Duffin is Brendan Behan, Potato *3202;* OC.
2 She Loves Me, D. Massey, B. Cook, B. Barley, J. Cassidy, MGM 4118, *4118* (2 LPs); OC.
5 Shelter, M. Rodd, T. Kiser, S. Browning, Columbia, no # (private pressing); OC.
3 Shoestring '57, B. Arthur, F. DeWitt, D. Goodman, Offbeat 4012; OC.
3 Shoestring Revue, B. Arthur, F. DeWitt, D. Goodman, Offbeat 4011; OC.
√2 Show Girl, C. Channing, J. Munshin, Roulette 80001, *80001;* OC.
√1 Show Girl, reissue of above; Forum 9054, *9054.*
√2 Showboat (1946 revival cast), J. Clayton, C. Bruce, Columbia 4058; OC.
3 Showboat, B. Crosby, L. Wiley, K. Baker, Decca 5060 (10" LP); SC.
1 Showboat, R. Merrill, P. Munsel, R. Stevens, RCA 2008; SC.
2 Shuffle Along, F. Miller, A. Lyles, E. Blake, New World 260; OC.
1 Shuffle Along/Blackbirds of 1928, A. Long, T. Carpenter, C. Calloway, RCA 3154 (10" LP); OC.
1 Siamsa, National Folk Theatre of Ireland, Rex *1016;* OC.
3 Silk Stockings, D. Ameche, H. Neff, G. Wyler, RCA 1016; OC.
1 Silk Stockings, reissue of above, "fake" stereo; RCA 1102, *1102e.*
3 Simply Heavenly, C. McNeil, M. Stewart, Columbia 5240; OC.
5 Sing, Muse!, K. Morrow, no label, no # (private pressing); OC.
√2 Sing Out Sweet Land, A. Drake, Decca 4304, *74304;* OC.
1 Skyscraper, J. Harris, C. N. Reilly, P. Marshall, Capitol 2422, *2422;* OC.
5 Smiling the Boy Fell Dead, D. Meehan, P. Leeds, Sunbeam 549/550 (private pressing, no cover ever made); OC.
2 Something For Everybody's Mother, D. Goggin, M. Solley, JGR *3000* (private pressing); OC.
2 Song of Norway, J. Reardon, B. Lewis, Columbia 1328, *8135;* OC (Jones Beach).
1 Song of Norway, L. Brooks, K. Carlisle, R. Shafer, Decca 8002; OC.
5 Sophie, L. Staiger, S. Allen, no label, no # (private pressing); OC.
1 The Sound of My Own Voice and Other Noises, S. Darden, Mercury 2202, *6202;* OC.

✓ 1 South Pacific, S. Deel, D. Eastham, T. Carpenter, J. Carroll (understudies of the original Broadway cast), RCA Camden 421; SC.
✓ 3 The Stingiest Man in Town, V. Damone, P. Munsel, B. Rathbone, R. Weede, J. Desmond, Columbia 950; TVC.
1 Story Theater, H. Camp, P. Sand, M. Dillon, V. Harper, Columbia 30415 (2 LPs); OC.
✓ 1 Street Scene, A. Jeffreys, B. Sullivan, P. Stoska, Columbia 4139; OC.
5 Streets of New York, D. Cryer, G. Johnston, M. Hand, B. A. Grael, Capitol 450/451 (private pressing); OC
1 The Student Prince/The Vagabond King, L. Melchior, J. Wilson/A. Drake, M. Benzell, Decca 8362; SC.
2 The Survival of St. Joan, Smoke Rise, Paramount 9000 (2 LPs); OC.
✓ 1 Sweethearts, E. Wrightson, J. Carroll, F. Greer, RCA Camden 369; SC.

3 Take Five, R. Graham, J. Arnold, E. Hanley, C. Cabot, Offbeat 4013 (2 covers): OC.
✓ 2 Take Me Along, J. Gleason, W. Pidgeon, E. Herlie, RCA 1050, *1050*; OC.
1 Tamalpais Exchange, M. Brandt, M. Knight, S. Kay, Atlantic 8263; OC.
2 Tarot, Touchstone, United Artists 5563; OC.
✓ 3 Tenderloin, M. Evans, R. Husmann, E. Rodgers, Capitol 1492, *1492*; OC.
5 Texas Lil' Darlin', K. Delmar, M. Hatcher, D. Scholl, L. Smith, Decca 5188 (10" LP); OC.
3 Thirteen Daughters, K. F. Chun, N. Stevens, T. Long, Mahalo 3003, *3003*; OC (Hawaii).
✓ 5 This is the Army, I. Berlin, E. Stone, W. Horne, J. Oshing, Decca 5108 (10" LP); OC.
2 This Was Burlesque, A. Corio, Roulette 25185, *25185*; OC.
1 Three Billion Millionaires, B. Crosby, J. Garland, S. Davis, Jr., United Artists 4, *54*; SC.
✓ 3 Three Evenings With Fred Astaire, TVC, Choreo 1.
✓ 5 Three Wishes For Jamie, J. Raitt, A. Jeffreys, B. Wheeler, Capitol 317; OC.
2 A Time For Singing, L. Naismith, T. O'Shea, S. Wallis, Warner Bros. 1639, *1639*; OC.
1 Time Remembered, incidental music by V. Duke, Mercury 20380, *60023*; OC.
✓ 3 To Broadway With Love, M. Savin, D. Liberto, Columbia 8030, *2630*; OC.

4 Together With Music, N. Coward, M. Martin, no label 303; TVC.
1 Tom Jones, C. Revill, Theater Productions 59000, *9000*; SC.
3 Tom Sawyer, J. Sharpe, J. Boyd, Decca 8432; TVC.
5 Top Banana, P. Silvers, R. Marie, Capitol 308; OC.
3 Tovarich, V. Leigh, J. P. Aumont, Capitol 1940, *1940*; OC.
✓ 1 A Tree Grows in Brooklyn, S. Booth, J. Johnson, Columbia 4405; OC.
2 Tropicana Holiday, Las Vegas Revue, Capitol 1048, *1048*; OC.
2 Treasure Girl/Chee-Chee, B. Comden, Ava 26, *26*; SC.
2 Trouble in Tahiti, B. Wolff, D. Atkinson, MGM 3646; SC.
1 Trouble in Tahiti, reissue of above; Heliodor 25020, *25020*.
✓ 4 Two on the Aisle, B. Lahr, D. Gray, Decca 8040; OC.
1 Two by Two, D. Kaye, M. Kahn, Columbia 30338; OC.
5 Two's Company, B. Davis, D. Burns, E. Hanley, RCA 1009; OC.

2 Up in Central Park/The Red Mill, E. Farrell, W. Evans, Decca 8016; SC.

1 Walking Happy, N. Wisdom, L. Troy, G. Rose, Capitol 2631, *2631*; OC.
1 What Makes Sammy Run?, S. Lawrence, S. A. Howes, Columbia 6040, *2440*; OC.
5 Whispers on the Wind, D. Cryer, N. Dussault, K. Morrow, no label, no # (private pressing); OC.
3 Whoop Up, S. Johnson, P. Ford, R. Young, S. Syms, MGM 3745, *3745* (stereo issue lacks overture); OC.
✓ 2 Wildcat, L. Ball, K. Andes, RCA 1060, *1060*; OC.
3 Wish You Were Here, J. Cassidy, S. Bond, P. Marand, RCA 1007; OC.
1 Wish You Were Here, reissue of above, "fake" stereo; RCA 1108, *1108*.
2 The Wonderful "O", B. Meredith, Colpix 6000; SC.

2 Young Abe Lincoln, D. Sandeen, T. Hudson, J. Blackton, Golden 76; OC.
1 Your Own Thing, L. Palmer, R. Thacker, M. Rodd, T. Ligon, RCA 1148, *1148*; OC.

✓ 2 Ziegfeld Follies, F. Brice, W. Rogers, B. Williams, Veritas 107; OC/SC.
1 The Zulu and the Zayda, M. Skulnik, O. Davis, L. Gossett, Columbia 6480, *2880*; OC.

6. ENGLISH CAST RECORDINGS

5 After the Ball, M. Ellis, V. Lee, G. Payn, Philips 7005; OC.
4 Aladdin (Cole Porter score), B. Monkhouse, R. Shiver, I. Wallace, D. Morrow, Columbia 1211, *3296*; OC.
1 Aladdin, C. Richard and the Shadows, A. Ashley, Columbia 1676, *3522*; OC.
1 Ambassador, H. Keel, D. Darrieux, RCA *5618*; OC.
2 Amy, D. Kay, A. Simpson, T. Cook, Custom *006*; OC.
1 Ann Veronica, M. Millar, H. Hazell, A. Lowe, P. Reeves, CBS *70052*; OC.
1 Anne of Green Gables, P. James, H. Sherman, B. Hamilton, CBS *70053*; OC.
5 Anything Goes (1969), M. Montgomery, V. Verdon, J. Kenney, L. Grant, Decca 5031 (private pressing); OC.
2 Anything to Declare, Moral Rearmament cast, MRA 1; OC.
1 At the Drop of a Hat, M. Flanders, D. Swann; Angel 65042 (US pressing).
1 At the Drop of Another Hat, M. Flanders, D. Swann; Angel 36388, *36388* (US pressing).

1 Babes in the Wood, F. Ifield, A. Askey, S. James, Columbia 6009, *6009*; OC.
2 The Beggar's Opera, H. Hazell, J. Waters, P. Gilmore, A. Richards, CBS *70046*; OC.
1 Beyond the Fridge, P. Cook, D. Moore, Atlantic *40503*; OC.
4 Belle, G. Benson, R. Hill, J. Desmonde, N. Roeg, Decca 4397, *4136*; OC.
2 Bitter Sweet, V. Lee, R. Cardinali, Angel 35814, *35814* (US pressing); SC.
1 Bitter Sweet, A. Leigh, J. Pease, S. Hampshire, MFP 1091; SC.
1 The Black Mikado, M. Denison, G. Griffiths, A. Tucker, Transatlantic *300*; OC.
1 Bless the Bride, M. Miller, R. Cardinali, MFP 1263, *1263*; SC.
3 Blitz, A. Bayntun, G. Frame, B. Grant, HMV 1569, *1441*; OC.
1 The Boy Friend, C. Kennedy, T. Adams, A. Beach, Parlophone 7044, *7044*; OC.
3 The Boys From Syracuse, D. Monkhouse, M. Fitzgibbon, D. Quilley, Decca 4564, *4564*; OC.
3 Braziliana, N. Ferraz and cast from Brazil,[2] Oriole 20006 (10" LP); OC.
5 The Buccaneer, T. Ruby, K. Williams, B. Clifton, HMV 1064; OC.
2 Bye Bye Birdie, C. Rivera, P. Marshall, A. Baddeley, Philips 3383, *205*; OC.
1 Bye Bye Birdie, same as above; Mercury/Wing 13000, *17000* (US pressing).

3 Call Me Madam, B. Worth, A. Walbrook, S. Wallis, A. Lowe,[3] Columbia 1002; OC.
3 Cambridge Circus, T. Brooke-Taylor, J. Cleese, D. Hatch, B. Oddie, Parlophone 1208, *3046*; OC.
3 Camelot, L. Harvey, E. Lauren, B. Kent, N. Henson, HMV 1756, *1559*; OC.
3 Can Can, A. Marks, I. Hilda, E. Mockridge, G. Lynne,[4] Parlophone 1017 (10" LP); OC.
2 Canterbury Tales, W. Brambell, J. Evans, K. Warren, Decca *4956*; OC.
1 The Card, J. Dale, M. Martin, M. Webb, Pye 18408; OC.
2 Carnival, S. Logan, B. Harris, J. Mitchell, HMV 1612, *1476*; OC.
1 Cat and the Fiddle/Hit the Deck, D. Hume, D. Quilley, Fontana 5028; SC.
1 Cat and the Fiddle/Hit the Deck, same as above; Epic 3569 (US pressing).
1 Charlie Girl, A. Neagle, D. Nimmo, J. Brown, H. Hazell, S. Damon, CBS 62627, *62627*; OC.
2 Charlie Girl, J. Mathews, MFP 1032; SC.
1 The Chocolate Soldier/The Firefly, L. Payne, S. Voss, WRC 210; SC.
5 Chrysanthemum, P. Kirkwood, H. Gregg, P. Moore, Nixa 18026; OC.
1 Chu Chin Chow, I. TeWiata, J. Bryan, HMV 1268, *1268*; SC.
1 Chu Chin Chow, H. Alan, M. Grimaldi, MFP 1012; SC.
1 Cinderella, C. Richard and the Shadows, Columbia 6103, *6103*; OC.
4 Cinderella (Richard Rodgers score), T. Steele, J. Edwards, K. Williams, B. Marsden, Decca 4303, *4050*; OC.
3 Cinderella (Richard Rodgers score), E. Larner, D. Quilley, Saga 9101 (10" LP); SC.
4 Cindy Ella, C. Laine, E. Welch, G. Brown, Decca 4559, *4559*; OC.
2 Come Spy With Me, D. LaRue, B. Windsor, R. Wattis, Decca 4810, *4810*; OC.
5 Cranks, H. Bryant, A. Newley, A. Ross, G. Vernon, HMV 1082, *1082*; OC.
4 The Crooked Mile, E. Welch, M. Martin, A. Rodgers HMV 1298, *1284*; OC.
2 The Crowning Experience, M. Smith, A. Buckles, MRA 101; OC.

1 Dames at Sea, J. Blair, R. Burton, S. White, K. Scott, CBS *70063*; OC.
1 The Dancing Years, A. Rogers, A. Cole, Columbia *188*; SC.

[2] Issued in the US as "Drums of Brazil"—Tempo 2258 (10" LP).
[3,4] Both of these LPs have been partially reissued in US on Monmouth-Evergreen 7073.

91

SHOW BUSINESS

2 The Dancing Years, I. Novello, M. Ellis, O. Gilbert, HMV 1028 (10" LP) ; OC.
1 The Dancing Years, D. Knight, J. Bronhill, RCA 7958; OC.
1 The Dancing Years, reissue of RCA 7958; RCA International *1049.*
5 Divorce Me Darling, C. Young, A. Sharley, J. Wren, J. Heal, Decca *4675;* OC.
3 Do Re Mi, M. Bygraves, M. Fitzgibbon, J. Waters, S. Arlen, Decca 4413, *4145;* OC.
2 Emma, A. Rogers, E. Molloy, J. Webb, President *1028, 1029* (2 LPs) ; SC.
1 Emma, excerpts of above; President *1031.*
2 The Establishment, J. Bird, E. Bron, J. Geidt, J. Fortune, Parlophone 1198; OC.
2 The Establishment, same as above; Riverside 850 (US pressing).
3 An Evening With Beatrice Lillie, OC; Decca 4129.
5 Expresso Bongo, P. Scofield, M. Martin, H. Hazell, V. Spinetti, Nixa 18016; OC.
1 Fiddler on the Roof, A. Bass, A. Bunnage, Hallmark *589;* SC.
2 Fings Ain't Wot They Used T'Be, M. Karlin, B. Windsor, J. Booth, T. Palmer, Decca 4346, *4092;* OC.
3 Fings Ain't Wot They Used T'Be, A. Bass, L. Bart, A. Faith, T. Tanner, J. Heal, HMV 1358, *1298;* SC.
2 Fings Ain't Wot They Used T'Be, same as Decca 4346; London 5763 (US pressing).
2 Flower Drum Song, same as below; Angel 35886, *35886* (US pressing).
2 Flower Drum Song, T. Herbert, Y. S. Tung, K. Scott, HMV 1359, *1305;* OC.
3 Follow That Girl, P. Gilmore, S. Hampshire, P. Routledge, M. Grimaldi, HMV 1366, *1307;* OC.
1 40 Years On, J. Gielgud, A. Bennett, D. Reynolds, Decca *4987;* OC.
3 Four Degrees Over, D. Wood, J. Gould, B. Scott, A. Weston, Parlophone 7014; OC.
1 The Four Musketeers, H. Secombe, S. Voss, A. Woods, E. Larner, Philips 3655, *3655;* OC.
3 Four to the Bar, B. Blackburn, P. Reeves, R. Hill, I. Wallace, Philips 7555, *678;* OC.
3 Free as Air, D. Reynolds, M. Aldredge, G. Harper, P. Bredin, Oriole 20016; OC.
1 Funny Game Politics, M. Martin, R. Kinnean, Parlophone 1225; OC.
3 A Funny Thing Happened on the Way to the Forum, F. Howard, E. Gray, J. Pertwee, HMV 1685, *1518;* OC.
3 Gentlemen Prefer Blondes, D. Bryan, A. Hart, D. Stewart, B. Love, HMV 1602, *1464;* OC.
1 Gilbert & Sullivan Go Kosher, R. Cowen, I. Kerr, Golden Guinea *0145;* OC.
2 Glamorous Night/Careless Rapture, M. Ellis, T. Jones, D. Dickson, O. Gilbert, HMV 1095 (10" LP) ; OC.
1 Gone With the Wind, H. Presnell, J. Ritchie, Columbia 9252; OC.
1 The Good Companions, J. Mills, J. Dench, C. Gable, R. Davis, EMI *3042;* OC.
1 The Good Old Bad Old Days, A. Newley, P. Bacon, C. Villiers, EMI *751;* OC.
4 Grab Me a Gondola, J. Heal, J. Wenham, D. Quilley, J. Blair, HMV 1103; OC.
1 The Great Waltz, S. Barabas, W. Cassel, D. Todd, Columbia 6429; OC.
4 Gulliver's Travels, Instrumentals, basis for subsequent musical, Instant 003; SC.

1 Gypsy, K. Medford, MFP *1308;* SC.
1 Half a Sixpence, T. Steele, C. Kennedy, M. Webb, Decca 4521, *4521;* OC.
1 Happy as a Sandbag, M. Duncan, G. Wright, T. Jones, Decca *5217;* OC.
5 Harmony Close, R. Hill, B. Kent, B. Cribbins, B. Ferris, Oriole 20014; OC.
1 Hello Dolly, D. Bryan, B. Spear, J. Dawn, HMV 3545, *3545;* SC.
2 Hello Dolly, M. Martin, L. Smith, RCA 7768, *7768;* OC.
2 Hello Dolly, same as RCA 7768; RCA 2007, *2007* (US pressing)
1 Hello Dolly, reissue of HMV 3545; WRC *1027.*
3 High Spirits, C. Courtneidge, M. Stevens, D. Quilley, J. Waters, Pye 18100, *83022;* OC.
2 His Monkey Wife, R. Swann, J. Ritchie, B. Armstrong, President *1051* (issued in plain white cover) ; OC.
5 Hooray For Daisy, D. Reynolds, A. Mackay, E. Drew, R. Hunter, HMV 1434; OC.
3 How to Succeed in Business Without Really Trying, W. Berlinger, B. DeWolfe, E. Gourlay, P. Michael, RCA 7564, *7564;* OC.

2 I Do! I Do!, A. Rogers, I. Carmichael, RCA *7938;* OC.
2 Innish, J. Kavanagh, A. Newman, Rex 1014; OC (Dublin).
3 Instant Marriage, J. Sims, B. Grant, P. Whitsun-Jones, S. Voss, Oriole 40062; OC.
2 Irma La Douce, E. Seal, K. Michell, C. Revill, Philips 7274; OC.
1 Isabel's a Jezebel, M. Sergides, M. Mowbray, M. Popkiewitz, United Artists *29148;* OC.

1 Jeeves, D. Hemmings, H. Aldridge, MCA 2726; OC.
2 Joe Lives!, J. Woodvine, MWM *1003;* OC.
1 John, Paul, George, Ringo . . . and Bert, B. Dickson, RSO 2394 *141;* OC.
5 Johnny the Priest, J. Brett, S. Voss, B. May, Decca 4352; OC.[5]
3 Jorrocks, J. Ashland, C. Kennedy, T. Ruby, P. Eddington, HMV 3591, *3591;* OC.
5 Joyce Grenfell Requests the Pleasure, J. Grenfell, B. Kaye, P. Stone, I. Davies, Philips 7004; OC.

1 The King and I, J. Matthews, F. Lucas, MFP 1257; SC.
4 The King and I, V. Hobson, H. Lom, M. Smith, Philips 7002; OC.
2 King Kong, N. Mdledle, P. Phango, J. Mogotsi, Decca 4392, *4132;* OC.
2 King Kong, same as above; London 5762 (US pressing).
2 King's Rhapsody, I. Novello, V. Lee, P. Dare, HMV 1010 (10" LP) ; OC.
1 Kiss Me Kate, P. Routledge, D. Holliday, MFP 1126; SC.

2 Late Joys, Music hall performers: A. Bayntun, P. Ashton, M. Browning, R. Hunter, Decca 4628, *4628;* OC.[6]
1 Lay Off, D. Charles, H. McRae, T. Henderson, 7:84 Theater Co. England 784001; OC.
1 Leave Him to Heaven, B. Protheroe, Chrysalis, *1118;* OC.
2 Lilac Time, J. Bronhill, T. Round, J. Cameron, Angel 35817, *35817* (US pressing) ; SC.
4 Little Mary Sunshine, P. Routledge, B. Cribbins, J. Blair, Pye 18071; OC.

[5] Rarest of all original cast LPs; estimated price: $400.
[6] Reissued as *A Night of Music Hall*—Ace of Clubs 1238.

ENGLISH CAST RECORDINGS

3 Little Me, B. Forsythe, E. Gourlay, B. Spear, S. Swenson, Pye 18107; OC.
2 Little Me, reissue of above; WRC 789.
4 Living For Pleasure, D. Bryan, G. Rose, D. Massey, HMV 1223; OC.
1 Liza of Lambeth, A. Richards, M. Robbins, P. Hayes, Thames 100; OC.
4 London Sketches, D. Swann, S. Shaw, Pye 34002 (10" LP); OC.
3 Look Who's Here, B. Young, A. Quayle, T. Tanner, G. Wright, HMV 1357, 1302; OC.
3 The Lord Chamberlain Regrets . . . , R. Stevens, J. Sims, M. Martin, A. Woods, Pye 18065; OC.
3 Maggie May, R. Roberts, K. Haigh, B. Humphries, Decca 4643, 4643; OC.
2 Maid of the Mountains, J. Edwards, L. Kennington, G. Clyde, Columbia 6504; OC.
1 Maid of the Mountains, M. Stephens, L. Fyson, Saga 8115; SC.
2 Maid of the Mountains/Balalaika, V. Bagnell, N. Williams, WRC 794; SC.
4 Make Me An Offer, D. Massey, S. Hancock, V. Spinetti, HMV 1333, 1295; OC.
1 Mame, B. Reid, J. Turner, Major Minor 5005; SC.
1 A Man Dies, V. Mountain, R. Forde, The Strangers, Columbia 1609; OC.
1 Man of Magic, S. Damon, J. Brice, S. Kaye, CBS 70027, 70027; OC.
1 Mardi Gras, N. Henson, D. Gillespie, P. Maycock, L. Satton, EMI 3123; OC.
5 Marigold, S. Smith, J. Brett, J. Kent, HMV 1275; OC.
3 The Matchgirls, V. Martin, G. Mely, M. Grimaldi, Pye 30172; OC.
2 The Mayflower, M. Rivers, P. Tyler, J. Rose, Avenue International 800; OC.
1 The Merry Widow, J. Bronhill, J. Brett, Columbia 234; SC.
5 Mine Fair Sadie, A. Fogel, B. Altman, S. Fishman, Oriole 20054; OC.
3 The Most Happy Fella, same as below; Angel 35887, 35887 (US pressing).
3 The Most Happy Fella, I. TeWiata, H. Scott, A. Lund, HMV 1365, 1306; OC
1 Mr. & Mrs., H. Blackman, J. Neville, A. Breeze, CBS 70048; OC.
2 Mrs. Wilson's Diary, M. Jenn, P. Reeves, B. Grant, B. Wallis, Parlophone 7043, 7043; OC.
1 Music in the Air/Roberta, A. Grimaldi, A. Cole, M. Fitzgibbon, WRC 121; SC.
1 My Fair Lady, same as below; Avon 3001 (US pressing).
1 My Fair Lady, E. Larner, H. Gregg, J. Slater, Society 942; OC (Knightsbridge Co.).
5 New Cranks, B. Cribbins, G. Lynne, C. Shelley, B. Wilson, HMV 1375; OC.
1 No No Nanette, A. Neagle, A. Rogers, T. Hird, CBS 70126; OC.
1 No No Nanette, V. Martin, A. Beach, Columbia 278; SC.
3 No Strings, A. Lund, B. Todd, H. Hazell, M. Stevens, Decca 4576, 4576; OC.
2 Oh What a Lovely War, A. Bunnage, V. Spinetti, J. Gower, Decca 4542, 4542; OC.
4 Old Chelsea, R. Tauber, C. Lynn, no label, no number (private pressing); OC.
1 Oliver, S. Holloway, A. Cogan, Capitol 1784, 1784 (US pressing); SC.
2 Oliver, R. Moody, G. Brown, Decca 4105; OC.
1 Oliver in the Overworld, F. Garrity, CBS 70096; TVC.
2 On the Brighter Side, S. Baxter, B. Marsden, P. Minton, D. Kernan, Decca 4395, 4134; OC.
2 On the Brighter Side, same as above; London 5767 (US pressing).
2 On the Level, S. White, B. Ingham, A. Richards, G. Bond, CBS 70021, 70021; OC.
4 On the Town, D. McKay, E. Gould, A. MacDonald, A. Jaffe, CBS 60005, 60005; OC.
5 Once Upon a Mattress, J. Connell, T. Ruby, M. Wall, P. Grant, HMV 1410; OC.
2 One Over the Eight, K. Williams, S. Hancock, J. Davies, Decca 4133, 4393; OC.
2 One Over the Eight, same as above; London 5760 (US pressing).
4 Our Man Crichton, M. Martin, K. More, P. Lambert, D. Kernan, Parlophone 1246, 3066; OC.
1 The Owl and the Pussycat Went to See . . . , H. Secombe, H. Jacques, R. Castle, Philips 6382 068; SC.
4 The Pajama Game, M. Wall, J. Nichols, E. Mockridge, E. Seal, HMV 1062; OC.
3 Pal Joey, English reissue of Capitol (US) 310, see p. 88; Capitol/WRC T; OC.
3 Passion Flower Hotel, N. Henson, J. Clyde, P. Collins, CBS 62598, 62598; OC.
3 Perchance to Dream/Salad Days (SC), M. Barron, R. Beaumont, Ace of Clubs 1112; OC.
1 Perchance to Dream, E. Robinson, P. Lambert, Columbia 250; TVC.
2 Phil the Fluter, S. Baxter, E. Laye, M. Wynter, J. Gower, Philips 7916; OC.
1 Pickwick, H. Secombe, T. Green, A. Rodgers, J. Evans, Philips 3431; OC.
2 Pieces of Eight, F. Fielding, K. Williams, P. Reeves, Decca 4337, 4084; OC.
2 Pieces of Eight, same as above; London 5761 (US pressing).
4 Plain and Fancy, S. Conway, R. Derr, J. Hovis, I. Emmanuel, Oriole 20009 (10" LP); OC.
3 Plain and Fancy/The Water Gypsies (SC), reissue of above; Dot 3048 (US pressing).
1 Promises, Promises, A. Roberts, B. Buckley, K. Britt, J. Kruschen, United Artists 29075; OC.
3 Quillow and the Giant, J. Carson, B. McGuire, Philips 7524; TVC.
1 Ride! Ride!, G. Gostelow, C. Villiers, B. Barry, Grapevine 101; OC.
2 Robert and Elizabeth, K. Michell, J. Bronhill, J. Clements, A. Richards, HMV 1820, 1575; OC.
3 Sail Away, E. Stritch, T. Adams, D. Holliday, HMV 1572, 1445; OC.
2 1776, L. Fiander, D. Kernan, B. Lloyd, Columbia 6424; OC.
4 Shave My Lettuce, M. Smith, K. Williams, R. Cook, Pye 18011; OC.
4 She Loves Me, R. Moreno, G. Miller, G. Raymond, A. Rogers, HMV 1745, 1546; OC.
2 Sing a Rude Song, B. Windsor, D. Quilley, M. Gibb, Polydor 2383-018; OC.
1 Smike, B. Reid, A. Keir, Pye 18423; TVC.
1 Smilin' Through, J. Hanson, L. Wynters, Philips 6308-095; OC.
1 Song of Norway, V. Elliott, N. Hughes, T. Round, Angel 35904 (US pressing); SC.

3 Space Is So Startling, C. Broadhurst, L. Holland, F. Cameron, H. Allen, Philips 632-303, *840-629;* OC.
2 The Stirrings in Sheffield on a Saturday Night, F. Canby, R. Wordsworth, EMI 1019; OC.
1 Stop the World I Want to Get Off, A. Newley, A. Quayle, Decca 4408, *4142;* OC.
4 Summer Song, S. A. Howes, D. Hughes, T. Griffiths, Philips 7070; OC.
3 Summer Song, reissue of above; Philips/Wing 1172.
1 Sweet Charity, J. Prowse, R. McLennan, P. Kelly, CBS *70035;* OC.

1 The Tailors of Poznance, M. Karlin, R. Cowen, I Kerr, Eyemark *1005;* OC.
4 Takeover, A. Fogel, S. Frome, Oriole 20095; OC.
4 The Teitelbaum File, A. Fogel, S. Frome, CBS, no number (private pressing) ; OC.
5 Three's Company, E. Shilling, M. Dobson, E. Boyd, Argo 51, 52 (2 LPs) ; OC.
1 Tom Brown's Schooldays, R. Dotrice, J. Bruce, L. Greene, Decca *5137;* OC.
1 Trelawny, I. Richardson, M. Adrian, G. Craven, Decca *5144;* OC.
4 Twang!, J. Booth, B. Breslaw, B. Windsor, United Artists 1116, *1116;* OC.
5 Twenty Minutes South, J. Bailey, J. Gordon, R. Hunter, J. LeMesurier, Oriole 20007; OC.
2 Two Cities, E. Woodward, N. Roeg, E. Power, K. Colson, EMI *6330;* OC.
1 Two Gentlemen of Verona, B. J. Arnau, R. C. Davis, D. Griffiths, J. Gilbert, RSO *2394-110;* OC.
1 Tyger, J. Lucas, D. Quilley, G. James, RCA *5612;* OC.

5 Valmouth, C. Laine, F. Fielding, B. Couper, D. Hare, Pye Nixa 18029; OC.

5 The Vanishing Island, Moral Rearmament cast, Philips 99538/99539 (2 LPs) ; OC.
3 Virtue in Danger, J. Moffat, B. Inghan, P. Routledge, Decca 4536, *4536;* OC.
1 Wait a Minim!, A. Tracey, P. Tracey, Decca 4610, *4610;* OC.
1 Wait a Minim!, same as above; London 58002, *88002* (US pressing) .
2 Waltzes From Vienna (English version of *The Great Waltz*) , J. Bronhill, HMV 1330; SC.
2 Waltzes From Vienna, reissue of above; Encore 185.
3 The Water Gypsies/Plain and Fancy, reissue of below; Dot 3048 (US pressing)
3 The Water Gypsies, D. Bryan, P. Charles, P. Graves, L. Payne, HMV 1097 (10" LP) ; OC.
3 The Wayward Way, J. Gower, D. Holliday, J. Dale, C. Kennedy, HMV 1834, *1587;* OC.
1 We Were Happy There (40 Years On) , J. Gielgud, G. Howe, Decca *75145* (U.S. pressing) ; OC.
5 Wedding in Paris, A. Walbrook, E. Laye, Parlophone 1011 (10" LP) ; OC.
2 What a Way to Run a Revolution, D. Angadi, M. Hucks, J. Smith, Grosvenor *1010;* OC.
1 What's a Nice Country Like U.S. Doing in a State Like This?, B. Boyle, J. Toye, P. Blake, Galaxy *6004;* OC.
3 Where's Charley?, N. Wisdom, P. Hinton, M. Grimaldi, Columbia 1085; OC.
2 White Horse Inn, A. Cole, R. Williams, Angel 35815, *35815* (US pressing) ; SC.
5 Wild Grows the Heather, P. Sinclair, M. Christie, V. Miller, B. O'Conner, HMV 1125 (10" LP) ; OC.
3 Wildest Dreams, D. Reynolds, A. Dawson, J. Baddeley, HMV 1467, *1377;* OC.

3 Young Visitors, A. Marks, A. Sharkey, J. Waters, J. Riddick, RCA *6792;* OC.

7. COLLECTING MOVIE SOUNDTRACKS

THE NUMBER OF film music enthusiasts is quite small, but many collectors and dealers look to the soundtrack market for its investment potential, owing to the utter scarcity of many important titles and the fact that they are unlikely candidates for reissue. (Although, in line with the recent reissue boom, it must be noted that a few American soundtracks—especially from the Decca catalog—have been reissued with original covers by the Japanese.) Consequently, speculation is rampant, and rare soundtracks tend to change hands frequently before winding up in someone's private collection.

About seventy-five percent of those soundtracks considered valuable are collected for the composer. Of primary interest are those composers who literally established the film music forms and created personal styles within them. This group includes Max Steiner, Erich Wolfgang Korngold, Alfred Newman, David Raksin, Bronislau Kaper, Franz Waxman, Hugo Friedhofer, Miklos Rosza, Bernard Herrmann, Victor Young, and Dmitri Tiomkin. The fact that most of these composers are either dead or inactive only enhances their collectibility. Also in demand are those composers who broke new ground in intelligent film scoring in the Fifties, such as Alex North, Elmer Bernstein, Ernest Gold, Jerome Moross, and Leonard Rosenman, as well as foreign composers like Nino Rota, Mario Nascimbene, and Georges Auric. Other composers whose recorded scores may command high prices include Malcolm Arnold, George Duning, John Barry, George Delerue, Maurice Jarre, Andre Previn, Frank Skinner, Henry Mancini (his early works), Leith Stevens, Jerry Goldsmith, and John Williams.

The rest of the market is made up of soundtrack specialists

—those who collect, say, only circus music, or music from horror films, or westerns; or perhaps they collect the soundtrack of any film in which a particular favorite star appears. Then, of course, there are the many film musicals, which would attract collectors of original cast material.

Mention must also be made of the glorious artwork covers of many rare soundtracks. Indeed, to one not necessarily enamored of film music, but who appreciates a rare record when he sees one, certain soundtracks may prove irresistible. He may be less interested, for example, in Steiner's score for *Band of Angels* than the cover picture of Clark Gable nuzzling up against Yvonne DeCarlo; or, for him, the ethereal, princess-like portrait of Grace Kelly on the cover of *The Swan* may override his feelings for Bronislau Kaper's music.

With so many diverse reasons at play, it's no wonder many collectors and dealers find the soundtrack market so intriguing.

Price Key: 1 = $5 to $10; 2 = $10 to $15; 3 = $15 to $25; 4 = $25 to $40; 5 = over $40.

8. MOVIE SOUNDTRACK RECORDINGS

4 Aaron Slick From Punkin Crick (J. Livingston, R. Evans), RCA 3006 (10")
3 Adrift (A. Liska), MPO *1001* (limited release)
5 Adventures of a Young Man (F. Waxman), RCA 1074, *1074* (very rare in stereo)
1 Advise and Consent (J. Fielding), RCA 1068, *1068*
3 An Affair to Remember (H. Friedhofer), Columbia 1013
1 Africa (A. North), MGM 4462, *4462* (TV soundtrack)
1 Africa Addio (R. Ortolani), United Artists 4141, *5141*
1 After the Fox (B. Bachrach), United Artists 4148, *5148*
3 The Agony and the Ecstasy (A. North), Capitol 2427, *2427*
3 Air Power (N. Dello Joio), Columbia 5214, *6029* (TV soundtrack)
2 Alakazam the Great (L. Baxter), Vee Jay 6000
5 Alexander the Great (M. Nascimbene), Mercury 20148
1 All Night Long (P. Green), Epic 16032, *17032*
1 An American in Paris/In the Good Old Summertime (G. Gershwin), MGM 3232
2 The Americanization of Emily (J. Mandel), Reprise 6151, *6151*
2 The Amorous Adventures of Moll Flanders (J. Addison), RCA 1113, *1113*
2 Anastasia (A. Newman), Decca 8460
3 Anatomy of a Murder (D. Ellington), Columbia 1360, *8166*
3 And God Created Woman (P. Misraki, w/dialogue), Decca 8685
1 Annie Get Your Gun/Easter Parade (I. Berlin), MGM 3227
3 Another Time, Another Place (D. Gamley), Columbia 1180
1 Anything Goes (C. Porter) Decca 8318
2 The Apartment (A. Deutsch), United Artists 3105, *6105*
2 April Love (var.), Dot 9000
1 Arabesque (H. Mancini), RCA 3623, *3623*
5 Athena (H. Martin, R. Blane), Mercury 25202 (10")
3 Atlantis, the Forbidden Island (A. Laszlo), Carlton 106
4 Auntie Mame (B. Kaper), Warner Bros. 1242, *1242*

2 Baby Doll (K. Hopkins), Columbia 958
3 Baby Face Nelson (V. Alexander), Jubilee 1021
1 Baby the Rain Must Fall (E. Bernstein), Mainstream 56056, *6056* or Ava 53, *53*
3 Back Street (F. Skinner), Decca 9097, *79097*
5 The Bad Seed (A. North), RCA 1395
1 Bambi (F. Churchill, E. Plumb), Disneyland 4009
5 Band of Angels (M. Steiner), RCA 1557
1 Bandolero (J. Goldsmith), Project 3 *5026*
2 Barabbas (M. Nascimbene), Colpix 510, *510*
4 The Barbarian and the Geisha (H. Friedhofer), 20th Century Fox 3004
1 Barefoot Adventure (B. Shank), Pacific Jazz 35, *35*
3 Battle of the Bulge (B. Frankel), Warner Bros. 1617, *1617*
1 Beach Blanket Bingo (var.), Capitol 2323, *2323*

1 Beach Party (var.), Buena Vista 3316, *3316*
3 Beau James (var.), Imperial 9041
1 Bebo's Girl (C. Rustichelli), Capitol 2316, *2316*
2 Because You're Mine (var.), RCA 7015 (10")
2 Beckett (L. Rosenthal), Decca 9117, *79117*
2 Beckett (L. Rosenthal, w/dialogue), RCA 1091, *1091* (2 LPs)
2 Bedazzled (D. Moore), London 82009
1 Behold a Pale Horse (M. Jarre), Colpix 519, *519*
3 Bell, Book and Candle (G. Duning), Colpix 502, *502*
2 The Belle of New York (H. Warren, J. Mercer), MGM 108 (10")
2 Bells of St. Mary's (var.), Decca 5052 (10")
2 Ben Hur (M. Rozsa), MGM 1E1, *1SE1* (Deluxe box set)
1 (More Music From) Ben Hur (M. Rozsa), MGM 3900, *3900*
2 Beneath the Planet of the Apes (L. Rosenman), Amos *8001*
2 The Best Things in Life Are Free (var., L. Newman Orch.), Liberty 3017
2 Beyond the Great Wall (trad. Chinese music), Capitol 10401
1 The Bible (T. Mayuzumi), 20th Century Fox 4184, *4184*
3 The Big Circus (P. Sawtell, B. Shefter), Todd 5001, *5001*
1 The Big Country (J. Moross), United Artists 40004, *5004*
1 Big Valley (G. Duning), ABC 527, *527* (TV soundtrack)
1 Billion Dollar Brain (R.R. Bennett), United Artists 4174, *5174*
2 Bird With the Crystal Plumage, Capitol *642*
1 The Birds, the Bees and the Italians (C. Rustichelli), United Artists 4157, *5157*
3 Black Orchid (A. Cicognini), Dot 3178, *25178*
2 Black Tights (var.), RCA International 3, *3*
3 Blood and Sand (V. Gomez), Decca 5380 (10")
2 Blood and Sand (V. Gomez), Decca 8279
Blow-Up (H. Hancock), see *Yardbirds*, p. 77.
1 Blue (M. Hadjidakis), Dot 3855, *25855*
Blue Hawaii, see *Elvis Presley*, p. 69.
3 Blue Max (J. Goldsmith), Mainstream 56081, *6081*
2 Boccaccio '70 (N. Rota, A. Trovajoli), RCA International 5, *5*
3 Bonjour Tristesse (G. Auric), RCA 1040
4 Boy on a Dolphin (H. Friedhofer), Decca 8580
3 The Brave One (V. Young), Decca 8344
3 Breath of Scandal (A. Cicognini), Imperial 9132, *9132*
2 The Buccaneer (E. Bernstein), Columbia 1278, *8096*
2 Bundle of Joy (J. Myrow), RCA 1399
1 Bunny Lake is Missing (P. Glass), RCA 1115, *1115*
1 Burke's Law (H. B. Gilbert), Liberty 3374, *7374* (TV soundtrack)
2 By the Light of the Silvery Moon (var.), Capitol 422 (10")
2 By the Light of the Silvery Moon (var.), Columbia 6248 (10")

97

5 The Caine Mutiny (M. Steiner w/dialogue), RCA 1013[7]
√1 Calamity Jane (S. Fain), Columbia 6273 (10")
2 Call Me Madam (I. Berlin), Decca 5465 (10")
1 Candidate (S. Karmen), Jubilee 5029, *5029*
2 Captain From Castille (A. Newman), Mercury 20005
2 Captain From Castille (A. Newman), Mercury 25072 (10")
3 The Cardinal (J. Moross), RCA 1084, *1084*
1 The Caretakers (E. Bernstein), Ava 31, *31*
√1 Carmen Jones (G. Bizet), RCA 1881
1 The Carpetbaggers (E. Bernstein), Ava 45, *45*
1 Casanova '70/Darling/Marriage Italian Style (A. Trovaioli/J. Dankworth), Epic 24195, *26195*
1 Casino Royale (B. Bachrach), Colgems 5005, *5005*
3 A Certain Smile (A. Newman), Columbia 1194, *8068*
2 The Chapman Report (L. Rosenman), Warner Bros. 1478, *1478*
1 The Charge of the Light Brigade (J. Addison), United Artists 5177
3 The Chase (J. Barry), Columbia 6560, *2960*
1 Checkmate (J. Williams), Columbia 1591, *8391* (TV soundtrack)
√1 Cinderella (J. Livingston), Disneyland 4007
2 Cinderfella (W. Scharf), Dot 8001, *3801*
1 Cinerama Holiday (M. Gould), Mercury 20059
1 Circle of Love (M. Magne), Monitor 602, *602*
3 Circus of Horrors (M. Mathieson), Imperial 9132, *9132*
Clambake, see *Elvis Presley*, p. 69.
1 The Clowns (N. Rota), Columbia 30772
5 Cobweb/Edge of the City (L. Rosenman), MGM 3501
2 The Collector (M. Jarre), Mainstream 56053, *6053*
2 College Confidential (D. Elliott), Chancellor 6015, *6015*
5 Comanche (H. B. Gilbert), Coral 57046
1 Come Blow Your Horn (N. Riddle), Reprise 6071, *6071*
1 Cool Hand Luke (L. Schiffrin), Dot 3833, *25833*
The Cool World (M. Waldron), See *Dizzy Gillespie*, p. 146.
1 The Corrupt Ones (G. Garvarentz), United Artists 4158, *5158*
3 Country Girl (H. Arlen), Decca 5556 (10")
3 Court Jester (S. Fine, S. Cahn), Decca 8212
3 Cowboy (G. Duning), Decca 8684
2 Crime in the Streets (F. Waxman), Decca 8376
3 Cyrano de Bergerac (P. Bowles, w/dialogue), Capitol 283

1 Damn the Defiant (C. Parker), Colpix 511, *511*
2 Damn Yankees (R. Adler, J. Ross), RCA 1047
3 Danger (T. Mottola), MGM 111 (10"; TV soundtrack)
2 Dark of the Sun (J. Loussier), MGM 4544, *4544*
5 David Copperfield (M. Arnold), GRT *10008* (TV soundtrack; limited release)
2 Davy Crockett (G. Bruns), Columbia 666
1 Day of the Dolphin (G. Delerue), Avco-Embassy *11014*

[7] The Holy Grail of all Recordom; worth approximately $3000. The most reliable story goes that author Herman Wouk threatened to sue RCA because his name was inadvertently left off the record jacket. About twenty copies are known to have been sold in a New York City record store before the entire shipment was recalled and subsequently destroyed. A word of warning: There also exists a pirate edition of *The Caine Mutiny* with a black and white facsimile of the original cover and the following printed information: "Private pressing, 1000 copies. Not for commercial use." The value of this bootleg (as with all bootlegs) is highly suspect, but some dealers have been known to charge as much as $100 per copy. If you stumble across one (and the boot is more plentiful than its "1000 copies" would indicate), and hope to make a profit by reselling it, consider the following: Yes, Max Steiner is one of the great film composers, but the record—one side of which is the entire courtmartial scene—contains, perhaps, ten minutes of music. Then there is the problem of the fidelity of the bootleg, which must certainly suffer compared to the original. And what is to prevent some budding entrepreneur from pressing up another thousand or so copies using one of the pirated releases as a master disc, thereby damaging the fidelity even further? Certainly, *The Caine Mutiny* is unique in its rarity, but in the case of a pirated edition, *caveat emptor*.

1 The Day the Fish Came Out (M. Theodorakis), 20th Century Fox 4194, *4194*
1 Daydreamer (M. Laws), Columbia 6540, *2940*
2 Dead Ringer (A. Previn), Warner Bros. 1536, *1536*
2 Deadfall (J. Barry), 20th Century Fox *4203*
1 Deep in My Heart (S. Romberg), MGM 3153
5 Desire Under the Elms (E. Bernstein), Dot 3095
3 Destination Moon (L. Stevens), Columbia 6151 (10")
4 Destination Moon (L. Stevens), Omega 1003, 3 (complete score)
3 The Devil at 4 O'Clock (G. Duning), Colpix 509, *509*
2 Diamond Head (J. Williams), Colpix 440, *440*
3 Diary of Anne Frank (A. Newman), 20th Century Fox 3012, *3012*
3 Dino (G. Fried), Epic 3404
1 The Dirty Dozen (DeVol), MGM 4445, *4445*
1 Divorce American Style (D. Grusin), United Artists 4163, *5163*
1 Divorce Italian Style (C. Rustichelli), United Artists 4106, *5106*
1 (The Abominable) Dr. Phibes (B. Kirchin), American International *1040*
3 Dog of Flanders (P. Sawtell, B. Shefter), 20th Century Fox 3026, *3026*
1 La Dolce Vita (N. Rota), RCA International 1, *1*
Double Trouble, see *Elvis Presley*, p. 69.
3 Dragnet (J. Scott, w/dialogue), RCA 3199 (10"; TV soundtrack)
5 Drango (E. Bernstein), Liberty 3036
3 The Dunwich Horror (L. Baxter), American International *1028*

2 East of Eden/Rebel Without a Cause (L. Rosenman), Columbia 940
3 East of Eden/Rebel Without a Cause (L. Rosenman), Imperial 9021
1 East Side, West Side (K. Hopkins), Columbia 2123, *8923* (TV soundtrack)
1 Easter Parade/Annie Get Your Gun (I. Berlin), MGM 3227
1 Ecco (R. Ortolani), Warner Bros. 1600, *1600*
2 The Eddie Cantor Story (var.), Capitol 467 (10")
5 Edge of the City/Cobweb (L. Rosenman), MGM 3501
3 8½ (N. Rota), RCA International 6, *6*
2 El Cid (M. Rozsa), MGM 3977, *3977*
3 El Dorado (N. Riddle), Epic 13114, *15114*
2 Eleven Against the Ice (K. Hopkins), RCA 1618 (TV soundtrack)
2 Elizabeth Taylor in London (J. Barry), Colpix 459, *459* (TV soundtrack)
3 Elmer Gantry (A. Previn), United Artists 4069, *5069*
2 Everything I Have Is Yours/Lili (B. Kaper), MGM 187 (10")
2 Experiment in Terror (H. Mancini), RCA 2442, *2442* (2 covers)

1 A Face in the Crowd (T. Glazer), Capitol 872
3 Fall of the Roman Empire (D. Tiomkin), Columbia 6660, *2460*
The Family Way, see *Paul McCartney*, p. 65.
3 A Farewell to Arms (M. Nascimbene), Capitol 918
1 Fellini Satyricon (N. Rota), United Artists 5208
1 Fellini's Roma (N. Rota), United Artists 052
3 Fifty-Five Days at Peking (D. Tiomkin), Columbia 2028, *8828*
3 Fire Down Below (var.), Decca 8597
2 Flea in Her Ear (B. Kaper), 20th Century Fox *4200*

MOVIE SOUNDTRACK RECORDINGS   99

Forbidden Island, see Atlantis, the Forbidden Island
3 For Whom the Bell Tolls/Golden Earrings (V. Young), Decca 8008 (original)
2 For Whom the Bell Tolls/Golden Earrings (V. Young), Decca 8481 (reissue)
3 Four Girls in Town (A. North)/Written on the Wind (F. Skinner), Decca 8424
1 Four Horsemen of the Apocalypse (A. Previn), MGM 3993, *3993*
1 Four in the Morning (J. Barry), Roulette 801, *801*
3 The Fox (L. Schiffrin), Warner Bros. *1738*
5 Francis of Assisi (M. Nascimbene), 20th Century Fox 3053, *3053* (very rare in stereo)
Frankie and Johnny, see *Elvis Presley*, p. 69.
3 French Line (J. Myrow), Mercury 25182 (10")
3 Friendly Persuasion (D. Tiomkin), RKO-Unique 110 or Venise 7026
3 The Fugitive Kind (K. Hopkins), United Artists 4065, *5065*
Fun in Acapulco, see *Elvis Presley*, p. 69.
✓ Funeral in Berlin (K. Elfers), RCA 1136, *1136*
✓2 Funny Face (G. Gershwin), Verve 15001
2 Fuzzy Pink Nightgown (B. May), Imperial 9042, *9042*

4 Games (F. Lai), Viking *105* (limited release)
2 Gay Purr-ee (H. Arlen), Warner Bros. 1479, *1479*
2 Geisha Boy (W. Scharf), Jubilee 1096, *1096*
2 The Gene Krupa Story (L. Stevens), Verve 15010, *6105*
3 (Themes From) The General Electric Theater (E. Bernstein), Columbia 1395, *8190* (TV soundtrack)
3 Genghis Khan (D. Radic), Liberty 3412, *7412*
2 Gentlemen Marry Brunettes (var.), Coral 57013
1 Gentlemen Prefer Blondes/Till the Clouds Roll By (var.), MGM 3231
G.I. Blues, see *Elvis Presley*, p. 69.
3 The Gift of Love (W. Mockridge), Columbia 1113
1 Gigot (J. Gleason), Capitol 1754, *1754*
2 Girl Crazy (G. Gershwin), Decca 5412 (10")
Girl Happy, see *Elvis Presley*, p. 69.
4 The Girl in the Bikini (J. Yatove), Poplar 1002
3 The Girl Most Likely (H. Martin, R. Blane), Capitol 930
Girls! Girls! Girls!, see *Elvis Presley*, p. 69.
5 God's Little Acre (E. Bernstein), United Artists 40002
5 The Golden Coach (A. Vivaldi), MGM 3111
2 Golden Earrings/For Whom the Bell Tolls (V. Young), Decca 8008 or 8481
3 Goliath and the Barbarians (L. Baxter), American International 1001, *1001*
1 Goodbye Again (G. Auric), United Artists 4091, *5091*
1 Goodbye Charlie (A. Previn), 20th Century Fox 3165, *4165*
4 The Gospel According to St. Matthew (var.), Mainstream 54000, *4000*
2 Goya (V. Gomez), Decca 8996
2 The Great Race (H. Mancini), RCA 3402, *3402*
3 The Greatest Show on Earth (var.), RCA 3018 (10")
1 The Greatest Story Ever Told (A. Newman), United Artists 4120, *5120*
1 The Green Hornet (B. May), 20th Century Fox 3186, *3186* (TV soundtrack)
3 Grounds For Marriage (var.), MGM 536 (10")
3 Guns For San Sebastian (E. Morricone), MGM 4565, *4565*
1 The Guns of Navarone (D. Tiomkin), Columbia 1655, *8455*
1 Gypsy Girl (M. DeLugg), Mainstream 56090, *6090*

2 The Hallelujah Trail (E. Bernstein), United Artists 4127, *5127*
2 Hamlet (W. Walton), RCA 5 (10")

2 Harlow (N. Hefti), Columbia 6390, 2790[8]
1 Harper (J. Mandel), Mainstream 56078, *6078*
Harum Scarum, see *Elvis Presley*, p. 69.
✓2 The Harvey Girls/Meet Me in St. Louis (var.), Decca 8498
Head, see *The Monkees*, p. 66.
2 The Helen Morgan Story (var.), RCA 1030
3 Hell to Eternity (L. Stevens), Warwick 2030, *2030*
1 Hennesey (S. Burke), Signature 1049, *1049* (TV soundtrack)
5 Hercules (E. Masetti, w/dialogue), RCA 1036
1 The Heroes of Telemark (M. Arnold) Mainstream 56064, *6064*
1 Hey Boy, Hey Girl (var.), Capitol 1160
2 High Time (H. Mancini), RCA 2314, *2314*
✓3 Hit the Deck (V. Youmans), MGM 3163
1 The Honey Pot (J. Addison), United Artists 4159, *5159*
3 The Horse Soldiers (D. Buttolph), United Artists 4035, *5035*
1 The Horsemen (G. Delerue), Sunflower 5007
4 Hot Rod Rumble (A. Courage), Liberty 3048
1 Hotel (J. Keating), Warner Bros. 1682, *1682*
1 Hour of the Gun (J. Goldsmith), United Artists 4166, *5166*
1 A House is Not a Home (B. Bachrach), Ava 50, *50*
3 Houseboat (G. Duning), Columbia 1222
1 How to Steal a Million (J. Williams), 20th Century Fox 4183, *4183*
1 How to Stuff a Wild Bikini (var.), Wand 671, *671*
2 Hurry Sundown (H. Montenegro), RCA 1133, *1133*
3 The Hustler (K. Hopkins), Kapp 1264, *3264*

2 I Could Go On Singing (H. Arlen), Capitol 1861, *1861*
2 I Love Melvin (J. Myrow), MGM 190 (10")
4 I Never Sang For My Father (A. Gorgoni, B. Mann), Bell 1204 (limited release)
1 Ice Station Zebra (M. Legrand), MGM *S1E-14*
2 Ichabod/Rip Van Winkle (var.), Decca 9106
2 I'll See You in My Dreams (var.), Columbia 6198 (10")
2 Imitation of Life (F. Skinner), Decca 8879, *78879*
1 In Cold Blood (Q. Jones), Colgems 107, *107*
3 In Harm's Way (J. Goldsmith), RCA 1100, *1100*
3 In Like Flint (J. Goldsmith), 20th Century Fox 4193, *4193*
1 In the Good Old Summertime/An American in Paris (G. Gershwin), MGM 3232
4 Indiscretion of an American Wife (A. Cicognini), Columbia 6277 (10")
4 Inn of Sixth Happiness (M. Arnold), 20th Century Fox 3011, *3011*
1 Inside Daisy Clover (A. Previn), Warner Bros. 1616, *1616*
2 Interlude (G. Delerue), Colgems 5007
3 Interlude/Tammy and the Bachelor (F. Skinner), Coral 57159
1 The Interns (L. Stevens), Colpix 427, *427*
3 Interrupted Melody (var.), MGM 3185
3 Invitation to the Dance (A. Previn), MGM 3207
1 The Ipcress File (J. Barry), Decca 9124, *79124*
2 Is Paris Burning? (M. Jarre), Columbia 6630, *3030*
4 Island in the Sky (H. Friedhofer, w/dialogue), Decca 7029 (10")
It Happened at the World's Fair, see *Elvis Presley*, p. 69.
3 It Started in Naples (A. Cicognini), Dot 3324, *25324*
3 It's Always Fair Weather (A. Previn), MGM 3241
4 Ivanhoe/Plymouth Adventure (M. Rozsa), MGM 179 (10")
4 Ivanhoe/Madame Bovary/Plymouth Adventure (M. Rozsa), MGM 3507

---

[8] This version stars Carol Lynley; not to be confused with Warner Bros. 1599 (N. Riddle), starring Carroll Baker.

SHOW BUSINESS

1 Jack the Ripper (P. Rugolo), RCA 2199, *2199*
3 The James Dean Story (L. Stevens), Capitol 881
3 The Joe Louis Story (G. Bassman), MGM 221 (10")
4 John Paul Jones (M. Steiner), Warner Bros. 1293, *1293*
1 Johnny Cool (B. May), United Artists 4111, *5111*
1 Johnny Tremain (G. Bruns), Disneyland 4014
2 Judgement at Nuremberg (E. Gold), United Artists 4095, *5095*
1 Judith (S. Kaplan), RCA 1119, *1119*
3 Juliet of the Spirits (N. Rota), Mainstream 56062, *6062*
4 Julius Caesar (M. Rozsa, w/dialogue), MGM 3033
3 Jungle Book/Thief of Bagdad (M. Rozsa), RCA 2118
1 Justine (J. Goldsmith), Monument *18123*

4 The Key (M. Arnold), Columbia 1185
1 Khartoum (F. Cordell), United Artists 4140, *5140*
King Creole, see *Elvis Presley*, p. 69.
2 King of Kings (M. Rozsa), MGM 1E-2, S1E-2 (Deluxe set w/book)
1 King Rat (J. Barry), Mainstream 56061, *6061*
5 Kings Go Forth (E. Bernstein), Capitol 1063
3 Kiss Them For Me (L. Newman), Coral 57160
Kissin' Cousins, see *Elvis Presley*, p. 69.
3 Knock on Wood (S. Fine), Decca 5527 (10")
1 Kraft Television Theater (V. Selinsky), RKO 127 (TV soundtrack)

2 The Land Raiders (B. Nicolai), Beverly Hills *21*
3 The Leopard (N. Rota), 20th Century Fox 5015, *5015*
Let No Man Write My Epitaph, see *Ella Fitzgerald*, p. 144.
Les Liaisons Dangereuses, see *Art Blakey*, p. 134.
2 Lili/Everything I Have is Yours (B. Kaper), MGM 187 (10")
3 Lilies of the Field (J. Goldsmith), Epic 24094, *26094*
2 Lillith (K. Hopkins), Colpix 520, *520*
5 The Lion (M. Arnold), London 76001
1 The Lively Set (B. Darin), Decca 9119, *79119*
1 Lolita (N. Riddle), MGM 4050, *4050*
4 The Long Hot Summer (A. North), Roulette 25026
5 Long John Silver (D. Buttolph), RCA 3279 (10")
3 The Long Ships (D. Radic), Colpix 517, *517*
2 The Longest Day (various, w/dialogue), 20th Century Fox 5007, *5007*
2 Lord Jim (B. Kaper), Colpix 521, *521*
3 Loss of Innocence (R. Addinsell), Colpix 508
5 The Lost Continent (A. F. Lavagnino), MGM 3635
3 Love is My Profession (R. Cloerec)/Where the Hot Winds Blow (R. Vlad), Everest 5076, *1076*
2 Lullaby of Broadway (var.), Columbia 6168 (10")
2 Lust For Life Suite/Background to Violence (M. Rozsa), Decca 10015, *710015*

4 Madame Bovary/Ivanhoe/Plymouth Adventure (M. Rozsa), MGM 3507
1 Madame X (F. Skinner), Decca 9152, *79152*
1 Madron (R. Ortolani), Quad *5001*
3 The Magnificent Obsession (F. Skinner), Decca 8078
1 Major Dundee (D. Amfitheatrof), Columbia 6380, *2780*
2 The Making of the President 1960 (E. Bernstein, w/dialogue), United Artists 9, *9* (2 LPs; TV soundtrack)
1 Malamondo (E. Morricone), Epic 24126, *26126*
1 A Man Called Adam (B. Carter), Reprise 6180, *6180*
2 A Man For All Seasons (G. Delerue, w/dialogue), RCA 116 (2 LPs)
2 Man in the Middle (L. Bart), 20th Century Fox 3128, *4128*
3 Man of a Thousand Faces (F. Skinner), Decca 8623

1 Mannix (L. Schifrin), Paramount 5004 (TV soundtrack)
4 Maracaibo (L. Almeida), Decca 8756
1 Marco the Magnificent (G. Garvarentz), Columbia 6470, *2780*
2 Mardi Gras (S. Fain), Bell 11, *11*
4 Marjorie Morningstar (M. Steiner), RCA 1044
1 Mary Queen of Scots (J. Barry), Decca *79186*
2 Master of the World (L. Baxter), Vee Jay 4000, *4000*
2 The Mating Urge (S. Wilson), International 7777
1 A Matter of Innocence (M. Legrand), Decca 9160, *79160*
2 McLintock (DeVol), United Artists 4112, *5112*
3 Me and the Colonel (G. Duning), RCA 1046, *1046*
2 Mediterranean Holiday (R. Ortolani), London 76003, *82003*
3 The Medium (G. Menotti, w/dialogue), Mercury 7 (2 LPs)
2 Meet Me in St. Louis/The Harvey Girls (var.), Decca 8498
3 Melba (var.), RCA 7012 (10")
5 Men in War (E. Bernstein), Imperial 9032
2 Merry Andrew (S. Chaplin), Capitol 1016
1 A Milanese Story (J. Lewis), Atlantic 1388, *1388*
5 Miss Sadie Thompson (G. Duning), Mercury 25181 (10")
5 Moby Dick (P. Sainton), RCA 1247
1 Modesty Blaise (J. Dankworth), 20th Century Fox 3182, *4182*
1 Molly Maguires (H. Mancini), Paramount *6000*
1 The Moon is Blue (H. B. Gilbert), Crown 5095, *130*
1 The Moon Spinners (R. Grainer), Buena Vista 3323
3 The Mountain (D. Amphtheatrof)/Omar Khayyam (V. Young), Decca 8449
4 Mr. Imperium (H. Arlen), RCA 61 (10")
1 M-Squad (var.), RCA 2062, *2062* (TV soundtrack)
3 Murder, Inc. (DeVol, G. Weiss), Canadian-American 1003
2 Murderer's Row (L. Schiffrin), Colgems 5003, *5003*
1 Muscle Beach Party (var.), Buena Vista 3314, *3314*
1 Music For Loretta (H. Lubin), Decca 4124, *74124*
1 Mutiny on the Bounty (B. Kaper), MGM 1E4, S1E4 (boxed set w/book)
3 My Geisha (F. Waxman), RCA 1070, *1070*
5 Myra Breckinridge (J. Phillips), 20th Century Fox *4210* (limited release)

1 Naked City (G. Duning), Colpix 505, *505* (TV soundtrack)
3 Naked Maja (A. F. Lavagnino), United Artists 4031, *5031*
2 Nevada Smith (A. Newman), Dot 3718, *25718*
1 The New Interns (E. Hagen), Colpix 473, *473*
1 Nicholas & Alexandria (R. R. Bennett), Bell *1103*
2 Night of the Generals (M. Jarre), Colgems 5002, *5002*
5 Night of the Hunter (W. Schumann, w/dialogue), RCA 1136
1 The Night They Raided Minsky's (C. Strouse, P. Adams), United Artists 5191
5 Nine Hours to Rama (M. Arnold), London 76002
1 No Sun in Venice (J. Lewis), Atlantic 1284, *1284*
1 Not With My Wife You Don't (J. Williams), Warner Bros. 1668, *1668*
1 Nothing But the Best (R. Grainer), Colpix 477, *477*
3 The Nun's Story (F. Waxman), Warner Bros. 1306, *1306*

2 Odds Against Tommorow (J. Lewis), United Artists 4061, *5061*
2 Of Love and Desire (R. Stein), 20th Century Fox 5014, *5014*
3 Oh, Rosalinda (var.), Mercury 20145
2 The Old Man and the Sea (D. Tiomkin), Columbia 1183, *8013*
3 Omar Khayyam (V. Young)/The Mountain (D. Amtheatrof), Decca 8449
2 On Moonlight Bay (var.), Columbia 6186 (10")

MOVIE SOUNDTRACK RECORDINGS

5 On the Beach (E. Gold), Roulette 25098, *25098*
2 One Eyed Jacks (H. Friedhofer), Liberty 16001, *17001*
1 One Step Beyond (H. Lubin), Decca 8970, *78970* (TV soundtrack)
3 1001 Arabian Nights (G. Duning), Colpix 410, *410*
1 Our Man Flint (J. Goldsmith), 20th Century Fox 3179, *4179*

3 Painting the Clouds With Sunshine (var.), Capitol 291 (10")
Pajama Party, see *Annette*, p. 46.
1 Palm Springs Weekend (F. Perkins), Warner Bros. 1519, *1519*
3 Panic Button (G. Garvarentz), Musicor 2036, *3026*
Paradise Hawaiian Style, see *Elvis Presley*, p. 69.
1 Paris Holiday (J. Van Heusen, J. Lilley), United Artists 40001
✓1 Paris When it Sizzles (N. Riddle), Reprise 6113, *6113*
2 Parrish (M. Steiner), Warner Bros. 1413, *1413*
2 A Patch of Blue (J. Goldsmith), Mainstream 56068, *6068*
1 The Pawnbroker (Q. Jones), Mercury 21011, *61011*
2 Pepe (var.), Colpix 507, *507*
Performance, see *Mick Jagger*, p. 61.
✓1 Petulia (J. Barry), Warner Bros. *1755*
3 Peyton Place (F. Waxman), RCA 1042, *1042* ("fake" stereo)
2 The Pleasure Seekers (L. Newman, J. Van Heusen), RCA 1101, *1101*
4 Plymouth Adventure/Ivanhoe (M. Rozsa), MGM 179 (10")
4 Plymouth Adventure/Ivanhoe/Madame Bovary (M. Rozsa), MGM 3507
1 Pretty Boy Floyd (D. Serino, W. Sanford), Audio Fidelity 1936, *5936*
4 The Pride and the Passion (G. Anthiel), Capitol 873
3 Private Hell 36 (L. Stevens), Coral 56122 (10")
3 The Professionals (M. Jarre), Colgems 5001, *5001*

2 The Quiet Man (V. Young), RCA 3089 (10")
3 The Quiet Man/Samson and Delilah (V. Young), Decca 8566
3 The Quiller Memorandum (J. Barry), Columbia 6660, *3060*
2 Quo Vadis Suite/Red House/Spellbound (M. Rozsa), Capitol 456
3 Quo Vadis (M. Rozsa, w/dialogue), MGM 134 (2 10" LPs)
3 Quo Vadis (M. Rozsa, w/dialogue), MGM 3524

1 Railway Children (J. Douglas), Capitol 871
4 The Rainmaker (A. North), RCA 1434
3 (Highlights From) Raintree County (J. Green), RCA 1038, *1038*
✓5 Raintree County (J. Green), RCA 6000 (2 LPs)
2 Rebel Without a Cause/East of Eden (L. Rosenman), Columbia 940
3 Rebel Without a Cause/East of Eden (L. Rosenman), Imperial 9021
3 Red Garters (J. Livingston, R. Evans), Columbia 6282 (10")
2 Red House/Spellbound/Quo Vadis Suite (M. Rozsa), Capitol 456
1 The Reivers (J. Williams), Columbia 3510
2 The Reporter (K. Hopkins), Columbia 2269, *9069* (TV soundtrack)
4 Return to Paradise (D. Tiomkin, w/dialogue), Decca 5489 (10")
5 Rhapsody of Steel (D. Tiomkin), US Steel 502 (limited release)[9]

[9] Industrial film for US Steel; not a commercial release.

1 Richard Diamond (P. Rugolo), Mercury 36162, *80045* (TV soundtrack)
3 Richard III (W. Walton, w/dialogue), RCA 6126 (3 LP boxed set)
1 Rider on the Rain (F. Lai), Capitol *584*
Riot on Sunset Strip, see *Chocolate Watchband*, p. 51.
2 Rip Van Winkle/Ichabod (var.), Decca 9106
2 The River (V. Thompson), Polymusic 5003
1 Robbery (J. Keating), London 76008, *82008*
✓1 Robin and the 7 Hoods (J. Van Heusen), Reprise 2021, *2021*
3 Rocco and His Brothers (N. Rota), RCA International 2, *2*
2 Rock Pretty Baby (H. Mancini), Decca 8429
Rock, Rock, Rock, see p. 78.
1 The Rogues (N. Riddle), RCA 2976, *2976* (TV soundtrack)
3 Romance of a Horsethief (M. Shuman), Allied Artists 110-100 (limited release)
1 Rome Adventure (M. Steiner), Warner Bros. 1458, *1458*
✓3 Romeo and Juliet (N. Rota, w/dialogue), Capitol 289 (4 LP boxed set)
2 Romeo and Juliet (R. Vlad, w/dialogue), Epic 3126
1 Romeo and Juliet (R. Vlad, w/dialogue), Epic 13104, *15104* (reissue; "fake" stereo)
5 Roots of Heaven (M. Arnold), 20th Century Fox 3005
3 The Rose Tatoo (A. North), Columbia 727
Roustabout, see *Elvis Presley*, p. 69.
3 Run of the Arrow (V. Young), Decca 8620

1 The Sacred Idol (L. Baxter), Capitol 1293, *1293*
4 St. Joan (M. Spoliansky), Capitol 865
2 St. Louis Blues (W. C. Handy), Capitol 993
4 Salome (G. Duning), Decca 6026 (10")
1 Samoa (O. Wallace)/Switzerland (P. Smith), Disneyland 4003
3 Samson and Delilah/The Quiet Man (V. Young) Decca 8566
2 The Sand Castle (A. Wilder), Columbia 1455, *8249*
3 The Sand Pebbles (J. Goldsmith), 20th Century Fox 4189, *4189*
1 Satan in High Heels (M. Lowe), Charlie Parker 406, *406*
1 The Savage Wild (J. Mendoza-Nava), American International *1032*
3 Sayonara (F. Waxman), RCA 1041, *1041*
2 Say One For Me (J. Van Heusen, S. Cahn), Columbia 1337, *8147*
2 The Scalphunters (E. Bernstein), United Artists 4176, *5176*
3 Scent of Mystery (M. Nascimbene), Ramrod 6001, *6001*
1 Search For Paradise (D. Tiomkin), RCA 1034
1 Sebastian (J. Goldsmith), Dot 3845, *25845*
1 Secrets of Life (P. Smith), Disneyland 4006
2 Seduced and Abandoned (C. Rusticelli), CAM 100001
2 Sergeants 3 (B. May), Reprise 2013, *2013*
3 The Seven Little Foys (var.), RCA 3275 (10")
3 The 7th Voyage of Sinbad (B. Herrmann), Colpix 504, *504*
1 Sex and the Single Girl (N. Hefti), Warner Bros. 1570, *1570*
3 Shake Hands With the Devil (W. Alwyn), United Artists 4043, *5043*
1 Shakespeare Wallah (S. Ray), Epic 13110, *15110*
1 Shenandoah (F. Skinner), Decca 9125, *79125*
3 Ship of Fools (E. Gold), RCA 2817, *2817*
2 The Shop on Main Street (Z. Liska), Mainstream 56082, *6082*
1 Shotgun Slade (G. Fried), Mercury 20575, *60235* (TV soundtrack)
1 The Silencers (E. Bernstein), RCA 1120, *1120*
3 Sincerely Yours (var.), Columbia 800

Sing Boy Sing, see *Tommy Sands*, p. 71.
2 Single Room Furnished (J. Sheldon), Sidewalk 5917
1 Slaughter on 10th Avenue (R. Rodgers), Decca 8657, 78657
3 Slave Trade in the World Today (T. Usuelli), London 76006
1 Smashing Time (J. Addison), ABC 6, 6
1 The Snow Queen (F. Skinner, w/dialogue), Decca 8977, 78977
2 Snow White and the Three Stooges (var.), Columbia 1650, 8450
3 So This is Love (var.), RCA 3000 (10")
2 So This is Paris (Sherell, Moody), Decca 5553 (10")
5 Sodom and Gomorrah (M. Rozsa), RCA 1076, 1076 (very rare in stereo)
4 Solomon and Sheba (M. Nascimbene), United Artists 4051, 5051
4 Some Came Running (E. Bernstein), Capitol 1109, 1109
3 Somebody Loves Me (var.), RCA 3097 (10")
3 Song of Bernadette (A. Newman), Decca 5358 (10")
1 Song Without End (F. Liszt), Colpix 506, 506
4 The Sons of Katie Elder (E. Bernstein), Columbia 6420, 2820
2 Sophia Loren in Rome (J. Barry), Columbia 6310, 2710 (TV soundtrack)
3 The Sound and the Fury (A. North), Decca 8885, 78885
2 South Seas Adventure (A. North), Audio Fidelity 1899, 5899
1 Southern Star (G. Garvarentz), Colgems 5009
4 The Spanish Affair (D. Amfitheatrof), Dot 3078
2 Spellbound/Red House/Quo Vadis Suite, Capitol 456
Spinout, see *Elvis Presley*, p. 69.
3 The Spirit of St. Louis (F. Waxman), RCA 1472
2 Staccato (E. Bernstein), Capitol 1287, 1287 (TV soundtrack)
2 Stagecoach (J. Goldsmith), Mainstream 56077, 6077
2 Stars and Stripes Forever (var.), MGM 3508
2 The Stooge (var.), Capitol 401 (10")
✓ 1 Stop the World, I Want to Get Off (L. Bricusse, A. Newley), Warner Bros. 1643, 1643
3 The Strange One (K. Hopkins), Coral 57132
2 A Streetcar Named Desire (A. North) Now Voyager/The Informer/Since You Went Away (M. Steiner), Capitol 387
1 Study in Terror (J. Scott), Roulette 801, 801
2 The Subterraneans (A. Previn), MGM 3812, 3812
4 Summer and Smoke (E. Bernstein), RCA 1067, 1067
Summer Holiday, see *Cliff Richard*, p. 70.
2 Summer Love (H. Mancini), Decca 8714
✓ 2 Summer Magic (R. Sherman), Buena Vista 4025, 4025
3 The Sun Also Rises (H. Friedhofer), Kapp 7001
5 The Swan (B. Kaper), MGM 3399
1 Sweet Love, Bitter (M. Waldron), Impulse 9142, 9142
2 The Sweet Smell of Success (E. Bernstein), Decca 8610
The Sweet Smell of Success (jazz version), see *Chico Hamilton*, p. 149.
2 The Swimmer (M. Hamlisch), Columbia 3210
Swinger's Paradise, see *Cliff Richard*, p. 70.
1 Switzerland (P. Smith) Samoa (O. Wallace), Disneyland 4003

3 Tammy and the Bachelor/Interlude (F. Skinner), Coral 57159
3 Taras Bulba (F. Waxman), United Artists 4100, 5100
Tarzan, see *Shorty Rogers*, p. 168.
1 Tell Me Lies (R. Peaslee, w/dialogue), Gregar 5000, 5000
1 The Ten Commandments (E. Bernstein), Dot 3054, 25054 (2 LPs)

5 Tender is the Night (B. Herrmann, others), 20th Century Fox 3054, 3054 (very rare in stereo)
1 The 10th Victim (P. Piccioni), Mainstream 56071, 6071
2 That Midnight Kiss/Toast of New Orleans (var.), RCA 2422
✓ 2 There's No Business Like Show Business (I. Berlin), Decca 8091
3 Thief of Bagdad/Jungle Book (M. Rozsa, w/dialogue), RCA 2118
1 36 Hours (D. Tiomkin), Vee Jay 1131, 1131
3 This Could Be the Night (var.), MGM 3530
5 This Earth is Mine (H. Friedhofer), Decca 8915, 78915
1 This Property is Condemned (K. Hopkins), Verve 8664, 68664
1 Those Magnificent Men in Their Flying Machines (R. Goodwin), 20th Century Fox 3174, 4174
3 Three For the Show (var.), Mercury 25204 (10")
3 Three Sailors and a Girl (S. Fain), Capitol 485 (10")
3 Three Worlds of Gulliver (B. Herrmann, w/dialogue), Colpix 414
1 Thriller (P. Rugolo), Time 52034, 2034 (TV soundtrack)
2 A Time to Love, a Time to Die (M. Rozsa), Decca 8778
1 To Bed or Not to Bed (P. Piccioni), London 76005
2 To Kill a Mockingbird (E. Bernstein), Ava 20, 20
2 Toast of New Orleans/That Midnight Kiss (var.), RCA 2422
1 Tom Thumb (F. Spielman, w/dialogue), Lion 70084
2 Tonight We Sing (var.), RCA 7016
2 Too Late Blues/Will Penny (D. Raksin), Dot 3844, 25844
3 Too Much, Too Soon (E. Gold), Mercury 20381, 60019
3 Torch Song (var.), MGM 214 (10")
1 Torn Curtain (J. Addison), Decca 9155, 79155
1 Touch of Evil (H. Mancini), Challenge 602 (original)
2 Touch of Evil (H. Mancini), Challenge 615 (reissue)
1 The Train (M. Jarre), United Artists 4122, 5122
1 The Trap (R. Goodwin), Atco 204, 204
2 Trapeze (M. Arnold), Columbia 870
3 The Trouble With Angels (J. Goldsmith), Mainstream 56073, 6073
3 The True Story of the Civil War (E. Gold, w/dialogue), Coral 59100
1 Tunes of Glory (M. Arnold), United Artists 4086, 5086
Turn On, Tune In, Drop Out, see *Dr. Timothy Leary*, p. 63.
2 Two for the Seesaw (A. Previn), United Artists 4103, 5103
1 Two Mules For Sister Sara (E. Morricone), Kapp 5512
3 Two Tickets to Broadway (var.), RCA 39 (10")

3 The Unforgiven (D. Tiomkin), United Artists 4068, 5068
1 The Untouchables (N. Riddle), Capitol 1430, 1430 (TV soundtrack)

5 Vertigo (B. Herrmann), Mercury 20384
3 The Virgin and the Gypsy (P. Gowers), Steady 122 (limited release)
1 Viva Maria (G. Delerue), United Artists 4135, 5135

1 Wagon Train (var.), Mercury 20502, 60179 (TV soundtrack)
1 Walk on the Wild Side (E. Bernstein), Mainstream 56083, 6083 or Ava 4, 4
2 War and Peace (N. Rota), Columbia 930
2 War and Peace (V. Ovchinnikov), Capitol 2918
1 The War Lord (J. Moross), Decca 9146, 79149
1 The Way West (B. Kaper), United Artists 4149, 5149
1 What Did You Do in the War, Daddy? (H. Mancini), RCA 3648, 3648

MOVIE SOUNDTRACK RECORDINGS

3 Where the Hot Winds Blow (R. Vlad) /Love is My Profession (R. Cloerec), Everest 5076, *1076*
1 Where's Jack (E. Bernstein), Paramount 5005
1 The Whisperers (J. Barry), United Artists 4161, *5161*
4 Who's Afraid of Virginia Woolf? (A. North, w/dialogue), Warner Bros. 1657, *1657* (2 LPs; soundtrack and complete film play)
3 The Wild Bunch (J. Fielding), Warner Bros. *1814*
3 Wild is the Wind (D. Tiomkin), Columbia 1090
3 (Jazz Themes From) The Wild One (L. Stevens), Decca 8349
2 Will Penny/Too Late Blues (D. Raksin), Dot 3844, *25844*
2 With a Song in My Heart (var.), Capitol 309
1 Woman Times Seven (R. Ortolani), Capitol 2800, *2800*
1 Women of the World (R. Ortolani), Decca 9112, *79112*

3 Wonderful Country (A. North), United Artists 4050, *5050* ("fake" stereo)
Wonderful to be Young, see *Cliff Richard*, p. 70.
3 The World of Suzie Wong (G. Duning), RCA 1059, *1059*
3 Written on the Wind (F. Skinner) /Four Girls in Town (A. North), Decca 8424
2 The Wrong Box (J. Barry), Mainstream 56088, *6088*

1 Yesterday, Today & Tomorrow (A. Trovaioli), Warner Bros. 1552, *1552*
3 Yojimbo (M. Sato), MGM 4096, *4096*
2 Young at Heart (var.), Columbia 6339 (10")
3 The Young Lions (H. Friedhofer), Decca 8719, *78719*
2 Young Man With a Horn (var.), Columbia 582
3 The Young Savages (D. Amram), Columbia 1672, *8472*

9. PERSONALITIES AND VOCALISTS

THE RECORDS IN THIS SECTION include those by popular singers, jazz singers, cabaret singers, records by stage and screen stars, and the like. A word of warning: Many of the one-star records listed here are not fast-sellers; they will sell eventually, but the demand for them is less insistent than for one-star records in other categories. They are included to indicate that the artist does have a following, however small, and it is simply a question of when the right buyer surfaces.

Price Key: 1 = $5 to $10; 2 = $10 to $15; 3 = $15 to $20; 4 = $20 to $35; 5 = over $35

Anna Maria Alberghetti
1 I Can't Resist You, Capitol 887
1 Warm and Willing, Capitol 1379, *1379*
1 Songs by Anna Maria Alberghetti, Mercury 20056 or Wing 12135
1 Love Makes the World Go Round, MGM 4001, *4001*

Lorez Alexandria
1 Early in the Morning, Argo 663, *663*
1 Sing No Sad Songs For Me, Argo 682, *682*
1 Deep Roots, Argo 694, *694*
1 For Swingers Only, Argo 720, *720*
1 This is Lorez, King 542
1 Lorez Sings Pres, King 565
1 The Band Swings, Lorez Sings, King 657
1 Songs Everybody Knows, King 676

Muhammad Ali, See Cassius Clay.

David Allen
1 My Lucky Day, Everest 5224, *1224*
2 I Only Have Eyes For You, Warner Bros. 1268, *1268*
2 David Allen Sings Jerome Kern, World Pacific 408, *1006*
2 Let's Face the Music and Dance, World Pacific 1250
2 David Allen Sings the Music of Jerome Kern, World Pacific 1295 (reissue of World Pacific 408)

Woody Allen
1 Woody Allen, Vol. 2, Colpix 488
1 Woody Allen, Colpix 518, *518*

Ernestine Anderson
2 Hot Cargo, Mercury 20354
2 Toast of the Nation's Critics, Mercury 20400, *60074*
2 Fascinating Ernestine, Mercury 20492, *60171*
2 My Kinda Swing, Mercury 20496, *60175*
2 Moanin' Moanin' Moanin', Mercury 20582, *60242*

Julie Andrews
1 Tell It Again (w/M. Green), Angel 65041
1 Broadway's Fair Julie Andrews, Columbia 1712, *8512*
1 Don't Go In the Lion's Cage Tonight, Columbia 1886, *8686*
3 The Lass With the Delicate Air, RCA 1403, *1403*
3 Julie Andrews Sings, RCA 1681, *1681*

Annette (Funicello), see p. 46.

Ann-Margret[10]
2 And Here She Is, RCA 2399, *2399*
1 On the Way Up, RCA 2453, *2453*
1 Vivacious One, RCA 2551, *2551*

George K. Arthur
2 George K. Arthur's Prize Package, MGM 3151

Fred Astaire
3 Three Evenings With Fred Astaire, Choreo 1
2 The Best of Fred Astaire, Epic 3137
1 Nothing Thrilled Us Half As Much, Epic 13103, *15103*

[10] See also *David Merrick.*

PERSONALITIES AND VOCALISTS

2 Now Fred Astaire, Kapp 1165
1 Fred Astaire Sound Tracks, Lion 70121
5 The Fred Astaire Story, Mercury 1001/02/03/03 (4 LP boxed set) [11]
4 The Fred Astaire Story #1, Mercury 1001 (single volume issue)
4 The Fred Astaire Story #2, Mercury 1002 (single volume issue)
4 The Fred Astaire Story #3, Mercury 1003 (single volume issue)
4 The Fred Astaire Story #4, Mercury 1004 (single volume issue)
3 Mr. Top Hat, Verve 2010
3 Easy to Dance With, Verve 2114
3 An Evening With Fred Astaire, no label, no number (private pressing) [12]
3 Another Evening With Fred Astaire, no label, no number (private pressing) [13]

Claire Austin
1 When Your Lover Has Gone, Contemporary 5002

Mildred Bailey, see p. 132.

Pearl Bailey
1 The Definitive Pearl Bailey, Columbia 985
1 Pearl Bailey, Coral 57037
1 Cultured Pearl, Coral 57162

Josephine Baker
1 Josephine Baker, Columbia 9532 (10")
1 Chansons Americaines, Columbia 9533 (10")
1 The Fabulous Josephine Baker, RCA 2475, *2475*

Kenny Baker
2 Song Hits Through the Years, RCA Camden 131

Kaye Ballard
2 The Fanny Brice Story in Song, MGM 3704, *3704*
2 Kaye Ballard Swings, United Artists 3043, *6043*
2 Kaye Ballard Live?, United Artists 3155, *6155*
2 Ha-Ha Boo-Hoo, United Artists 3165, *6165*

Brigitte Bardot
2 Special Bardot, Burlington Cameo 1000 (private pressing from 1968 TV broadcast)
3 Brigitte Bardot Sings, Philips 204, *604*
2 Behind Brigitte Bardot (themes from her films by P. Rugolo Orchestra), Warner Bros. 1371, *1371*

Harry Belafonte
1 Midnight Special (w/B. Dylan on harmonica), RCA 2449, *2449*

Betty Bennett
2 Nobody Else But Me, Atlantic 1226
3 Betty Bennett Sings Previn Arrangements, Trend 1006 (10")
2 I Love to Sing (w/A. Previn), United Artists 3070, *6070*

Tony Bennett
3 Cloud 7 (w/C. Wayne), Columbia 621
1 Tony, Columbia 938

1 The Beat of My Heart, Columbia 1079
2 Tony Bennett Sings Songs For Two (w/R. Sharon), Columbia 1446, *8242*
1 My Heart Sings, Columbia 1658, *8458*

Polly Bergen
1 Bergen Sings Morgan, Columbia 994
1 The Party's Over, Columbia 1031
1 Polly and Her Pop, Columbia 1138
1 My Heart Sings, Columbia 1171, *8018*
1 All Alone By the Telephone, Columbia 1300, *8100*
1 Four Seasons of Love, Columbia 1451, *8246*
1 Polly Bergen Sings the Hit Songs From Do Re Mi and Annie Get Your Gun, Columbia 1632, *8432*
2 Little Girl Blue, Jubilee 14 (10")

Vivian Blaine
1 Vivian Blaine Sings Songs From the Ziegfeld Follies, Mercury 20233 or Wing 12166
1 Songs From the Great White Way, Mercury 20234
1 Vivian Blaine Singing Pal Joey and Annie Get Your Gun, Mercury 20321

Mel Blanc
2 Party Panic!, Capitol 436 (10")

Blue Stars of France
2 Blue Stars of France, EmArcy 36067
2 Pardon My English, Mercury 20329

Dirk Bogarde
3 Lyrics For Lovers, London 3147, *210*

Shannon Bolin
3 Songs For Patricia (and Other Music of Alec Wilder), Riverside 805
3 Rare Wine, Vanguard 9003

Connee Boswell
3 Bing and Connee, Decca 5390 (10")
2 Connee, Decca 8356
1 Connee Boswell Sings Irving Berlin, Design 68
1 The New Sound of Connee Boswell (Sings the Rodgers and Hart Song Folio), Design 101
3 Connee Boswell and the Original Memphis Five, RCA 1426

Teresa Brewer
1 Music, Music, Music, Coral 57027
1 Teresa, Coral 57053
1 For Teenagers in Love, Coral 57135

Fannie Brice/Helen Morgan
1 Fannie Brice/Helen Morgan, RCA Vintage 561 (reissue of Vik 997)
2 Torch Songs, Vik 997

Georgia Brown
1 The Many Shades of Georgia Brown, Capitol 2329, *2329*
1 Georgia Brown, Coral 57436, *757436*
1 Georgia Brown, London 3286
1 Georgia Brown Loves Gershwin, London 3331, *331*

Lenny Bruce, see p. 49.

Joy Bryan
2 Make the Man Love Me, Contemporary 3604, *7604*
3 Joy Bryan Sings, Mode 108

---

[11] Very rare limited edition (1,384 printed) on blue plastic in red portfolio with pictures and sketches; estimated value $200.
[12] and [13] Excerpts from TV broadcasts presented by Chrysler Corporation.

Carol Burnett
1 Carol Burnett Remembers How They Stopped the Show, Decca 4049, *74049*
1 Let Me Entertain You, Decca 4437
1 Carol Burnett Sings, RCA 3879, *3879*
1 Together Again For the First Time (w/M. Raye), Tetragrammaton 106, *106*
1 Here's Carol, Vocalion *73824*

Abe Burrows
2 Abe Burrows Sings, Columbia 6128 (10")
2 The Girl With the Three Blue Eyes, Decca 5288 (10")

Jackie Cain and Roy Kral
3 The Glory of Love, ABC-Paramount 120
3 Bits and Pieces, ABC-Paramount 163
3 Free and Easy, ABC-Paramount 207
3 In the Spotlight, ABC-Paramount 267, *267*
4 Jackie Cain and Roy Kral, Brunswick 54026
2 Sweet and Low Down, Columbia 1469, *8260*
2 Double Take, Columbia 1704, *8504*
2 Like Sing (the songs of Dory and Andre Previn), Columbia 1934, *8734*
3 By Jupiter/Girl Crazy, Roulette 25278, *25278*
4 Storyville Presents Jackie and Roy, Storyville 904
4 Sing! Baby Sing!, Storyville 915
1 Lovesick, Verve 8688, *68688*

Cab Calloway, see p. 136.

Eddie Cantor
1 Concert at Carnegie Hall, Audio Fidelity 702
1 Original Recordings, RCA Camden 870, *870*
1 The Best of Eddie Cantor, Vik 1119

Hoagy Carmichael
1 I Can Dream, Can't I, Capitol 1819, *1819*
2 The Stardust Road, Decca 8588
2 Hoagy Sings Carmichael, Jazztone 1266 (reissue of Pacific Jazz 1223)
3 Ole' Buttermilk Sky, Kapp 1086
1 Legend of Hoagy Carmichael, Kimberley 2023, *11023* (reissue of Pacific Jazz 1223)
3 Hoagy Sings Carmichael, Pacific Jazz 1223

Helen Carr
2 Why Do I Love You, Bethlehem 45
3 Down in the Depths on the 90th Floor, Bethlehem 1027 (10")

Diahann Carroll
1 Fun Life, Atlantic 8048, *8048*
2 Diahann Carroll Sings Harold Arlen Songs, RCA 1467
1 Diahann Carroll and the André Previn Trio, United Artists 3069, *6069*
1 Fabulous Diahann Carroll (w/A. Previn Trio), United Artists 3229, *6229*
1 Porgy and Bess (w/A. Previn Trio), United Artists 4021, *5021*

Betty Carter, see p. 137.

Jack Carter
2 Broadway a la Carter, Aamco 319, *65*

Carol Channing
1 Carol Channing Entertains, Command 880, *880*
1 Carol Channing, Vanguard 9056, *2041*

June Christy
2 Something Cool, Capitol 516
2 The Misty Miss Christy, Capitol 725
2 June Fair and Warmer, Capitol 833
2 Gone For the Day, Capitol 902
2 This is June Christy, Capitol 1006
2 June's Got Rhythm, Capitol 1006
1 The Song is June, Capitol 1114, *1114*
2 June Christy Recalls Those Kenton Days, Capitol 1202, *1202*
3 Ballads For Night People, Capitol 1308, *1308*
3 The Cool School, Capitol 1398, *1398*
2 Off Beat, Capitol 1498, *1498*
2 Do Re Mi (w/B. Cooper), Capitol 1586, *1586*
3 That Time of Year, Capitol 1605, *1605* (original Christmas songs)
1 Big Band Specials, Capitol 1845, *1845*
1 The Intimate Miss Christy, Capitol 1953, *1953*
1 Something Broadway, Something Latin, Capitol 2410, *2410*

Petula Clark
1 Uptown With Petula Clark, Imperial 9281, *12281*
1 In Love!, Laurie 2032, *2032*

Robert Clary
1 Meet Robert Clary, Epic 3171
1 Hooray For Love, Epic 3281

Cassius Clay (Muhammad Ali)
3 I Am the Greatest, Columbia 2093, *8893*

Eldridge Cleaver
1 Soul on Wax, More 4000

Rosemary Clooney
1 That Travelin' Two Beat (w/B. Crosby), Capitol 2300, *2300*
1 Hollywood's Best (w/H. James), Columbia 585
1 Blue Rose (w/D. Ellington), Capitol 872
2 Clooney Tunes, Columbia 969
2 Ring Around Rosie (w/Hi-Los), Columbia 1006
1 Rosie's Greatest Hits, Columbia 1230
3 A Date with the King (w/B. Goodman), Columbia 2572 (10")
2 Swing Around Rosie, Coral 57266, *757266*
3 Clooney Sisters With Tony Pastor (w/B. Clooney), Epic 3160
1 Rosemary Clooney in High Fidelity, Harmony 7123
1 Young at Heart, Harmony 7236
3 "Oh, Captain" (w/J. Ferrer), MGM 3687
1 The Ferrers at Home, MGM 3709
1 Hymns From the Heart, MGM 3782, *3782*
2 Rosemary Clooney Swings Softly, MGM 3834, *3834*
1 Fancy Meeting You Here (w/B. Crosby), RCA 1854, *1854*
2 A Touch of Tabasco (w/P. Prado), RCA 2133, *2133*
2 Clap Hands, Here Comes Rosie!, RCA 2212, *2212*
2 Rosie Solves the Swinging Riddle (w/N. Riddle), RCA 2265, *2265*
2 Love, Reprise 6088, *96088*
1 Thanks For Nothing, Reprise 6108, *96108* (*6108*)

PERSONALITIES AND VOCALISTS

Nat King Cole
4 Nat King Cole at the Piano, Capitol 156 (10")
3 Harvest of Hits, Capitol 213
3 Penthouse Serenade, Capitol 332
1 Unforgettable, Capitol 357
2 Nat King Cole Sings For Two in Love, Capitol 420
2 Tenth Anniversary Album, Capitol 514
2 Vocal Classics, Capitol 591
2 Instrumental Classics, Capitol 592
2 Ballads of the Day, Capitol 680
2 The Piano Style of Nat King Cole, Capitol 689
1 After Midnight, Capitol 782
1 Love Is the Thing, Capitol 824, *824*
2 This is Nat King Cole, Capitol 870
2 Just One of Those Things, Capitol 903, *903*
2 St. Louis Blues, Capitol 993, *993*
1 The Very Thought of You, Capitol 1084, *1084*
1 Welcome to the Club, Capitol 1120, *1120*
1 To Whom It May Concern, Capitol 1190, *1190*
1 Tell Me All About Yourself, Capitol 1331, *1331*
1 Wild Is Love, Capitol 1392, *1392*
1 The Magic of Christmas, Capitol 1444, *1444*
1 The Touch of Your Lips, Capitol 1574, *1574*
3 The Nat King Cole Story, Capitol 1613, *1613* (3 LP boxed set)
1 The Swinging Side of Nat King Cole, Capitol 1724, *1724*
1 Where Did Everyone Go?, Capitol 1859, *1859*
1 Nat King Cole Sings the Blues, Capitol 1929, *1929*
1 Let's Face the Music, Capitol 2008, *2008*
1 Nat King Cole Trio, Capitol 2311
1 Nat King Cole at the Sands, Capitol 2434, *2434*
2 In the Beginning, Decca 8260
3 Nat King Cole Trio (w/L. Young, R. Callender), Score 4019

Dorothy Collins
1 At Home With Dorothy and Raymond (Scott), Coral 57105
1 Songs by Dorothy Collins, Coral 57106
1 Picnic, Coral 57150
1 A New Way to Travel, Top Rank 340
1 Dorothy Collins With the Barney Kessel Trio, Vocalion 3724

Chris Connor
1 Gentle Bossa Nova, ABC-Paramount 529, *529*
4 Chris Connor Sings the George Gershwin Almanac of Song, Atlantic 2-601 (2 LPs)
3 Chris Connor, Atlantic 1228, *1228*
2 He Loves Me, He Loves Me Not, Atlantic 1240, *1240*
1 A Jazz Date With Chris Connor, Atlantic 1286
2 Chris Craft, Atlantic 1290
3 Chris Connor Sings Ballads of the Sad Cafe, Atlantic 1307, *1307*
2 I Miss You So, Atlantic 8014
2 Witchcraft, Atlantic 8032, *8032*
3 Chris In Person, Atlantic 8040, *8040*
2 A Portrait of Chris, Atlantic 8046, *8046*
2 Double Exposure (w/M. Ferguson), Atlantic 8049, *8049*
3 Free Spirits, Atlantic 8061, *8061*
2 This is Chris, Bethlehem 20
2 Chris, Bethlehem 56
2 Chris Connor Sings Lullabys of Birdland, Bethlehem 6004
3 Chris Connor at the Village Gate, FM 300, *300*
3 A Weekend in Paris, FM 312, *312*
2 Two's Company (w/M. Ferguson), Roulette 52068, *52068*

Barbara Cook
4 Barbara Cook Sings Songs of Perfect Propriety, Urania 113, *1020*
4 From the Heart (Songs of Rodgers & Hart), Urania 9026, *1026*

Noel Coward—see page 120.

Bing Crosby
2 The Voice of Bing in the 1930's, Brunswick 54005
1 That Travelin' Two Beat (w/R. Clooney), Capitol 2300, *2300*
5 A Musical Autobiography, DXK 151 (5 LP boxed set)
4 Old Masters, DXL 152 (3 LP boxed set)
1 My Golden Favorites, Decca 4086
3 Easy to Remember, Decca 4250[14]
3 Pennies From Heaven, Decca 4251
3 Pocket Full of Dreams, Decca 4252
3 East Side of Heaven, Decca 4253
3 The Road Begins, Decca 4254
3 Only Forever, Decca 4255
3 Holiday Inn, Decca 4256
3 Swinging On a Star, Decca 4257
3 Accentuate the Positive, Decca 4258
3 Blue Skies, Decca 4259
3 But Beautiful, Decca 4260
3 Sunshine Cake, Decca 4261
3 Cool of the Evening, Decca 4262
3 Zing a Little Zong, Decca 4263
3 Anything Goes, Decca 4264
1 Holiday in Europe, Decca 4281, *74281*
1 Songs Everybody Knows, Decca 4415, *74415*
2 Go West Young Man (w/Andrew Sisters), Decca 5302 (10")
3 Bing and Connee (Boswell), Decca 5390 (10")
2 The Man Without a Country/What So Proudly We Hail, Decca 8020
1 Merry Christmas, Decca 8128, *78128*
1 Shillelaghs and Shamrocks, Decca 8207, *78207*
1 Home on the Range, Decca 8210
1 When Irish Eyes Are Smiling, Decca 8262, *78262*
1 Drifting and Dreaming, Decca 8268
1 Blue Hawaii, Decca 8269
1 Songs I Wish I Had Sung the First Time Around, Decca 8352, *78352*
1 Twilight on the Trail, Decca 8365
2 Some Fine Old Chestnuts, Decca 8374
1 A Christmas Sing with Bing, Decca 8419
2 Bing and the Dixieland Bands, Decca 8493
2 New Tricks (w/B. Cole Trio), Decca 8575
1 Around the World With Bing Crosby, Decca 8687
1 Bing in Paris, Decca 8780
1 That Christmas Feeling, Decca 8781
1 In a Little Spanish Town, Decca 8846
2 A Musical Autobiography of Bing Crosby (1927-1934), Decca 9054[15]
2 A Musical Autobiography of Bing Crosby (1934-1941), Decca 9064
2 A Musical Autobiography of Bing Crosby (1941-1944), Decca 9067
2 A Musical Autobiography of Bing Crosby (1944-1947), Decca 9077
2 A Musical Autobiography of Bing Crosby (1947-1953), Decca 9078

---

[14] Decca 4250-4264 known as Bing's Hollywood series; songs from his films.
[15] Decca 9054, 9064, 9067, 9077, 9078 are single volume issues of DXK 151.

1 Bing and Satch (w/L. Armstrong), MGM 3882, *3882*
1 Senor Bing, MGM 3890, *3890*
1 Great Standards, MGM 4129
1 The Very Best of Bing Crosby, MGM 4203, *4203*
2 Bing With a Beat (w/B. Scobey), RCA 1473
1 Fancy Meeting You Here (w/R. Clooney), RCA 1854, *1854*
2 Young Bing Crosby, RCA 2071
3 Bing Sings Whilst Bregman Swings (w/B. Bregman Orchestra), Verve 2020
2 Young Bing Crosby, Vik 995
3 Young Bing Crosby, "X" 1000

Dan Dailey
1 Mr. Musical Comedy, Tops 1598

Vic Damone
2 Linger Awhile, Capitol 1646, *1646*
2 Strange Enchantment, Capitol 1691, *1691*
2 The Lively Ones, Capitol 1748, *1748*
2 My Baby Loves to Swing, Capitol 1811, *1811*
2 The Liveliest, Capitol 1944, *1944*
2 On the Street Where You Live, Capitol 2133, *2133*
3 That Towering Feeling, Columbia 900
2 Angela Mia, Columbia 1088, *8046*
3 Closer Than a Kiss, Columbia 1174, *8019*
3 This Game of Love, Columbia 1368, *8168*
3 On the Swingin' Side, Columbia 1573, *8373*
3 Young and Lively, Columbia 1912, *8712*
2 Yours For a Song, Mercury 20163
2 Vic Damone, Mercury 20193
2 The Voice of Vic Damone, Mercury 20194
1 Stay With Me, RCA 3671
1 On the South Side of Chicago, RCA 3765
1 The Damone Type of Thing, RCA 3916
1 Why Can't I Walk Away?, RCA 3984

Billy Daniels
1 You Go to My Head, Verve 2072
1 The Masculine Touch, Verve 2085

Bobby Darin, see p. 53.

Sammy Davis, Jr.
1 Mr. Entertainment, Decca 4153, *74153*
1 Sammy Davis, Jr. Sings Forget-Me-Nots for First-Nighters, Decca 4381, *74381*
1 Starring Sammy Davis Jr., Decca 8118
1 Just For Lovers, Decca 8170
1 Here's Lookin' at You, Decca 8351
1 Sammy Swings, Decca 8486
1 Boy Meets Girl (w/C. McRae), Decca 8490
1 It's All Over But the Swingin', Decca 8641
1 Mood to Be Wooed, Decca 8676
1 All the Way, Decca 8779
1 Sammy Davis, Jr. at Town Hall, Decca 8841, *78841*
1 Porgy and Bess (w/C. McRae), Decca 8854, *78854*
1 Sammy Awards, Decca 8921, *78921*
1 I Gotta Right to Swing, Decca 8981, *78981*
1 The Sammy Davis, Jr. All-Star Spectacular (impersonations), Reprise 6033, *96033*
1 California Suite, Reprise 6126, *6126*

Dennis Day
1 Here's Dennis Day, Capitol 741

Doris Day
2 Hooray For Hollywood, Columbia C2L5 (2 LPs)
2 Day Dreams, Columbia 624
1 Day in Hollywood, Columbia 749
1 Day By Day, Columbia 942
1 Day By Night, Columbia 1053, *8089*
1 Greatest Hits, Columbia 1210, *8635*
1 Cuttin' Capers, Columbia 1232, *8078*
1 What Every Girl Should Know, Columbia 1438, *8234*
1 Show Time, Columbia 1470, *8261*
1 Bright and Shiny, Columbia 1614, *8414*
1 I Have Dreamed, Columbia 1660, *8460*
1 Duet (w/A. Previn), Columbia 1752, *8552*
1 Latin For Lovers, Columbia 2310, *9110*

James Dean
3 The James Dean Story, Capitol 881 (movie sound track)
3 The James Dean Story, Coral 57099 (music and narration w/S. Allen, B. Randle, G. Perreau, others)
3 A Tribute to James Dean, Imperial 9021 (East of Eden/Rebel Without a Cause soundtracks)
2 Music Lived By James Dean, RKO 109

Blossom Dearie
2 Blossom Time, Fontana 27562, *67562*
5 Blossom Dearie Sings Rootin' Songs, Hires 1111
5 Blossom Dearie, Verve 2037
5 Give Him the Ooh-La-La, Verve 2081
4 Blossom Dearie Sings Comden and Green, Verve 2109, *6050 (62109)*
4 Once Upon a Summertime, Verve 2111, *6020 (62111)*
4 My Gentleman Friend, Verve 2125, *6112 (62125)*
4 Blossom Dearie Sings Broadway Hit Songs, Verve 2133, *62133*

Yvonne DeCarlo
2 Yvonne DeCarlo Sings, Masterseal (no number)

Matt Dennis
1 Welcome Matt Dennis, Jubilee 1105, *1105*
2 Matt Dennis Plays and Sings Matt Dennis, Kapp 1024
3 She Dances Overhead (Songs of Rodgers & Hart), RCA 1065
2 Dennis Anyone?, RCA 1134
2 Play Melancholy Baby, RCA 1322
1 Saturday Date, Tops 1596

Fay Dewitt
2 Through Sick and Sin, Epic 3776

Marlene Dietrich
2 American Songs in German for the O.S.S., Columbia 105 (10")
1 Dietrich in Rio, Columbia 164
1 Lili Marlene, Columbia 1275
2 Marlene Dietrich Souvenir Album, Decca 5100 (10")
1 Marlene Dietrich, Decca 8465

Diana Dors
1 Swinging Dors, Columbia 1436

Frank D'Rone
1 New Morning, Cadet 806
2 Frank D'Rone Sings, Mercury 20418, *60074*
2 Try a Little Tenderness, Mercury 20497, *60174*
2 After the Ball, Mercury 20586, *60246*
2 In Person, Mercury 20721, *60721*

PERSONALITIES AND VOCALISTS

Patty Duke, see p. 55.

Jimmy Durante
1 Club Durante (radio broadcast w/B. Crosby, B. Hope, E. Barrymore, A. Jolson, others), Decca 9049

Billy Eckstine
3 Mr. "B", Audio Lab 1549 (includes Deluxe 265-12)
3 Great Mr. B. and His All-Star Band, Deluxe 265-12 (10")
2 I Surrender Dear, EmArcy 36010
2 Blues For Sale, EmArcy 36029
2 The Love Songs of Mr. B., EmArcy 36030
2 Imagination, EmArcy 36129
2 Billy Eckstine and Sarah Vaughan Sing the Best of Irving Berlin, Mercury 20316, *60002*
1 Billy's Best, Mercury 20333
1 Billy Eckstine and Quincy Jones at Basin St. East, Mercury 20674, *60674*
3 Mr. B With a Beat, MGM 3176 (w/W. Herman, G. Shearing, Metronome All Stars)
1 Rendezvous, MGM 3209
1 That Old Feeling, MGM 3275
4 Billy Eckstine Sings, National 2001 (10")
1 Prisoner of Love, Regent 6052
1 The Duke, the Blues and Me, Regent 6053
1 My Deep Blue Dream, Regent 6054
1 You Call it Madness, Regent 6058
1 No Cover No Minimum, Roulette 52052, *52052*

Anita Ellis
3 The World in My Arms, Elektra 179, *7179*
3 I Wonder What Became of Me, Epic 3280
3 Hims, Epic 3419

Ethel Ennis
1 Change of Scenery, Capitol 941
1 Have You Forgotten?, Capitol 1078
1 Ethel Ennis Sings Lullabys For Losers, Jubilee 1021
1 Ethel Ennis Sings, Jubilee 5024

Ken Errair
1 Solo Session, Capitol 807

Eileen Farrell
2 Here I Go Again, Columbia 1653, *8553*
2 This Fling Called Love, Columbia 1739, *8539*
2 Together With Love (w/A. Previn), Columbia 1920, *8720*
2 Franz Lehar Memorial (w/C. Fredericks), RCA 1004

Alice Faye
1 Alice Faye in Hollywood, Columbia 3068
1 Alice Faye Sings Her Famous Movie Hits, Reprise 6029, *96029*

Frances Faye
1 No Reservations, Capitol 512
1 Frances Faye Swings Fats Domino, Imperial 9059, *12007*
1 You Gotta Go! Go! Go!, Regina 315
1 In Frenzy, Verve 2147

Benny Fields
2 Benny Fields and His Minstrel Men (w/J. Benny, M. Berle, G. Burns, P. Silvers), Colpix 501, *501*
1 Two a Day at the Palace (w/B. Seeley), Mercury 20224

Gracie Fields
1 Our Gracie, Liberty 3059

Ella Fitzgerald, see p. 144.

Rhonda Fleming
3 Rhonda, Columbia 1080

Errol Flynn, see Basil Rathbone.

Helen Forrest
1 Voice of the Name Bands, Capitol 704

Four Freshmen
2 Voices in Modern, Capitol 522
1 Four Freshmen and 5 Trombones, Capitol 683, *683*
1 Freshmen Favorites, Capitol 743, *743*
2 Four Freshmen and 5 Trumpets, Capitol 763
2 Four Freshmen and 5 Saxes, Capitol 844
2 Voices in Latin, Capitol 922
1 Four Freshmen in Person, Capitol 1008, *1008*
1 Voices in Love, Capitol 1074, *1074*
1 Freshmen Favorites, Vol. 2, Capitol 1103
1 Love Lost, Capitol 1189, *1189*
1 Four Freshmen and 5 Guitars, Capitol 1255, *1255*
1 Voices & Brass, Capitol 1295, *1295*
1 First Affair, Capitol 1378, *1378*
1 The Freshman Year, Capitol 1485, *1485*
1 Voices in Fun, Capitol 1543, *1543*
1 Stars in Our Eyes, Capitol 1682, *1682*
2 The Swingers, Capitol 1753, *1753*
1 In Person, Vol. 2, Capitol 1860, *1860*
1 Got That Feelin', Capitol 1950, *1950*
1 Funny How Time Slips Away, Capitol 2067, *2067*

Stan Freberg
3 A Child's Garden of Freberg, Capitol 777
2 The Best of the Stan Freberg Shows, Capitol 1035 (2 LPs)
1 Stan Freberg With the Original Cast, Capitol 1242, *1242*
1 Stan Freberg Presents the United States of America, Capitol 1573, *1573*
3 Face the Funnies, Capitol 1694
3 Madison Avenue Werewolf, Capitol 1816
1 Freberg Underground! Show #1, Capitol 2551, *2551*
4 Oregon! Oregon! (original musical comedy presented at the Oregon State Centennial, 1959; book, music, and lyrics by Freberg; starring Freberg and Stubby Kaye), no label, no number (private pressing)

Greta Garbo
2 Garbo! (scenes from original soundtracks), MGM 4201

Judy Garland
4 Miss Show Business, Capitol 676
4 Judy, Capitol 734
2 Alone, Capitol 835
3 Judy in Love, Capitol 1036, *1036*
3 Judy Garland at the Grove, Capitol 1118, *1118*
4 The Letter (w/letter attached to cover), Capitol, 1188, *1188*
2 That's Entertainment!, Capitol 1467, *1467*
1 Judy Garland at Carnegie Hall, Capitol 1569, *1569* (2 LPs)
3 The Garland Touch, Capitol 1710, *1710*
3 Our Love Letter, Capitol 1941, *1941*
2 Just For Openers, Capitol 2062, *2062*

SHOW BUSINESS

1 Live at the London Palladium (w/L. Minnelli), Capitol 2295, *2295* (2 LPs)
1 The Best of Judy Garland, Decca 172, *7172* (2 LPs)
1 The Magic of Judy Garland, Decca 4199
2 Judy at the Palace, Decca 6020 (10")
2 Greatest Performances, Decca 8190
3 If You Feel Like Singing, Sing, MGM 3149
1 The Judy Garland Story (The Star Years), MGM 3989
1 The Judy Garland Story, Vol. 2 (The Hollywood Years), MGM 4005
2 Judy in Hollywood, Radiant 711-0102 (TV soundtrack)
2 Unforgettable!, Radiant 711-0105 (TV soundtrack)
2 Portrait in Song, Radiant 711-0106 (TV soundtrack)

Mitzi Gaynor
3 Mitzi, Verve 2110, *6014*
3 Mitzi Gaynor Sings the Lyrics of Ira Gershwin, Verve 2115, *6049*

Genevieve
1 Genevieve, Columbia 633

Georgia Gibbs
1 Her Nibs, Coral 57183
1 Georgia Gibbs's Greatest Hits, Epic 24059, *24059*
1 Something's Gotta Give!, Imperial 9107, *10264*
1 Music and Memories, Mercury 20071
1 Song Favorites, Mercury 20114
1 Swinging With Her Nibs, Mercury 20170

Ann Gilbert
2 The Many Moods of Ann Gilbert, Groove 1004
2 In a Swingin' Mood, Vik 1090

Hermione Gingold
1 Facade (w/R. Oberlin; music by W. Walton), Decca 710097, *710097*
3 La Gingold, Dolphin 7

Jackie Gleason
3 And Awaaay We Go! (comedy songs), Capitol 511 (10")

Dody Goodman
1 Dody Goodman Sings?, Coral 57196

Honi Gordon
2 Honi Gordon Sings, Prestige 7230, *7230*

Gogi Grant
2 The Wayward Wind, Era 106
2 Suddenly There's Gogi Grant, Era 20001
1 Welcome to My Heart, RCA 1717, *1717*
1 Torch Time, RCA 1940, *1940*

Dolores Gray
2 Warm Brandy, Capitol 897

Kathryn Grayson
3 Kathryn Grayson Sings, MGM 3257

Buddy Greco
2 Buddy Greco at Mister Kelly's, Coral 57022
1 My Buddy, Epic 3660, *557*
1 Songs For Swinging Losers, Epic 3746, *585*
1 Buddy's Back in Town, Epic 3771, *593*
2 I Like It Swinging, Epic 3793, *602*

1 Let's Love, Epic 3820, *615*
1 Buddy and Soul, Epic 24010, *26010*
2 Broadway Melodies, Kapp 1033
2 Buddy, Kapp 1107

Joyce Grenfell
2 Presenting Joyce Grenfell, Elektra 184

Tammy Grimes
2 Tammy Grimes, Columbia 1789, *8589*
1 The Unmistakable Tammy Grimes, Columbia 1984, *8784*
4 Julius Monk Presents Tammy Grimes, Off Broadway 401

Hilda Gueden
2 My Secret Heart (songs of Ivor Novello and Noel Coward), London 1703

Connie Haines
2 Connie Haines Sings, Coral 56055 (10")
1 Faith, Hope and Charity, RCA 2264, *2264*

Juanita Hall
3 Juanita Hall Sings the Blues, Counterpoint 564, *556*

Toni Harper
2 Lady Lonely, RCA 2092, *2092*
2 Night Mood, RCA 2253, *2253*
3 Toni, Verve 2001

Nancy Harrow
3 You Never Know, Atlantic 8075, *8075*
3 Wild Women Don't Have the Blues, Candid 8008, *9008*

Johnny Hartman
3 Songs From the Heart, Bethlehem 43
2 All of Me, Bethlehem 6014
1 Just You, Just Me, Regent 6048
2 And I Thought About You, Roost 2232

Dick Haymes
3 Rain or Shine, Capitol 713
3 Moondreams, Capitol 787
2 Dick Haymes Sings (w/C. Cavallaro), Decca 5023 (10")
1 Little Shamrocks, Decca 5038 (10")
1 Little White Lies, Decca 8773
2 The Name's Haymes, Hallmark 301
2 Look at Me Now, Hollywood 138
2 Richard the Lion-Hearted, Warwick 2023, *2023*

Bill Henderson
2 Bill Henderson With the Oscar Peterson Trio, MGM 4128, *4128*
2 Bill Henderson Sings, Vee Jay 1015
1 Bill Henderson, Vee Jay 1031, *1031*

Al Hibbler
1 Melodies by Al Hibbler, Argo 601 (reissue of Marterry 601)
1 After the Lights Go Down Low, Atlantic 1251
2 Al Hibbler With the Ellingtonians, Brunswick 54036
1 Starring Al Hibbler, Decca 8328
1 Here's Hibbler!, Decca 8420
1 Torchy and Blue, Decca 8697
1 Hits by Hibbler, Decca 8757
1 Al Hibbler Remembers Big Songs of the Big Bands, Decca 8862, *78862*

PERSONALITIES AND VOCALISTS

2 Al Hibbler With the Roland Hanna Trio, LMI 10001
3 Melodies by Al Hibbler, Marterry 601
1 Monday Every Day, Reprise 2005, *92005*
3 I Surrender Dear, Score 4013
1 Al Hibbler Sings Love Songs, Verve 4000

Dwayne Hickman
2 Dobie!, Capitol 1441, *1441*

Hildegarde
2 Souvenir Album, Decca 8656
1 The Incomparable Hildegarde, Design 77
2 Hildegarde, Seeco 400

Hi-Los
1 Suddenly It's the Hi-Los, Columbia 952
2 Ring Around Rosie (Clooney), Columbia 1006
1 Now Hear This, Columbia 1023
1 Hi-Los and All That Jazz, Columbia 1259, *8077*
1 Broadway Playbill (Gypsy, Fiorello, Sound of Music), Columbia 1416, *8213*
1 Hi-Los All Over the Place, Columbia 1509, *8300*
1 This Time It's Love, Columbia 1723, *8523*
2 The Hi-Los (w/J. Fielding Orchestra), Kapp 1027
1 Under Glass, Kapp 1184 (reissue of Starlite 7005)
1 The Hi-Los On Hand, Kapp 1194 (reissue of Starlite 7008)
1 Hi-Los in Stereo, Omega *11*
2 Under Glass, Starlite 7005
2 Listen to the Hi-Los, Starlite 7006
2 The Hi-Los I Presume, Starlite 7007
2 The Hi-Los On Hand, Starlite 7008

Mimi Hines
1 Mimi Hines Sings, Decca 4709, *74709*
1 Mimi Hines is a Happening, Decca 4834, *74834*

Alfred Hitchcock
2 Alfred Hitchcock Presents Music to be Murdered By, Imperial 9052, *12005*

Billie Holliday, see p. 152.

Judy Holliday
3 Trouble is a Man, Columbia 1153, *8041*

Shirley Horn
2 Travelin' Light, ABC-Paramount 538, *538*
1 Loads of Love, Mercury 20761, *60761*
2 With Horns, Mercury 20835, *60835*
1 Where Are You Going?, Perception *31*
1 Embers and Ashes, Stereocraft *16*

Lena Horne
1 Lena Horne Sings Your Requests, Charter 101, *101*
1 Like Latin, Charter 106, *106*
1 Lena and Ivie (Anderson), Jazztone 1262
1 I Feel So Smoochie, Lion 70050
1 Once in a Lifetime, Movietone 71005, *72005*
2 Lena Horne at the Waldorf Astoria, RCA 1028, *1028*
3 It's Love, RCA 1148
3 Stormy Weather, RCA 1375 (includes RCA 3061)
3 Give the Lady What She Wants, RCA 1879, *1879*
3 Songs of Burke and Van Heusen, RCA 1895, *1895*
2 Lena at the Sands, RCA 2364, *2364*
2 Lena On the Blue Side, RCA 2465, *2465*

2 Lovely and Alive, RCA 2587, *2587*
3 This is Lena Horne, RCA 3061 (10")
2 Here's Lena Now!, 20th Century Fox 3115
2 Feelin' Good, United Artists 3433, *6433*
2 Lena in Hollywood, United Artists 3470, *6470*
2 Soul, United Artists 3496, *6496*

Helen Humes, see p. 153.

Alberta Hunter, see p. 153.

Lurlean Hunter
2 Blue and Sentimental, Atlantic 1344, *1344*
2 Lonesome Gal, RCA 1151
2 Night Life, Vik 1061
2 Stepping Out, Vik 1116

Tab Hunter
1 Young Love, Dot 3370, *25370*
1 Tab Hunter, Warner Bros. 1221, *1221*
1 When I Fall in Love, Warner Bros. 1292, *1292*
1 R.F.D. Tab Hunter, Warner Bros. 1367, *1367*

Betty Hutton
2 Betty Hutton at the Saints and Sinners Ball, Warner Bros. 1267, *1267*

June Hutton
1 Afterglow, Capitol 643
1 Dream, Venise 10017

Ink Spots, see p. 61.

Jackie and Roy, see Jackie Cain and Roy Kaal.

Florence Foster Jenkins
1 A Faust Travesty, RCA 2597
1 A Florence! Foster!! Jenkins!!! Recital!!!!, RCA 7000 (10")

Inez Jones
2 Have You Met Inez Jones (w/O. Moore), Riverside 819

Spike Jones
1 Omnibust, Liberty 3140, *7140*
1 60 Years of "Music America Hates Best", Liberty 3154, *7154*
3 Musical Depreciation, RCA 1893/4/5 (3 LP boxed set)
1 Thank You Music Lovers, RCA 2224
1 Bottoms Up, RCA 3054
2 Let's Sing a Song of Christmas, Verve 2021
2 Dinner Music For People Who Aren't Very Hungry, Verve 4005
1 Spike Jones in Hi-Fi/Stereo, Warner Bros. 1332, *1332*

T.C. Jones
1 T.C. Jones Himself, GNP Crescendo 602, *602*

Sheila Jordan
4 Portrait of Sheila, Blue Note 9002, *89002*

Stubby Kaye
2 Music For Chubby Lovers, Seeco 421, *4210*

Greta Keller
3 This is My Vienna, Dolphin 8
1 Remember Me, London 1305

Beverly Kenney
2 Beverly Kenney Sings For Playboys, Decca 8743
2 Born to Be Blue, Decca 8850
2 Like Yesterday, Decca 8948, *78948*
3 Beverly Kenney Sings for Johnny Smith, Roost 2206
3 Come Swing With Me, Roost 2212
3 Beverly Kenney with Jimmy Jones and the Basie-ites, Roost 2218

Jack Kerouac
3 Poetry for the Beat Generation, Hanover 5000
4 Blues and Haikus (w/A. Cohn, Z. Sims), Hanover 5006
3 On the Beat Generation, Verve 15005

Larry Kert
2 Larry Kert Sings, Epic 3409
2 Larry Kert Sings Leonard Bernstein, Seeco 467, *4670*

Morgana King
2 The Winter of My Discontent, Ascot 13014, *16014*
1 The End of a Love Affair, Ascot 13019, *16019* (reissue of United Artists 30020)
1 Everybody Loves Saturday Night, Ascot 13020, *16020* (reissue of United Artists 3028)
1 For You, For Me, Forever More, EmArcy 36079
2 Morgana King Sings the Blues, Mercury 20231 or Wing 60007
2 The Greatest Songs Ever Swung, RCA Camden 543, *543*
1 It's A Quiet Thing, Reprise 6192, *6192*
1 Wild is Love, Reprise 6205, *6205*
1 Gemini Changes, Reprise 6257, *6257*
3 Folk Songs a la King, United Artists 3028, *6028*
3 Let Me Love You, United Artists 30020, *30020*
1 More Morgana King, Wing 12307, *16307*

Teddi King
3 All the King's Songs, Coral 57278, *757278*
3 Bidin' My Time, RCA 1147
3 To You From Teddi King, RCA 1313
3 A Girl and Her Songs, RCA 1454
4 Round Midnight, Storyville 302 (10")
4 Storyville Presents Teddi King, Storyville 314 (10")
4 Now in Vogue, Storyville 903

Lisa Kirk
2 Lisa Kirk at the Plaza, MGM 3737, *3737*

Eartha Kitt
2 Fabulous Eartha Kitt, Kapp 1162, *3046*
2 Eartha Kitt Revisited, Kapp 1192, *3192*
2 Bad But Beautiful, MGM 4009, *4009*
3 Down to Eartha, RCA 1109
3 That Bad Eartha, RCA 1183
3 Thursday's Child, RCA 1300
3 St. Louis Blues (w/S. Rogers), RCA 1661, *1661*

Irene Kral
2 Better Than Anything, Ava 33, *33*
1 Wonderful Life, Mainstream 56058, *6058*
3 SteveIreneO! (Steve Allen songs), United Artists 3052, *6052*
3 The Band and I (w/H. Pomeroy Orchestra), United Artists 4016, *5016*

Frankie Laine
2 A Musical Portrait of New Orleans (w/J. Stafford), Columbia 578
1 Frankie Laine and the Four Lads, Columbia 861
1 Rockin', Columbia 975
1 Foreign Affair, Columbia 1116
1 Torchin', Columbia 1176, *8024*
1 Songs By Frankie Laine, Mercury 20069
1 That's My Desire, Mercury 20080
1 Songs For People Together, Mercury 20083
1 With All My Heart, Mercury 20105

Dorothy Lamour
2 The Road to Romance, Design 45

Elsa Lanchester
1 Songs For a Smoke-Filled Room, Hi Fi 405, *405*
1 Songs For a Shuttered Parlor, Hi Fi 406, *406*
1 Cockney London, Verve 15015, *615015*
2 Elsa Lanchester Herself, Verve 15024, *615024*

Dory Langdon (Previn)
3 Leprechauns Are Upon Me, Verve 2101

Eddie Lawrence
2 The Old Philosopher, Coral 57103
2 Eddie "The Old Philosopher" Lawrence, Coral 57155
2 The Kingdom of Eddie Lawrence, Coral 57203
2 The Side-Splitting Personality of Eddie Lawrence, Coral 57371, *757371*
2 7 Characters in Search of Eddie Lawrence, Coral 57411, *757411*
4 The Garden of Eddie Lawrence, Signature 1003

Gertude Lawrence
1 The Star Gertrude Lawrence, Audio Fidelity 709
1 A Bright Particular Star, Decca 4940, *74940* (reissue of Decca 8673)
2 Gertrude Lawrence Souvenir Album, Decca 5418 (10")
2 A Remembrance, Decca 8673
2 Noel and Gertie, RCA 1156

Barbara Lea
3 Barbara Lea (w/J. Windhurst), Prestige 7065
2 Lea in Love, Prestige 7100
3 A Woman in Love, Riverside 2518 (10")

Dr. Timothy Leary—see p. 63.

Brenda Lee—see p. 63.

Gypsy Rose Lee
1 Gypsy Rose Lee Remembers Burlesque, Stereoddities *1*

Jeanne Lee
3 The Newest Sound Around (w/R. Blake), RCA 2500, *2500*

Peggy Lee
2 Rendezvous, Capitol 151
2 The Man I Love (orchestra conducted by F. Sinatra), Capitol 864
1 Jump For Joy, Capitol 979, *979*

PERSONALITIES AND VOCALISTS

  2 Things Are Swingin', Capitol 1049, *1049*
  2 I Like Men, Capitol 1131, *1131*
  1 Beauty and the Beat (w/G. Shearing), Capitol 1219, *1219*
  2 Christmas Carousel, Capitol 1423, *1423*
  1 Mink Jazz, Capitol 1850, *1850*
  1 Lover, Decca 4458, *74458*
  1 The Fabulous Peggy Lee, Decca 4461, *74461*
  2 Pete Kelly's Blues (w/E. Fitzgerald), Decca 8166
  2 Black Coffee, Decca 8358
  2 Dream Street, Decca 8411
  2 Songs From Walt Disney's "Lady and the Tramp", Decca 8462
  2 Sea Shells, Decca 8591
  1 Miss Wonderful, Decca 8816
  1 Peggy Lee Sings with Benny Goodman, Harmony 7005

Robert Q. Lewis
  2 Robert Q. Lewis and His Gang, "X" 1033

Beatrice Lillie
  3 Beatrice Lillie Souvenir Album, Decca 5453 (10")
  3 Beatrice Lillie Sings, JJC 3003
  4 Thirty Minutes With Beatrice Lillie, Liberty Music Shop 1002 (10")
  3 An Evening With Beatrice Lillie, London 1373 or 5212 (original cast album)
  3 Auntie Bea, London 5471
  1 Beatrice Lillie in Peter and the Wolf and Carnival of the Animals, London *6187*

Abbey Lincoln—see p. 157.

Sophia Loren
  3 Peter Sellers and Sophia Loren, Angel 35910, *35910*
  2 Sophia Loren in Rome, Columbia 6310, *2710* (TV sound track)

Dorothy Loudon
  3 Live at the Blue Angel, Coral 57265, *757265*

Gisele Mackenzie
  1 Gisele Mackenzie in Person at the Empire Room, Everest 5069, *1069*
  1 Gisele, RCA 1790
  1 Gisele Mackenzie, Vik 1055
  1 Mam'selle Gisele, Vik 1075

Gordon MacRae
  1 Memory Songs (w/J. Stafford), Capitol 423
  1 Romantic Ballads, Capitol 537
  1 Operetta Favorites, Capitol 681
  1 The Best Things In Life Are Free, Capitol 765
  1 Cowboy's Lament, Capitol 834
  1 Motion Picture Soundstage, Capitol 875
  1 In Concert, Capitol 980
  1 This Is Gordon MacRae, Capitol 1050

Miriam Makeba
  1 The Many Voices of Miriam Makeba, Kapp 1274, *3274*
  1 The Magnificent Miriam Makeba, Mercury 21082, *61082*
  1 Miriam Makeba, RCA 2267, *2267*
  1 The World of Miriam Makeba, RCA 2750, *2750*
  1 The Voice of Africa, RCA 2845, *2845*
  1 Makeba Sings, RCA 3321, *3321*
  1 The Magic of Makeba, RCA 3512, *3512*
  1 Miriam Makeba in Concert, Reprise 6253, *6253*
  1 Pata Pata, Reprise 6274, *6274*

Jayne Mansfield
  2 Shakespeare, Tchaikovsky and Me, MGM 4202
  3 Jayne Mansfield Busts Up Las Vegas, 20th Century Fox 3049 (original cast album)

Charles Manson—see p. 65.

Marion Marlowe
  1 TV Sweethearts (w/F. Parker), Columbia 576
  1 Dearly Beloved, Design 117, *1006*

Mary Martin
  2 Mary Martin Sings For You, Columbia 2061 (10")
  3 Ford 50th Anniversary Show (w/E. Merman), Decca 7027 (10")
  1 Mary Martin Sings a Musical Love Story, Disneyland 3031, *3031*
  1 Hi-Ho, Disneyland 4016, *3038*
  1 Guideposts For Living (w/N. V. Peale), Guideposts 100
  2 Mary Martin Sings, Richard Rodgers Plays, RCA 1539

Harpo Marx
  3 Harpo in Hi-Fi, Mercury 20232

Mary Ann McCall[16]
  2 Melancholy Baby, Coral 57276
  3 Mary Ann McCall Sings, Discovery 3011 (10")
  2 Detour to the Moon, Jubilee 1078
  1 Easy Living, Regent 6040

Marie McDonald
  2 The Body Sings, RCA 1585

Carmen McRae
  3 Carmen McRae, Bethlehem 1023 (10")
  1 Tonight's the Night (w/D. Brubeck Quartet), Columbia 1609, *8409*
  1 Lover Man, Columbia 1730, *8530*
  2 Something Wonderful, Columbia 1943, *8743*
  3 By Special Request, Decca 8173
  2 Torchy, Decca 8267
  2 Blue Moon, Decca 8347
  1 Boy Meets Girl (w/S. Davis, Jr.), Decca 8490
  3 After Glow, Decca 8583
  1 Mad About the Man (Noel Coward songs), Decca 8662
  3 Carmen For Cool Ones, Decca 8738
  3 Birds of a Feather, Decca 8815, *78815*
  2 Bittersweet, Focus 334, *334*
  2 Book of Ballads, Kapp 1117, *3001*
  2 When You're Away, Kapp 1135, *3018*
  2 Something to Swing About, Kapp 1169, *3053*
  1 This is Carmen McRae, Kapp 1541, *1541*
  1 Live at Sugar Hill, Time 52104, *2104*

Mabel Mercer
  1 Mabel Mercer Sings Cole Porter, Atlantic 1213
  1 Midnight at Mabel Mercer's, Atlantic 1244

Ethel Merman
  4 A Musical Autobiography, Decca 153 (2 LP boxed set)
  3 Songs She Made Famous, Decca 5053 (10")
  3 Ford 50th Anniversary Show (w/M. Martin), Decca 7027 (10")

[16] See also Charlie Ventura (p. 175).

114   SHOW BUSINESS

  2 12 Songs From Call Me Madam, Decca 8035
  2 A Musical Autobiography, Vol. 1, Decca 8178 (single volume issue of Decca 153)
  2 A Musical Autobiography, Vol. 2, Decca 8179 (single volume issue of Decca 153)
  1 12 Songs From Call Me Madam, Decca 9022 (reissue of Decca 8035)
  2 Ethel Merman Memories, Decca 9028
  3 Ethel Merman Sings Cole Porter, JJC 3004, *3004*
  2 Her Greatest!, Reprise 6032, *96032*
  2 Merman in Vegas, Reprise 6062, *96062*
  4 Ethel Merman and Gertrude Niesen, "X" 1004

David Merrick
  1 David Merrick Presents Hits from His Broadway Hits (w/J. Gary, Ann-Margaret), RCA 2947, *2947*

Helen Merrill
  2 American Country Songs, Atco 112, *112*
  2 Helen Merrill, EmArcy 36006
  1 Helen Merrill with Strings, EmArcy 36057
  3 Dream of You, EmArcy 36078
  2 Merrill at Midnight, EmArcy 36107
  3 The Nearness of You, EmArcy 36134
  1 The Artistry of Helen Merrill, Mainstream 56014, *6014*
  3 You've Got a Date With the Blues, Metrojazz 1010, *1010*

Sal Mineo
  3 Sal, Epic 3405

Liza Minnelli
  2 Liza! Liza!, Capitol 2174, *2174*
  2 It Amazes Me, Capitol 2271, *2271*
  1 Live at the London Palladium (w/J. Garland), Capitol 2295, *2295* (2 LPs)

Robert Mitchum
  1 Calypso is Like So, Capitol 853
  1 That Man, Monument 8086, *18086*

Matt Monro
  1 My Kind of Girl, Warwick 2045, *2045*

Marilyn Monroe
  1 Marilyn Monroe, Ascot 13008, *16008*
  1 The Unforgettable Marilyn Monroe Sings (songs from her original motion picture sound tracks), Movietone 71016, *72016* (reissue of 20th Century Fox 5000)
  2 Marilyn, 20th Century Fox 5000

Joe Mooney
  3 Lush Life, Atlantic 1255
  2 The Greatest of Joe Mooney, Columbia 2186
  2 The Happiness of Joe Mooney, Columbia 2345, *9145*
     You Go to My Head, Decca 5555 (10")
  3 On the Rocks, Decca 8468

Grace Moore
  2 Grace Moore Sings, Decca 9593
  1 The Art of Grace Moore, RCA Camden 519

Marilyn Moore
  3 Moody, Bethlehem 73

Rita Moreno
  2 Rita Moreno Sings, Strand 1039, *1039*
  1 Warm, Wild and Wonderful, Wynne 103

Helen Morgan, see Fanny Brice.

Henry Morgan and Isobel Robins
  2 The Saint and the Sinner, Offbeat 3004

Robert Morse and Charles Neslon Reilly
  1 A Jolly Theatrical Season, Capitol 1862, *1862*

Zero Mostel
  1 Zero Mostel Sings Harry Ruby's Songs My Mother Never Sang, Vanguard 9229, *79229*

Mark Murphy
  3 This Could Be the Start of Something, Capitol 1177, *1177*
  3 Hip Parade, Capitol 1299, *1299*
  3 Meet Mark Murphy, Decca 8390
  3 Let Yourself Go, Decca 8632
  1 Rah!, Riverside 395, *9395*
  1 That's How I Love the Blues, Riverside 441, *9441*

Rose Murphy
  1 Jazz, Joy and Happiness (w/S. Stewart), United Artists 14025, *15025*
  1 Not Cha-Cha, But Chi-Chi, Verve 2070

Portia Nelson
  3 Love Songs For a Late Evening, Columbia 4722
  3 Autumn Leaves, Dolphin 4

Anthony Newley
  1 Love is a Now and Then Thing, London 3156
  1 Tony, London 3252, *244*
  1 This is Tony, London 3262
  1 Peak Performances, London 3283
  1 In My Solitude, RCA 2925, *2925*
  1 Who Can I Turn To, RCA 3347, *3347*
  1 Newley Recorded, RCA 3614, *3614*
  1 Anthony Newley Sings the Songs From Doctor Doolittle, RCA 3839, *3839*

Nicholas Brothers
  2 We Do Sing Too, Mercury 20355

Mike Nichols and Elaine May
  1 An Evening With Mike Nichols and Elaine May, Mercury 2200, *6200*
  2 Improvisations to Music, Mercury 20376, *60040*
  2 Mike Nichols and Elaine May Examine Doctors, Mercury 20680, *60680*

Gertrude Niesen
  3 Gertrude Niesen, Decca 5138 (10")
  4 Ethel Merman and Gertrude Niesen, "X" 1004

Ken Nordine
  2 Word Jazz, Dot 3075
  2 Son of Word Jazz, Dot 3096, *25096*

Helen O'Connell
  1 An Era Reborn, Cameo 1045, *1045*
  1 Here's Helen, RCA Camden 706, *706*
  2 Green Eyes, Vik 1093

Anita O'Day[17]
  4 Anita O'Day Specials, Advance 8 (10")
  2 Singin' and Swingin', Coral 56073 (10") (reissue of Advance 8)

[17] See also *Gene Krupa* (p. 156).

PERSONALITIES AND VOCALISTS

4 Anita O'Day Sings Jazz, Norgran 1049
4 An Evening With Anita O'Day, Norgran 1057 or Verve 2050
3 Anita, Verve 2000
3 Pick Yourself Up, Verve 2043
3 The Lady is a Tramp, Verve 2049 (reissue of Norgran 1049)
3 Anita O'Day at Mister Kelly's, Verve 2113, *6043* or *62113*
3 Anita O'Day Swings Cole Porter, Verve 2118, *6059* or *62118*
3 Anita O'Day Swings Rodgers and Hrt, Verve 2141, *62141*
3 Waiter, Make Mine Blues, Verve 2145, *62145*
4 Trav'lin Light, Verve 2157, *62157*
3 Anita Sings the Most, Verve 8259
3 Anita Sings the Winners, Verve 8283, *6002* or *68283*
4 Cool Heat (Anita O'Day Sings Jimmy Giuffre Arrangements), Verve 8312, *6046* or *68312*
3 All the Sad Young Men, Verve 8442, *68442*
2 Time for Two (w/C. Tjader), Verve 8472, *68472*
2 This is Anita, Verve 8483, *68483* (reissue of Verve 2000)
1 Anita Sings the Winners, Verve 8485, *68485* (reissue of Verve 8283)
2 Anita O'Day and the Three Sounds, Verve 8514, *68514*
3 Incomparable, Verve 8572, *68572*

Jerry Orbach
3 Off Broadway, MGM 4056, *4056*

Patti Page
1 In the Land of Hi-Fi (w/P. Rugolo), EmArcy 36074, Mercury *80000*
2 The East Side (w/P. Rugolo), EmArcy 36116
2 The West Side (w/P. Rugolo), EmArcy 36136
1 Manhattan Tower, Mercury 20226

Jackie Paris
5 Skylark, Brunswick 54019
5 That Paris Mood, Coral 56118 (10")
5 The Jackie Paris Sound, East-West 4002
3 Songs By Jackie Paris, EmArcy 36095
1 The Song is Paris, Impulse 17, *17*
4 Jackie Paris Sings the Lyrics of Ira Gershwin, Time 70009
1 I Can't Get Started With You, Wing 60004 (reissue of EmArcy 36095)

Les Paul and Mary Ford
2 New Sound, Vol. 1, Capitol 226
1 New Sound, Vol. 2, Capitol 286
2 Bye Bye Blues, Capitol 356
2 The Hit Makers, Capitol 416
2 Les and Mary, Capitol 577
2 Time to Dream, Capitol 802
1 Lovers' Luau, Columbia 1276, *8086*
1 Warm and Wonderful, Columbia 1688, *8488*
1 Bouquet of Roses, Columbia 1821, *8621*
1 Swingin' South, Columbia 1928, *8728*

Tony Perkins
2 Tony Perkins, Epic 3394
1 From My Heart, RCA 1679, *1679*
1 On a Rainy Afternoon, RCA 1853, *1853*

Edith Piaf
1 Piaf, Capitol 10210
1 More Piaf of Paris, Capitol 10283, *10283*
1 Potpourri par Piaf, Capitol 10295, *10295*
1 Chansons, Capitol 10328, *10328*
1 Piaf and Sarapo at the Bobino, Capitol 10348, *10348*
1 Piaf at the Olympia, Capitol 10368, *10368*
2 La Vie En Rose, Columbia 898
2 La Petite Lili, Columbia 2160 (10")
2 Chansons, Columbia 4779
2 Chansons de Cafes de Paris, Decca 6004 (10")

Lucy Ann Polk
3 Lucky Lucy Ann, Mode 115 (original) or Interlude 504, *1004* (reissue)
4 Lucy Ann Polk (w/D. Pell), Trend 1008 (10")

Dick Powell
1 Dick Powell in Hollywood, Columbia C2L-44 (2 LPs)
1 Dick Powell Song Book, Decca 8837
2 Dick Powell Presents Themes From Original TV Soundtracks (music by J. Goldsmith, L. Rosenman, L. Stevens, J. Fielding), Dot 3421

Jane Powell
2 Romance, Columbia 2034 (10")
2 A Date With Jane Powell, Columbia 2045 (10")
2 Alice in Wonderland, Columbia 4148
2 Can't We Be Friends?, Verve 2023

Dory Previn, see Dory Langdon.

Ruth Price
2 Live and Beautiful, Ava 54, *54*
2 Ruth Price with Shelly Manne & His Men at the Manne Hole, Contemporary 3590, *7590*
3 My Name is Ruth Price, I Sing, Kapp 1006
3 The Party's Over, Kapp 1054
3 Ruth Price Sings (w/J. Smith), Roost 2217

Louis Prima
1 The Wildest (w/K. Smith), Capitol 755
1 The Call of the Wildest (w/K. Smith), Capitol 836
1 The Wildest Show at Tahoe (w/K. Smith), Capitol 908
1 Las Vegas Prima Style (w/K. Smith), Capitol 1010
1 Strictly Prima!, Capitol 1132
1 Hey Boy! Hey Girl! (w/K. Smith), Capitol 1160 (movie soundtrack)
1 The Wildest Comes Home!, Capitol 1723, *1723*
1 Louis and Keely!, Dot 3210, *25210*

Charlotte Rae
3 Songs I Taught My Mother, Vanguard 9004, *9004*

John Raitt
1 Highlights of Broadway, Capitol 583
1 Mediterranean Magic, Capitol 714
1 Under Open Skies, Capitol 1058, *1058*

Basil Rathbone
2 Treasure Island/Robin Hood, Columbia 673
2 The Three Musketeers (E. Flynn)/Oliver Twist (Rathbone), Columbia 674 or 4162
2 Peter and the Wolf/Treasure Island, Columbia 4038
2 Sinbad the Sailor/Oliver Twist, Columbia 4072
1 The Three Musketeers/Robin Hood, Harmony 9558 (reissue of Columbia 4162)

SHOW BUSINESS

Johnnie Ray
1 The Big Beat, Columbia 961
1 'Til Morning (w/B. Taylor Trio), Columbia 1225, *8034*
1 Johnnie Ray's Greatest Hits, Columbia 1227
2 Johnny Ray, Epic 1120 (10")

Martha Raye
4 The Voice of Martha Raye, Discovery 3010 (10")
3 Here's Martha Raye, Epic 3061
1 Together Again For the First Time (w/C. Burnett), Tetragrammaton 106, *106*

Della Reese
1 Melancholy Baby, Jubilee 1026
1 The Story of the Blues, Jubilee 1095
1 Della By Starlight, RCA 2204, *2204*
1 Special Delivery, RCA 2391, *2391*

Lucy Reed
3 The Singing Reed, Fantasy 3212
3 This is Lucy Reed, Fantasy 3243

Rita Reys
4 The Cool Sound of Rita Reys (w/Jazz Messengers), Columbia 903
2 New Voices (w/S. Pierce, P. Serra), Dawn 1125
2 Her Name is Rita Reys, Epic 3522

Ann Richards
1 Ann, Man!, Atco 136, *136*
1 The Many Moods of Ann Richards, Capitol 1406, *1406*

Chita Rivera
2 Chita, Wing 1095

Mavis Rivers
1 The Simple Life, Capitol 1408, *1408*
1 Mavis, Reprise 2002, *9-2002*
1 Swing Along, Reprise 2009, *9-2009*
1 Mavis Rivers Meets Shorty Rogers, Reprise 6074, *6074*
1 We Remember Mildred Bailey (w/R. Norvo), Vee Jay 1132, *1132*

Joan Roberts
4 Joan Roberts Sings, Quality 719-26 (10")

Sugar Ray Robinson
1 I'm Still Swinging, Continental 16009

Betty Roche[18]
2 Take the "A" Train, Bethlehem 64
3 Singin' & Swingin', Prestige 7187
2 Lightly and Politely, Prestige 7198

Ginger Rogers
3 Ginger Rogers as Alice in Wonderland (music by V. Young), Decca 5040 (10")

Mickey Rooney
3 Mickey Rooney Sings George M. Cohan, RCA 1520

Annie Ross, see p. 168.

[18] See also *Dinah Washington* (p. 176).

Lillian Roth
2 I'll Cry Tomorrow, Epic 3206
1 Lillian Roth Sings, Tops 1567

Anna Russell
2 Anna Russell Sings?, Columbia 4594
2 Anna Russell Sings Again?, Columbia 4733
2 Anna Russell's Guide to Concert Audiences, Columbia 4928
2 A Square Talk on Popular Music, Columbia 5036
2 Anna Russell in Darkest Africa, Columbia 5195
2 A Practical Banana Promotion, Columbia 5295

Betty St. Claire
3 Hal McKusick Plays/Betty St. Claire Sings, Jubilee 15 (10")
2 Cool and Clearer, Jubilee 23 (10")
2 What is There to Say?, Jubilee 1011
2 Betty St. Claire at Basin St. East, Seeco 456, *456*

Felicia Sanders
2 Felicia Sanders at the Blue Angel, Columbia 654
1 That Certain Feeling, Decca 8762, *78762*
1 Songs of Kurt Weill, Mainstream 65016, *6016* or Time 52007, *2007*
1 Felicia Sanders, Time 52110, *2110*

George Sanders
3 The George Sanders Touch, ABC-Paramount 231

Catherine Sauvage
1 Songs of Kurt Weill, Epic 3489

Little Jimmy Scott
2 Very Truly Yours, Savoy 12027
2 The Fabulous Songs of Little Jimmy Scott, Savoy 12150
2 If You Only Knew, Savoy 14003
2 Little Jimmy Scott, Tangerine 1501, *1501*

Lizabeth Scott
2 Lizabeth, Vik 1130

Peter Sellers
2 Best of Peter Sellers, Angel 35884, *35884*
3 Peter Sellers and Sophia Loren, Angel 35910, *35910*

Hugh Shannon
4 Hugh Shannon Plays and Sings, Atlantic 406 (10")

Jean Shepard[19]
2 Into the Unknown With Jazz, Abbott 5003
1 Jean Shepard and Other Foibles, Elektra 172

Joya Sherrill
1 Joya Sherrill Sings Duke Ellington, 20th Century Fox 3170, *4170*

Dinah Shore
2 Dinah, Yes Indeed!, Capitol 1247, *1247*
2 Somebody Loves Me, Capitol 1296, *1296*
3 Dinah Sings Some Blues With Red (Norvo), Capitol 1354, *1354*
2 Dinah Sings, Previn Plays, Capitol 1422, *1422*

[19] See also *Charles Mingus* (p. 159).

PERSONALITIES AND VOCALISTS

2 Dinah, Down Home!, Capitol 1655, *1655*
1 Fabulous Hits Newly Recorded, Capitol 1704, *1704*
2 S'Wonderful (w/B. Clark), Columbia 6015 (10")
1 Dinah Shore Sings Cole Porter and Richard Rodgers, Harmony 7010
1 Love Songs, Harmony 7099
2 Holdings Hands at Midnight, RCA 1154
2 Bouquets of Blues, RCA 1214
2 Moments Like These, RCA 1719, *1719*
2 Dinah Shore Sings the Blues, RCA 3130 (10")
2 Dinah Shore TV Show, RCA 3214 (10")
1 I'm Your Girl, RCA Camden 477
1 Vivacious, RCA Camden 572
2 Dinah (Exclusive Limited Edition), S&H Green Stamps 1 (private pressing LP; from 1962 TV show)

Nina Simone
1 Nina Simone, Bethlehem 6028, *6028*
1 The Amazing Nina Simone, Colpix 407, *407*
1 Nina at Town Hall, Colpix 409, *409*
1 Nina Simone at Newport, Colpix 412, *412*
1 Forbidden Fruit, Colpix 419, *419*
1 Nina at the Village Gate, Colpix 421, *421*
1 Nina Simone Sings Ellington, Colpix 425, *425*

Frank Sinatra
1 In the Wee Small Hours, Capitol 581
2 Swings Easy (Songs for Young Lovers), Capitol 587
1 Songs For Swingin' Lovers, Capitol 653
3 Tone Poems of Color (non-vocal; Sinatra conducting original compositions of V. Young, A. Wilder, E. Bernstein, others), Capitol 735
1 This is Sinatra, Capitol 768
2 Close to You, Capitol 789
1 A Swingin' Affair, Capitol 803
2 Where Are You?, Capitol 855, *855*
2 A Jolly Christmas, Capitol 894
1 This is Sinatra, Vol. 2, Capitol 982
1 Look to Your Heart, Capitol 1164
1 Swing Easy, Capitol 1429
1 Songs For Young Lovers, Capitol 1432
1 Point of No Return, Capitol 1676, *1676*
1 Of Love and Things, Capitol 1729, *1729*
1 Frank Sinatra Sings Rodgers and Hart, Capitol 1825, *1825*
2 Frankie, Columbia 606
2 The Voice, Columbia 743
3 Frank Sinatra Conducts the Music of Alec Wilder (non-vocal), Columbia 884
2 That Old Feeling, Columbia 902
2 Adventures of the Heart, Columbia 953
2 Christmas Dreaming, Columbia 1032
2 Put Your Dreams Away, Columbia 1136
2 Love Is A Kick, Columbia 1241
2 The Broadway Kick, Columbia 1297
2 Come Back to Sorrento, Columbia 1359
2 Reflections, Columbia 1448
1 Frankie and Tommy (Dorsey), RCA 1569
1 We 3 (w/T. Dorsey, A. Stordahl), RCA 1632
5 A Man and His Music, Reprise 1016, *1016* (2 LP boxed set; limited edition)
1 Frank Sinatra Conducts Music From Pictures and Plays, Reprise 6045, *96045*

Carol Sloane
3 Out of the Blue, Columbia 1766, *8566*
3 Live at 30th Street, Columbia 1923, *8723*

Cornelia Otis Skinner
2 Cornelia Otis Skinner with Otis Skinner, RCA Camden 190

Keely Smith[20]
1 I Wish You Love, Capitol 914, *914*
1 Politely!, Capitol 1073, *1073*
1 Swingin' Pretty, Capitol 1145, *1145*

Joanie Sommers
2 Joanie Sommers, Columbia 2495, *9295*
3 Positively the Most, Warner Bros. 1346, *1346*
2 Voice of the 60's, Warner Bros. 1412, *1412*
2 For Those Who Think Young, Warner Bros. 1436, *1436*
2 Johnny Get Angry, Warner Bros. 1470, *1470*
2 Let's Talk About Love, Warner Bros. 1474, *1474*
2 Sommers' Season, Warner Bros. 1504, *1504*
1 Softly (w/L. Almeida), Warner Bros. 1575, *1575*

Jeri Southern
3 Jeri Southern Meets Cole Porter, Capitol 1173
3 Jeri Southern at the Crescendo, Capitol 1278
3 Warm (w/D. Barbour Trio), Decca 5331 (10")
2 You Better Go Now, Decca 8214
3 When Your Heart's On Fire, Decca 8394
3 Jeri Gently Jumps, Decca 8472
3 Prelude to a Kiss, Decca 8745
3 Southern Hospitality, Decca 8761
3 Coffee, Cigarettes and Memories, Roulette 25039
3 Southern Breeze, Roulette 52010, *52010*
3 Jeri Southern Meets Johnny Smith, Roulette 52016, *52016*

Dusty Springfield, see p. 73.

Jo Stafford
2 Autumn in New York, Capitol 197
1 Memory Songs (w/G. MacRae), Capitol 428
1 Starring Jo Stafford, Capitol 435
2 A Musical Portrait of New Orleans (w/F. Laine), Columbia 578
1 Broadway's Best, Columbia 584
1 Happy Holiday, Columbia 691
1 Ski Trails, Columbia 910
1 Once Over Lightly (w/A. Van Damme Quintet), Columbia 968
1 Swingin' Down Broadway, Columbia 1124
1 Jo's Greatest Hits, Columbia 1228
1 I'll Be Seeing You, Columbia 1262, *8080*
1 Ballad of the Blues, Columbia 1332, *8139*
3 Jo + Jazz, Columbia 1561, *8361*

Kay Starr
2 Songs by Kay Starr, Capitol 211
2 Kay Starr Style, Capitol 363
1 Hits of Kay Starr, Capitol 415
2 In a Blue Mood, Capitol 580
1 Movin', Capitol 1254, *1254*
1 Losers, Weepers, Capitol 1303, *1303*
1 One More Time, Capitol 1358
1 Movin' On Broadway, Capitol 1374, *1374*
1 Jazz Singer, Capitol 1438, *1438*
1 All Starr Hits, Capitol 1468
2 I Cry By Night, Capitol 1681, *1681*
1 Fabulous Favorites Newly Recorded, Capitol 2106, *2106*

[20] See also Louis Prima.

SHOW BUSINESS

  3 Swingin' with the Starr, Liberty 9001
  2 The One and Only, RCA 1149
  2 Blue Starr, RCA 1549

Dakota Staton
  1 The Late Late Show, Capitol 876
  1 Dynamic!, Capitol 1054, *1054*
  2 Crazy He Calls Me, Capitol 1170
  2 Time to Swing, Capitol 1241, *1241*
  2 More Than the Most, Capitol 1325, *1325*
  2 Ballads and Blues, Capitol 1387, *1387*
  2 Softly, Capitol 1427, *1427*
  2 Dakota, Capitol 1490, *1490*
  2 'Round Midnight, Capitol 1597, *1597*
  2 Dakota at Storyville, Capitol 1649, *1649*
  1 With Love, United Artists 3292, *6292*
  1 Live and Swinging, United Artists 3312, *6312*

Helyne Stewart
  2 Love Moods, Contemporary 3601, *7601*

Gale Storm
  1 Gale Storm, Dot 3011
  1 Sentimental Me, Dot 3017
  1 Gale's Great Hits, Dot 3098

Elaine Stritch
  4 Stritch, Dolphin 3

Maxine Sullivan
  1 Flow Gently Sweet Rhythm, Jazztone 1229 (reissue of various Period titles)
  3 Maxine Sullivan, Vol. 2, Period 1207
  3 Maxine Sullivan 1956, Period 1909

Inga Swenson
  1 I'm Old Fashioned, Liberty 3379, *7379*

Sylvia Syms
  3 Sylvia Syms Sings, Atlantic 1243
  1 Torch Song, Columbia 1447, *8243*
  3 Sylvia Syms Sings, Decca 8188
  2 Songs of Love, Decca 8639
  3 That Man (Love Letter to Frank Sinatra), Kapp 1236
  2 Sylvia is with Kenny Burrell, Prestige *7439*
  1 For Once in My Life, Prestige *7489*
  1 The Fabulous Sylvia Syms, 20th Century Fox 3123
  5 After Dark, Version 103 (10")

John Charles Thomas
  2 John Charles Thomas Sings Songs You Love, RCA Camden 208
  2 I Hear America Singing, RCA Camden 367

Kay Thompson
  4 Kay Thompson, MGM 3146
  3 Let's Talk About Russia, Signature 1017

Mike Todd
  2 Mike Todd's Broadway, Everest 5011 (1 LP in box w/photos)

Mel Torme[21]
  3 Mel Torme at the Red Hill, Atlantic 8066, *8066*
  3 Comin' Home Baby!, Atlantic 8069, *8069*

[21] See also *Artie Shaw* (p. 170).

  3 Sunday in New York, Atlantic 8091, *8091*
  3 It's a Blue World, Bethlehem 34
  3 Mel Torme and the Marty Paich Dek-tette, Bethlehem 52
  3 Mel Torme Sings Fred Astaire, Bethlehem 6013
  3 California Suite, Bethlehem 6016
  3 Mel Torme at the Crescendo, Bethlehem 6020
  3 Songs For Any Taste, Bethlehem 6031
  4 Mel Torme at the Crescendo December 15, 1954, Coral 57012
  4 Musical Sounds Are the Best Songs, Coral 57044
  1 Prelude to a Kiss, Mayfair 9615, *9615*
  2 Mel Torme Sings, Strand 1076, *1076*
  3 Torme, Verve 2105, *6015* or *62105*
  3 Olé Torme, Verve 2117, *6058* or *62117*
  3 Back in Town, Verve 2120, *6063* or *62120*
  3 Mel Torme Swings Shubert Alley, Verve 2132, *6146* or *62132*
  3 Swingin' On the Moon, Verve 2144, *62144*
  3 Broadway Right Now! (w/M. Whiting), Verve 2146, *62146*
  3 My Kind of Music, Verve 8440, *68440*
  3 I Dig the Duke, I Dig the Count, Verve 8491, *68491*

Bobby Troup
  3 Bobby Troup Sings Johnny Mercer, Bethlehem 19
  2 The Distinctive Style of Bobby Troup, Bethlehem 35
  3 Bobby!, Capitol 484
  1 Cool, Interlude 501, *1001* (reissue of Mode 111)
  2 Bobby Troup and His Trio, Liberty 3002
  2 Do Re Mi (Words and Music by Bobby Troup), Liberty 3026
  1 Here's to My Lady, Liberty 3078
  3 Bobby Swings Tenderly, Mode 111
  3 Bobby Troup and His Stars of Jazz, RCA 1959, *6494*

Sarah Vaughan, see p. 175.

Gwen Verdon
  3 The Girl I Left Home For, RCA 1152

Millie Vernon
  3 Introducing Millie Vernon, Storyville 901

Nancy Walker
  3 I Can Cook Too, Dolphin 2
  2 I Hate Men, RCA Camden 561, *561*

Dinah Washington, see p. 176.

Ethel Waters
  3 Ethel Waters Sings, Continental 16008
  4 Singing Her Best, Jay 3010 (10")
  2 The Favorite Songs of Ethel Waters, Mercury 20051
  4 Ethel Waters, "X" 1009

Frances Wayne
  2 The Warm Sound, Atlantic 1263
  2 Frances Wayne, Brunswick 54022
  2 Songs For My Man, Epic 3222

Mae West
  2 Wild Christmas, Dagonet 4, *4*
  1 The Fabulous Mae West, Decca 9016
  1 Way Out West, Tower 5028, *5028*

PERSONALITIES AND VOCALISTS

Kitty White
- 1 A New Voice in Jazz, EmArcy 36020
- 1 Cold Fire, EmArcy 36068
- 1 A Moment of Love, Pacifica 2002
- 1 Sweet Talk, Roulette 52020
- 1 Intimate, World Pacific 1406 (reissue of Pacifica 2002)

Margaret Whiting
- 3 Margaret Whiting Sings Rodgers & Hart, Capitol 209 (10")
- 2 Love Songs by Margaret Whiting, Capitol 410
- 2 Margaret Whiting Sings for the Starry-Eyed, Capitol 685
- 1 Goin' Places, Dot 3072, *25072*
- 1 Margaret, Dot 3113, *25113*
- 1 Margaret Whiting's Great Hits, Dot 3176, *25176*
- 1 Ten Top Hits, Dot 3235, *25235*
- 1 Just a Dream, Dot 3337
- 1 Past Midnight, MGM 4006, *4006*
- 3 Broadway Right Now (w/M. Torme), Verve 2146, *62146*
- 3 Margaret Whiting Sings the Jerome Kern Songbook, Verve 4038-2, *64038-2* (2 LPs)

Lee Wiley
- 2 Lee Wiley Sings/Lennie Tristano Plays (one side each), Allegro-Elite 4049 (10")
- 1 Night in Manhattan, Columbia 656
- 3 Lee Wiley Sings Vincent Youmans, Columbia 6125 (10")
- 3 Lee Wiley Sings Irving Berlin, Columbia 6126 (10")
- 4 Songs by Cole Porter, Liberty Music Shop 1003 (10")
- 4 Songs by Irving Berlin, Liberty Music Shop 1004 (10")
- 3 West of the Moon, RCA 1408
- 3 A Touch of the Blues, RCA 1566, *1566*
- 4 Lee Wiley Sings Rodgers & Hart, Storyville 312 (10")
- 4 Duologue (Lee Wiley Sings Rodgers & Hart), Storyville 911 (reissue of Storyville 312 plus 4 titles by E. Larkins)

Billy Dee Williams
- 1 Let's Misbehave, Prestige 30001

Joe Williams, see p. 177.

Julie Wilson
- 1 Meet Julie Wilson, Cameo 1021
- 3 Love, Dolphin 6
- 2 My Old Flame, Vik 1095
- 2 Julie Wilson at the St. Regis, Vik 1118

Marie Wilson
- 1 Gentlemen Prefer Marie Wilson, Design 76

Gretchen Wyler
- 2 Wild, Wyler, Wildest, Jubilee 1100, *1100*

10. COMPOSERS AND LYRICISTS

Price Key: 1 = $5 to $10; 2 = $10 to $15; 3 = $15 to $20; 4 = $20 to $35; 5 = over $35.

Harold Arlen
- 3 Harold Arlen and His Songs, Capitol 635
- 1 Blues Opera (w/A. Kostelanetz), Columbia 1099
- 4 Music of Harold Arlen, Walden 306/307 (2 LPs)
- 5 Composers at Play (w/C. Porter), "X" 1003

Malcolm Arnold
- 3 Homage to the Queen, RCA 2037

John Barry
- 1 John Barry Plays Film and TV Themes, Capitol 2527, *2527*
- 1 Ready When You Are J.B., Columbia *1003*
- 1 Great Movie Sounds of John Barry, Columbia 2493, *9293*
- 1 John Barry Conducts the Greatest Movie Hits, Columbia 2708, *9508*

Elmer Bernstein
- 1 Movie and TV Themes, Ava 11, *11*
- 2 Blues and Brass, Decca 8686
- 1 Love Scene, Dot 3097, *25097*
- 3 Backgrounds For Brando, Dot 3107, *25107*
- 1 A Man and His Movies, Mainstream 56094, *6094*

Marc Blitzstein
- 2 Marc Blitzstein Discusses his Theatre Compositions: The Cradle Will Rock, No For An Answer, Regina, Spoken Arts 717

Michael Brown
- 2 Michael Brown Sings His Own Songs With Norman Paris, Jubilee 2010 (10")

Irving Caesar
- 3 And Then I Wrote, Coral 57083

Hoagy Carmichael, see p. 106.

Betty Comden
- 2 Remember These (*Treasure Girl/Chee Chee*), Ava 26, 26

Betty Comden and Adolph Green
- 2 A Party With Comden and Green, Capitol 1197, *1197* (original cast LP)
- 4 Comden and Green Perform Their Own Songs, Heritage 0057
- 4 Comden and Green Perform Their Own Songs From *It's Always Fair Weather*, Heritage 0058 (10")

J. Fred Coots
- 3 And Then I Wrote, Coral 57084

Aaron Copland
- 3 Music for the Movies/Theatre/Radio, MGM 3367
- 1 Music for the Theatre/Suite from *Three Penny Opera* (K. Weill), MGM 9034

Noel Coward
- 2 Noel Coward Sings "Sail Away," Capitol 1667, *1667*
- 1 Noel Coward at Las Vegas, Columbia 5063
- 1 Noel Coward in New York, Columbia 5163
- 3 World Weary (The Songs of Noel Coward sung by Harry Noble, with Stuart Ross at the piano), Heritage 0054 (10")
- 2 Noel and Gertie (w/G. Lawrence), RCA 1156

Vernon Duke
- 2 This is My Beloved (poetry w/original musical score), Atlantic 110 (10")
- 3 Vernon Duke Plays Vernon Duke, Atlantic 407 (10")
- 1 Time Remembered, Mercury 20380, *60023*
- 3 Souvenir de Monte Carlo (Duke) /Mediterranean Suite (R. Cobert), MGM 3497

George Gershwin
- 3 George Gershwin (Gershwin at the piano w/F. Astaire, Hildegarde, others), Columbia 39 (10")
- 3 The Gershwin Years (G. Bassman Orch.), Decca 160, *160* (3 LP boxed set)
- 2 An American in Paris/Rhapsody in Blue (Gershwin at the piano w/RCA Victor Symphony Orch./P. Whiteman Orch.), RCA 29 (10")
- 3 Music by George Gershwin/Victor Herbert, RCA Camden 177
- 1 George Gershwin at the Piano, 20th Century Fox 3013
- 3 George Gershwin Piano Transcriptions, Walden 200
- 4 Gershwin Rarities, Vol. 1, Walden 302
- 4 Gershwin Rarities, Vol. 2, Walden 303

Ira Gershwin
- 4 Tryout, Kurt Weill and Ira Gershwin, Heritage 0051
- 4 Lyrics by Ira Gershwin, Walden 300

COMPOSERS AND LYRICISTS

Johnny Green
- 2 The Johnny everGreens (R. Garcia Orch.), ABC-Paramount 147
- 2 Johnny Green on the Hollywood Sound Stage, MGM 3694
- 1 Out of Nowhere, Regent 6028

Oscar Hammerstein II
- 2 Richard Rodgers and Oscar Hammerstein II in Conversation With Arnold Michaelis, MGM 2E4 (2 LP boxed set)
- 2 Oscar Hammerstein II A Xerox Recorded Portrait, Xerox 1004 (private pressing)

Victor Herbert
- 3 Music by George Gershwin/Victor Herbert, RCA Camden 177
- 3 Music of Victor Herbert, RCA Camden 228

Bernard Herrmann
- 5 Piano Concerto From "Hangover Square" (Herrmann) Scenario for Orchestra on Themes From "Show Boat" (J. Kern), RCA Camden 205

Bronislau Kaper
- 2 Movie Themes by Bronislau Kaper, MGM 3511

Jerome Kern[22]
- 3 The Music of Jerome Kern, RCA Camden 243
- 4 The Melodies of Jerome Kern, Vol. 1, Walden 308
- 4 The Melodies of Jerome Kern, Vol. 2, Walden 309

Erich Wolfgang Korngold
- 1 Much Ado About Nothing Suite, Boston 411
- 4 Music by Korngold (conducted by L. Newman), Warner Bros. 1438, *1438*

Michel Legrand, see p. 157.

Alan Jay Lerner
- 4 Lyrics by Lerner, Heritage 0060

Hugh Martin and Ralph Blane
- 4 Martin and Blane Sing Martin and Blane, Harlequin 701

Johnny Mercer
- 1 Two of a Kind (w/B. Darin), Atco 126, *126*
- 2 Johnny Mercer Sings, Capitol 214 (10″)
- 2 Accentuate the Positive, Capitol 907
- 3 Johnny Mercer Sings Just For Fun, Jupiter 1001

Bob Merrill
- 3 And Then I Wrote, Coral 57081

Alfred Newman
- 1 Ports of Paradise, Capitol 1447, *1447*
- 2 Alfred Newman Themes, Capitol 1652, *1652*
- 2 Love Scenes, Capitol 8516, *8516* (2 LPs)
- 3 Serenade to the Stars, Decca 8123
- 2 String Enchantment, Decca 8194
- 2 Love Dreams, Decca 8299
- 2 Popular Classics, Mercury 20000
- 2 Music For Orchestra and Invitation to the Ballet, Mercury 20036
- 3 Music For Motion Pictures, Mercury 20037
- 2 For Your Listening Pleasure, Mercury 20038

[22] See also *Bernard Herrmann*.

Lionel Newman[23]
- 1 Silver Screen '63, 20th Century Fox 3102, *4102*
- 1 Silver Screen/Magic Screen, 20th Century Fox 3105, *4105*

Alex North
- 3 North of Hollywood, RCA 1445, *1445*

Cole Porter
- 4 Cole Porter Songs (sung by Louise Carlyle and Bob Shaver), Walden 301
- 5 Composers at Play (w/H. Arlen), "X" 1003

Robert Prince
- 2 Ballets U.S.A., RCA 2435, *2435*
- 2 Ballets U.S.A., Warner Bros. 1240

Richard Rodgers
- 1 Richard Rodgers (conducting the Philharmonic Symphony Orchestra of New York), Columbia 810
- 2 Richard Rodgers and Oscar Hammerstein II in Conversation with Arnold Michaelis, MGM 2E4 (2 LP boxed set)
- 2 The Sounds of Richard Rodgers (interview LP w/script for radio use), RCA 33-345 (noncommercial release)
- 2 Mary Martin Sings, Richard Rodgers Plays, RCA 1539
- 4 Rodgers and Hart (sung by Louise Carlyle and Bob Shaver), Walden 304

Harold Rome
- 1 Harold Rome's Gallery, Columbia 6091, *6691*
- 3 And Then I Wrote, Coral 57082
- 4 A Touch of Rome, Heritage 0053
- 4 Fanny, Heritage 0055 (10″)
- 4 Rome-Antics, Heritage 0063

Miklos Rozsa
- 1 Miklos Rozsa Conducts His Great Film Themes, Capitol 2837, *2837*
- 2 Piano Sonata, Capitol 8376
- 1 Danube Waves, Capitol 8540, *8540*
- 1 To Everything There Is a Season, Dot 3304, 25304
- 1 Great Movie Themes by Miklos Rozsa, MGM 4112, *4112*

Arthur Schwartz
- 4 Songs by Schwartz, Walden 305

Max Steiner
- 3 Great Love Themes From Motion Pictures, RCA 1170

Leith Stevens
- 3 Jazz Themes For Cops and Robbers, Coral 57083, *57283*[24]

Jule Styne
- 1 My Name is Jule, United Artists 3469, *6469*

Dmitri Tiomkin
- 3 Movie Themes From Hollywood, Coral 57006

Franz Waxman
- 2 Humoresque (violin selections w/I. Stern, O. Levant, conducted by Waxman), Columbia 2103 (10″)
- 2 Music by Franz Waxman, Decca 8376
- 1 Sinfonietta for Strings and Timpani, Decca 9889

[23] See also *Erich Wolfgang Korngold*.
[24] Includes the complete soundtrack of *Private Hell 36*.

Kurt Weill

4 Tryout: Kurt Weill and Ira Gershwin, Heritage 0051
1 The World of Kurt Weill in Song (sung by M. Schlamme), MGM 4052, *4052*
1 Suite from "Three Penny Opera"/Music for the Theatre (A. Copeland), MGM 9034

Alec Wilder[25]

1 The World's Most Beautiful Girls, Golden Crest 3026

Meredith Willson

1 Dance to the Music Man, Capitol 966
2 And Then I Wrote "The Music Man," Capitol 1320, *1320*

[25] See also *Shannon Bolin* (p. 105), *Mundell Lowe* (p. 157), *George Russell* (p. 169), *Frank Sinatra* (p. 117).

Tommy Wolf

2 Wolf at Your Door, Fraternity 1002
2 Spring Can Really Hang You Up the Most, Fraternity 1010

Victor Young[26]

2 Cinema Rhapsodies, Decca 8051
1 Gypsy Magic, Decca 8052
2 Hollywood Rhapsodies, Decca 8060
2 Night Music, Decca 8085
2 Victor Young's Musical Sketchbook, Decca 8140
1 April in Paris, Decca 8243
1 Imagination, Decca 8278
1 Valentino Tangos, Decca 8279
2 Pearls on Velvet, Decca 8285
1 After Dinner Music, Decca 8350
2 Love Themes From Hollywood, Decca 8364
1 Sugar and Spice and Melodies Nice, Decca 8466
1 Soft Lights and Sweet Music, Decca 8789
1 Forever Young, Decca 8798

[26] See also *Ginger Rogers*.

11. ANTHOLOGIES, VARIOUS ARTISTS

Capitol
- 2 Composer's Holiday (L. Brown Orchestra; original compositions by A. Newman, G. Duning, A. Previn, etc.), Capitol 886, *886*
- 1 Capital of the World (ballet score by G. Anthiel based on Hemingway story), Capitol 8278
- 1 The Hollywood Bowl Symphony Orchestra Plays Music from Motion Pictures (conducted by A. Newman, M. Rozsa), Capitol 8598, *8598*
- 1 Soap Symphony (radio themes orchestrated by A. Newman, M. Rozsa), Capitol 8633, *8633*

Carlton
- 2 Memories Aux Bruxelles (official music of Brussels World's Fair, 1958; composed by A. Laszlo), Carlton 112, *112*

Columbia
- 1 Music From Hollywood (P. Faith Orchestra), Columbia 577
- 1 Sound Stage Music From Hollywood (P. Weston Orchestra), Columbia 612
- 1 Love Music From Hollywood (P. Weston Orchestra), Columbia 794
- 1 Twilight Zone (M. Manning Orchestra), Columbia 1586
- 2 Music for Jennifer (Jones; themes from her films played by P. Weston Orchestra), Columbia 6281 (10")

Coral
- 1 Main Title (Themes from Motion Pictures; D. Jacobs Orchestra), Coral 57065
- 2 Themes From Horror Movies (D. Jacobs Orchestra), Coral 57240, *757240*

Decca
- 2 Modern American Music (compositions by V. Duke, H. Arlen, D. Ellington, etc. conducted by M. Willson), Decca 8025
- 1 Fifty Years of Movie Music, Decca 9079, *79079*
- 1 Music to Read Life's Year-End Issue By, Decca 34155

Heritage
- 3 Saturday Matinee (composers and lyricists sing their own songs), Heritage 0061 (10")

Mainstream
- 1 Golden Original Sound Tracks and Movie Themes, Mainstream 56063, *6063*

Mercury
- 1 Serenade to a Princess (themes from Grace Kelly films played by D. Carroll Orchestra), Mercury 20156

Philips
- 2 Film Music from France (original soundtrack excerpts from "Jules et Jim," "Cleo from 5 to 7," etc.), Philips 200–071, *600–071*

RCA
- 2 Music From Hollywood (A. Goodman Orchestra), RCA 1007
- 2 Theme Music From Great Motion Pictures (A. Goodman Orchestra), RCA 1008
- 1 The Great Music Themes of Television (H. Winterhalter Orchestra), RCA 1020
- 1 Impact (TV themes), RCA 2042, *2042*
- 2 Double Impact (TV themes), RCA 2180, *2180*
- 1 Music of the Young Hollywood Composers (w/A. Previn), RCA 3491, *3491*

Walden
- 2 Show Tune Treasury, Walden 1

123

PART III

JAZZ

12. COLLECTING JAZZ RECORDS

WHEN COLLEGE AUDIENCES switched their allegiance from the "cool" Fifties jazz of Chet Baker, Dave Brubeck, and Miles Davis to the protest music and heavy-metal sounds of the turbulent Sixties, the jazz record market, dominated by independent labels, suffered severe setbacks. Many companies went under completely or were absorbed by conglomerates with indifferent record policies, and only the most marketable jazz musicians were afforded the opportunity to record. Records by less popular artists were promptly deleted and sold for $1.98 or less in bargain bins throughout the country, only to emerge many years later as high-priced collectors' items.

Today jazz is on the uptake. The amount of new product, especially from abroad, is staggering, and virtually every catalog from the past has undergone at least a partial reissue program.

One might think such reissue activity would wreak havoc in the collectors' market, but that has not really been the case. Although it varies from title to title, most legitimate jazz rarities retain a solid portion of their original value when reissued. For one thing, about 60% of the collectors' market concerns itself solely with original issues, regardless of the music's availability. And it is not uncommon for those interested primarily in the music—members of the remaining 40%—to relinquish their original copies in favor of reissues, which often sound better. Certainly there is a general diminution of interest when a rare record is reissued, but for dealers previously unable to locate some of the scarcer titles and who have customers waiting to buy the originals, reissues may actually prove to be a plus.

The following information is provided to indicate how the

original issue may be determined for a few major jazz labels. That is not to say that later pressings are not desirable (for certain hard-to-find titles there is little price difference), but for records that have remained in print over the years only the original issue is, generally speaking, of value.

Blue Note

1500 series: Blue Note 1501 to early 1540's (at least through 1543) were originally issued with the Lexington Avenue address on the label. Blue Note 1544 (?) to 1599 were originally issued with the W. 63rd St. address on the label.

4000 series: Blue Note 4000 through (at least) 4077 were originally issued with the W. 63rd St. address. Blue Note 4078 (?), etc. reads "New York USA." Later pressings may read "A Division of United Artists, Inc." or "A Division of Liberty Records, Inc."

Original label color is blue and white.

Prestige

Prestige 7001 through 7141 were originally issued with the New York City address on the label. Prestige 7142, etc. were originally issued with the Bergenfield, N.J. address on the label.

Original label color is yellow (black for stereo).

Riverside

Riverside 201 through 242 were originally issued with white labels. Riverside 243, etc. were originally issued with blue labels (black for stereo). White label issues are reported to be noisier than later, blue-label pressings of the same titles, but are nevertheless in demand, particularly among foreign collectors. Many records from the Riverside catalog have been reissued by the Japanese with original covers and liner notes, and are currently available in the U.S. at domestic prices.

Verve (Clef Series)

There is only a slight price difference between records originally issued on Clef that later appeared on Verve. However, the Verve "Clef Series" should have a drawing of a trumpet player on the label. There is a noticeable drop in value for later pressings, which have no drawing and may read "A Division of Metro-Goldwyn-Mayer, Inc."

As a general rule of thumb, only those 10" LPs that did not appear on 12" disks are included in the listings. When the transition to the 12" LP occurred in the early to mid-Fifties, most 10" LPs—certainly those by major artists—appeared on 12" disks, and although the earlier incarnations are, indeed, valuable, for the sake of convenience and clarity they are not included in this discography.

Price Key: 1 = $5 to $10; 2 = $10 to $15; 3 = $15 to $20; 4 = $20 to $35; 5 = over $35.

13. JAZZ RECORDINGS

Ahmed Abdul-Malik (aka Sam Gill)
- 1 The Music of Ahmed Abdul-Malik, New Jazz 8266
- 1 Sounds of Africa, New Jazz 8282
- 1 East Meets West, RCA 2015, *2015*
- 2 Jazz Sahara (w/J. Griffin), Riverside 287, *1121*
- 1 Spellbound, Status 8303

Pepper Adams[1]
- 2 Motor City Scene (w/D. Byrd), Bethlehem 6056, *6056*
- 2 Pepper Adams 5, Interlude 502, *1002* (reissue of Mode 112)
- 4 Pepper-Knepper Quintet, Metrojazz 1004, *1004*
- 4 Pepper Adams Quintet, Mode 112
- 2 The Cool Sound of Pepper Adams, Regent 6066
- 2 10 to 4 at the 5 Spot (w/D. Byrd), Riverside 265, *1104*
- 4 Out of This World (w/D. Byrd), Warwick 2041, *2041*
- 4 Pepper Adams Plays the Compositions of Charles Mingus, Workshop 219, *219*
- 3 Critic's Choice, World Pacific 407

Julian "Cannonball" Adderley[2]
- 2 Somethin' Else, Blue Note 1595
- 2 Julian "Cannonball" Adderley, EmArcy 36043
- 1 Julian "Cannonball" Adderley and Strings, EmArcy 36063
- 1 In the Land of Hi-Fi, EmArcy 36077
- 2 Sophisticated Swing, EmArcy 36110
- 1 Cannonball's Sharpshooters, EmArcy 36135 or Mercury 20531, 60208 *(80018)*
- 1 Jump For Joy (songs from the Duke Ellington musical), EmArcy 36146 or Mercury 20530, 60207 *(80017)*
- 2 Cannonball Adderley Quintet in Chicago, Mercury 20449, *60134*
- 2 Cannonball Enroute, Mercury 20616, *60616*
- 1 Portrait of Cannonball, Riverside 269
- 2 Things Are Getting Better, Riverside 286, *1128*
- 1 Cannonball Takes Charge, Riverside 303, *1148*
- 1 Cannonball Adderley Quintet in San Francisco, Riverside 311, *1157*
- 1 Them Dirty Blues, Riverside 322, *1170*
- 1 Cannonball Adderley Quintet at the Lighthouse, Riverside 344, *9344*
- 2 Cannonball Adderley and the Poll-Winners (w/R. Brown, W. Montgomery), Riverside 355, *9355*
- 2 Cannonball Adderley Quintet Plus, Riverside 388, *9388*
- 1 Cannonball Adderley Sextet in New York, Riverside 404, *9404*
- 1 Know What I Mean (w/B. Evans), Riverside 433, *9433*

[1] See also *Curtis Fuller*.
[2] See also *John Benson Brooks, Ray Brown*.

Nat Adderley[3]
- 2 Introducing Nat Adderley, EmArcy 36091 or Wing 60000
- 2 To the Ivy League from Nat, EmArcy 36100
- 1 Naturally, Jazzland 47, *947*
- 1 In the Bag, Jazzland 75, *975*
- 2 Branching Out, Riverside 285
- 2 Much Brass, Riverside 301, *1143*
- 1 Work Song, Riverside 318, *1167*
- 2 That's Right, Riverside 330, *9330*
- 1 Little Big Horn, Riverside 474, *9474*
- 1 That's Nat, Savoy 12021

Toshiko Akiyoshi (Mariano)
- 4 Toshiko-Mariano Quartet, Candid 8012, *9012*
- 2 Country & Western Sound of Jazz (w/S. Kuhn), **Dauntless** 4308, *6308*
- 2 United Notions, Metrojazz 1001, *1001*
- 5 Toshiko's Piano, Norgran 22 (10")
- 5 The Toshiko Trio, Storyville 912
- 5 Her Trio/Her Quartet, Storyville 918
- 1 Jazz in Japan, Vee Jay 2505
- 2 Toshiko and Leon Sash at Newport (one side each), Verve 8236
- 3 The Many Sides of Toshiko, Verve 8273

Manny Albam
- 3 The Jazz Greats of Our Time, Vol 2, Coral 57142
- 3 The Jazz Greats of Our Time, Vol. 1, Coral 57173
- 2 West Side Story, Coral 57207
- 2 The Blues is Everybody's Business, Coral 59101
- 3 Down Beat Jazz Concert, Vol. 2, Dot 3188
- 3 Down Beat Jazz Concert, Dot 9003
- 3 Jazz New York, Dot 9004, *29004*
- 3 The Jazz Workshop, RCA 1211
- 1 The Drum Suite (w/E. Wilkins), RCA 1279
- 1 I Had the Craziest Dream, RCA *2508*

Joe Albany
- 2 The Right Combination (w/W. Marsh), Riverside 270

Max Albright
- 1 Mood For Max, Motif 502

Tony Aless
- 2 Long Island Suite (w/S. Powell), Roost 2202

Joe Alexander
- 1 Blue Jubilee, Jazzland 23, *923*

[3] See also *Harry Arnold*.

JAZZ RECORDINGS

Roland Alexander
1 Pleasure Bent, New Jazz 8267

Lorez Alexandria, see p. 104.

Henry "Red" Allen
1 Feeling Good, Columbia 2447, *9247*
2 Ride, Red, Ride, RCA 1509
1 Mr. Allen, Swingville 2034
2 Red Allen Meets Kid Ory, Verve 1018, 6076 (*61018*)
2 We've Got Rhythm (w/K. Ory), Verve 1020, *6121* (*61020*)
2 Red Allen Plays King Oliver, Verve 1025, *61025*
3 Red Allen With Jack Teagarden and Kid Ory at Newport, Verve 8233

Steve Allen[4]
2 The Jazz Story (w/L. Feather; music and narration), Coral 100 (3 LP boxed set)

Mose Allison
1 Back Country Suite, Prestige 7091
1 Local Color, Prestige 7121
1 Young Man Mose, Prestige 7137
1 Creek Bank, Prestige 7152
1 Autumn Song, Prestige 7189
1 Ramblin' With Mose, Prestige 7215

Trigger Alpert
2 Trigger Happy, Riverside 225

Albert Ammons
2 Memorial Album, Blue Note 7017 (10")
2 Albert Ammons, Mercury 25012 (10")
2 Eight to the Bar (w/P. Johnson), RCA 9 (10")

Gene Ammons
1 Nice and Cool, Moodsville 18
1 The Soulful Moods of Gene Ammons, Moodsville 28
1 Groovin' With Jug (w/R. Holmes), Pacific Jazz 32, *32*
5 Hi Fidelity Jam Session, Prestige 7039 (original)
2 The Happy Blues, Prestige 7039 (reissue)
5 All Star Sessions, Prestige 7050 (original)
2 Woofin' & Tweetin', Prestige 7050 (reissue)
5 Jammin' With Gene, Prestige 7060 (original)
2 Not Really the Blues, Prestige 7060 (reissue)
5 Funky, Prestige 7083
4 Jammin' in Hi Fi With Gene Ammons, Prestige 7110
3 The Big Sound, Prestige 7132[5]
3 Blue Gene, Prestige 7146
1 "The Twister," Prestige 7176 (reissue of Prestige 7110)
2 Boss Tenor, Prestige 7180
2 Jug, Prestige 7192
3 Groove Blues, Prestige 7201[5]
1 UpTight, Prestige 7208
1 Juggin' Around, Vee Jay 3024

David Amram
2 Jazz Studio No. 6 (w/J. Barrow), Decca 8558

Curtis Amy
1 Groovin' Blue (w/F. Butler), Pacific Jazz 19, *19*
1 Way Down (w/V. Feldman), Pacific Jazz 46, *46*
1 Tippin' on Through, Pacific Jazz 62, *62*
2 Katanga! (w/D. Bolton), Pacific Jazz 70, *70*

Cat Anderson
1 Cat on a Hot Tin Horn, EmArcy 36142 or Mercury 20522, *60199 (80008)*

Ernestine Anderson, see p. 104.

Earl Anderza
1 Outa Sight, Pacific Jazz 65, *65*

Lil Armstrong
1 Satchmo and Me (documentary), Riverside 120
1 Lil Armstrong, Riverside 401, *9401*

Louis Armstrong
1 Louis Armstrong and Eddie Condon at Newport (one side each), Columbia 931
2 Satchmo at Symphony Hall, Decca 108 (2 LP boxed set w/program notes)
1 Satchmo at Symphony Hall, Vol. 1, Decca 8037 (single record issue)
1 Satchmo at Symphony Hall, Vol. 2, Decca 8038 (single record issue)
3 Satchmo . . . A Musical Autobiography, Decca 155 (4 LP boxed set w/illustrated book; recreations of early hits and reminiscences)
2 Satchmo at Pasadena, Decca 8041
1 Satchmo Sings, Decca 8126
1 Louis Armstrong at the Crescendo, Vol. 1, Decca 8168
1 Louis Armstrong at the Crescendo, Vol. 2, Decca 8169
1 Satchmo Serenades, Decca 8211
1 New Orleans Nights, Decca 8329
1 Satchmo on Stage, Decca 8330
1 Bing and Satch, MGM 3882, *3882*
2 Louis Armstrong Sings the Blues, RCA 1005
1 Town Hall Concert Plus, RCA 1443
1 Young Louis Armstrong, Riverside 101
1 Louis Armstrong: 1923, Riverside 122
2 Ella and Louis, Verve 4003
2 Ella and Louis Again, Verve 4006-2 (2 LPs)
2 Porgy and Bess (w/E. Fitzgerald), Verve 4011-2, *6040-2 6401-2* (2 LPs)
1 Louis Under the Stars, Verve 4012, *6044* (*64012*)
1 Ella and Louis Again, Vol. 1, Verve 4017 (single record issue)
1 Ella and Louis Again, Vol. 2, Verve 4018 (single record issue)
2 Louis Armstrong Meets Oscar Peterson, Verve 8322, *6062 (68322)*

Buddy Arnold
3 Wailing, ABC-Paramount 114

Harry Arnold
1 Harry Arnold + Big Band + Quincy Jones = Jazz, EmArcy 36139 or Mercury *80006*
1 Great Big Band and Friends (w/C. Hawkins, L. Thompson, B. Bailey, N. Adderley, T. Thielemans), Jazzland 65, *965*

Dorothy Ashby
1 Dorothy Ashby, Argo 690, *690*

---
[4] See also *Jack Kerouac, Irene Kral* (p. 112).
[5] With John Coltrane on alto saxophone.
NOTE: All Prestige LPs yellow label.

1 Soft Winds (w/T. Pollard), Jazzland 61, *961*
1 In a Minor Groove, New Jazz 8209
1 Hip Harp (w/F. Wess), Prestige 7140
1 The Jazz Harpist, Regent 6039

Georgie Auld
3 Concert in Jazz, Apollo 102 (10″)
2 That's Auld, Discovery 3007 (10″)
1 Georgie Auld in the Land of Hi-Fi, EmArcy 36060
1 Dancing in the Land of Hi-Fi, EmArcy 36090
2 Georgie Auld Plays the Winners, Philips 200–096, *600–096*
1 Here's to the Losers, Philips 200–116, *600–116*
2 Georgie Auld Quintet, Roost 403 (10″)

Albert Ayler
5 My Name is Albert Ayler, Debut 140 (Danish pressing) [6]
5 Ghosts, Debut 144 (Danish pressing) [6]
5 Spirits, Debut 146 (Danish pressing) [6]
1 Spiritual Unity, ESP 1002
1 Bells, ESP 1010, *1010* (music on one side only)
1 New York Eye and Ear Control, ESP 1016, *1016*

Harry Babasin
2 Jazz in Hollywood Series, Nocturne 3 (10″)

Don Bagley
3 Basically Bagley, Dot 3070, *25070*
2 Soft Sell, Dot 9007, *29007*
2 Jazz on the Rocks, Regent 6061

Benny Bailey[7]
1 The Music of Quincy Jones (w/J. Harris, A. Persson), Argo 668, *668*
4 Big Brass, Candid 8011, *9011*

Buster Bailey
3 All About Memphis, Felsted 7003, *2003*

Davie Bailey
1 One Foot in the Gutter, Epic 16008, *17008*
1 Gettin' Into Somethin', Epic 16011, *17011*
1 2 Feet in the Gutter, Epic 16021, *17021*
4 Bash!, Jazzline 33–01, *33–01*
3 Reaching Out, Jazztime 003

Mildred Bailey
1 A Mildred Bailey Serenade, Columbia 6094 (10″)
1 The Rockin' Chair Lady, Decca 5387 (10″)
1 Me and the Blues, Regent 6032

Chet Baker[8]
2 The Most Important Jazz Album of 1964/1965, Colpix 476, *476*
1 Chet Baker in Milan, Jazzland 18, *918*
1 Chet Baker With Fifty Italian Strings, Jazzland 21, *921*
1 Polka Dots and Moonbeams, Jazzland 88, *988*
1 Baby Breeze, Limelight 82003, *86003*
3 Chet Baker Ensemble, Pacific Jazz 9 (10″)
3 Chet Baker Sextet, Pacific Jazz 15 (10″)

2 Picture of Heath (w/A. Pepper), Pacific Jazz 18 (reissue of Pacific Jazz 1234)
2 Chet Baker Sings and Plays, Pacific Jazz 1202
2 Jazz at Ann Arbor, Pacific Jazz 1203
2 The Trumpet Artistry of Chet Baker, Pacific Jazz 1206
3 Chet Baker in Europe, Pacific Jazz 1218
2 Chet Baker Sings, Pacific Jazz 1222
3 Chet Baker and Crew, Pacific Jazz 1224, *1004*
2 Chet Baker Big Band, Pacific Jazz 1229
2 Quartet: Russ Freeman and Chet Baker, Pacific Jazz 1232
3 Playboys (w/A. Pepper), Pacific Jazz 1234
2 It Could Happen to You, Riverside 278, *1120*
1 Chet Baker in New York, Riverside 281, *1119*
2 Chet, Riverside 299, *1135*
2 Chet Baker Plays the Best of Lerner and Loewe, Riverside 307, *1152*
2 Stan Meets Chet (w/S. Getz), Verve 8263
2 Pretty/Groovy, World Pacific 1249
3 Music From "James Dean Story", World Pacific 2005

Harold "Shorty" Baker[9]
1 Broadway Beat, King 608, *608*
1 Shorty and Doc (Cheatham), Swingville 2021

Ronnie Ball
2 All About Ronnie, Savoy 12075

Paul Barbarin
1 Paul Barbarin and his New Orleans Jazz, Atlantic 1215
1 Paul Barbarin and his New Orleans Band, Circle 408 (10″)
1 New Orleans Contrasts (w/S. Bonano; one side each), Riverside 217 (partial reissue of Circle 408)

Charlie Barnet
1 Classics in Jazz, Capitol 624
2 One Night Stand, Clef 638
1 Town Hall Concert, Columbia 639
1 Hop on the Skyliner, Decca 8098
1 Redskin Romp, RCA 1091
1 Charlie's Choice, RCA Camden 389
2 Dance Bash, Verve 2007
2 Dancing Party, Verve 2027 (reissue of Clef 638)
2 For Dancing Lovers, Verve 2031
1 Lonely Street, Verve 2040

Count Basie[10]
2 Count Basie, Brunswick 54012
3 Dance Session, Clef 626
3 Basie Jazz, Clef 633
3 Dance Session #2, Clef 647
3 Basie, Clef 666
2 Count Basie Swings, Joe Williams Sings, Clef 678 or Verve 8063
3 The Count!, Clef 685
2 The Swinging Count, Clef 706 or Verve 8090
2 Basie Roars Again, Clef 723 or Verve 8018 (partial reissue of Clef 626 and Clef 647)
2 King of Swing, Clef 724 or Verve 8104 (partial reissue of Clef 626 and Clef 647)
2 Basie Rides Again, Clef 729 or Verve 8108 (partial reissue of Clef 633 and Clef 685)
1 Count Basie Classics, Columbia 754

---

[6] Considering Ayler's stature and the prices these records fetch, I have chosen to include them in this discography despite the fact that they are not American LPs.
[7] See also *Harry Arnold*.
[8] See also *Gerry Mulligan*.
[9] See also *Bud Freeman*.
[10] See also *Eddie "Lockjaw" Davis, Illinois Jacquet, Lester Young*.

JAZZ RECORDINGS

1 Blues By Basie, Columbia 901
2 Count Basie and His Orchestra, Decca 8049
2 Basie's Back in Town, Epic 3169
2 Count Basie, RCA 1112
1 The Count, RCA Camden 395
1 Basie's Basement, RCA Camden 497
2 Count Basie in Kansas City, RCA Vintage 514
2 The Count Basie Story, Roulette RB-1, *1* (2 LP boxed set w/illustrated booklet)
1 Basie (e=mc²), Roulette 52003, *52003*
1 Basie Plays Hefti, Roulette 52011, *52011*
1 One More Time, Roulette 52024, *52024*
1 Breakfast Dance and Barbecue, Roulette 52028, *52028*
1 Dance With Basie, Roulette 52036, *52036*
1 Not Now, I'll Tell You When, Roulette 52044, *52044*
1 String Along With Basie, Roulette 52051, *52051*
1 Basie at Birdland, Roulette 52065, *52065*
1 The Legend (From the Pen of Benny Carter), Roulette 52086, *52086*
1 Basie in Sweden, Roulette 52099, *52099*
2 The Greatest! (w/J. Williams), Verve 2016, *6006* (*62016*)
1 Ella and Basie, Verve 4061, *64061*
1 April in Paris, Verve 8012
2 The Count!, Verve 8070 (partial reissue of Clef 685)
2 The Band of Distinction, Verve 8103 (reissue of Clef 666)
2 Basie in London, Verve 8199
2 Count Basie at Newport (w/J. Rushing, L. Young, J. Jones, I. Jacquet, R. Eldridge), Verve 8243, *6024* (*68243*)
2 Dizzy Gillespie With Mary Lou Williams at Newport (Count Basie With Joe Williams at Newport), Verve 8244
2 One O'Clock Jump (w/E. Fitzgerald, J. Williams), Verve 8288
2 Hall of Fame, Verve 8291

Billy Bauer
5 Let's Have a Session, Ad Lib 5501 (10")
5 Plectrist, Norgran 1082 or Verve 8172

Sidney Bechet
2 Sidney Bechet Solos, Atlantic 118 (10")
3 Duets (w/M. Spanier), Atlantic 1206
1 Grand Master of the Soprano Saxophone and Clarinet, Columbia 836
1 Sidney Bechet in Concert at the Brussels Fair, 1958, Columbia 1410
5 Sidney Bechet (original cover), Dial 301 (10")
5 Blackstick (2nd cover), Dial 301 (10")
5 Sidney Bechet with Wally Bishop's Orchestra, Dial 302 (10")
1 King of the Soprano Saxophone, Good Time Jazz 12013
2 Jazz à la Creole, Jazztone 1213 (w/O. Simeon; one side each)
3 Young Ideas (w/M. Solal), Pacific Jazz 1236
1 Bechet of New Orleans, RCA Vintage 510
1 The Blue Bechet, RCA Vintage 535
1 The Immortal Sidney Bechet, Reprise 6076
3 In Memoriam, Riverside 138/139 (2 LPs)
2 Bechet, Riverside 149
2 Creole Reeds, Riverside 216 (w/A. Nicholas; one side each)
1 Sidney Bechet, Savoy 15013 (10")
4 Sidney Bechet at Storyville, Storyville 902

Bix Beiderbecke[11]
1 The Bix Beiderbecke Legend, RCA 2323
1 Bix Beiderbecke and the Wolverines, Riverside 123

Aaron Bell
4 Three Swinging Bells, Herald 0100
2 After the Party's Over, RCA 1876

Marty Bell, see Don Elliott.

Louis Bellson[12]
1 The Just Jazz All Stars, Capitol 348
4 Journey Into Love, Norgran 1007
4 The Louis Bellson Quintet, Norgran 1011
3 The Hawk Talks, Norgran 1020, Norgran 1099, or Verve 8186
3 Skin Deep, Norgran 1046 or Verve 8137
1 Big Band Jazz at the Summit, Roulette 52087, *52087*
1 The Mighty Two (w/G. Krupa), Roulette 52098, *52098*
2 The Brilliant Bellson Sound, Verve 2123, *6093* (*62123*)
2 Louis Bellson Swings Jule Styne, Verve 2131, *6138* (*62131*)
3 Concerto For Drums, Verve 8016 (reissue of Norgran 1011)
3 Drumorama, Verve 8193
3 Louis Bellson at the Flamingo, Verve 8256
3 Let's Call it Swing, Verve 8258
3 Music, Romance and Especially Love, Verve 8280
1 Drummer's Holiday, Verve 8354

Max Bennett
3 Max Bennet, Bethlehem 48
3 Max Bennett Plays, Bethlehem 50

Walter Benton
2 Out of This World, Jazzland 28, *928*

Bunny Berigan
1 Bunny Berigan Plays Again, RCA 1003
1 Bunny Berigan and His Orchestra, RCA 2078
1 Bunny, RCA Camden 550

Sonny Berman
3 Jazz Immortal 1946, Esoteric 532

Milt Bernhart
1 The Sound of Bernhart, Decca 8823 or 9214
2 Modern Brass, RCA 1123

Bill Berry
1 Jazz and Swinging Percussion, Directional Sounds 5002

Eddie Bert
3 Eddie Bert Quintet, Discovery 3020 (10")
1 Musician of the Year, Savoy 12015
2 Encore, Savoy 12019
1 Like Cool, Somerset 5200 (reissue of Transworld 208)
3 Let's Dig Bert, Transworld 208

Barney Bigard[13]
9 Barney Bigard, Liberty 3072 (felt cover)

[11] See also *Jean Goldkette.*
[12] See also *Meade Lux Lewis, Art Tatum.*
[13] See also *Benny Carter.*

JAZZ

Walter Bishop, Jr.
4 Speak Low, Jazztime 002

Ran Blake
1 Ran Blake Plays Solo Piano, ESP 1011
3 The Newest Sound Around (w/J. Lee), RCA 2500, *2500*

Art Blakey (and the Jazz Messengers)[14]
1 Art Blakey's Jazz Messengers With Thelonious Monk, Atlantic 1278 (black label)
3 Hard Drive, Bethlehem 6023
3 Art Blakey's Big Band, Bethlehem 6027, *6027*
3 The Jazz Messengers at the Cafe Bohemia, Vol. 1, Blue Note 1507
3 The Jazz Messengers at the Cafe Bohemia, Vol. 2, Blue Note 1508
5 A Night at Birdland, Vol. 1, Blue Note 1521 (original art cover)
2 A Night at Birdland, Vol. 1, Blue Note 1521 (photo cover)
5 A Night at Birdland, Vol. 2, Blue Note 1522 (original art cover)
2 A Night at Birdland, Vol. 2, Blue Note 1522 (photo cover)
1 Indestructible!, Blue Note 4193, *84193*
1 The Witch Doctor, Blue Note 4258, *84258*
5 Max Roach Quintet (3 titles) / Art Blakey and His Band (4 titles), Blue Note 5010 (10")
2 Golden Boy, Colpix 478, *478*
2 The Jazz Messengers, Columbia 897
2 Drum Suite, Columbia 1002
3 Hard Bop, Columbia 1040
2 Midnight Session, Elektra 120, *120*
3 Blakey, EmArcy 26030 (10")
2 Art Blakey in Paris, Epic 16017, *17017*
2 Les Liaisons Dangereuses, Epic 16022, *17022* (movie soundtrack)
2 Cu-Bop (w/Sabu), Jubilee 1049
1 'S Make It, Limelight 82001, *86001*
3 The Jazz Messengers/Elmo Hope Quintet (one side each), Pacific Jazz 33
2 Ritual, Pacific Jazz 402
1 A Night in Tunisia, RCA 2654, *2654 (e)* (reissue of Vik 1115; "fake" stereo)
1 Three Blind Mice, United Artists 14002, *15002*
2 Plays Lerner and Loewe, Vik 1103
3 A Night in Tunisia, Vik 1115

Paul Bley
5 Introducing Paul Bley, Debut 7 (10")
2 Paul Bley, EmArcy 36092

Blue Stars of France, see p. 105.

Peter Bocage
1 Peter Bocage with his Creole Serenaders and the Love-Jiles Ragtime Orchestra, Riverside 379, *9379*

Francy Boland, see Kenny Clark-Francy Boland Band.

Claude Bolling
2 Claude Bolling All Stars, Bally 12003
1 Rolling With Bolling, Omega 6

Beryl Booker
1 Beryl Booker Trio, Cadence 1000 (10")
2 Beryl Booker Trio, Discovery 3021 (10")
3 Beryl Booker Trio with Don Byas, Discovery 3022 (10")
2 Girl Met a Piano, EmArcy 26007 (10")

Earl Bostic, see p. 49.

Johnny Bothwell
1 Presenting Johnny Bothwell and his Orchestra, Brunswick 58033 (10")

Rocky Boyd
4 Ease It, Jazztime 001

Will Bradley
3 Boogie-Woogie (w/R. McKinley), Epic 3115
2 House of Bradley (w/W. Bradley, Jr.), Epic 3199
1 Dixieland Jazz, Grand Award 310 (w/B. Byrne; one side each)
1 Big Band Boogie (w/J. Guarnieri), RCA 2098, *2098*

Ruby Braff[15]
3 Ruby Braff Featuring Dave McKenna, ABC-Paramount 141
2 A Ruby Braff Omnibus, Bethlehem 5
2 The Best of Ruby Braff, Bethlehem 6043
2 Braff!!, Epic 3377
1 Swinging With Ruby Braff, Jazztone 1210
3 Hi-Fi Salute to Bunny, RCA 1510
3 Easy Now, RCA 1966, *1966*
1 You're Getting to Be a Habit With Me, Stereocraft 507, *507* or Bell *43*
3 Hustlin' and Bustlin', Storyville 908
2 Blowing Around the World, United Artists 3045, *6045*
1 Ruby Braff-Marshall Brown Sextet, United Artists 4093, *5093*
1 Ruby Braff Special, Vanguard 8504
1 2 x 2 (Ruby Braff and Ellis Larkins Play Rodgers and Hart), Vanguard 8507
1 Pocketfull of Dreams (w/E. Larkins), Vanguard 8516
1 Buck Meets Ruby (w/B. Clayton), Vanguard 8517
2 Ruby Braff Octet with Pee Wee Russell/Bobby Henderson at Newport (one side each), Verve 8241
2 Ruby Braff Goes Girl Crazy, Warner Bros. 1273, *1273*

Dollar Brand
3 Duke Ellington Presents the Dollar Brand Trio, Reprise 6111, *6111*

Lenny Breau
2 Guitar Sounds From Lenny Breau, RCA *4076*
2 Lenny Breau Live, RCA 4199

Buddy Bregman[16]
2 Swinging Kicks, Verve 2042, *6013 (62042)*
1 The Gershwin Anniversary Album, Verve 2093
1 Dig Buddy in Hi-Fi, Verve 2094
1 Swingin' Standards, World Pacific 1263, *1024*

---
[14] See also *Kenny Burrell, Rita Reys, Sonny Rollins, Randy Weston.*
NOTE: All Blue Note LPs with original address on label; see p. 128.

[15] See also *George Wein.*
[16] See also *Bing Crosby* (p. 107), *Annie Ross.*

JAZZ RECORDINGS

Bob Brookmeyer[17]
3 Portrait of the Artist, Atlantic 1320, *1320*
4 Bob Brookmeyer Plays Bob Brookmeyer and Some Others, Clef 644
1 Bob Brookmeyer and Friends, Columbia 2237, *9037*
1 Jazz is a Kick, Mercury 20600, *60600*
2 Revelation, New Jazz 8294 (reissue of Prestige 7066)
3 Bob Brookmeyer Quartet, Pacific Jazz 16 (10")
3 Traditionalism Revisited, Pacific Jazz 1233
4 The Street Swingers (w/J. Hall, J. Raney), Pacific Jazz 1239
4 The Dual Role of Bob Brookmeyer, Prestige 7066
5 Bob Brookmeyer featuring Al Cohn, Storyville 305 (10")
5 Tonight's Jazz Today (w/Z. Sims), Storyville 907
5 Whooecee (w/Z. Sims), Storyville 914
3 Kansas City Revisited, United Artists 4008, *5008*
4 The Ivory Hunters (w/B. Evans; piano duets), United Artists 4044, *5044*
3 The Modernity of Bob Brookmeyer, Verve 8111 (reissue of Clef 644)
3 The Blues Hot and Cold, Verve 8385, *68385*
3 7 x Wilder, Verve 8413, *68413*
2 Gloomy Sunday, Verve 8455, *68455*
2 Brookmeyer, Vik 1071

Hadda Brooks, see p. 49.

John Benson Brooks
3 Alabama Concerto (w/C. Adderley, A. Farmer), Riverside 276, *1123*
3 Folk Jazz, U.S.A., Vik 1083

Roy Brooks
1 Roy Brooks Beat, Workshop 220, *220*

Tina Brooks
5 True Blue, Blue Note 4041

Boots Brown (pseudonym for Shorty Rogers)
1 Rock That Beat, Groove 1000

Boyce Brown (aka Brother Matthew)
2 Brother Matthew with Eddie Condon's Jazz Band, ABC-Paramount 121

Clifford Brown[18]
3 Memorial Album, Blue Note 1526 (Lexington Ave. address on label)
5 Clifford Brown Sextet (New Star on the Horizon), Blue Note 5032 (10")
2 Clifford Brown and Strings EmArcy 36005
2 Clifford Brown All Stars, EmArcy 36102
2 Jazz Immortal (w/Z. Sims), Pacific Jazz 3 (reissue of Pacific Jazz 1214; see *Jack Montrose*)
4 Clifford Brown Memorial, Prestige 7055

Clifford Brown-Max Roach Quintet
2 Brown and Roach Inc., EmArcy 36008
2 Clifford Brown and Max Roach, EmArcy 36036
2 A Study in Brown, EmArcy 36037
2 Clifford Brown and Max Roach at Basin Street, EmArcy 36070

Lawrence Brown
4 Slide Trombone, Clef 682 or Verve 8067

Pete Brown
2 Jazz Kaleidoscope, Bethlehem 4 (w/Jonah Jones; one side each)
2 From the Heart, Verve 8365, *6133* (*68365*)

Ray Brown[19]
3 Bass Hit, Verve 8022
3 This is Ray Brown, Verve 8290
2 Jazz Cello, Verve 8390, *68390*
1 Ray Brown With the All-Star Big Band (w/C. Adderley), Verve 8444, *68444*

Ted Brown
5 Free Wheeling (w/A. Pepper, W. Marsh), Vanguard 8515

Dave Brubeck
1 Dave Brubeck at Storyville: 1954, Columbia 590
1 Jazz Impressions of the U.S.A., Columbia 984
1 Dave Digs Disney, Columbia 1059
1 Jazz Impressions of Eurasia, Columbia 1251, *8058*
1 The Riddle (w/B. Smith), Columbia 1454
1 Tonight Only (w/C. McRae), Columbia 1609, *8409*
1 Dave Brubeck Trio, Fantasy 3204
1 Dave Brubeck Trio (Distinctive Rhythm Instrumentals), Fantasy 3205
1 Jazz at the Blackhawk, Fantasy 3210
1 Jazz at College of Pacific, Fantasy 3223, *8078*
1 Dave Brubeck Quartet (w/P. Desmond), Fantasy 3229, *8092*
1 Dave Brubeck Quartet (w/P. Desmond), Fantasy 3230, *8093*
1 Dave Brubeck Octet, Fantasy 3239, *8094*
1 Jazz at Storyville, Fantasy 3240, *8080*
1 Jazz at Oberlin, Fantasy 3245, *8069*
1 Dave Brubeck & Paul Desmond at Wilshire-Ebell, Fantasy 3249, *8095*
1 Dave Brubeck Plays & Plays, Fantasy 3259
1 Reunion, Fantasy 3268, *8007*
1 Jazz at the Blackhawk, Fantasy 3298, *8081*
1 Brubeck a la Mode, Fantasy 3301, *8047*
1 Near Myth (w/B. Smith), Fantasy 3319, *8063*

George Brunis
1 King of the Tailgate Trombone, Commodore 30015

Clora Bryant
1 Gal With a Horn, Mode 106

Ray Bryant
1 Little Susie, Columbia 1449, *8244*
1 Madison Time, Columbia 1476, *8276*
2 Con Alma, Columbia 1633, *8433*
2 Dancing the Big Twist, Columbia 1746, *8546*
5 Meet Betty Carter and Ray Bryant, Epic 3202
3 Ray Bryant Trio, Epic 3279
3 Alone With the Blues, New Jazz 8213
1 The Ray Bryant Trio, New Jazz 8227 (reissue of Prestige 7098)
4 Ray Bryant Trio, Prestige 7098
4 Ray Bryant Plays, Signature 6008, *6008*

---
[17] See also *Al Cohn, Stan Getz, Gerry Mulligan, Jimmy Raney, Bud Shank, Phil Sunkel*.
[18] See also *Gigi Gryce*.
[19] See also *Julian "Cannonball" Adderley*.

JAZZ

Milt Buckner[20]
1 Rockin' with Milt, Capitol 642
1 Rockin' Hammond, Capitol 722

Vinnie Burke[21]
3 Vinnie Burke All Stars, ABC-Paramount 139
2 String Jazz Quartet, ABC-Paramount 170
3 Bass by Pettiford/Burke (one side each), Bethlehem 6
1 Vinnie Burke Trio, Josie 3509 (reissue of Jubilee 1025)
3 The Eddie Costa-Vinnie Burke Trio, Jubilee 1025

Ralph Burns
2 Bijou, Bethlehem 68
3 Jazz Recital, Clef 718 or Verve 8098[22]
2 Jazz Studio 5, Decca 8235
1 The Masters Revisited, Decca 8555
1 Very Warm For Jazz, Decca 9207
1 Porgy and Bess, Decca 9215, *9215*
1 Spring Sequence, Jazztone 1228 (reissue of Bethlehem 68)
2 The Swinging Seasons, MGM 3616 (one side D. Hyman; other side L. Feather-R. Burns Orchestra)
3 Ralph Burns Among the JATP's, Norgran 1028 or Verve 8121
1 Where There's Burns There's Fire, Warwick 5001

Kenny Burrell[23]
4 Introducing Kenny Burrell, Blue Note 1523
2 Kenny Burrell, Blue Note 1543
2 Blue Lights, Vol. 1, Blue Note 1596
2 Blue Lights, Vol. 2, Blue Note 1597
3 On View at the Five Spot (w/A. Blakey), Blue Note 4021
4 Weaver of Dreams (vocals), Columbia 1703, *8503*
1 Lotsa Bossa Nova, Kapp 1326, *3326*
2 Bluesy Burrell (w/C. Hawkins), Moodsville 29
3 Kenny Burrell with John Coltrane, New Jazz 8276
4 Kenny Burrell, Prestige 7088
4 Two Guitars (w/J. Raney), Prestige 7119
1 Guitar Forms (w/G. Evans), Verve 68612
1 A Generation Ago Today, Verve 68656

Gary Burton
2 New Vibe Man in Town, RCA 2420, *2420*
2 Who is Gary Burton?, RCA 2665, *2665*
3 Something's Coming! (w/J. Hall), RCA 2880, *2880*
1 The Groovy Sound of Music, RCA 3360, *3360*
2 A Genuine Tong Funeral, RCA *3988*

Jaki Byard
3 Here's Jaki, New Jazz 8256
3 Hi-Fly, New Jazz 8273

Don Byas[24]
3 Tenor Saxophone Solos, Atlantic 117 (10")
5 Saxophone Moods, Dial 216 (10")
2 Jazz From Saint Germain Des Pres (w/B. Peiffer; one side each), Verve 8119

Billy Byers
1 Impressions of Duke Ellington, Mercury 2028, *6028*
2 The Jazz Workshop, RCA 1269

Donald Byrd[25]
2 Motor City Scene (w/P. Adams), Bethlehem 6056, *6056*
3 Off to the Races, Blue Note 4007
3 Byrd in Hand, Blue Note 4019
2 Fuego, Blue Note 4026
2 Byrd in Flight, Blue Note 4048
2 Donald Byrd at the Half-Note Cafe, Vol. 1, Blue Note 4060, *84060*
2 Donald Byrd at the Half-Note Cafe, Vol. 2, Blue Note 4061, *84061*
1 The Cat Walk, Blue Note 4075, *84075*
1 Mustang!, Blue Note 4238, *84238*
5 2 Trumpets (w/A. Farmer), Prestige 7062
5 Youngbloods (w/P. Woods), Prestige 7080
5 3 Trumpets (w/A. Farmer, I. Sulieman), Prestige 7092
1 Byrd's Word, Savoy 12032
5 Donald Byrd in Paris, Vol. 1, Signature 1039
5 Byrd's Eye View, Transition 4
5 Byrd Jazz, Transition 5
5 Byrd Blows on Beacon Hill, Transition 17
4 Out of This World (w/P. Adams), Warwick 2041, *2041*

Red Callender
1 Callender Speaks Low (w/B. Collette), Crown 5012
1 Swingin' Suite, Crown 5025 or Modern 1201
2 The Lowest, Metrojazz 1007, *1007*

Cab Calloway
1 Blues Make Me Happy, Coral 57408, *757408*
1 Cab Calloway, Epic 3265
3 Cotton Club Revue 1958, Gone 101
1 Hi De Hi, Hi De Ho, RCA 2021, *2021*

Conte Candoli[26]
2 West Coast Wailers (w/L. Levy), Atlantic 1268
2 West Coasting With Conte Candoli and Stan Levey, Bethlehem 9
2 Conte Candoli, Bethlehem 30
2 The Brothers Candoli (w/P. Candoli), Dot 3062
2 Conte Candoli Quartet, Mode 109

Mutt Carey
2 Mutt Carey Plays the Blues (w/H. Thomas), Riverside 1042 (10")
1 Jazz, New Orleans, Vol 1, Savoy 12038 (w/P. Miller; one side each)
1 Jazz, New Orleans, Vol. 2, Savoy 12050 (w/P. Miller; one side each)

Harry Carney
4 Harry Carney with Strings, Clef 640
4 Moods for Girl and Boy, Verve 2028 (reissue of Clef 640)

Helen Carr, see p. 106.

Barbara Carroll
3 Ladies in Jazz, Atlantic 1271 (w/M. L. Williams; one side each)

[20] See also *Terry Gibbs*.
[21] See also *Mike Cuozzo*.
[22] One side reissue of 10" LP "Free Forms" (Clef 115) w/L. Konitz; other side reissue of 10" LP "Billie Holiday at Jazz at the Philharmonic" (Clef 169).
[23] See also *Sylvia Syms* (p. 118), *Frank Wess*.
[24] See also *Beryl Booker*.
NOTE: All Blue Note LPs with original addresses on label; see p. 128.

[25] See also *Pepper Adams, Red Garland, Jazz Lab, Hank Mobley, Jackie Cain and Roy Kral*—see p. 106.
[26] See also *Jack Montrose, Frank Morgan*.

JAZZ RECORDINGS

4 Barbara Carroll Trio, Livingston 1081 (10")
2 Barbara Carroll Trio, RCA 1001
2 Lullabies in Rhythm, RCA 1023
1 Have You Met Miss Carroll?, RCA 1137
1 We Just Couldn't Say Goodbye, RCA 1296
1 It's a Wonderful World, RCA 1396
3 Why Not?, Sesac 3201/02
1 Funny Face, Verve 2063
1 Barbara Carroll Trio Plays the Best of George and Ira Gershwin, Verve 2092 (reissue of Verve 2063)
1 Barbara, Verve 2095

Joe Carroll
1 Man With a Happy Sound, Charlie Parker 802, *802*
2 Joe Carroll, Epic 3272

Benny Carter[27]
3 The Fabulous Benny Carter Band, Audio Lab 1505
3 Benny Carter Plays Pretty, Norgran 1015
4 New Jazz Sounds (w/D. Gillespie, B. Harris), Norgran 1044 or Verve 8137
3 Alone Together (w/O. Peterson), Norgran 1058 or Verve 8148
3 Cosmopolite, Norgran 1070 or Verve 8160
3 B.B.B. and Co. (w/B. Bigard, B. Webster), Swingville 2032
2 Aspects, United Artists 4017, *5017*
1 Jazz Calendar, United Artists 4080, *5080* (reissue of United Artists 4017)
2 Sax a la Carter, United Artists 4094, *5094*
2 Moonglow, Verve 2025 (reissue of Norgran 1015)
4 The Urbane Jazz of Roy Eldridge and Benny Carter, Verve 8202

Betty Carter
4 The Modern Sound of Betty Carter, ABC-Paramount 363, *363*
3 Ray Charles and Betty Carter, ABC-Paramount 385, *385*
4 Round Midnight, Atco 152
5 Meet Betty Carter and Ray Bryant, Epic 3202
5 Out There, Peacock 90
5 Inside Betty Carter, United Artists 3379, *6379*
2 Inside Betty Carter, United Artists 5639 (reissue of above)

Ron Carter
3 Where (w/E. Dolphy), New Jazz 8265

Dick Carey
1 Dixieland Goes Progressive, Golden Crest 3024
1 Hot and Cool, Stereocraft *106*

Al Casey
2 Al Casey Quartet, Moodsville 12
3 Buck Jumpin', Swingville 2007

Lee Castle
2 Dixieland Heaven, Davis 105

Serge Chaloff
5 Blue Serge, Capitol 742
5 Boston Blow-Up, Capitol 6510
5 New Stars, New Sounds, Vol. 2 (w/O. Pettiford), Mercer 1003 (10")
5 Serge Chaloff and Boots Mussulli, Storyville 310 (10")
5 The Fable of Mabel, Storyville 317 (10")

[27] See also *Count Basie, Art Tatum*.

Paul Chambers[28]
2 Whims of Chambers, Blue Note 1534
3 Paul Chambers Quintet, Blue Note 1564
2 Bass on Top, Blue Note 1569
5 A Jazz Delegation From the East, Jazz West 7
3 A Jazz Delegation From the East, Score 4033 (reissue of Jazz West 7)
1 Go, Vee Jay 1014, *1014*
1 1st Bassman, Vee Jay 3012

Eddie Chamblee
2 Chamblee Music, EmArcy 36124 or Mercury *60127*
2 Doodlin', EmArcy 36131 or Mercury *80007*

Jim Chapin
1 Jim Chapin Sextet, Classic Editions 6 (includes Prestige 213)
1 Skin Tight (w/B. Wilber), Classic Editions 7
2 Jim Chapin Ensemble (w/P. Woods), Prestige 213 (10")

Ray Charles[29]
1 The Genius Hits the Road, ABC-Paramount 335, *335*
1 Dedicated to You, ABC-Paramount 355, *355*
3 Ray Charles and Betty Carter, ABC-Paramount 385, *385*
1 Modern Sounds in Country and Western Music, ABC-Paramount 410, *410*
1 More Modern Sounds in Country and Western Music, ABC-Paramount 435, *435*
1 Ingredients in a Recipe For Soul, ABC-Paramount 465, *465*
1 Sweet and Sour Tears, ABC-Paramount 480, *480*
1 Have a Smile With Me, ABC-Paramount 495, *495*
1 Live in Concert, ABC-Paramount 500, *500*

Teddy Charles (aka Ted Cohen)[30]
4 Teddy Charles Tentet, Atlantic 1229
4 Word From Bird, Atlantic 1274
3 A Salute to Hamp, Bethlehem 6032, *6032*
3 On Campus (w/Z. Sims), Bethlehem 6044, *6044*
3 Vibe-Rant, Elektra 136
1 Teddy Charles Trio Plays Duke Ellington, Josie 3505, *3505* (reissue of Jubilee 1047)
3 Three for Duke, Jubilee 1047
4 Teddy Charles and his Trio, Prestige 132 (10")
5 Collaboration West (w/S. Rogers), Prestige 7028
5 Evolution, Prestige 7078
2 Russia Goes Jazz, United Artists 3365, *6365*
4 Metronome Presents Jazz in the Garden at the Museum of Modern Art, Warwick 2033, *2033*

Doc Cheatham, see *Shorty Baker*.

Buddy Childers
1 Sam Songs, Liberty 6009
1 Buddy Childers Quartet, Liberty 6013

Charlie Christian
3 Jazz Immortal 1941, Counterpoint 548 (red plastic; includes Esoteric 1)
4 Jazz Immortal, Esoteric 1 (10") (red plastic)
2 Jazz Immortal, Esoteric 548 (reissue of Counterpoint 548)

[28] See also *Roy Haynes*.
[29] See also p. 51.
[30] See also *Prestige Jazz Quartet*.
NOTE: All Blue Note LPs with original addresses on label; see p. 128.

June Christy, see p. 106.

Sonny Clark[31]
3 Dial "S" for Sonny, Blue Note 1570
4 Sonny's Crib, Blue Note 1576, *81576*
4 Sonny Clark Trio, Blue Note 1579, *81579*
3 Cool Struttin', Blue Note 1588, *81588*
5 Leapin' and Lopin', Blue Note 4091, *84091*
4 Max Roach, Sonny Clark, George Duviver, Time 52101, *2101* (reissue of Time 70010)
5 Sonny Clark Trio, Time 70010

Kenny Clarke
2 Kenny Clarke Plays Andre Hodeir, Epic 3376
1 Kenny Clarke's Sextet, Savoy 12006
1 Wilkins-Clarke Septet, Savoy 12007
1 Klook's Clique, Savoy 12065

Kenny Clarke-Francy Boland Band
2 Jazz is Universal, Atlantic 1401, *1401*
2 Clarke-Boland Big Band, Atlantic 1404, *1404*
2 The Golden 8, Blue Note 4092, *84092*
2 Now Hear Our Meaning, Columbia 2314, *9114*

James Clay[32]
2 Sound of the Wide Open Spaces (w/D. Newman), Riverside 327, *1178*
2 A Double Dose of Soul, Riverside 349, *9349*

Buck Clayton[33]
1 The Huckebuck and Robbins' Nest, Columbia 546
1 How High the Fi, Columbia 567
  Buck Clayton Jams Benny Goodman Favorites, Columbia 614
1 Jumpin' at the Woodside, Columbia 701
1 Cat Meets Chick (w/J. Rushing, A. Moore), Columbia 778
1 All the Cats Join In, Columbia 882
1 Songs for Swingers, Columbia 1320, *8123*
2 The Classic Swing of Buck Clayton, Riverside 142
3 Harry Edison Swings Buck Clayton and Vice-Versa, Verve 8293, *6016*

Jimmy Cleveland[34]
1 Introducing Jimmy Cleveland and His All Stars, EmArcy 36066
1 Cleveland Style, EmArcy 36126 or Mercury 20553, *60121*
1 A Map of Cleveland, Mercury 20442, 60117
1 Rhythm Crazy, Mercury/EmArcy 26003, *66003*

Claude Cloud, see p. 52.

Arnett Cobb
4 Swinging With Arnett Cobb, Apollo 105 (10")
2 Ballads by Cobb, Moodsville 14
2 Blow, Arnett, Blow (w/E. Davis), Prestige 7151
2 Party Time, Prestige 7165
2 More Party Time, Prestige 7175
2 Smooth Sailing, Prestige 7184

2 Movin' Right Along, Prestige 7216
2 Sizzlin', Prestige 7227 (yellow label), 7227 (black label)

Al Cohn[35]
4 Al Cohn Quintet (w/B. Brookmeyer), Coral 57118
4 Cohn on the Saxophone, Dawn 1110
5 Al Cohn Quartet, Progressive 1003
5 Al Cohn Quartet, Progressive 3002 (10")
5 Al Cohn Quintet, Progressive 3004 (10")
3 East Coast-West Coast (w/S. Rogers; one side each), RCA 1020
3 Mr. Music, RCA 1024
3 The Natural Seven, RCA 1116
3 Four Brass, One Tenor, RCA 1161
3 That Old Feeling, RCA 1207
1 Al Cohn's Tones, Savoy 12048 (reissue of Progressive 3002 and 3004)

Al Cohn-Zoot Sims[36]
4 Al and Zoot, Coral 57171
3 Either Way, Fred Miles 1
1 You 'N Me, Mercury 20606, *60606*
3 From A to Z, RCA 1282

Jerry Coker
1 Modern Music From Indiana University, Fantasy 3214

Cozy Cole[37]
2 Hot and Cozy, Continental 16007 (4 titles by Cole, 7 titles by Hot Lips Page)
1 After Hours, Grand Award 334
1 Concerto for Cozy, Savoy 14010

Nat King Cole, see p. 107.

Earl Coleman
4 Earl Coleman Returns, Prestige 7045

Ornette Coleman
1 At the "Golden Circle" Stockholm, Vol. 1, Blue Note 4224, *84224* (label reads New York USA)
1 At the "Golden Circle" Stockholm, Vol. 2, Blue Note 4225, *84225* (label reads New York USA)
1 Town Hall—1962, ESP 1006, *1006*
1 The Music of Ornette Coleman, RCA 2982

Johnny Coles
1 Little Johnny C, Blue Note 4144, *84144*
2 The Warm Sound, Epic 16015, *17015*

Buddy Collette[38]
1 Calm, Cool and Collette, ABC-Paramount 179
1 Aloha to Jazz, Bel Canto 1002, *1002* (one side unrelated Hawaiian music; two Collette titles from Dooto 245)
3 Jazz on the Bounce (w/C. Counce; one side each), Bel Canto 1004, *1004* (1 LP in a box; includes two titles from Dooto 245)
1 Everybody's Buddy, Challenge 603
2 Man of Many Parts, Contemporary 3522
1 Nice Day With Buddy Collette, Contemporary 3531

[31] See also *Buddy DeFranco*.
[32] See also *Lawrence Marable*.
[33] See also *Duke Ellington, Tommy Gwaltney, Flip Philips, Paul Quinichette, Buddy Tate*.
[34] See also *Seldon Powell*.
NOTE: All Blue Note LPs with original oddresses on label; see p. 128.

[35] See also *Bob Brookmeyer, Zoot Sims*.
[36] See also *Jack Kerouac*, p. 112.
[37] See also p. 52.
[38] See also *Red Callender, Chico Hamilton, Herbie Mann*.

JAZZ RECORDINGS

4 Tanganyika (w/J. Hall, C. Hamilton), Dig 101
2 Buddy's Best, Dooto 245
2 Jazz Loves Paris, Specialty 5002
1 Star Studded Cast, Tampa 34 (reissue of Dig 101)

Al "Jazzbo" Collins
4 East Coast Jazz Scene, Coral 57035
1 In the Purple Grotto, Old Town 2001

Dick Collins[39]
2 Horn of Plenty, RCA 1019
2 King Richard the Swing Hearted, RCA 1027

John Coltrane[40]
2 Blue Trane, Blue Note 1577 (W. 63rd St. address on label)
5 Cosmic Music, Coltrane Records *4950* (private pressing)
5 Cosmic Music, Coltrane Records 5000 (private pressing)
5 Coltrane, Prestige 7105
5 John Coltrane With the Red Garland Trio, Prestige 7123
4 Soultrane, Prestige 7142
4 Cattin' With Coltrane and Quinichette, Prestige 7158
3 Lush Life, Prestige 7188
2 Settin' the Pace, Prestige 7213
2 Standard Coltrane, Prestige 7243
2 Stardust, Prestige 7268
3 Dakar, Prestige 7280
2 Coltrane Time, United Artists 14001, *15001* (reissue of United Artist 4014; see *Cecil Taylor*)

Eddie Condon[41]
1 Bixieland, Columbia 719
1 Louis Armstrong and Eddie Condon at Newport (one side each), Columbia 913
1 The Roaring Twenties, Columbia 1089
1 Chicago Jazz Album, Decca 8029
1 A Night at Eddie Condon's, Decca 8281
1 Ivy League Jazz, Decca 8282
1 Eddie Condon is Uptown Now, MGM 3651

Chris Connor, see p. 107.

Junior Cook
1 Junior's Cookin', Jazzland 58, *958*

Bob Cooper[42]
3 Kenton Presents Bob Cooper, Capitol 6501 (10")
3 Shifting Winds (w/J. Giuffre, C. Williamson), Capitol 6513
2 Coop!, Contemporary 3511, *7012*

Chick Corea
1 Tones for Joan's Bones, Vortex *2004*

Bob Corwin
2 Bob Corwin Quartet (w/D. Elliott), Riverside 220

---
[39] See also *Nat Pierce*.
[40] See also *Gene Ammons, Kenny Burrell, Ray Draper, Wilbur Harden, Thelonious Monk, Mal Waldron*.
[41] See also *Boyce Brown*.
[42] See also *June Christy* (p. 106), *Bud Shank*.
NOTE: All Prestige LPs, yellow label.

Eddie Costa[43]
3 Guys and Dolls Like Vibes, Coral 57230
5 House of Blue Lights, Dot 3206, *25206*
2 The Eddie Costa Quintet, Interlude 508, *1008* (reissue of Mode 118)
3 Eddie Costa—Vinnie Burke Trio, Jubilee 1025
4 Eddie Costa Quintet, Mode 118
2 The Eddie Costa Trio with Rolf Kuhn and Dick Johnson (4 titles) /Mat Mathews/Don Elliott at Newport, Verve 8237

Curtis Counce
3 Jazz on the Bounce (w/B. Collette; one side each), Bel Canto 1004, *1004* (1 LP in a box)
3 The Curtis Counce Group, Contemporary 3526
3 You Get More Bounce with Curtis Counce, Contemporary 3539
3 Carl's Blues, Contemporary 3574, *7574*
3 Landslide, Contemporary *7526* (stereo issue of Contemporary 3526)
3 Exploring the Future, Dooto 247

Ida Cox
1 The Moanin' Groanin' Blues, Riverside 147
2 Blues for Rampart Street (w/C. Hawkins), Riverside 374, *9374*

Sonny Criss[44]
5 Jazz U.S.A., Imperial 9006
5 Go Man! It's Sonny Criss and Modern Jazz, Imperial 9020
5 Sonny Criss Plays Cole Porter, Imperial 9024
5 Criss-Cross, Imperial 9205, *12205*
5 At the Crossroads, Peacock 91
1 This is Criss, Prestige 7511, *7511*
2 Up, Up & Away, Prestige *7530*

Bob Crosby
1 Bob Crosby's Bobcats, Capitol 293
1 The Bob Cats Ball, Coral 57005
1 Bobcats Blues, Coral 57060
1 Bobcats on Parade, Coral 57061
1 Bob Crosby in Hi-Fi, Coral 57062
1 Bob Crosby and his Orchestra (1936–1956), Coral 57089
1 Bobcats in Hi-Fi, Coral 57170
1 Five Feet of Swing, Decca 8042
1 Bob Cats, Decca 8061

Mike Cuozzo
3 Mike Cuozzo with the Costa-Burke Trio, Jubilee 1027
2 Mighty Mike Cuozzo, Savoy 12051

Ted Curson
5 Plenty of Horn, Old Town 2003 (blue plastic)

Bert Dahlander (aka Bert Dale)
1 Skal, Verve 8253

Joe Daley
1 Joe Daley Trio, RCA 2763, *2763*

Tadd Dameron[45]
2 Classics in Modern Jazz, Vol. 2, Jazzland 68, *968*

---
[43] See also *Mike Cuozzo, John Mehegan*.
[44] See also *The Six*.
[45] See also *Fats Navarro*.

140 JAZZ

5 Fontainebleau, Prestige, 7037
5 Mating Call, Prestige 7070
3 The Magic Touch, Riverside 419

Hank D'Amico
2 We Brought Our Axes, Bethlehem 7 (w/A. Sachs; one side each)

Dartmouth Indian Chiefs
1 Chiefly Jazz, Transition 23

Kenny Davern
1 In the Gloryland, Elektra *201*

Eddie "Lockjaw" Davis[46]
1 Best of Eddie "Lockjaw" Davis (w/S. Scott), Bethlehem 6069 (reissue of various King titles)
1 Kickin' & Wailin', Continental 16001
1 Alma Alegre, Jazzland 97, *997* (reissue of Riverside 373)
2 Modern Jazz Expressions, King 506
2 Jazz With a Horn, King 526
2 Jazz With a Beat, King 566
2 Big Beat Jazz, King 599
2 Uptown, King 606
2 Eddie "Lockjaw" Davis with Shirley Scott, Moodsville 4
2 Misty, Moodsville 30
2 The Eddie "Lockjaw" Davis Cookbook, Vol. 1 (w/S. Scott, J. Richardson), Prestige 7141
2 Jaws (w/S. Scott), Prestige 7154
2 The Eddie "Lockjaw" Davis Cookbook, Vol. 2 (w/ S. Scott, J. Richardson), Prestige 7161
1 Jaws in Orbit (w/Scott), Prestige 7171
1 Bacalao (w/S. Scott), Prestige 7178
3 Trane Whistle, Prestige 7206
1 The Eddie "Lockjaw" Davis Cookbook, Vol. 3, Prestige 7219
1 Goin' to the Meeting, Prestige 7242
2 Lock the Fox, RCA 3652, *3652*
2 The Fox and the Hounds, RCA 3741, *3741*
2 Love Calls (w/P. Gonsalves), RCA 3882, *3882*
3 Afro-Jaws, Riverside 373, *9373*
2 Jawbreakers (w/H. Edison), Riverside 430, *9430*
2 Eddie "Lockjaw" Davis Trio, Roost 2227
1 Eddie "Lockjaw" Davis Trio (w/S. Scott), Roost 2227 (different LP than above)
2 Count Basie Presents Eddie Davis Trio & Joe Newman, Roulette 52007, *52007*
1 Eddie Davis Trio, Roulette 52019, *52019*

Eddie "Lockjaw" Davis-Johnny Griffin
2 Tough Tenors, Jazzland 31, *931*
2 Lookin' at Monk, Jazzland 39, *939*
2 Griff and Lock, Jazzland 42, *942*
2 Blues Up and Down, Jazzland 60, *960*
2 Tough Tenor Favorites, Jazzland 76, *976*
2 The Tenor Scene, Prestige 7191
2 Battle Stations, Prestige 7282

Miles Davis
4 Miles Davis Vol. 1, Blue Note 1501 (Lex. Ave. address on label)
4 Miles Davis Vol. 2, Blue Note 1502 (Lex. Ave. address on label)
2 Birth of the Cool, Capitol 762
2 Miles Ahead & 19, Columbia 1041 (original "boat" cover)
1 Jazz Track, Columbia 1268[47]
5 Blue Moods, Debut 120
5 The Musings of Miles, Prestige 7007
5 Dig (w/S. Rollins), Prestige 7012
5 Miles, Prestige 7014
5 Miles Davis and Horns, Prestige 7025
4 Quintet/Sextet (w/M. Jackson), Prestige 7034
4 Collectors' Items, Prestige 7044
4 Blue Haze, Prestige 7054
3 Walkin', Prestige 7076
3 Cookin', Prestige 7094
3 Bags' Groove, Prestige 7109
3 Relaxin', Prestige 7129
3 Miles Davis and the Modern Jazz Giants, Prestige 7150
3 Workin', Prestige 7166
2 Early Miles, Prestige 7168 (reissue of Prestige 7025)
3 Steamin', Prestige 7200

Walter Davis, Jr.
4 Davis Cup, Blue Note 4018 (W. 63rd St. address on label)

Wild Bill Davison
1 Swingin' Dixie, Bear 10002
1 Pretty Wild, Columbia 871
1 With Strings Attached, Columbia 983
1 Mild and Wild Dixieland Jazz, Commodore 30009
2 Sweet and Hot, Riverside 211

Blossom Dearie, see p. 108.

Rusty Dedrick
1 Salute to Bunny, Counterpoint 552
2 Counterpoint For Six Valves (w/D. Elliott), Riverside 218

Buddy DeFranco[48]
2 University of New Mexico Stage Band, Advance Guard 1001
1 Pacific Standard (Swingin'!) Time (w/T. Gumina), Decca 4031, *74031*
1 Presenting the Buddy DeFranco-Tommy Gumina Quartet, Mercury 20685, *60685*
1 Kaleidoscope (w/T. Gumina), Mercury 20743, *60743*
1 Polytones (w/T. Gumina), Mercury 20833, *60833*
1 The Girl From Ipanema (w/T. Gumina), Mercury 20900, *60900*
5 The King of the Clarinet, MGM 177 (10")
4 Buddy DeFranco With Strings, MGM 253 (10")
4 Buddy DeFranco, MGM 3396 (includes MGM 177)
5 The Progressive Mr. DeFranco, Norgran 1006
5 The Artistry of Buddy DeFranco, Norgran 1012
4 Buddy DeFranco and Oscar Peterson Play George Gershwin, Norgran 1016
5 Buddy DeFranco Quartet, Norgran 1026
5 Jazz Tones, Norgran 1068 or Verve 8158
4 Mr. Clarinet, Norgran 1069 or Verve 8159 (partial reissue of Norgran 1026)

---

[46] See also *Arnett Cobb, Red Garland, Coleman Hawkins, Sonny Stitt.*
NOTE: All Prestige LPs yellow label.

[47] One side original soundtrack for the film *L'Ascenseur pour l'echafaud* (*Elevator to the Scaffold*); other side Miles Davis Sextet.
[48] See also *Art Tatum.*
NOTE: All Prestige LPs yellow label.

5 In a Mellow Mood, Norgran 1079 or Verve 8169
4 The Buddy DeFranco Wailers, Norgran 1085 or Verve 8175
4 Odalisque, Norgran 1094 or Verve 8182 (reissue of Norgran 1006)
4 Autumn Leaves, Norgran 1096 or Verve 8183 (reissue of Norgran 1012)
1 Blues Bag, Vee Jay 2506
3 The George Gershwin Song Book (w/O. Peterson), Verve 2022 (reissue of Norgran 1016)
3 Broadway Showcase, Verve 2033
3 Buddy DeFranco Plays Benny Goodman, Verve 2089
3 Buddy DeFranco Plays Artie Shaw, Verve 2090
3 I Hear Benny Goodman and Artie Shaw, Verve 2108, *6032* (*62108*)
3 Buddy DeFranco and the Oscar Peterson Quartet, Verve 8210
5 Cooking the Blues (w/S. Clark), Verve 8221
5 Sweet and Lovely, Verve 8224
3 Bravura, Verve 8315, *6051* (*68315*)
3 Generalissimo, Verve 8363, *6132* (*68363*)
3 Wholly Cats, Verve 8375, *6150* (*68375*)
3 Closed Session, Verve 8382, *68382*
3 Live Date!, Verve 8383, *68383*

John Dennis
2 New Jazz Expressions, Debut 121

Wilbur DeParis
1 Wilbur DeParis and his New Orleans Jazz, Atlantic 1219, *1219*
1 Marchin' and Swingin', Atlantic 1233, *1233*
1 Wilbur DeParis at Symphony Hall, Atlantic 1253, *1253*
1 New Orleans Blues (w/J. Witherspoon), Atlantic 1266
1 Wilbur DeParis Plays Cole Porter, Atlantic 1288
1 Wilbur DeParis Plays Something Old, New, Gay, Blue, Atlantic 1300, *1300*
1 That's a Plenty, Atlantic 1318, *1318*
1 The Wild Jazz Age, Atlantic 1336, *1336*
1 Wilbur DeParis on the Riviera, Atlantic 1363, *1363*

Paul Desmond
2 Gerry Mulligan Quartet/Paul Desmond Quintet (one side each), Fantasy 3220
2 Paul Desmond Quartet (w/D. Elliott), Fantasy 3235
1 Desmond Blue, RCA 2438, *2438*
2 Take Ten, RCA 2569, *2569*
1 Two of a Mind (w/G. Mulligan), RCA 2624, *2624*
2 Bossa Antigua, RCA 3320, *3320*
2 Glad to Be Unhappy, RCA 3407, *3407*
2 Easy Living, RCA 3480, *3480*
3 The Gerry Mulligan-Paul Desmond Quartet, Verve 8246
1 Blues in Time, Verve 8478, *68478* (reissue of Verve 8246)
2 Paul Desmond and Friends, Warner Bros. 1356, *1356*

Jimmy Deuchar
1 Pub Crawling, Contemporary 3529
2 Showcase, Discovery 2004 (10")

Vic Dickenson
2 Mainstream (w/J. Thomas; one side each), Atlantic 1303, *1303*
4 Vic's Boston Story, Storyville 920
1 Vic Dickenson Septet, Vol. 1, Vanguard 8520
1 Vic Dickenson Septet, Vol. 2, Vanguard 8521

Walt Dickerson
2 Unity, Audio Fidelity 2131, *6131*
2 Jazz Impressions of "Lawrence of Arabia", Dauntless 4313, *6313*
4 This is Walt Dickerson, New Jazz 8254
4 A Sense of Direction, New Jazz 8268
4 Relativity, New Jazz 8275
4 To My Queen, New Jazz 8283

Bill Dixon
1 Intents and Purposes, RCA 3844, *3844*

Baby Dodds
1 Talking and Drum Solos, Folkways 30 (10")

Johnny Dodds
1 The King of New Orleans Clarinets, Brunswick 58016 (10")
1 Johnny Dodds and Kid Ory, Epic 3207 or Epic 16004
1 Johnny Dodds, RCA Vintage 558
1 New Orleans Clarinet, Riverside 104
1 In the Alley, Riverside 135
2 Washboard Band, "X" 3006 (10")

Jerry Dodgian, see Charlie Marian.

Eric Dolphy[49]
2 Iron Man, Douglas 785
5 Conversations, FM 308
2 Last Date, Limelight 82013, *86013* (fold-out cover w/photos)
5 Outward Bound, New Jazz 8236 (original art cover)
2 Outward Bound, New Jazz 8236 (photo cover)
3 Caribe (w/Latin Jazz Quintet), New Jazz 8251
5 Out There, New Jazz 8252 (original art cover)
2 Out There, New Jazz 8252 (photo cover)
3 Eric Dolphy at the Five Spot, Vol. 1, New Jazz 8260
3 Far Cry, New Jazz 8270

Lou Donaldson
4 Quartet/Quintet/Sextet, Blue Note 1537
3 Wailing With Lou, Blue Note 1545
3 Swing and Soul, Blue Note 1566
5 Lou Takes Off, Blue Note 1591
2 Lou Takes Off, Blue Note *81591* (later pressing)
2 Blues Walk, Blue Note 1593
2 The Time is Right, Blue Note 4025
2 Sunny Side Up, Blue Note 4036
1 Down Home, Sunset 5258 ("fake" stereo; reissue of Blue Note 1537)

Kenny Dorham
4 The Jazz Prophets, ABC Paramount 122
4 'Round About Midnight at the Cafe Bohemia, Blue Note 1524
3 Afro-Cuban, Blue Note 1535
2 Trompeta Toccata, Blue Note 4181, *84181*
5 Kenny Dorham Quintet, Debut 9 (10")
5 The Arrival of Kenny Dorham, Jaro 5007, *8007*
4 Quiet Kenny, New Jazz 8225
3 Inta Somethin' (w/J. McLean), Pacific Jazz 41, *41*
2 Jazz Contrasts (w/S. Rollins), Riverside 239, *1105*
4 2 Horns/2 Rhythm (w/E. Henry), Riverside 255
4 This is the Moment (Kenny Dorham Sings and Plays), Riverside 275

[49] See also Ron Carter, Ken McIntyre, Oliver Nelson, Mal Waldron.

3 Blue Spring, Riverside 297, *1139*
2 Jazz Contemporary, Time 52004, *2004*
3 Showboat, Time 52024, *2024*
1 Matador, United Artists 14007, *15007*

Bob Dorough
1 Devil May Care, Bethlehem 11
1 Just About Everything, Focus *336*

Jimmy Dorsey
1 Dixie By Dorsey, Columbia 608
1 The Fabulous Jimmy Dorsey, Fraternity 1008

Tommy Dorsey
1 Yes, Indeed!, RCA 1229
1 Hawaiian War Chant, RCA 1234
1 Tribute to Dorsey, Vol 1, RCA 1432
1 Tribute to Dorsey, Vol. 2, RCA 1433
1 Frankie and Tommy (w/F. Sinatra), RCA 1569
1 Tommy Dorsey and His Clambake Seven, RCA 1643
1 This is Tommy Dorsey and His Orchestra, RCA 3005
2 That Sentimental Gentleman, RCA 6003 (2 LP boxed set)
2 Greatest Band, 20th Century Fox 101-2 (2 LPs)

Dorsey Brothers
4 Last Moments of Greatness, Top Rank RTJ 1 (4 LP deluxe album w/illustrated booklet)
1 The Fabulous Dorseys in Hi-Fi, Columbia C2L-8 (2 LPs)

Double Six of Paris
1 Double Six of Paris, Capitol 10259, *10259*
1 Swingin' Singin', Philips 200-026, *600-026*
1 Dizzy Gillespie & the Double Six of Paris, Philips 200-106, *600-106*
1 Double Six of Paris Sing Ray Charles, Philips 200-141, *600-141*

Ray Draper
1 Ray Draper, Josie 3504, *3504* (reissue of Jubilee 1090)
3 Tuba Jazz, Jubilee 1090
4 Ray Draper Quintet (w/J. Coltrane), New Jazz 8228
5 Tuba Sounds, Prestige 7096

Kenny Drew[50]
5 Undercurrent, Blue Note 4059
5 Kenny Drew Trio, Blue Note 5023 (10″)
5 Talkin' & Walkin', Jazz West 4
1 Hard Bop, Jazzland 6 (reissue of Riverside 236)
1 Tough Piano Trio, Jazzland 9 (reissue of Riverside 224)
5 The Modernity of Kenny Drew, Norgran 1002
4 Kenny Drew and His Progressive Piano, Norgran 1066 or Verve 8156 (includes Norgran 1002)
5 Kenny Drew Trio, Riverside 224 (white label)
2 Kenny Drew Trio, Riverside 224 (blue label)
4 This is New, Riverside 236 (white label)
2 This is New, Riverside 236 (blue label)
2 Pal Joey, Riverside 249, *1112*

Allen Eager
2 New Trends of Jazz, Vol. 2, Savoy 9015 (10″)
2 Allen Eager, Vol. 2, Savoy 15044 (10″)

[50] See also *Jane Fielding, Sonny Rollins.*

Jon Eardley[51]
4 Jon Eardley in Hollywood, New Jazz 1105 (10″) or Prestige 205 (10″)
4 Hey There, Prestige 207 (10″)
5 Jon Eardley Seven, Prestige 7033

Billy Eckstine, see p. 109.

Harry "Sweets" Edison[52]
2 Ben Webster–Sweets Edison, Columbia 1891, *8691*
4 Sweets, Clef 717 or Verve 8097
3 Buddy Rich and Sweets Edison, Norgran 1038 or Verve 8129
2 The Inventive Mr. Edison, Pacific Jazz 11
2 Jawbreakers (w/E. Davis), Riverside 430, *9430*
1 Sweetenings, Roulette 52023, *52023*
1 Patented by Edison, Roulette 52041, *52041*
4 Gee Baby, Ain't I Good to You, Verve 8211
3 Harry "Sweets" Edison Swings Buck Clayton and Vice Versa, Verve 8293, *6016 (68293)*
3 The Swinger, Verve 8295, *6037 (68295)*
3 Mr. Swing, Verve 8353, *6118 (68353)*

Teddy Edwards
1 It's About Time (w/L. McCann), Pacific Jazz 6, *6*
2 Sunset Eyes, Pacific Jazz 14, *14*

Roy Eldridge[53]
3 Roy and Diz, Clef 641
3 Roy and Diz #2, Clef 671
3 Little Jazz, Clef 683 or Verve 8068
3 Rockin' Chair, Clef 704 or Verve 8088
3 Dale's Wail, Clef 705 or Verve 8089
1 Trumpet Battle (w/D. Gillespie), Clef 730 or Verve 8109
1 The Trumpet Kings (w/D. Gillespie), Clef 731 or Verve 8110
5 Little Jazz Four, Dial 304 (10″)
4 Little Jazz, Discovery 2009 (10″)
1 Roy's Got Rhythm, EmArcy 36084
4 Swing Goes Dixie, Verve 1010
3 That Warm Feeling, Verve 2088
4 The Urbane Jazz of Roy Eldridge and Benny Carter, Verve 8202
3 Swingin' on the Town, Verve 8389, *68389*

Duke Ellington[54]
2 Historically Speaking, Bethlehem 60
2 Duke Ellington Presents, Bethlehem 6005
2 Early Ellington, Brunswick 54007
3 Premiered by Ellington, Capitol 440 (10″)
3 Dance to the Duke, Capitol 637
3 Ellington Showcase, Capitol 679
3 The Ellington Era, Vol. 1, Columbia C3L-27 (3 LP boxed set)
5 The Ellington Era, Vol. 2, Columbia C3L-39 (3 LP boxed set)
2 Blue Light, Columbia 663
1 Liberian Suite, Columbia 848
2 Duke Ellington and the Buck Clayton All Stars at Newport, Columbia 933

[51] See also *Phil Woods.*
[52] See also *Cy Touff, Joe Williams, Lester Young.*
[53] See also *Count Basie, Coleman Hawkins, Gene Krupa, Oscar Peterson, Art Tatum, Lester Young.*
[54] See also *Ella Fitzgerald, Billy Strayhorn.*

JAZZ RECORDINGS

3 The Cosmic Scene, Columbia 1198
1 Newport 1958, Columbia 1245, *8072*
2 Duke Ellington at the Bal Masque, Columbia 1282, *8098*
3 Anatomy of a Murder (movie soundtrack), Columbia 1360, *8166*
2 Blues in Orbit, Columbia 1445, *8241*
3 Piano in the Background, Columbia 1546, *8346*
1 "Peer Gynt" Suite, Columbia 1597, *8397*
2 All American, Columbia 1790, *8590*
1 Midnight in Paris, Columbia 1907, *8707*
3 Piano in the Foreground, Columbia 2029, *8829*
3 Masterpieces by Ellington, Columbia 4418
3 Ellington Uptown, Columbia 4639
1 My People, Contact 1, *1*
3 Seattle Concert, RCA 1002
2 Duke Ellington's Greatest, RCA 1004
2 The Duke and His Men, RCA 1092
1 In a Mellotone, RCA 1364
1 At His Very Best, RCA 1715
2 Duke Ellington's Concert of Sacred Music, RCA 3582, *3582*
2 Far East Suite, RCA 3782, *3782*
3 And His Mother Called Him Bill, RCA 3906, *3906*
3 The Indispensable Duke Ellington, RCA 6009-2 (2 LPs)
1 Duke Ellington at the Cotton Club, RCA Camden 459
1 Daybreak Express, RCA Vintage 506
1 Jumpin' Punkins, RCA Vintage 517
1 Johnny Come Lately, RCA Vintage 541
1 Pretty Woman, RCA Vintage 553
1 Flaming Youth, RCA Vintage 568
2 Afro-Bossa, Reprise *6069*
2 The Symphonic Ellington, Reprise *6097*
1 Will Big Bands Ever Come Back?, Reprise *6168*
2 Concert in the Virgin Islands, Reprise *6185*
2 Birth of Big Band Jazz, Riverside 129 (w/F. Henderson; one side each)
1 Duets (w/B. Strayhorn), Riverside 475
2 Ellington Moods, Sesac 2701/2702
1 Blackbirds of 1928, Sutton 270
2 Money Jungle (w/C. Mingus, M. Roach), United Artists 14017, *15017*
2 Back to Back (w/J. Hodges), Verve 8317, *6055 (68317)*
2 Side by Side (w/J. Hodges), Verve 8345, *6109 (68345)*
1 Soul Call, Verve 8701, *68701*
3 Early Recordings, "X" 3037 (10")

Mercer Ellington
2 Stepping Into Swing Society, Coral 57225, *757225*
2 Colors in Rhythm, Coral 57293, *757293*

Don Elliott*
1 A Musical Offering, ABC-Paramount 106
1 Don Elliott at the Modern Jazz Room, ABC-Paramount 142
2 Jamaica Jazz (w/G. Evans, arr.), ABC-Paramount 008, *008*
2 Don Elliott: Mellophone, Bethlehem 12
2 Don Elliott Sings, Bethlehem 15
2 Don Elliott Quintet, RCA 1007
2 The Voice of Marty Bell, The Quartet of Don Elliott, Riverside 206
2 Counterpoint For Six Valves (w/R. Dedrick), Riverside 218
1 Vib-Rations, Savoy 12054

* See also *Bob Corwin, Eddie Costa, Paul Desmond, Sam Most.*

Don Ellis
1 How Time Passes, Candid 8004, *9004*
2 New Ideas. New Jazz 8257
2 Essence, Pacific Jazz 55, *55*

Herb Ellis
1 The Midnight Roll, Epic 16034, *17034*
1 Three Guitars in Bossa Nova Time, Epic 16036, *17036*
2 Together (w/S. Smith), Epic 16039, *17039*
3 Ellis in Wonderland, Norgran 1081 or Verve 8171
4 Nothing But the Blues, Verve 8252
3 Herb Ellis Meets Jimmy Giuffre, Verve 8311, *6045 (68311)*
2 Thank You Charlie Christian, Verve 8381, *68381*
1 Softly, Verve 8448, *68448*

Bob Enevoldsen
1 Smorgasbord, Liberty 6008
2 Bob Enevoldsen Quintet, Nocturne 6 (10")
1 Bob Enevoldsen Reflections in Jazz, Tampa 14

Rolf Ericson
2 Rolf Ericson and His All American Stars, EmArcy 36106

Booker Ervin
2 The Book Cooks, Bethlehem 6048
1 The In-Between, Blue Note 4283, *84283*
2 That's It, Candid 8014, *9014*
1 Structurally Sound, Pacific Jazz 10199, *20199*

Bill Evans[55]
5 New Jazz Conceptions, Riverside 223 (photo cover)
3 New Jazz Conceptions, Riverside 223 (art cover)
2 Everybody Digs Bill Evans, Riverside 291, *1129*
2 Portrait in Jazz, Riverside 315, *1162*
1 Explorations, Riverside 351, *9351*
2 Sunday at the Village Vanguard, Riverside 376, *9376*
1 Waltz for Debby, Riverside 399, *9399*
2 Moonbeams, Riverside 428, *9428*
2 Interplay, Riverside 445, *9445*
2 How My Heart Sings, Riverside 473, *9473*
1 Bill Evans Trio at Shelly's Manne-Hole, Riverside 487, *9487*
4 The Ivory Hunters (w/B. Brookmeyer, piano), United Artists 3044, *6044*
2 Undercurrent (w/J. Hall), United Artists 14003, *15003*
1 Undercurrent, United Artists 5640 (reissue of United Artists 14003)
2 Empathy (w/S. Manne), Verve 8497, *68497*
1 Trio '64, Verve 8578, *68578*
2 Trio '65, Verve 8613, *68613*
1 Bill Evans Trio with Symphony Orchestra, Verve 8640, *68640*
1 Intermodulation (w/J. Hall), Verve 8655, *68655*

Gil Evans[56]
1 Big Stuff, New Jazz 8215 (reissue of Prestige 7120)
3 Gil Evans and Ten, Prestige 7120
1 The Individualism of Gil Evans, Verve 8555, *68555*
1 New Bottle, Old Wine, World Pacific 1246, *1246*
1 Great Jazz Standards, World Pacific 1270, *1270*

Don Fagerquist
2 Music to Fill a Void, Mode 124

[55] See also *Cannonball Adderley, George Russell.*
[56] See also *Kenny Burrell, Don Elliott.*

JAZZ

Tal Farlow[57]
- 5 Tal Farlow Quartet, Blue Note 5042 (10")
- 5 The Artistry of Tal Farlow, Norgran 1014
- 5 The Interpretations of Tal Farlow, Norgran 1027
- 5 A Recital by Tal Farlow, Norgran 1030 or Verve 8123
- 5 The Tal Farlow Album, Norgran 1047 or Verve 8138
- 5 Autumn in New York, Norgran 1097 or Verve 8184 (reissue of Norgran 1014)
- 5 Tal, Norgran 1102 or Verve 8021
- 5 Fascinatin' Rhythm, Verve 8011 (reissue of Norgran 1027)
- 5 The Swingin' Guitar of Tal Farlow, Verve 8201
- 5 This is Tal Farlow, Verve 8289
- 4 The Guitar Artistry of Tal Farlow, Verve 8370, *6143* (*68370*)
- 4 Tal Farlow Plays the Music of Harold Arlen, Verve 8371, *68371*

Art Farmer[58]
- 1 Last Night When We Were Young, ABC-Paramount 200
- 1 Art, Argo 678, *678*
- 1 Perception, Argo 738, *738*
- 2 Interaction (w/J. Hall), Atlantic 1412, *1412*
- 3 "Live" at the Half-Note (w/J. Hall), Atlantic 1421, *1421*
- 2 To Sweden With Love (w/J. Hall), Atlantic 1430, *1430*
- 1 Sing Me Softly of the Blues, Atlantic 1442, *1442*
- 1 The Time and the Place, Columbia 2649, *9449*
- 2 Listen to Art Farmer and the Orchestra, Mercury 20766, *60766*
- 3 Early Art, New Jazz 8258
- 1 Work of Art, New Jazz 8278 (reissue of Prestige 7031)
- 1 Evening in Casablanca, New Jazz 8289 (reissue of Prestige 7017)
- 5 Art Farmer Quintet (w/G. Gryce), Prestige 7017
- 5 Art Farmer Septet, Prestige 7031
- 5 When Farmer Met Gryce, Prestige 7085
- 5 2 Trumpets (w/D. Byrd), Prestige 7062
- 5 3 Trumpets (w/D. Byrd, I. Sulieman), Prestige 7092
- 3 Farmer's Market, Prestige/New Jazz 8203
- 1 The Many Faces of Art Farmer, Scepter 521, *521*
- 3 Modern Art, United Artists 4007, *5007*
- 3 Brass Shout, United Artists 4047, *5047*
- 3 Aztec Suite, United Artists 4062, *5062*
- 2 Brass Shout, United Artists 4079, *5079* (reissue of United Artists 4047)
- 2 Aztec Suite, United Artists 4082, *5082* (reissue of United Artists 4062)

Leonard Feather[59]
- 2 Leonard Feather Presents 52nd Street, Interlude 511, *1011* (reissue of Mode 127)
- 2 Hi-Fi Suite (w/D. Hyman), MGM 3494
- 3 Oh Captain, MGM 3650
- 4 Leonard Feather Presents Bop, Mode 127

Victor Feldman[60]
- 2 Suite Sixteen, Contemporary 3541
- 2 With Mallets a Fore Thought, Interlude 510, *1010* (reissue of Mode 120)
- 3 Victor Feldman on Vibes, Mode 120
- 2 Merry Olde Soul, Riverside 366, *9366*

Maynard Ferguson[61]
- 2 Jam Session, EmArcy 36009
- 2 Maynard Ferguson Octet, EmArcy 36021
- 2 Dimensions, EmArcy 36044
- 2 Maynard Ferguson's Hollywood Party, EmArcy 36046
- 1 Around the Horn With Maynard Ferguson, EmArcy 36076
- 1 Boy With Lots of Brass, EmArcy 36114 or Mercury 20556, *60124*
- 3 Birdland Dream Band, Vik 1070
- 3 Birdland Dream Band, Vol. 2, Vik 1077

Jane Fielding
- 4 Jazz Trio for Voice, Piano and Bass, Jazz West 3
- 4 Embers Glow (w/K. Drew), Jazz West 5

Herbie Fields
- 2 Blow Hot, Blow Cool, Decca 8130 (w/Melrose Ave. Conservatory Orch; one side each)
- 2 A Night at Kitty's, RKO-Unique 124

Clare Fischer[62]
- 3 Thesaurus, Atlantic *1520*
- 2 First Time Out, Pacific Jazz 52, *52*
- 2 Surging Ahead, Pacific Jazz 67, *67*
- 1 Extension, Pacific Jazz 77, *77*
- 1 Manteca, Pacific Jazz 10096, *20096*

Ella Fitzgerald[63]
- 1 Songs in a Mellow Mood, Decca 8068
- 1 Lullabies of Birdland, Decca 8149
- 1 Sweet and Hot, Decca 8155
- 2 Pete Kelly's Blues (w/P. Lee), Decca 8166
- 1 Ella Sings Gershwin, Decca 8378
- 2 Ella and Her Fellas, Decca 8477
- 1 The First Lady of Song, Decca 8695
- 1 Miss Ella Fitzgerald and Mr. Nelson Riddle Invite You to Listen and Relax, Decca 8696
- 1 For Sentimental Reasons, Decca 8832
- 2 Ella Fitzgerald Sings the Cole Porter Songbook, Verve 4001-2 (2 LPs)
- 2 Ella Fitzgerald Sings the Rodgers and Hart Songbook, Verve 4002-2 (2 LPs)
- 2 Like Someone in Love, Verve 4004, *6000* (*64004*)
- 2 Ella Fitzgerald Sings the Duke Ellington Songbook, Vol. 1, Verve 4008-2 (2 LPs)
- 3 Ella Fitzgerald Sings the Duke Ellington Songbook, Vol. 2, Verve 4009-2 (2 LPs)
- 5 Ella Fitzgerald Sings the Duke Ellington Songbook, Verve 4010-4 (4 LP boxed set w/illustrated booklet; includes Verve 4008, 4009)
- 2 Ella Fitzgerald Sings the Irving Berlin Songbook, Verve 4019-2, *6005*-2 (*64019*-2) (2 LPs)
- 1 Ella Swings Lightly, Verve 4021, *6019* (*64021*)
- 5 Ella Fitzgerald Sings the George & Ira Gershwin Song Books, Verve 4029-5, *6082*-5 (*64029*-5) (Deluxe 5 LP boxed set containing single volume issues 4024-4028, album cover art, hard cover book entitled *The*

---

[57] See also *Gil Melle*.
[58] See also *John Benson Brooks, Curtis Fuller, Bennie Green, The Jazztet, Hal McKusick, Gerry Mulligan*.
[59] See also *Steve Allen, Ralph Burns*.
[60] See also *Curtis Amy*.
[61] See also *Chris Connor*, p. 107.
[62] See also *Joe Pass*.
[63] See also *Louis Armstrong, Count Basie, Chick Webb*.

JAZZ RECORDINGS

Gershwins and a 7" LP of Gershwin instrumentals arranged and conducted by N. Riddle) [64]
1 Ella Fitzgerald Sings Sweet Songs for Swingers, Verve 4023, 6072 *(64032)*
1 Hello Love, Verve 4034, 6100 *(64034)*
1 Get Happy, Verve 4036
2 Ella Fitzgerald Sings Songs from "Let No Man Write My Epitaph," Verve 4043, *64043* (movie soundtrack)
1 Ella Fitzgerald Sings Cole Porter, Verve 4049
1 Ella Fitzgerald Sings More Cole Porter, Verve 4050
1 Clap Hands Here Comes Charlie, Verve 4053, *64053*
1 Ella Fitzgerald Sings the Harold Arlen Songbook, Vol. 1, Verve 4057, *64057*
1 Ella Fitzgerald Sings the Harold Arlen Songbook, Vol. 2, Verve 4058, *64058*
1 Ella Fitzgerald Sings the Jerome Kern Songbook, Verve 4060, *64060*
1 These Are the Blues, Verve 4062
2 Ella Fitzgerald and Billie Holiday at Newport (one side each), Verve 8234, 6022 *(68234)*
2 Ella Fitzgerald at the Opera House, Verve 8264, 6026 *(68264)*

Tommy Flanagan
3 The Tommy Flanagan Trio, Moodsville 9
5 Overseas, Prestige 7134
2 Jazz . . . It's Magic, Regent 6055

Med Flory
1 Big Band, Josie 3506, *3506* (reissue of Jubilee 1066)
2 Jazz Wave, Jubilee 1066

Jimmy Forrest
2 Forrest Fire, New Jazz 8250
2 Soul Street, New Jazz 8293
2 Out of the Forrest, Prestige 7202
2 Most Much, Prestige 7218
2 Sit Down and Relax, Prestige 7235

Frank Foster
4 Here Comes Frank Foster, Blue Note 5043 (10")
5 Hope Meets Foster (w/E. Hope), Prestige 7021 (original)
4 Wail, Frank, Wail, Prestige 7021 (reissue)
1 No Count, Savoy 12078

Four Freshmen, see p. 109.

Bud Freeman
1 Bud Freeman, Bethlehem 29
1 Bud Freeman and his Summa Cum Laude Trio, Dot 3166
1 Midnight Session, Dot 3254, *25254*
1 Midnight at Eddie Condon's, EmArcy 36019
1 All Star Jazz, Harmony 7046
2 Chicago/Austin High School Jazz in Hi-Fi, RCA 1508
2 Bud Freeman All Stars (w/S. Baker), Swingville 2012
2 Something Tender & a Guitars (w/G. Barnes, K. Kress), United Artists 14003, *15003*

Russ Freeman
4 Russ Freeman/Richard Twardzik Trio (one side each), Pacific Jazz 1212
2 Quartet: Russ Freeman and Chet Baker, Pacific Jazz 1232

Don Friedman
2 A Day in the City, Riverside 384, *9384*
1 Circle Waltz, Riverside 431, *9431*
1 Flashback, Riverside 463, *9463*
1 Dreams and Explorations, Riverside 485, *9485*

Tony Fruscella
5 Tony Fruscella, Atlantic 1220

Curtis Fuller
3 The Opener, Blue Note 1567
3 Bone and Bari, Blue Note 1572
4 Curtis Fuller, Vol. 3 (w/A. Farmer), Blue Note 1583
3 The Magnificent Trombone of Curtis Fuller, Epic 16013, *17013*
3 South American Cookin', Epic 16020, *17020*
4 Curtis Fuller With Red Garland, New Jazz 8277
5 New Trombone, Prestige 7107
1 Blues-ette, Savoy 12141
2 Curtis Fuller Jazztet, Savoy 12143
2 Imagination, Savoy 12144
2 Curtis Fuller, Savoy 12151
2 Images, Savoy 12164
3 Jazz Conference Abroad, Smash 27034, *67034*
3 Curtis Fuller and Hamp Hawes With French Horns, Status 8305
4 Sliding Easy, United Artists 4041, *5041*
4 Boss of the Soul Stream Trombone, Warwick 2038, *2038*

Gil Fuller
1 Gil Fuller and the Monterey Jazz Festival Orchestra (w/Dizzy Gillespie), Pacific Jazz 93, *93*

Jerry Fuller
1 Clarinet Portrait, Andex 3008, *3008*

Slim Gaillard
3 Opera in Vout (Gaillard)/Boogie-Woogie at the Philharmonic (M. L. Lewis), Clef 506 (10")
3 Slim Gaillard Rides Again, Dot 3190, *25190*
3 Mish Mash, Mercury 126 (10")
3 Slim Gaillard and his Musical Aggregations, Wherever He May Be, Norgran 13 (10")
1 Rhythm and Boogie, Royale 75 (10")
4 Smorgasbord, Verve 2013 (reissue of various Mercury and Norgran titles)

Barry Galbraith
2 Guitar and the Wind, Decca 9200

Dick Garcia
3 A Message From Garcia, Dawn 1100 (1–Seeco 428)

Russ Garcia
2 The Johnny everGreens, ABC-Paramount 147
2 Four Horns and a Lush Life, Bethlehem 46
3 Wigville, Bethlehem 1040 (10")
2 Jazz Music for Birds and Hep Cats (w/M. Paich), Bethlehem 6039
2 Listen to the Music of Russell Garcia and His Orchestra, Kapp 1050

---

[64] Verve also released 200 "limited edition" sets of the Gershwin songbooks, each in a solid walnut box with pearlized leather pockets for the 5 LPs. The original price of the limited edition set was $100.

NOTE: All Blue Note LPs with original addresses on label; see p. 128.

146   JAZZ

Red Garland[65]
- 1 The Nearness of You, Jazzland 62, *962*
- 1 Solar, Jazzland 73, *973*
- 2 Red's Good Groove, Jazzland 87, *987*
- 2 Red Garland Plus Eddie "Lockjaw" Davis, Moodsville 1
- 1 Red Alone, Moodsville 3
- 1 The Red Garland Trio, Moodsville 6
- 1 Alone With the Blues, Moodsville 10
- 4 A Garland of Red, Prestige 7064
- 4 Red Garland's Piano, Prestige 7086
- 4 Groovy, Prestige 7113
- 5 All Mornin' Long (w/J. Coltrane), Prestige 7130
- 2 Manteca (w/R. Barreto), Prestige 7139
- 5 All Kinds of Weather, Prestige 7148
- 1 Red in Bluesville, Prestige 7157
- 1 Red Garland at the Prelude, Prestige 7170
- 3 Soul Junction, Prestige 7181
- 1 Rojo, Prestige 7193
- 3 High Pressure, Prestige 7209
- 3 Dig It, Prestige 7229
- 1 When There Are Grey Skies, Prestige 7258
- 1 Can't See For Lookin', Prestige 7276
- 1 Soul Burnin', Prestige 7307 (blue label)
- 4 Sugan (w/P. Woods), Status 8304
- 1 Little Darlin', Status 8314
- 1 Live, Status 8326

Erroll Garner[66]
- 2 Errol Garner Rhapsody, Atlantic 109 (10")
- 2 Piano Solos, Vol. 1, Atlantic 112 (10")
- 2 Passport to Fame, Atlantic 128 (10")
- 2 Piano Solos, Vol. 2, Atlantic 135 (10")
- 2 Overture to Dawn, Vol. 1, Blue Note 5007 (10")
- 2 Overture to Dawn, Vol. 2, Blue Note 5008 (10")
- 2 Overture to Dawn, Vol. 3, Blue Note 5014 (10")
- 2 Overture to Dawn, Vol. 4, Blue Note 5015 (10")
- 2 Overture to Dawn, Vol. 5, Blue Note 5016 (10")
- 1 Erroll Garner, Columbia 535
- 1 Erroll Garner Gems, Columbia 583
- 1 Gone Garner Gonest, Columbia 617
- 1 Erroll Garner Contrasts, EmArcy 36001
- 1 Erroll, EmArcy 36069
- 3 Erroll Garner, Dial 205 (10")
- 3 By Gaslight, Dial 902
- 1 Piano Variations, King 540
- 1 Mambo Moves Garner, Mercury 20055
- 1 Afternoon of an Elf, Mercury 20090
- 1 One World Concert, Reprise 6080, *9-6080*
- 1 Giants of the Piano, Roost 2213 (w/A. Tatum; one side each)

Matthew Gee
- 3 Jazz by Gee, Riverside 221

Herb Geller
- 2 Herb Geller Plays Gypsy, Atco 109, *109*
- 2 The Gellers (w/L. Geller), EmArcy 36024
- 2 Herb Geller Sextette, EmArcy 36040
- 2 Herb Geller Plays, EmArcy 36045
- 1 Alto Saxophone, Josie 3502, *3502* (reissue of Jubilee 1044)

- 3 Fire in the West, Jubilee 1044, *1044*
- 2 Stax of Saxes, Jubilee 1094, *1094*

Stan Getz[67]
- 3 Stan Getz Plays, Clef 137 (10")
- 3 The Artistry of Stan Getz, Clef 143 (10")
- 5 In Retrospect, Dale 21 (10")
- 5 Billie and Stan (w/B. Holiday), Dale 25 (10")
- 1 Long Island Sound, New Jazz 8214 (reissue of Prestige 7002)
- 3 Interpretations by the Stan Getz Quintet, Norgran 1000
- 3 Interpretations by the Stan Getz Quintet, #2, Norgran 1008
- 3 Interpretations by the Stan Getz Quintet, #3, Norgran 1029 or Verve 8122
- 3 West Coast Jazz, Norgran 1032 or Verve 8028
- 3 Hamp and Getz, Norgran 1037 or Verve 8128
- 3 Stan Getz Plays, Norgran 1042 or Verve 8133
- 3 Diz and Getz, Norgran 1050 or Verve 8141
- 3 Stan Getz '57, Norgran 1087 or Verve 8029
- 3 More West Coast Jazz, Norgran 1088 or Verve 8177
- 4 Stan Getz at the Shrine, Norgran 2000-2 or Verve 8188-2 (2 LP boxed set)
- 5 Quartets, Prestige 7002
- 2 The Sound, Roost 2207
- 2 Stan Getz at Storyville, Roost 2209
- 2 At Storyville, Vol. 2, Roost 2225
- 3 Highlights in Modern Jazz (w/W. Gray; one side each), Seeco 7 (10")
- 3 Stan Getz and the Cool Sounds, Verve 8200
- 2 Stan Getz in Stockholm, Verve 8213
- 2 Getz Meets Mulligan in Hi-Fi, Verve 8249, *6003* (*68249*)
- 2 Stan Getz and the Oscar Peterson Trio, Verve 8251, *6027*
- 2 Stan Meets Chet (Baker), Verve 8263
- 2 Stan Getz and J.J. Johnson at the Opera House, Verve 8265, *6027* (*68265*)
- 2 The Steamer, Verve 8294
- 1 Award Winner, Verve 8296
- 1 The Soft Swing, Verve 8321
- 1 Imported From Europe, Verve 8331
- 1 Stan Getz with Gerry Mulligan and Oscar Peterson, Verve 8348
- 2 At Large, Verve 8393-2, *68393-2* (2 LPs)
- 1 Stan Getz and Bob Brookmeyer, Verve 8418, *68418*

Terry Gibbs
- 1 Swingin' With Terry Gibbs and His Orchestra, EmArcy 36103
- 1 Launching a New Sound in Music, Mercury 20440, *60112*
- 1 Explosion, Mercury 20704, *60704*
- 1 Swing is Here!, Verve 2134, *6140* (*62134*)
- 1 Music from Cole Porter's Can-Can, Verve 2136, *6145* (*62136*)
- 1 Live at the Summit, Verve 2151, *62151*

Dizzy Gillespie[68]
- 1 Dizzy at Home and Abroad, Atlantic 1257
- 3 Horn of Plenty, Blue Note 5017 (10")
- 3 Roy and Diz (w/R. Eldridge), Clef 641
- 3 Roy and Diz #2, Clef 671
- 1 Trumpet Battle (w/R. Eldridge), Clef 730 or Verve 8109
- 1 The Trumpet Kings (w/R. Eldridge), Clef 731 or Verve 8110

---
[65] See also *John Coltrane, Curtis Fuller, Coleman Hawkins*.
[66] See also *Woody Herman*.
NOTE: All Prestige LPs yellow label (except Prestige 7307) and with original addresses on label; see p. 128.
[67] See also *Johnny Smith, Cal Tjader*.
[68] See also *Benny Carter, Gil Fuller, Charlie Parker*.

JAZZ RECORDINGS

2 Dizzy in Paris, Contemporary 2504 (10")
5 Dizzy Gillespie and Modern Trumpets, Dial 212 (10")
3 Afro, Norgran 1003 or Verve 8191
3 Diz Big Band, Norgran 1023, Norgran 1090, or Verve 8178
3 Diz and Getz, Norgran 1050 or Verve 8141
2 The Modern Jazz Sextet, Norgran 1076 or Verve 8166
3 Jazz Recital, Norgran 1083 or Verve 8173
3 World Statesman, Norgran 1084 or Verve 8174
1 Dizzy Gillespie and the Double Six of Paris, Philips 200-106, *600-106*
2 Cool World (w/M. Waldron), Philips 200-138, *600-138* (movie soundtrack)
2 Dizzier and Dizzier, RCA 1009
1 The Greatest of Dizzy Gillespie, RCA 2398
1 Dizzy Gillespie, RCA Vintage 530
1 Concert in Paris, Roost 2214
2 Jazz From Paris, Verve 8015 (w/D. Reinhardt; one side each)
3 Dizzy in Greece, Verve 8017
1 Manteca, Verve 8208 (reissue of Norgran 1003/Verve 8191 minus one title)
4 Dizzy Gillespie and Stuff Smith, Verve 8214
3 Birks' Works, Verve 8222
2 Dizzy Gillespie at Newport, Verve 8242, *6023 (68242)*
2 Dizzy Gillespie with Mary Lou Williams at Newport/Count Basie with Joe Williams at Newport, Verve 8244
3 Dizzy Gillespie Duets (w/S. Rollins, S. Stitt), Verve 8260
3 Sonny Side Up (w/S. Rollins, S. Stitt), Verve 8262
3 Have Trumpet, Will Excite, Verve 8313, *6047 (68313)*
2 The Ebullient Dizzy Gillespie, Verve 8328, *6068 (68328)*
3 The Greatest Trumpet of Them All, Verve 8352, *6117 (68352)*
3 A Portrait of Duke Ellington, Verve 8386, *68386*
3 Gillespiana, Verve 8394, *68394*
2 An Electrifying Evening, Verve 8401, *68401*
2 Perceptions, Verve 8411, *68411*
3 Carnegie Hall Concert, Verve 8423, *68423*

John Gilmore
3 Blowing in From Chicago (w/C. Jordan), Blue Note 1549

Jimmy Giuffre[69]
2 The Jimmy Giuffre Clarinet, Atlantic 1238
2 The Jimmy Giuffre 3, Atlantic 1254
2 The Music Man, Atlantic 1276, *1276*
2 Travelin' Light, Atlantic 1282, *1282*
2 The Four Brothers Sound, Atlantic 1295, *1295*
2 Western Suite, Atlantic 1330, *1330*
2 Jimmy Giuffre, Capitol 549
2 Tangents in Jazz, Capitol 634
2 Free Fall, Columbia 1964, *8764*
3 Seven Pieces, Verve 8307, *6039 (68307)*
3 Herb Ellis Meets Jimmy Giuffre, Verve 8311, *6045 (68311)*
5 Lee Konitz Meets Jimmy Giuffre, Verve 8335, *6073 (68335)*
3 The Easy Way, Verve 8337, *6095 (68337)*
3 Ad Lib, Verve 8361, *6130 (68361)*
3 In Person, Verve 8387, *68387*
2 Fusion, Verve 8397, *68397*
2 Thesis, Verve 8402, *68402*

[69] See also *Bob Cooper, Modern Jazz Quartet, Sonny Stitt.*

Johnny Glasel[70]
2 Jazz Session, ABC-Paramount 165
1 The John Glasel Brasstet, Jazz Unlimited 1002

Lloyd Glenn, see p. 58.

Sanford Gold
2 Piano D'or, Prestige 7019

Jean Goldkette
1 Dance Hits of the 20's, RCA Camden 548
2 Jean Goldkette and His Orchestra (w/B. Beiderbecke), "X" 3017

Benny Golson[71]
1 Take a Number from 1 to 10, Argo 681, *681*
1 Free, Argo 716, *716*
1 Pop + Jazz = Swing, Audio Fidelity 1978, *5978*[72]
3 Just Jazz, Audio Fidelity 2150, *6150* (reissue of Audio Fidelity 1978 minus strings and woodwinds) [73]
1 Reunion, Jazzland 85, *985* (reissue of Riverside 256)
2 Turning Point, Mercury 20801, *60801*
3 Groovin' with Golson, New Jazz 8220
3 Gone with Golson, New Jazz 8235
3 Gettin' With It, New Jazz 8248
2 The Modern Touch, Riverside 256
3 The Other Side of Benny Golson, Riverside 290
3 Benny Golson and the Philadelphians, United Artists 4020, *5020*
2 Benny Golson and the Philadelphians, United Artists 4076, *5076* (reissue of United Artists 4020)

Paul Gonsalves[74]
2 Cookin', Argo 626
2 Gettin' Together, Jazzland 36, *936*

Virgil Gonsalves
1 Jazz—San Francisco Style, Liberty 6010
2 Virgil Gonsalves Sextet (w/B. Wise, L. Levy), Nocturne 8 (10")

Babs Gonzales
2 Sunday at Small's Paradise, Dauntless 4311, *6311*
4 Tales of the Famous, Guess Who?, Expubidence 001
4 Voila!, Hope 001
3 Tales of Manhattan, Jaro 5000

Benny Goodman
1 B.G. 1927–1934, Brunswick 54010
2 Easy Does It, Capitol 295 (10")
2 Benny Goodman Trio, Capitol 343 (10")
2 Session For Six, Capitol 395
2 The Benny Goodman Band, Capitol 409
2 The Goodman Touch, Capitol 441
1 B.G. in Hi-Fi, Capitol 565

[70] See also *The Six.*
[71] See also *Roland Kirk, Jazztet, Lem Winchester.*
[72,73] As its title indicates, Audio Fidelity 1978 attempts to illustrate the fact that many jazz compositions are based on the chord structures of popular songs. Thus, one hears, for example, Charlie Parker's "Ornithology" (played by a sextet) from one speaker and "How High the Moon" (strings, woodwinds) from the other. Happily, the record was reissued without the gimmick, as the title of Audio Fidelity 1978 suggests. Golson does not play on the date, but is listed as leader for his arranging and conducting duties. Some of the musicians heard are Bill Evans, Eric Dolphy, Wayne Shorter, Freddie Hubbard, and Curtis Fuller.
[74] See also *Eddie "Lockjaw" Davis.*

1 Mostly Sextets, Capitol 668
1 Benny Goodman Combos, Capitol 669
1 Benny Rides Again, Chess 1440, *1440*
4 An Album of Swing Classics, Classics Record Library 7673 (3 LP boxed set)
2 Benny Goodman Combos, Columbia 500
2 The Benny Goodman Trio Plays for the Fletcher Henderson Fund, Columbia 516
1 Benny Goodman and His Orchestra, Columbia 534
1 The New Benny Goodman Sextet, Columbia 552
1 The Great Benny Goodman, Columbia 820
1 The Vintage Goodman, Columbia 821
3 A Date With the King (w/R. Clooney), Columbia 2572 (10")
1 Peggy Lee Sings With Benny Goodman, Harmony 7005
4 The Benny Goodman Treasure Chest, MGM 3E9 (3 LP boxed set)
5 The Golden Age of Swing, RCA 6703 (5 LP boxed set)

Bob Gordon[75]
2 Meet Mr. Gordon, Pacific Jazz 12 (10")
2 Jazz Impressions, Tampa 26

Dexter Gordon
2 Daddy Plays the Horn, Bethlehem 36
2 The Chase and Steeplechase (w/W. Gray), Decca 7025 (10")
5 Dexter Gordon Quintet, Dial 204 (10")
3 Dexter Blows Hot and Cool, Dooto 207
3 The Resurgence of Dexter Gordon, Jazzland 29, *929*

Honi Gordon, see p. 110.

Joe Gordon
1 Lookin' Good, Contemporary 3597, *7597*
1 Introducing Joe Gordon, EmArcy 36025

Conrad Gozzo
1 Goz the Great, RCA 1124

John Graas
2 Premiere in Jazz, Andex 3003
3 Jazz Studio 2, Decca 8079
3 Jazz Studio 3, Decca 8104
3 Jazz Lab 1, Decca 8343
3 Jazz Lab 2, Decca 8478
3 Jazzmantics, Decca 8677
2 Coup de Graas, EmArcy 36117
3 French Horn Jazz, Kapp 1046 (reissue of Trend 1005 plus 4 titles)
3 French Horn Jazz, Trend 1005 (10")

Norman Granz, see Jam Sessions, Jazz at the Philharmonic.

Stephane Grappelly
1 Feeling + Finesse = Jazz, Atlantic 1391, *1391*
1 Improvisations, EmArcy 36120
1 Musique Pour Arreter le Temps, Verve 20001

Wardell Gray
2 The Chase and Steeplechase (w/D. Gordon), Decca 7025 (10")
5 The Wardell Gray Memorial Album, Vol. 1, Prestige 7008
5 The Wardell Gray Memorial Album, Vol. 2, Prestige 7009

3 Highlights in Modern Jazz (w/S. Getz; one side each), Seeco 7 (10")

Bennie Green
2 Hornful of Soul, Bethlehem 6054, *6054*
3 Back on the Scene, Blue Note 1587
4 Soul Stirrin', Blue Note 1599
3 Walkin' and Talkin', Blue Note 4010
2 Blow Your Horn (w/P. Quinichette; one side each), Decca 8176
3 Bennie Green Swings the Blues, Enrica 2002
2 Glidin' Along, Jazzland 43, *943*
1 Bennie Green Swings the Blues, Mt. Vernon 121 (reissue of Enrica 2002)
4 Bennie Green and Art Farmer, Prestige 7041
4 Walkin' Down, Prestige 7049
4 Bennie Green Blows His Horn, Prestige 7052
2 Bennie Green Blows His Horn, Prestige 7160 (reissue of Prestige 7052)
4 Bennie Green, Time 5021, *2021*
1 The Swingin'est, Vee Jay 1005, *1005*

Freddie Green
3 Mr. Rhythm, RCA 1210

Urbie Green[76]
4 Blues and Other Shades of Green, ABC-Paramount 101
3 All About Urbie Green and his Big Band, ABC-Paramount 137
2 Urbie, Bethlehem 14
4 Urbie Green Septet, Blue Note 5036 (10")
1 Let's Face the Music and Dance, RCA 1667, *1667*
1 Jimmy McHugh in Hi-Fi, RCA 1741, *1741*
1 The Best of New Broadway Show Hits, RCA 1969, *1969*
4 A Cool Yuletide, "X" 3026 (10")

Al Grey
1 The Last of the Big Plungers, Argo 653, *653*
1 The Thinking Man's Trombone, Argo 677, *677*
1 Al Grey-Billy Mitchell Sextet at the Museum of Modern Art, Argo 689, *689*
1 Snap Your Fingers (w/B. Mitchell), Argo 700, *700*
1 Night Song (w/B. Mitchell), Argo 711, *711*
1 Having a Ball, Argo 718, *718*
1 Boss Bone, Argo 731, *731*
1 Shades of Grey, Tangerine 1504

Johnny Griffin[77]
2 Johnny Griffin, Argo 624 (split-cover jacket)
5 Introducing Johnny Griffin, Blue Note 1533
3 Johnny Griffin Vol. 2 (A Blowing Session), Blue Note 1559
4 The Congregation, Blue Note 1580
3 Johnny Griffin Sextet, Riverside 264
1 Way Out, Riverside 274
2 The Little Giant, Riverside 304, *1149*
1 The Big Soul Band, Riverside 331, *1179*
1 Johnny Griffin's Studio Jazz Party, Riverside 338, *9338*
2 Change of Pace, Riverside 368, *9368*
1 White Gardenia, Riverside 387, *9387*
3 The Kerry Dancers, Riverside 420, *9420*

[76] See also *Gil Melle*.
[77] See also *Ahmed Abdul-Malik, Eddie "Lockjaw" Davis–Johnny Griffin, Wilbur Ware*.
NOTE: All Blue Note LPs with original addresses on label; see p. 128.

[75] See also *Herbie Harper, Jack Montrose*.

1 Grab This!, Riverside 437, *9437*
1 Do Nothin' Till You Hear From Me, Riverside 462, *9462*

Tiny Grimes
3 Blues Groove, Prestige 7138[78]
3 Callin' the Blues, Prestige 7144
2 Tiny in Swingville, Swingville 2002
1 Callin' the Blues, Swingville 2004 (reissue of Prestige 7144)

Dave Grusin
1 Kaleidoscope, Columbia 2344, *9144*

Gigi Gryce[79]
4 Gigi Gryce-Clifford Brown Sextet, Blue Note 5048 (10")
4 Jazztime Paris (w/C. Brown), Blue Note 5049 (10")
4 Gigi Gryce and his Little Band (w/C. Brown), Blue Note 5050 (10")
4 Gigi Gryce Quintet/Sextet (w/C. Brown), Blue Note 5051 (10")
1 Reminiscin', Mercury 20628, *60628*
3 Gigi Gryce, Metrojazz 1006, *1006*
3 Sayin' Somethin', New Jazz 8230
3 Hap'nin's, New Jazz 8246
3 The Rat Race Blues, New Jazz 8262
5 When Farmer Met Gryce, Prestige 7085
1 Nica's Tempo, Savoy 12137 (reissue of Signal 1201)
5 Quartet/Orchestra, Signal 1201

Johnny Guarnieri[80]
2 Songs of Hudson and De Lange, Coral 57085
2 The Duke Again, Coral 57086
1 Johnny Guarnieri Plays, Golden Crest 3020
1 Cheerful Little Earful, RCA Camden 345
1 Side by Side, RCA Camden 391
1 An Hour of Modern Piano Rhythms, Royale 1296

Friedrich Gulda
2 From Vienna With Jazz, Columbia 2251, *9051*
2 The Ineffable Friedrich Gulda, Columbia 2346, *9146*
3 Friedrich Gulda at Birdland, RCA 1355
1 Piano and Big Band, Scepter 538

Lars Gullin
3 Baritone Sax, Atlantic 1246
2 Modern Sounds: Sweden, Contemporary 2505 (10")
4 Lars Gullin Swings, East-West 4003
2 Lars Gullin Quartet, EmArcy 26041 (10")
2 Gullin's Garden, EmArcy 26044 (10")
3 Lars Gullin, EmArcy 36012
1 Lars Gullin with the Moretone Singers, EmArcy 36059
2 New Sounds from Sweden, Vol. 2 (w/B. Hallberg), Prestige 121 (10")
2 New Sounds from Sweden, Vol. 3 (w/A. Domnerus), Prestige 133 (10")
2 New Sounds from Sweden, Vol. 5, Prestige 144 (10")
2 New Sounds from Sweden, Vol. 7, Prestige 151 (10")

Tommy Gumina, see Buddy DeFranco.

Tommy Gwaltney
1 Goin' to Kansas City (w/B. Clayton, D. Wells), Riverside 353, *9353*

Bobby Hackett
2 Trumpet Solos, Brunswick 58014 (10")
1 Soft Lights and Bobby Hackett, Capitol 458
1 Coast Concert, Capitol 692
1 Rendezvous, Capitol 719
1 Gotham Jazz Scene, Capitol 857
1 Don't Take Your Love From Me, Capitol 1002
2 Bobby Hackett at the Embers, Capitol 1077, *1077*
1 Blues With a Kick, Capitol 1172, *1172*
2 Bobby Hackett Quartet, Capitol 1235, *1235*
1 Easy Beat, Capitol 1413, *1413*
2 Jazz Session, Columbia 6156 (10")

Al Haig
5 Jazz Will-o-the-Wisp, Counterpoint 551 (includes Esoteric 7)
5 Al Haig Trio, Esoteric 7 (10")
5 Al Haig Today, Mint 711
5 Al Haig Trio, Pacific Jazz 18 (10")
5 Al Haig Quartet, Period 1104 (10")

Edmond Hall
1 Celestial Express, Blue Note 6505
2 Rumpus on Rampart St., Rae-Cox 1120
2 Petite Fleur, United Artists 4028, *5028*

Jim Hall[81]
4 Good Friday Blues (Modest Jazz Trio), Pacific Jazz 10
2 Jazz Guitar, Pacific Jazz 79 (reissue of Pacific Jazz 1227)
4 Jazz Guitar, Pacific Jazz 1227

Lenny Hambro
3 Lenny Hambro Quintet, Columbia 757
2 The Nature of Things, Epic 3361
1 Mambo Hambro, Savoy 15031 (10")

Chico Hamilton[82]
2 Jazz from "Sweet Smell of Success," Decca 8614
1 Spectacular!, Pacific Jazz 39 (reissue of Pacific Jazz 1209)
2 Chico Hamilton Quintet (w/B. Collette), Pacific Jazz 1209
2 Chico Hamilton Quintet in Hi-Fi, Pacific Jazz 1216
2 Chico Hamilton Trio, Pacific Jazz 1220
1 Chico Hamilton Quintet, Pacific Jazz 1225, *1005* (*1225*)
1 Music of Fred Katz, Pacific Jazz 1291
5 That Hamilton Man, Sesac 2901/2902
4 With Strings Attached, Warner Bros. 1245, *1245*
4 Gongs East, Warner Bros. 1271, *1271*
4 The Three Faces of Chico, Warner Bros. 1344, *1344*
1 South Pacific in Hi-Fi, World Pacific 1238, *1003* (*1238*)
1 Ellington Suite, World Pacific 1258, *1016* (*1258*)
1 The Original Chico Hamilton Quintet, World Pacific 1287

Jimmy Hamilton
1 Swing Low, Everest 5100, *1100*
1 It's About Time, Swingville 2022
1 Can't Help Swingin', Swingville 2028

[78] Reissued with same title under Coleman Hawkins' name on Swingville 2035; see p. 151.
[79] See also *Art Farmer, Jazz Lab.*
[80] See also *Will Bradley.*
[81] See also *Bob Brookmeyer, Gary Burton, Buddy Collette, Bill Evans, Art Farmer, Jimmy Raney.*
[82] See also *Buddy Collette.*

2 Accent on Clarinet, Urania 1204
2 Clarinet in Hi-Fi, Urania 1208

Lionel Hampton[83]
2 Jazztime Paris, Blue Note 5046 (10")
3 Lionel Hampton Quartet, Clef 611
3 Lionel Hampton Quintet, Clef 628
3 Lionel Hampton Quintet Album #2, Clef 642
3 Lionel Hampton Quartet/Quintet, Clef 667
3 Big Band, Clef 670
3 Hamp, Clef 673, Clef 738, or Verve 8114
2 Flying Home, Clef 735 or Verve 8112
2 Swinging With Hamp, Clef 736 or Verve 8113
2 Hamp's Big Four, Clef 744 or Verve 8117
2 Wailin' at the Trianon, Columbia 711
1 Hamp in Paris, EmArcy 36032
1 Crazy Rhythm, EmArcy 36034
1 Jam Session in Paris, EmArcy 36035
2 Apollo Hall Concert 1954, Epic 3190
2 Oh Rock, MGM 3386
3 Hamp and Getz, Norgran 1037 or Verve 8128
3 Lionel Hampton and his Giants, Norgran 1080 or Verve 8170
2 Lionel Hampton Swings, Perfect 12002
1 Hot Mallets, RCA 1000
1 Lionel Hampton Plays Love Songs, Verve 2018
2 Travelin' Band, Verve 8019 (reissue of Clef 670)
2 King of the Vibes, Verve 8105
2 Air Mail Special, Verve 8106
2 The Genius of Lionel Hampton, Verve 8215
2 Lionel Hampton '58, Verve 8223
2 Hallelujah Hamp, Verve 8226
2 The High and Mighty, Verve 8228

Slide Hampton
1 Sister Salvation, Atlantic 1339, *1339*
1 Somethin' Sanctified, Atlantic 1362, *1362*
2 Drum Suite, Epic 16030, *17030*
3 Slide Hampton and his Horn of Plenty, Strand 1006, *1006*

George Handy
4 Handyland U.S.A., "X" 1004
4 By George, Handy of Course, "X" 1032

Roland Hanna[84]
2 Destry Rides Again, Atco 108, *108*
2 Easy to Love, Atco 121, *121*

Bob Hardaway
2 Jazz Practitioners, Bethlehem 3 (w/E. Shu; one side each)

Wilbur Harden
1 Mainstream 1958 (w/J. Coltrane), Savoy 12127
1 Jazz Way Out (w/J. Coltrane), Savoy 12131, *13004*
1 The King and I, Savoy 12134, *13002*
1 Tanganyika Strut (w/J. Coltrane), Savoy 12136, *13005*

Bill Hardman
2 The Bill Hardman Quintet, Savoy 12170

Herbie Harper
3 Herbie Harper, Bethlehem 1025 (10")
2 Herbie Harper featuring Bud Shank and Bob Gordon, Liberty 6003 (reissue of Nocturne 1 and Nocturne 11)

[83] See also *Gene Krupa, Art Tatum.*
[84] See also *Al Hibbler,* p. 110.

2 Herbie Harper Sextet, Mode 100
2 Herbie Harper Quintet featuring Bob Gordon, Nocturne 1 (10")
2 Quartet/Quintet, Nocturne 7 (10")
1 Herbie Harper Quintet, Tampa 11

Barry Harris
1 Breakin' It Up, Argo 644, *644*
1 Barry Harris at the Jazz Workshop, Riverside 326, *1177*
1 Preminado, Riverside 354, *9354*
3 Listen to Barry Harris (Solo Piano), Riverside 392, *9392*
3 Newer Than New, Riverside 413, *9413*
3 Chasin' the Bird, Riverside 435, *9435*

Bill Harris[85]
2 Bill Harris and Friends, Fantasy 3263
2 The Ex-Hermanites, Mode 129
3 Bill Harris Herd, Norgran 1062 or Verve 8152

Nancy Harrow
1 You Never Know, Atlantic 8075, *8075*
3 Wild Women Don't Have the Blues, Candid 8008, *9008*

Johnny Hartman, see p. 110.

Hasaan
1 The Max Roach Trio featuring the Legendary Hasaan, Atlantic 1435, *1435*

Hampton Hawes
5 Piano East/Piano West, Prestige 7067 (4 titles by F. Redd/8 titles by Hawes)
3 Curtis Fuller and Hamp Hawes with French Horns, Status 8305
2 Movin', Status 8307 (reissue of Prestige 7067)
5 Hampton Hawes Trio, Vantage 1 (10")

Coleman Hawkins[86]
5 Coleman Hawkins and His Orchestra, Apollo 101 (10") [87]
1 Bean Bags (w/M. Jackson), Atlantic 1316, *1316*
4 The Big Sounds, Brunswick 54016 (w/B. Webster; one side each)
2 Jazz Reunion (w/Pee Wee Russell), Candid 8020, *9020*
2 The Gilded Hawk, Capitol 819
1 Back in Bean's Bag, Columbia 1991, *8791*
2 Classic Tenors, Contact 3 (8 titles by Hawkins, 4 titles by L. Young)
2 On the Bean, Continental 16003
1 Coleman Hawkins, Crown 5181, *206*
2 The Hawk Swings, Crown 5207, *224*
4 The Hawk Talks, Decca 8127
3 The High and Mighty Hawk, Felsted 7005, *2005*
4 Jazz Concert (w/G. Auld; one side each), Grand Award 316 (Hawkins side reissue of Apollo 101)
2 Timeless Jazz, Jazztone 1201
1 The Hawk and the Hunter, Mira 3003
3 At Ease with Coleman Hawkins, Moodsville 7
3 The Hawk Relaxes, Moodsville 15
3 Good Old Broadway, Moodsville 23
3 The Jazz Version of "No Strings," Moodsville 25
3 Make Someone Happy, Moodsville 31

[85] See also *Benny Carter.*
[86] See also *Harry Arnold, Kenny Burrell, Ida Cox, Clark Terry.*
[87] Generally acknowledged as the first bebop recording session; recorded in February, 1944, and features Dizzy Gillespie.

JAZZ RECORDINGS   151

   1 Jazz at the Metropole (w/S. Yaged), Philips 200–022, 600–022
   3 Soul, Prestige 7149
   3 Hawk Eyes, Prestige 7156
   2 The Hawk in Hi-Fi, RCA 1281
   2 Sonny Meets Hawk/ (w/Rollins), RCA 2712, *2712*
   1 Body and Soul, RCA Vintage 501
   4 Coleman Hawkins, A Documentary (spoken word), Riverside 117/118 (2 LPs)
   2 The Hawk Flies High, Riverside 233
   2 The Hawk Returns, Savoy 12013
   3 Coleman Hawkins with the Red Garland Trio, Swingville 2001
   2 Coleman Hawkins All Stars (w/J. Thomas, V. Dickenson), Swingville 2005
   2 Night Hawk (w/E. Davis), Swingville 2016
   1 Things Ain't What They Used to Be, Swingville 2024
   1 Years Ago, Swingville 2025
   1 Blues Groove, Swingville 2035 (reissue of Prestige 7138; see *Tiny Grimes*)
   1 Soul, Swingville 2038, (reissue of Prestige 7149)
   1 Hawk Eyes, Swingville 2039 (reissue of Prestige 7156)
   3 Accent on Tenor, Urania 1201
   4 The Genius of Coleman Hawkins, Verve 8261, *6033* (68261)
   4 Coleman Hawkins and Roy Eldridge at the Opera House, Verve 8266, *6028* (68266)
   4 Coleman Hawkins Encounters Ben Webster, Verve 8327, *6066* (68327)
   3 Coleman Hawkins and Confreres, Verve 8346, *6110* (68346)
   1 Hawkins, Eldridge, Hodges Alive at the Village Gate, Verve 8504, *68504*
   1 Hawkins! Alive! at the Village Gate, Verve 8509, *68509*
   1 The Essential Coleman Hawkins, Verve 8568, *68568* (includes "Picasso," unaccompanied tenor saxophone performance)
   2 The Hawk in Paris, Vik 1059
   2 Coleman Hawkins and the Saxophone Section, World Wide *2001*

Louis Hayes
   1 Louis Hayes, Vee Jay 3010

Tubby Hayes
   2 The Couriers of Jazz (w/R. Scott), Carlton 116
   2 Introducing Tubbs, Epic 16019, *17019*
   3 Tubby the Tenor, Epic 16023, *17023*
   2 Little Giant of Jazz, Imperial 9046
   2 Message From Britain (w/R. Scott), Jazzland 34, *934*
   3 Tubby's Back in Town, Smash 27026, *67026*

Roy Haynes
   2 Jazz Abroad, EmArcy 36083 (w/Q. Jones; one side each)
   3 We 3 (w/P. Newborn, P. Chambers), New Jazz 8210
   3 Just Us, New Jazz 8245
   3 Cracklin', New Jazz 8286
   3 Cymbalism, New Jazz 8287
   2 People (w/F. Strozier), Pacific Jazz 82, *82*

Jimmy Heath
   3 The Thumper, Riverside 314, *1160*
   3 Really Big!, Riverside 333, *1188*
   3 The Quota, Riverside 372, *9372*
   3 Triple Threat, Riverside 400, *9400*
   1 Swamp Seed, Riverside 465, *9465*
   2 On the Trail, Riverside 486, *9486*

Bob Helm, see Lu Watters.

Bill Henderson, see p. 110.

Bobby Henderson
   1 Handful of Keys, Vanguard 8511
   1 Call House Blues, Vanguard 9017
   2 Ruby Braff Octet with Pee Wee Russell/Bobby Henderson at Newport, Verve 8241 (one side each)

Fletcher Henderson
   5 A Study in Frustration, Columbia C4L19 (4 LP boxed set w/illustrated booklet)
   2 Birth of Big Band Jazz, Riverside 129 (w/D. Ellington; one side each)
   3 Connie's Inn Orchestra, "X" 3013 (10")

Joe Henderson
   1 Page One, Blue Note 4140, *84140*
   1 Our Thing, Blue Note 4152, *84152*
   1 In 'N Out, Blue Note 4166, *84166*
   1 Inner Urge, Blue Note 4189, *84189*
   1 Mode For Joe, Blue Note 4227, *84227*

Jon Hendricks[88]
   2 Evolution of the Blues Song, Columbia 1583, *8383*
   2 Fast Livin' Blues, Columbia 1805, *8605*
   1 Salud!, Reprise 6089, *6089*
   1 Recorded in Person at the Trident, Smash 27069, *67069*
   2 A Good Git-Together, World Pacific 1283, *1283*

Ernie Henry[89]
   4 Presenting Ernie Henry, Riverside 222 (white label)
   1 Presenting Ernie Henry, Riverside 222 (blue label)
   4 Seven Standards and a Blues, Riverside 248
   4 Last Chorus, Riverside 266

Woody Herman
   1 Woody Herman at the Monterey Jazz Festival, Atlantic 1328, *1328*
   2 The Swinging Herman Herd, Brunswick 54024
   1 Classics in Jazz, Capitol 324
   2 The Woody Herman Band, Capital 560
   2 Road Band, Capitol 658
   2 Jackpot, Capitol 748
   2 Blues Groove, Capitol 784
   1 The Three Herds, Columbia 592
   2 Songs for Tired Lovers (w/E. Garner), Columbia 651
   2 12 Shades of Blue, Columbia 683
   1 New Swingin' Herman Herd, Crown 5180, 205
   2 Woodchopper's Ball, Decca 8133
   5 Swinging with the Woodchoppers, Dial 210 (10")
   3 The Herdsmen Play Paris, Fantasy 3201
   2 The Fourth Herd, Jazzland 17, *917*
   5 Dance Date on Mars, Mars 1 (10")
   5 Woody Herman Goes Native, Mars 2 (10")
   3 Carnegie Hall 1946, MGM 3043
   2 Hi-Fi-ing Herd, MGM 3385
   3 Early Autumn, Verve 2030
   3 Songs for Hip Lovers, Verve 2069
   2 Love is the Sweetest Thing, Sometimes, Verve 2096
   3 Jazz the Utmost, Verve 8014

[88] See also *Lambert, Hendricks & Ross/Bavan*.
[89] See also *Kenny Dorham*.
NOTE: All Blue Note LPs w/New York label.

3 Men From Mars, Verve 8216
3 Woody Herman '58, Verve 8255

Eddie Heywood[90]
3 Featuring Eddie Heywood, Coral 57095
2 Lightly and Politely, Decca 8202
2 Swing Low Sweet Heywood, Decca 8270

Al Hibbler, see p. 110.

Andrew Hill
5 So in Love, Warwick 2002, *2002*

Hi-Los, see p. 111.

Earl "Fatha" Hines[91]
4 Fats Waller Memorial Set (w/N. Jaffe; one side each), Advance 4 (10")
2 Famous QRS Solos, Atlantic 120 (10")
2 Fats Waller Songs (w/N. Jaffe), Brunswick 58034 (10") (reissue of Advance 4)
1 Spontaneous Explorations, Contact 2
4 Earl Hines All-Stars, Dial 306 (10")
1 Oh, Father!, Epic 3223
1 In Concert, Focus 335, *335*
1 Earl's Pearls, MGM 3832, *3832*
1 Up to Date, RCA *3380*
1 Grand Terrace Band, RCA Vintage 512
1 A Monday Date, Riverside 398, *9398*
1 Stride Right (w/J. Hodges), Verve 8647, *68647*
1 Swing's Our Thing (w/J. Hodges), Verve 8732, *68732*
2 Piano Solos, "X" 3023

Milt Hinton
2 Milt Hinton, Bethlehem 10

Jutta Hipp
2 Jutta Hipp at the Hickory House, Vol. 1, Blue Note 1515
2 Jutta Hipp at the Hickory House, Vol. 2, Blue Note 1516
3 Jutta Hipp with Zoot Sims, Blue Note 1530
2 Jutta Hipp Quintet, Blue Note 5056 (10")
2 Cool Europe, MGM 3157

André Hodeir[92]
1 Jazz et Jazz, Philips 200–073, *600–073*
1 American Jazzmen Play André Hodeir's "Essais," Savoy 12104
1 The Paris Scene, Savoy 12113

Johnny Hodges[93]
1 Hodge Podge, Epic 3105
3 Memories of Ellington, Norgran 1004
3 More of Johnny Hodges and his Orchestra, Norgran 1009
3 Dance Bash, Norgran 1024 or Norgran 1091
3 Creamy, Norgran 1045 or Verve 8136
3 Castle Rock, Norgran 1048 or Verve 8139
3 Ellingtonia '56, Norgran 1055 or Verve 8145
3 In a Tender Mood, Norgran 1059 or Verve 8149
3 Used to Be Duke, Norgran 1060 or Verve 8150
3 The Blues, Norgran 1061 or Verve 8151

1 Things Ain't What They Used to Be (w/R. Stewart), RCA Vintage 533
3 Perdido, Verve 8179 (reissue of Norgran 1024)
3 In a Mellow Tone, Verve 8180 (reissue of Norgran 1004)
3 Duke's in Bed, Verve 8203
3 The Big Sound, Verve 8271, *6017*
3 Johnny Hodges and His Strings Play the Prettiest Gershwin, Verve 8314, *6048*
2 Back to Back (w/D. Ellington), Verve 8317, *6055* (*68317*)
2 Side by Side (w/D. Ellington), Verve 8345, *6109* (*68345*)
3 Not So Dukish, Verve 8355, *68355*
3 Blues-a-Plenty, Verve 8358, *68358*
2 Gerry Mulligan Meets Johnny Hodges, Verve 8367, *68367*
2 Johnny Hodges with Billy Strayhorn and the Orchestra, Verve 8452, *68452*
1 Stride Right (w/E. Hines), Verve 8647, *68647*
1 Swing's Our Thing (w/E. Hines), Verve 8732, *68732*

Billie Holiday
3 Music For Torching, Clef 669, or Verve 8026
3 A Recital, Clef 686 or Verve 8027
3 Solitude, Clef 690 or Verve 8074
3 Velvet Mood, Clef 713 or Verve 8096
3 Jazz Recital, Clef 718 or Verve 8098[94]
3 Lady Sings the Blues, Clef 721 or Verve 8099
5 Stan and Billie (w/Getz), Dale 25 (10")
3 Billie Holiday, MGM 3764, *3764* (her last recording session)
5 Billie Holiday Sings the Blues, Score 4014
1 Lady Love, United Artists 14014, *15014*
3 Body and Soul, Verve 8197
2 Ella Fitzgerald and Billie Holiday at Newport (one side each), Verve 8234, *6022* (*68234*)
2 Songs For Distingué Lovers, Verve 8257, *6021*
2 Stay With Me, Verve 8302
2 All or Nothing at All, Verve 8329

Bill Holman
2 In a Jazz Orbit, Andex 3004, *3004*
2 Jive For Five (w/M. Lewis), Andex 3005, *3005*
1 Bill Holman's Great Big Band, Capitol 1464, *1464*
2 Kenton Presents Bill Holman, Capitol 6500 (10")
2 The Fabulous Bill Holman, Coral 57188

Richard "Groove" Holmes[95]
1 Richard "Groove" Holmes (w/B. Webster, L. McCann), Pacific Jazz 23, *23*
1 Groovin' With Jug (w/G. Ammons), Pacific Jazz 32, *32*
1 After Hours, Pacific Jazz 59, *59*

Elmo Hope
4 Sounds from Rikers Island, Audio Fidelity 2119, *6119*
5 High Hopes, Beacon 401
5 Elmo Hope Trio, Blue Note 5029 (10")
5 Elmo Hope Quintet, Blue Note 5044 (10")
5 Elmo Hope Trio, Celebrity 209
3 Elmo Hope, Hi Fi 616
3 The Jazz Messengers/Elmo Hope Quintet (one side each), Pacific Jazz 33
5 Meditations, Prestige 7010
5 Hope Meets Foster, Prestige 7021 (original)
4 Wail, Frank, Wail, Prestige 7021 (reissue)

[90] See also *Teddy Wilson.*
[91] See also *Dinah Washington.*
[92] See also *Kenny Clarke.*
[93] See also *Coleman Hawkins.*
[94] One side reissue of 10" LP *Billie Holiday at Jazz at the Philharmonic* (Clef 169); other side reissue of 10" Ralph Burns LP *Free Forms* (Clef 115).
[95] See also *Gerald Wilson.*

JAZZ RECORDINGS

5 Informal Jazz, Prestige 7043
3 Homecoming, Riverside 381, *9381*
3 Hope-Full (w/B. Hope), Riverside 408, *9408*

Claude Hopkins
1 Yes Indeed, Swingville 2009
1 Let's Jam, Swingville 2020
1 Swing Time, Swingville 2041

Paul Horn
1 House of Horn, Dot 3091
1 Plenty of Horn, Dot 9002, *29002*
1 Impressions, World Pacific 1266

Freddie Hubbard
3 Open Sesame, Blue Note 4040, *84040*

Langston Hughes
3 The Weary Blues (poetry and music), MGM 3697 (1-VSP 36)

Helen Humes
3 Helen Humes, Contemporary 3571, *7571*
3 Songs I Like to Sing, Contemporary 3582, *7582*
3 Swingin' with Humes, Contemporary 3598, *7598*

Alberta Hunter
1 Alberta Hunter With Lovie Austin's Blues Serenaders, Riverside 418, *9418*

Dick Hyman, see Ralph Burns, Leonard Feather.

Chubby Jackson
1 Chubby's Back!, Argo 614, *614*
1 I'm Entitled to You, Argo 625, *625*
1 Chubby Takes Over, Everest 5009, *1009*
1 Jazz Then Till Now, Everest 5041, *1041*

Cliff Jackson, see D. Wellstood.

Milt Jackson[96]
1 Bags and Flutes, Atlantic 1294, *1294*
1 Bean Bags (w/C. Hawkins), Atlantic 1316, *1316*
3 Milt Jackson (w/T. Monk), Blue Note 1509 (Lexington Ave. address on label)
4 Milt Jackson Quartet, Prestige 7003
1 Invitation, Riverside 446, *9446*
1 Live at the Village Gate, Riverside 495, *9495*
3 Bags' Opus, United Artists 4022, *5022*

Illinois Jacquet[97]
5 Battle of the Saxes (w/L. Young; one side each), Aladdin 701 (10")
5 Illinois Jacquet and His Tenor Sax, Aladdin 708 (10")
5 Illinois Jacquet and His Tenor Sax, Aladdin 803
5 Jam Session, Apollo 104 (10")
4 Jazz Moods, Clef 622
4 Illinois Jacquet and His Orchestra, Clef 676 or Verve 8061
4 The Kid and the Brute (w/B. Webster), Clef 680 or Verve 8065
4 Jazz Moods (w/C. Basie), Clef 700 or Verve 8084 (different LP than Clef 622)
4 Port of Rico (w/C. Basie), Clef 701 or Verve 8085

4 Groovin' with Jacquet, Clef 702 or Verve 8086
4 Swing's the Thing, Clef 750 or Verve 8023
1 Illinois Jacquet, Epic 16003, *17003*
3 Black Velvet, RCA 3236
2 Illinois Jacquet Flies Again, Roulette 52035, *52035*
2 Illinois Jacquet, Savoy 15024 (10")

Nat Jaffe, see Earl "Fatha" Hines.

Jam Sessions (Norman Granz)
3 Jam Session #1, Clef 4001 (original)
2 Jam Session #1, Clef 601, 651, or Verve 8049 (reissues)
3 Jam Session #2, Clef 4002 (original)
2 Jam Session #2, Clef 602, 652, or Verve 8050 (reissues)
3 Jam Session #3, Clef 4003 (original)
2 Jam Session #3, Clef 653 or Verve 8051 (reissues)
3 Jam Session #4, Clef 4004 (original)
2 Jam Session #4, Clef 654 or Verve 8052 (reissues)
3 Jam Session #5, Clef 4005 (original)
2 Jam Session #5, Clef 655 or Verve 8053 (reissues)
2 Jam Session #6, Clef 656 or Verve 8054
2 Jam Session #7, Clef 677 or Verve 8062
2 Jam Session #8, Clef 711 or Verve 8094
2 Jam Session #9, Verve 8196

Bob James
1 Explosions, ESP 1009
1 Conceptions, Mercury 20768, *60768*

Conrad Janis
1 Tailgate Five, Jubilee 1010
1 Dixieland Jam Session, Riverside 215

Keith Jarrett
2 Life Between the Exit Signs, Vortex *2006*
1 Restoration Ruin, Vortex *2008*
2 Somewhere Before, Vortex *2012*

Bobby Jaspar[98]
2 Bobby Jaspar and his All Stars, EmArcy 36105
2 Tenor and Flute, Riverside 240

Jazz at the Philharmonic (Norman Granz)
1 Jazz at the Philharmonic, Verve Vol. 1
1 Jazz at the Philharmonic, Verve Vol. 2
1 Jazz at the Philharmonic, Verve Vol. 3
1 Jazz at the Philharmonic, Verve Vol. 4
1 Jazz at the Philharmonic, Verve Vol. 5
1 Jazz at the Philharmonic, Verve Vol. 6
1 Jazz at the Philharmonic, Verve Vol. 7
3 Jazz at the Philharmonic, Verve Vol. 8 (3 LP boxed set)
3 Jazz at the Philharmonic, Verve Vol. 9 (3 LP boxed set)
3 Jazz at the Philharmonic, Verve Vol. 10, 3 LP boxed set)
3 Jazz at the Philharmonic, Verve Vol. 11 (3 LP boxed set)

Jazz Lab (Donald Byrd-Gigi Gryce)
2 Jazz Lab, Columbia 998
2 Modern Jazz Perspectives, Columbia 1058
1 Jazz Lab, Jazzland 1 (reissue of Riverside 229)
3 Jazz Lab, Jubilee 1059
2 Gigi Gryce and the Jazz Lab Quintet, Riverside 229, *1110*
3 The Gigi Gryce-Donald Byrd Jazz Laboratory/Cecil Taylor Quintet at Newport (one side each), Verve 8238

---
[96] See also *Miles Davis, Modern Jazz Quartet.*
[97] See also *Count Basie, Rex Stewart.*
[98] See also *Herbie Mann.*

JAZZ

The Jazz Modes (Charlie Rouse-Julius Watkins)
- 2 The Most Happy Fella, Atlantic 1280
- 2 The Jazz Modes, Atlantic 1306, *1306*
- 3 Jazzville, Vol. 1, Dawn 1101 (w/G. Quill-D. Sherman Quintet; one side each)
- 3 Les Jazz Modes, Dawn 1108
- 2 Mood in Scarlet, Dawn 1117

The Jazztet (Art Farmer-Benny Golson)
- 1 Meet the Jazztet, Argo 664, *664*
- 1 Big City Sounds, Argo 672, *672*
- 1 The Jazztet and John Lewis, Argo 684, *684*
- 1 The Jazztet at Birdhouse, Argo 688, *688*
- 3 Here and Now, Mercury 20698, *60698*
- 3 Another Git Together, Mercury 20737, *60737*

Blind Lemon Jefferson
- 2 Classic Folk Blues, Riverside 125
- 2 Blind Lemon Jefferson, Vol. 2, Riverside 136

Eddie Jefferson
- 3 Letter From Home, Riverside 411, *9411*

John Jenkins
- 3 John Jenkins, Blue Note 1573
- 4 John Jenkins, Cliff Jordan and Bobby Timmons, New Jazz 8232

Bill Jennings
- 2 Guitar/Vibes, Audio Lab 1514
- 3 Billy in the Lion's Den (w/L. Parker), King 527
- 2 Enough Said, Prestige 7164
- 2 Glide On, Prestige 7177

Jack Jenney
- 3 Jack Jenney, Columbia 4803

Budd Johnson
- 1 French Cookin', Argo 721, *721*
- 1 Ya! Ya!, Argo 736, *736*
- 1 Off the Wall (w/J. Newman), Argo 748, *748*
- 3 Blues a la Mode, Felsted 7007, *2007*
- 2 Let's Swing, Swingville 2015
- 3 Budd Johnson and the 4 Brass Giants, Riverside 343, *9343*

Dick Johnson[99]
- 2 Music for Swinging Moderns, EmArcy 36081
- 3 Most Likely, Riverside 253

J.J. Johnson[100]
- 3 The Eminent J.J. Johnson, Vol. 1, Blue Note 1505 (Lexington Ave. address on label)
- 3 The Eminent J.J. Johnson, Vol. 2, Blue Note 1506 (Lexington Ave. address on label)
- 2 J is for Jazz, Columbia 935
- 1 First Place, Columbia 1030
- 2 Dial J.J. 5, Columbia 1084
- 2 J.J. in Person, Columbia 1161, *8009*
- 2 Blue Trombone, Columbia 1303, *8109*
- 2 Really Livin', Columbia 1383, *8178*
- 1 Trombone and Voices, Columbia 1547, *8347*
- 2 J.J. Inc., Columbia 1606, *8406*
- 2 A Touch of Satin, Columbia 1737, *8537*

J.J. Johnson-Kai Winding
- 1 K & JJ, Bethlehem 6001
- 2 Trombone For Two, Columbia 742
- 2 Jay & Kai + 6, Columbia 892
- 1 Dave Brubeck and Jay & Kai at Newport (one side each) Columbia 932
- 2 Jay and Kai, Columbia 973
- 3 Afternoon at Birdland, Vik 1040

James P. Johnson
- 2 Rent Party Piano, Blue Note 7011 (10″)
- 2 Jazz Band Ball, Blue Note 7012 (10″)
- 1 The Daddy of the Piano, Decca 5190 (10″)
- 1 Fats Waller Favorites, Decca 5228 (10″)
- 2 James P. Johnson: Rare Solos, Riverside 105
- 2 Backwater Blues, Riverside 151

Osie Johnson
- 2 The Happy Jazz of Osie Johnson, Bethlehem 66
- 1 A Bit of the Blues, RCA 1369

Pete Johnson[101]
- 2 Boogie Woogie Mood, Brunswick 58041 (10″)
- 2 Joe Turner and Pete Johnson, EmArcy 36014
- 2 Eight to the Bar (w/A. Ammons), RCA 9 (10″)

Plas Johnson, see p. 62.

Pete Jolly
- 1 Impossible, Metrojazz 1014, *1014*
- 2 Jolly Jumps In, RCA 1105
- 2 The Five, RCA 1121
- 1 Duo, Trio, Quartet, RCA 1125
- 1 When Lights are Low, RCA 1367

Carmell Jones[102]
- 2 The Remarkable Carmell Jones, Pacific Jazz 29, *29*
- 1 Brass Bag (w/T. Lofton), Pacific Jazz 49, *49*
- 2 Business Meetin', Pacific Jazz 53, *53*

Elvin Jones
- 1 Elvin, Riverside 409, *9409*

Hank Jones
- 1 This is Ragtime Now, ABC-Paramount 496, *496*
- 1 Here's Love, Argo 728, *728*
- 1 The Talented Touch, Capitol 1044, *1044*
- 1 Porgy and Bess, Capitol 1175, *1175*
- 4 Urbanity, Clef 707 or Verve 8091
- 1 Hank Jones Swings Gigi, Golden Crest 3042, *5002*
- 1 Arrival Time, RCA 2570, *2570*
- 2 The Trio, Savoy 12023
- 2 Quartet/Quintet, Savoy 12037
- 2 Blue Bird, Savoy 12053
- 2 Have You Met Hank Jones, Savoy 12084
- 2 Hank Jones Quartet, Savoy 12087

Jo Jones
- 1 Jo Jones Trio, Everest 5023, *1023*
- 2 Vamp 'Till Ready, Everest 5099, *1099*
- 1 Percussion and Bass, Everest 5110, *1110*

---

[99] See also *Eddie Costa*.
[100] See also *Sonny Stitt*.
[101] See also p. 62.
[102] See also *Bud Shank*.

JAZZ RECORDINGS

Jonah Jones
2 Jazz Kaleidoscope, Bethlehem 4 (w/P. Brown; one side each)
1 Jonah Jones at the Embers, Vik 1135

Philly Joe Jones
1 Philly Joe's Beat, Atlantic 1340, *1340*
2 Blues for Dracula, Riverside 282
3 Drums Around the World, Riverside 302, *1147*
2 Philly Joe Jones Showcase, Riverside 313, *1159*

Quincy Jones[103]
2 This is How I Feel About Jazz, ABC-Paramount 149
3 Go West, Man, ABC-Paramount 186
2 Jazz Abroad, EmArcy 36083 (w/R. Haynes; one side each)

Sam Jones
1 The Soul Society, Riverside 324, *1172*
1 The Chant, Riverside 358, *9358*
2 Down Home, Riverside 432, *9432*

Thad Jones[104]
4 Detroit–New York Junction, Blue Note 1513
4 The Magnificent Thad Jones, Blue Note 1527
4 The Magnificent Thad Jones, Vol. 3, Blue Note 1546
5 The Fabulous Thad Jones, Debut 12 (10″)
5 Jazz Collaborations, Vol. 1 (w/C. Mingus), Debut 17 (10″)
5 Thad Jones, Debut 127
4 Mad Thad, Period 1208
2 Touche (w/F. Wess), Status 8310 (reissue of Prestige 7084; see p. 182)
3 Motor City Scene, United Artists 4025, *5025*

Clifford Jordan[105]
1 These Are My Roots, Atlantic 1444, *1444*
3 Clifford Jordan, Blue Note 1565
4 Cliff Craft, Blue Note 1582
2 A Story Tale (w/S. Red), Jazzland 40, *940*
3 Starting Time, Jazzland 52, *952*
3 Bearcat, Jazzland 69, *969*
3 Spellbound, Riverside 340, *9340*

Duke Jordan
3 Flight to Jordan, Blue Note 4046
5 Jazz Laboratory, Vol. 1, Signal 101
5 Duke Jordan Trio/Quintet, Signal 1202

Louis Jordan, see p. 62.

Sheila Jordan
4 Portrait of Sheila, Blue Note 9002, *89002*

Taft Jordan
1 The Moods of Taft Jordan, Mercury 20429, *60101*
2 Mood Indigo, Moodsville 21

Max Kaminsky
1 Chicago Jazz, Jazztone 1208
1 When the Saints Go Marching In, MGM 261 (10″)

1 Ambassador of Jazz, Westminster 6125, *15060*
1 Max Goes East, United Artists 3174, *6174*

Richie Kamuca[106]
1 Jazz Erotica, Hi Fi 604, *604*
3 Richie Kamuca Quartet, Mode 102

Dick Katz
2 Piano & Pen, Atlantic 1314, *1314*

Roger Kellaway
2 Jazz Portrait of Roger Kellaway, Regina 298, *298*

Wynton Kelly
4 Wynton Kelly Trio, Blue Note 5025 (10″)
1 Whisper Not, Jazzland 83, *983* (reissue of Riverside 254)
2 Wynton Kelly, Riverside 254
2 Kelly Blue, Riverside 298, *1142*
1 Undiluted, Verve 8622, *68622*

Stan Kenton
4 The Kenton Era, Capitol 569 (4 LP boxed set)

Barney Kessel[107]
3 On Fire, Emerald 1201, *2401*

Morgana King, see p. 112.

Teddi King, see p. 112.

Andy Kirk
1 Instrumentally Speaking, Decca 79232 ("fake" stereo)
2 A Mellow Bit of Rhythm, RCA 1302

(Rahsaan) Roland Kirk
1 Introducing Rahsaan Roland Kirk (w/I. Sullivan), Argo 669, *669* (color cover)
2 Third Dimension, Bethlehem 6064 (reissue of King 539)
4 Triple Threat, King 539
1 I Talk With the Spirits, Limelight 82008, *86008*
1 We Free Kings, Mercury 20679, *60679*
1 Domino, Mercury 20748, *60748*
1 Reeds and Deeds, Mercury 20800, *60800*
3 Roland Kirk Quartet Meets the Benny Golson Orchestra, Mercury 20844, *60844*
1 Kirk's Works (w/J. McDuff), Prestige 7210

Jimmy Knepper[108]
2 A Swinging Introduction to Jimmy Knepper, Bethlehem 77
5 New Faces (w/C. Porter), Debut 129
4 Pepper-Knepper Quintet (w/P. Adams), Metrojazz 1004, *1004*

Lee Konitz[109]
4 Lee Konitz With Warne Marsh, Atlantic 1217
4 Inside Hi-Fi, Atlantic 1258, *1258*
4 The Real Lee Konitz, Atlantic 1273
5 Subconscious-Lee, Prestige 7004
4 Originalee, Roost 416 (10″)

---

[103] See also *Harry Arnold, Sonny Stitt.*
[104] See also *Billy Mitchell, Sonny Rollins.*
[105] See also *John Gilmore, John Jenkins.*
[106] See also *Bill Perkins, Cy Touff.*
[107] See also *Dorothy Collins,* p. 107.
[108] See also *Tony Scott.*
[109] See also *Ralph Burns, Gerry Mulligan.*

4 Lee Konitz at Storyville, Storyville 304 (10")
4 Konitz, Storyville 313 (10")
4 Lee Konitz in Harvard Square, Storyville 323 (10")
4 Jazz at Storyville, Storyville 901 (reissue of Storyville 304 and 313)
4 Very Cool, Verve 8209
4 Tranquility, Verve 8281
4 An Image, Verve 8286, *6035* (*68286*)
5 Lee Konitz Meets Jimmy Giuffre, Verve 8335, *6073* (*68335*)
4 You and Lee, Verve 8362, *6131* (*68362*)
2 Motion, Verve 8399, *68399*

Irene Kral, see p. 112.

Gene Krupa
3 The Gene Krupa Trio at JATP, Clef 600 or Verve 8031
3 The Rocking Mr. Krupa, Clef 627
3 The Gene Krupa Sextet #3, Clef 631 or Clef 728
2 Gene Krupa Quartet, Clef 668
3 Gene Krupa-Lionel Hampton-Teddy Wilson, Clef 681 or Verve 8066
3 Gene Krupa and Buddy Rich, Clef 684 or Verve 8069
3 The Exciting Gene Krupa, Clef 687 or Verve 8071
2 Drum Boogie, Clef 703 or Verve 8087
1 Swingin' With Krupa, RCA Camden 340
1 The Mighty Two (w/L. Bellson), Roulette 52098, *52098*
3 Drummer Man (w/R. Eldridge, A. O'Day), Verve 2008
3 The Driving Gene Krupa, Verve 8107 (reissue of Clef 631)
2 Sing Sing Sing, Verve 8190 (reissue of Clef 627)
2 The Jazz Rhythms of Gene Krupa, Verve 8204
2 Krupa Rocks, Verve 8276
3 Gene Krupa Plays Gerry Mulligan Arrangements, Verve 8292, *6008* (*68292*)
2 Hey! Here's Gene Krupa, Verve 8300
2 Big Noise From Winnetka, Verve 8310, *6042* (*68310*)
1 Percussion King, Verve 8414, *68414*
1 New Quartet (w/C. Ventura), Verve 8584, *68584*
2 The Gene Krupa Story, Verve 15010, *6105* (*615010*) (movie soundtrack)

Steve Kuhn
1 Three Waves, Contact 5, *5*
2 Country & Western Sounds of Jazz (w/T. Akiyoshi), Dauntless 4308, *6308*

Steve Lacy
4 The Straight Horn of Steve Lacy, Candid 8007, *9007*
5 Reflections, New Jazz 8206
5 Evidence, New Jazz 8271
5 Soprano Saxophone, Prestige 7125

Tommy Ladnier
2 Blues and Stomps, Riverside 154
3 Tommy Ladnier, "X" 3027 (10")

Dave Lambert[111]
2 Sing & Swing Along, United Artists 3084, *6084*

Donald Lambert
2 Giant Stride, Solo Art 18001

Lambert, Hendricks and Bavan
1 Live at Basin Street East, RCA 2635, *2635*

111 See also *Lambert, Hendricks and Bavan/Ross*.

2 At Newport '63, RCA 2747, *2747*
1 Live at the Village Gate, RCA 2861, *2861*

Lambert, Hendricks and Ross
1 Sing a Song of Basie, ABC-Paramount 223
3 The Swingers (w/Z. Sims), World Pacific 1264

Harold Land
2 Hear Ye! (w/R. Mitchell), Atlantic 1376, *1376*
2 Harold in the Land of Jazz, Contemporary 3550
2 Grooveyard, Contemporary 7550 (stereo issue of Contemporary 3550)
3 The Fox, Hi Fi 612, *612*
1 Jazz Impressions of Folk Music, Imperial 9247, *12247*
3 West Coast Blues (w/W. Montgomery), Jazzland 20, *920*
2 Harold Land in New York, Jazzland 33, *933*

John LaPorta
3 John LaPorta Quintet (w/L. Mucci), Debut 10 (10")
3 Three Moods, Debut 122
1 Most Minor, Everest 5037, *1037*
1 Conceptions, Fantasy 3228
1 South American Brothers, Fantasy 3237
1 The Clarinet Artistry of John LaPorta, Fantasy 3248

Ellis Larkins[112]
1 Manhattan at Midnight, Decca 8303
1 The Soft Touch, Decca 9205
1 Blue and Sentimental, Decca 9211
1 Perfume and Rain, Storyville 316 (10")
2 Do Nothin' Till You Hear From Me, Storyville 913

Pete LaRoca
1 Basra, Blue Note 4205, *84205*
1 Turkish Women at the Bath, Douglas 782

Yusef Lateef[113]
1 Eastern Sounds, Moodsville 22
1 Other Sounds, New Jazz 8218
1 Cry!, Tender, New Jazz 8234
1 Into Something, New Jazz 8272
1 The Sounds of Yusef, Prestige 7122
1 The Three Faces of Yusef Lateef, Riverside 325, *1176*
1 The Centaur and the Phoenix, Riverside 337, *9337*
3 Before Dawn, Verve 8217

Latin Jazz Quintet, see Eric Dolphy.

Elliot Lawrence
2 Elliott Lawrence Plays Gerry Mulligan Arrangements, Fantasy 3206
2 Elliot Lawrence Plays Tiny Kahn and Johnny Mandel Arrangements, Fantasy 3219
2 Swinging at the Steel Pier, Fantasy 3236
2 Jump Steady, Sesac 1153/54
2 Music For Trapping, Top Rank 304
2 Jazz Goes Broadway, Vik 1113

Barbara Lea, see p. 112.

Jeanne Lee
3 The Newest Sound Around (w/R. Blake), RCA 2500, *2500*

112 See also *Ruby Braff, Lee Wiley*, p. 119.
113 See also *Clark Terry, Doug Watkins*.

JAZZ RECORDINGS

Julia Lee
2 Party Time, Capitol 2038

Wade Legge
3 Wade Legge Trio, Blue Note 5031 (10")

Carmen Leggio
2 Carmen Leggio Group, Jazz Unlimited 1000

Michel Legrand
1 Legrand Jazz, Columbia 1250, *8079*
1 Michel Legrand Big Band Plays Richard Rodgers, Philips 200-074, *600-074*

Harlan Leonard
3 Harlan Leonard and his Rockets, RCA Vintage 531

Harvey Leonard
2 Jazz Ecstasy, Keynote 1102

Johnny Letman
1 The Many Angles of Johnny Letman, Bethlehem 6053, *6053*

Stan Levey
2 West Coasting (w/C. Candoli), Bethlehem 9
1 This Time the Drum's on Me, Bethlehem 37
3 Grand Stan, Bethlehem 71
3 Drummin' the Blues, Liberty 3064 (w/M. Roach; one side each)
2 Stan Levey Quintet, Mode 101

Alonzo Levister
2 Manhattan Monodrama, Debut 125

Rod Levitt
2 Insight, RCA 3372, *3372*
2 Solid Ground, RCA 3448, *3448*
2 Forty-Second Street, RCA 3615, *3615*
2 Dynamic Sound Patterns, Riverside 471, *9471*

Lou Levy[114]
2 West Coast Wailers (w/C. Candoli), Atlantic 1268
2 Baby Grand Jazz, Jubilee 1101, *1101*
3 Lou Levy Trio, Nocturne 10 (10")
1 The Hymn, Philips 200-056, *600-056*
3 Solo Scene, RCA 1267
2 Jazz in Four Colors, RCA 1319
2 A Most Musical Fella, RCA 1491

George Lewis
2 George Lewis and his New Orleans All Stars, Circle 421 (10")
4 Jazz at the Ohio Union, Disc Jockey 100 (2 lp boxed set)
2 Jazz in the Classic New Orleans Tradition, Riverside 207 (includes 4 titles from Circle 421)
2 Jazz at Vespers, Riverside 230
1 Original Zenith Brass Band and the Eclipse Alley Five, Riverside 283
1 George Lewis and Turk Murphy at Newport (one side each), Verve 8232
1 The Perennial George Lewis, Verve 8277
1 On Stage, Vol. 1, Verve 8303
1 On Stage, Vol. 2, Verve 8304
1 Oh, Didn't He Ramble, Verve 8325, *6064 (68325)*

114 See also *Virgil Gonsalves*.

John Lewis[115]
1 Afternoon in Paris (w/S. Distel), Atlantic 1267
1 The John Lewis Piano, Atlantic 1272
3 The Wonderful World of Jazz, Atlantic 1375, *1375*
1 A Milanese Story, Atlantic 1388, *1388* (movie soundtrack)
1 European Encounter (w/S. Asmussen), Atlantic 1392, *1392*
2 Animal Dance (w/A. Mangelsdorff), Atlantic 1402, *1402*
1 Essence, Atlantic 1425, *1425*

Meade Lux Lewis
2 Boogie-Woogie Interpretations, Atlantic 133 (10")
2 Boogie-Woogie Classics, Blue Note 7018 (10")
3 Opera in Vout (Slim Gaillard)/Boogie Woogie at the Philharmonic (Lewis), Clef 506 (10")
3 Boogie-Woogie Piano and Drums (w/L. Bellson), Clef 632
2 Meade Lux Lewis, Down Home 7 or Verve 1007 (reissue of Clef 632)
2 The Blues Piano Artistry of Meade Lux Lewis, Riverside 402, *9402*
2 Barrel House Piano, Tops 1533
2 Cat House Piano, Verve 1006

Mel Lewis[116]
3 Mel Lewis Sextet, Mode 103
3 Got Cha, San Francisco 2

Abbey Lincoln
1 Straight Ahead, Barnaby *31037* (reissue of Candid *9015*)
4 Straight Ahead, Candid 8015, *9015*
4 Affair, Liberty 3025
3 That's Him, Riverside 251, *1107*
3 It's Magic, Riverside 277
1 Abbey is Blue, Riverside 308, *1153*

Melba Liston
3 Melba Liston and her Bones, Metrojazz 1013, *1013*

Booker Little
4 Booker Little and Friend, Bethlehem 6061, *6061*
5 Out Front, Candid 8037, *9027*
5 Booker Little, Time 52011, *2011*
4 Booker Little 4 (w/M. Roach), United Artists 4034, *5034*

Hugo Loewenstern
2 Who Said Good Music is Dead? (w/J. Richards), Jazz Art 1103

Harry Lookofsky
2 Stringsville, Atlantic 1319, *1319*

Mundell Lowe
1 Satan In High Heels, Charlie Parker 406, *406* (movie soundtrack)
1 Low Down Guitar, Jazzland 8 (reissue of Riverside 238)
3 Tacet for Neurotics, Offbeat 3010, *93010* (reissue of Riverside 219; liner notes by Frank Sinatra)
3 The Mundell Lowe Quintet, RCA 3002 (10")
2 Mundell Lowe Quartet, Riverside 204
3 Guitar Moods, Riverside 208
3 New Music of Alec Wilder, Riverside 219 (liner notes by Frank Sinatra)
3 A Grand Night For Swinging, Riverside 238

115 See also *Modern Jazz Quartet, Orchestra U.S.A.*
116 See also *Bill Holman*.

Howard Lucraft
  2 Showcase for Modern Jazz, Decca 8679

Jimmy Lunceford
  1 Lunceford Special, Columbia 654
  2 Jimmy Lunceford and His Orchestra, Decca 8050

Johnny Lytle
  1 Nice and Easy, Jazzland 67, *967*

Teo Macero
  3 What's New (6 titles by Macero/5 titles by B. Prince), Columbia 842
  4 Explorations, Debut 6 (10″)
  4 Teo with the Prestige Jazz Quartet, Prestige 7104

Junior Mance
  1 Junior, Verve 8319, *6057* (*68319*)

Albert Mangelsdorff, see John Lewis.

Mangione Brothers (Chuck and Gap)
  1 Jazz Brothers, Riverside 335, *9335*
  1 Hey Baby, Riverside 371, *9371*
  1 Spring Fever, Riverside 405, *9405*

Herbie Mann
  1 The Herbie Mann Quartet, Bethlehem 24
  1 The Herbie Mann–Sam Most Quintet, Bethlehem 40
  1 Herbie Mann Plays, Bethlehem 58
  1 Love and the Weather, Bethlehem 63
  1 Flute Fraternity (w/B. Collette), Mode 114 or Interlude 503, *1003*
  1 Just Wailin', New Jazz 8211
  1 Flute Souffle (w/B. Jaspar), Prestige 7101
  1 Flute Flight (w/B. Jaspar), Prestige 7124
  1 Sultry Serenade, Riverside 234

Shelly Manne[117]
  1 Boss Sounds!, Atlantic 1469, *1469*
  1 Pepper-Manne, Charlie Parker 836 (w/A. Pepper; one side each)

Lawrence Marable
  5 Lawrence Marable Tenorman (w/J. Clay), Jazz West 8

Charlie Mariano
  4 Charlie Mariano, Bethlehem 25
  4 Charlie Mariano Plays, Bethlehem 49
  4 Toshiko–Mariano Quartet, Candid 8015, *9015*
  3 Charlie Mariano Sextet/Dick Collins–Nat Pierce Nonet (one side each), Fantasy 3224
  5 Charlie Mariano With His Jazz Group, Imperial 3006 (10″)
  5 Modern Saxophone Stylings, Imperial 3007 (10″)
  5 New Sounds From Boston, Prestige 130 (10″)
  5 Boston All Stars, Prestige 153 (10″)
  3 Jazz Portrait of Charlie Mariano, Regina 286, *286*
  3 Beauties of 1918 (w/J. Dodgian), World Pacific 1245, *1014*

Reese Markewich
  2 New Designs in Jazz, Modernage 134

[117] See also *Bill Evans, Jack Montrose, Gerry Mulligan, Ruth Price*, p. 115.

Dodo Marmarosa
  3 Dodo's Back, Argo 4012, *4012*
  5 Piano Contrasts, Dial 208 (10″)

Warne Marsh[118]
  4 Lee Konitz with Warne Marsh, Atlantic 1217
  4 Warne Marsh, Atlantic 1291, *1291*
  5 Jazz of Two Cities, Imperial 9027
  5 Music For Prancing, Mode 125

Pat Martino (aka Pat Azzara)
  2 El Hombre, Prestige 7513, *7513*
  2 Strings!, Prestige 7547, *7547*
  2 East, Prestige 7562, *7562*
  1 Baiyina, Prestige 7589

Mat Mathews[119]
  1 Accordian Solos, Brunswick 54013
  2 The Modern Art of Jazz, Dawn 1104

Mary Ann McCall, see p. 113.

Howard McGhee
  2 The Return of Howard McGhee, Bethlehem 42
  3 Life is Just a Bowl of Cherries, Bethlehem 61
  3 Dusty Blue, Bethlehem 6055, *6055*
  5 Howard McGhee's All Stars, Blue Note 5012 (10″)
  5 Howard McGhee All Stars, Vol. 2, Blue Note 5024 (10″)
  5 Night Music, Dial 217 (10″)
  5 Music From "The Connection", Felsted 7512
  2 Jazz Goes to the Battlefront, Vol. 1, Hi Lo 6001 (10″)
  2 Jazz Goes to the Battlefront, Vol. 2, Hi Lo 6002 (10″)
  1 Nobody Knows You When You're Down, United Artists 14028, *15028*

Ken McIntyre
  4 Looking Ahead (w/E. Dolphy), New Jazz 8247
  2 Stone Blues, New Jazz 8259
  2 Way, Way Out, United Artists 3336, *6336*
  1 Year of the Iron Sheep, United Artists 14015, *15015*

Dave McKenna[120]
  4 Solo Piano, ABC-Paramount 104
  3 Dual Piano Jazz (w/H. Overton), Bethlehem 6049, *6049*
  3 Dave McKenna, Epic 3558, *527*
  3 Lullabies in Jazz, Realm 923

McKinney's Cotton Pickers
  2 McKinney's Cotton Pickers, RCA 24 (10″)
  2 McKinney's Cotton Pickers, "X" 3031 (10″)

Hal McKusick
  5 Hal McKusick, Bethlehem 16
  4 Jazz at the Academy, Coral 57116
  4 Hal McKusick Quintet (w/A. Farmer), Coral 57131
  4 Cross Section—Saxes, Decca 9209, *79209*
  3 Hal McKusick Plays/Betty St. Claire Sings, Jubilee 15 (10″)
  5 Triple Exposure, Prestige 7135
  4 In a Twentieth Century Drawing Room, RCA 1164
  4 The Jazz Workshop, RCA 1366

[118] See also *Ted Brown*.
[119] See also *Eddie Costa*.
[120] See also *Ruby Braff*.

JAZZ RECORDINGS

Jackie McLean[121]
- 5 The New Tradition, Ad Lib 6601
- 3 Swing, Swang, Swingin', Blue Note 4024
- 2 Jackie's Bag, Blue Note 4051
- 5 A Fickle Sonance, Blue Note 4089, *4089*
- 1 Action, Blue Note 4218, *4218*
- 1 New and Old Gospel, Blue Note 4262, *4262*
- 2 Jackie McLean Quintet, Jubilee 1064 (reissue of Ad Lib 6601)
- 3 Fat Jazz, Jubilee 1093
- 4 McLean's Scene, New Jazz, 8212
- 4 Makin' the Changes, New Jazz 8231
- 4 A Long Drink of the Blues, New Jazz 8253
- 2 Lights Out, New Jazz 8263 (reissue of Prestige 7035)
- 2 4, 5 and 6, New Jazz 8279 (reissue of Prestige 7048)
- 2 Steeplechase, New Jazz 8290 (reissue of Prestige 7068)
- 2 Alto Madness, New Jazz/Status 8312 (reissue of Prestige 7114)
- 2 Jackie McLean and Company, New Jazz/Status 8323 (reissue of Prestige 7087)
- 5 Lights Out, Prestige 7035
- 5 4, 5 and 6, Prestige 7048
- 5 Jackie's Pals, Prestige 7068
- 5 Jackie McLean and Company, Prestige 7087
- 5 Alto Madness (w/J. Jenkins), Prestige 7114

Ted McNabb
- 2 Ted McNabb and Company, Epic 3663, *558*

Jimmy McPartland
- 2 Dixieland Band, Brunswick 54018
- 2 Jimmy McPartland's Dixieland, Epic 3371
- 2 Jimmy McPartland and his Dixieland Band, Epic 3463, *506*
- 1 That Happy Dixieland Jazz, RCA Camden 549, *549*

Marian McPartland
- 1 Marian McPartland at the London House, Argo 640, *640*
- 1 Marian McPartland at the Hickory House, Capitol 574
- 1 After Dark, Capitol 699
- 1 Marian McPartland Trio, Capitol 785

Carmen McRae, see p. 113.

Jay McShann
- 2 New York—1208 Miles, Decca 79236 ("fake" stereo) (includes Charlie Parker's first studio recordings while a sideman with McShann's band.)

Lou Mecca[122]
- 3 Lou Mecca Quartet, Blue Note 5067 (10")

John Mehegan
- 1 Reflections, Savoy 12020
- 2 A Pair of Pianos (w/E. Costa), Savoy 12049
- 1 How I Play Jazz Piano, Savoy 12076
- 3 Casual Affair, TJ 1

Gil Melle
- 4 Patterns in Jazz, Blue Note 1517
- 4 Gil Melle Quintet/Sextett, Blue Note 5020 (10")
- 4 Gil Melle Quintet (w/T. Farlow, U. Green), Blue Note 5033 (10")
- 3 Gil Melle Quartet (w/L. Mecca), Blue Note 5054 (10")
- 3 Five Impressions of Color (w/D. Butterfield), Blue Note 5063 (10")
- 4 Primitive Modern, Prestige 7040
- 5 Gil's Guests, Prestige 7063
- 4 Quadrama, Prestige 7097

Helen Merrill, see p. 114.

Metronome All Stars
- 3 Metronome All Stars 1956, Clef 743 or Verve 8030
- 2 Metronome All Stars, Harmony 7044
- 2 The Metronome All-Star Bands, RCA Camden 426

Mezz Mezzrow
- 2 Mezz Mezzrow and his Band, Blue Note 7023 (10")
- 2 Mezzin' Around (w/F. Newton), RCA 1006
- 2 Mezz Mezzrow, "X" 3027 (10")

Lizzie Miles[123]
- 1 A Night in Old New Orleans (w/S. Bonano), Capitol 792
- 1 Moans and Blues, Cook 1182, *1182*
- 1 Hot Songs, Cook 1183, *1183*
- 1 Torchy Lullabies, Cook 1184, *1184*
- 1 Clambake on Bourbon St., Cook 11815, *11815*

Big Miller
- 1 Did You Ever Hear the Blues?, United Artists 3047, *6047*

Punch Miller, see Mutt Carey.

Jack Millman
- 2 Jazz Studio 4, Decca 8156
- 2 Blowing Up a Storm, Era 20005
- 1 Shades of Things to Come, Liberty 6007

Charles Mingus[124]
- 5 Pithecanthropus Erectus, Atlantic 1237
- 5 The Clown (w/narration by J. Shepard), Atlantic 1260 (black label)
- 3 The Clown, Atlantic 1260 (multicolored label)
- 5 The Jazz Experiments of Charles Mingus, Bethlehem 65 (reissue of Period 1107 and 1111)
- 5 East Coasting, Bethlehem 6019, *6019*
- 5 A Modern Jazz Symposium of Music and Poetry, Bethlehem 6026, *6026*
- 5 Charles Mingus Presents Charles Mingus, Candid 8005, *9005*
- 5 Mingus, Candid 8021, *9021*
- 5 Strings and Keys (w/S. Givens), Debut 1 (10")
- 5 Mingus at the Bohemia, Debut 123
- 3 Mingus Three, Jubilee 1173
- 2 Pre-Bird, Mercury 20627, *60627*
- 5 Mingus at Monterey, Mingus Jazz Workshop 001/002 (2 LPs) [125]
- 5 Town Hall Concert, Vol. 1, Mingus Jazz Workshop 005
- 5 My Favorite Quintet, Vol. 1 (Tyrone Guthrie Theater), Mingus Jazz Workshop 009

[123] See also *Bob Scobey.*
[124] See also *Duke Ellington, Thad Jones.*
[125] Originally privately pressed for mail-order sales; all but MJW 0013/0014 were later released on commercial labels; other such private recordings are rumored to exist but are not included pending verification.

[121] See also *Kenny Dorham, Freddie Redd.*
[122] See also *Gil Melle.*
NOTE: Additional Blue Note LPs, all currently available, are collectible if they are original issues (W. 63rd St. address on label).

JAZZ

  5 Music Written for Monterey 1965 Not Heard Played in its Entirety at UCLA, Mingus Jazz Workshop 0013/0014 (2 LPs)
  5 Jazzical Moods, Vol. 1, Period 1107 (10″)
  5 Jazzical Moods, Vol. 2, Period 1111 (10″)
  1 Tiajuana Moods, RCA 2533, *2533*
  3 Jazz Portraits, United Artists 4036, *5036*
  2 Money Jungle (w/D. Ellington, M. Roach), United Artists 14017, *15017*

Billy Mitchell[126]
  1 This is Billy, Smash 27027, *67027*
  1 A Little Juicy (w/ T. Jones), Smash 27042, *67042*

Blue Mitchell[127]
  1 The Thing to Do, Blue Note 4178, *84178*
  1 Boss Horn, Blue Note 4257, *84257*
  3 Big 6, Riverside 273
  3 Out of the Blue, Riverside 293, *1131*
  3 Blue Soul, Riverside 309, *1155*
  1 Blue's Moods, Riverside 336, *9336*
  3 Smooth as the Wind, Riverside 367, *9367*
  3 A Sure Thing, Riverside 414, *9414*
  2 The Cup Bearers, Riverside 439, *9439*

Red Mitchell
  2 Hear Ye (w/H. Land), Atlantic 1376, *1376*
  3 Jazz Mainstream, Bethlehem 2 (w/O. Pettiford; one side each)
  2 Red Mitchell, Bethlehem 38
  2 Presenting Red Mitchell, Contemporary 3538
  2 Rejoice (Cello Debut at the Renaissance), Pacific Jazz 22

Whitey Mitchell
  3 Whitey Mitchell Sextette, ABC-Paramount 126

The Mitchells (Blue, Red and Whitey)
  2 Get Those Elephants Outa Here, Metrojazz 1012, *1012*

MJT + 3 (Bob Cranshaw, Walter Perkins, others)
  1 Daddy-O Presents MJT + 3, Argo 621
  1 MJT + 3, Vee Jay 1013, *1013*
  1 Make Everybody Happy, Vee Jay 3008
  1 MJT + 3, Vee Jay 3014, *3014*

Hank Mobley[128]
  4 Hank Mobley (w/D. Byrd, L. Morgan), Blue Note 1540
  3 Hank Mobley and his All Stars, Blue Note 1544 (W. 63rd St. address on label)
  4 Hank Mobley Quintet, Blue Note 1550
  4 Hank, Blue Note 1560
  5 Hank Mobley, Blue Note 1568
  5 Peckin' Time (w/L. Morgan), Blue Note 1574
  4 Soul Station, Blue Note, 4031
  2 Roll Call, Blue Note 4058, *84058*
  3 Workout, Blue Note 4080, *84080*
  2 The Turnaround, Blue Note 4186, *84186*
  2 Dippin', Blue Note 4209, *84209*
  5 Hank Mobley Quartet, Blue Note 5066 (10″)
  4 Mobley's Message, Prestige 7061
  4 Mobley's Second Message, Prestige 7082

[126] See also *Al Grey.*
[127] See also *Sonny Red.*
[128] See also *Max Roach.*
NOTE: All Blue Note LPs with original addresses on label; see p. 128.

Modern Jazz Quartet[129]
  2 The Modern Jazz Quartet at Music Inn (Guest Artist: Jimmy Giuffre), Atlantic 1247
  1 One Never Knows (Original Film Score for "No Sun in Venice"), Atlantic 1284, *1284*
  2 The Modern Jazz Quartet at Music Inn, Vol. 2 (Guest Artist: Sonny Rollins), Atlantic 1299, *1299*
  3 Concorde, Prestige 7005 (original photo cover)
  1 Concorde, Prestige 7005 (art cover)
  2 Django, Prestige 7057
  2 Modern Jazz Quartet/Milt Jackson Quintet, Prestige 7059
  2 Odds Against Tomorrow, United Artists 4063, *5063* (movie soundtrack)
  2 The Modern Jazz Quartet and the Oscar Peterson Trio at the Opera House (one side each), Verve 8269

Miff Mole
  1 Doorway to Dixie, Argo 606 (w/C. Touff; one side each)

Thelonious Monk[130]
  4 Genius of Modern Music, Vol. 1, Blue Note 1510 (Lexington Ave. address on label)
  4 Genius of Modern Music, Vol. 2, Blue Note 1511 Lexington Ave. address)
  3 Thelonious Monk with John Coltrane, Jazzland 46, *946*
  5 Thelonious Monk Trio, Prestige, 7027
  5 Featuring Thelonious Monk, Prestige 7053
  5 Thelonious Monk and Sonny Rollins, Prestige 7075
  2 Monk's Moods, Prestige 7159 (reissue of Prestige 7027)
  2 Work!, Prestige 7169 (reissue of Prestige 7075)
  2 We See, Prestige 7245 (reissue of Prestige 7053)
  5 Thelonious Monk Plays Duke Ellington, Riverside 201 (original photo cover)
  2 Thelonious Monk Plays Duke Ellington, Riverside 201 (art cover)
  5 The Unique Thelonious Monk, Riverside 209 (original photo cover)
  2 The Unique Thelonious Monk, Riverside 209 (art cover)
  4 Brilliant Corners, Riverside 226 (white label)
  3 Brilliant Corners, Riverside 226, *1174* (mono: blue label; stereo: black label)
  4 Thelonious Himself, Riverside 235 (white label)
  2 Thelonious Himself, Riverside 235 (blue label)
  4 Monk's Music, Riverside 242 (white label)
  3 Monk's Music, Riverside 242, *1102* (mono: blue label; stereo: black label)
  2 Mulligan Meets Monk, Riverside 247, *1106*
  2 Thelonious in Action, Riverside 262, *1190*
  2 Misterioso, Riverside 279, *1133*
  3 The Thelonious Monk Orchestra at Town Hall, Riverside 300, *1138*
  2 5 by Monk by 5, Riverside 305, *1150*
  3 Thelonious Alone in San Francisco, Riverside 312, *1158*
  3 Thelonious Monk Quartet + 2 at the Blackhawk, Riverside 323, *1171*

J.R. Monterose[131]
  4 J. R. Monterose (w/I. Sullivan), Blue Note 1536
  5 The Message, Jaro 5004, *8004*
  5 In Action, Studio 4

[129] See also *Sonny Rollins.*
[130] See also *Art Blakey, Clark Terry.*
[131] See also *Rene Thomas.*

JAZZ RECORDINGS

Montgomery Brothers (Wes, Buddy, and Monk)
2 Montgomery Brothers, Fantasy 3308, *8052*
2 Montgomery Brothers in Canada, Fantasy 3323, *8066*
2 Montgomeryland, Pacific Jazz 5, *5*
2 Wes, Buddy & Monk Montgomery (w/H. Land, F. Hubbard), Pacific Jazz 17
1 Grooveyard, Riverside 362, *9362*
2 The Montgomery Brothers and 5 Others, World Pacific 1240

Wes Montgomery[132]
2 Wes Montgomery Trio, Riverside 310, *1156*
2 The Incredible Jazz Guitar of Wes Montgomery, Riverside 320, *1169*
2 Movin' Along, Riverside 342, *9342*
1 So Much Guitar!, Riverside 382, *9382*
1 Bags Meets Wes (w/M. Jackson), Riverside 407, *9407*
1 Full House, Riverside 434, *9434*
1 Boss Guitar, Riverside 459, *9459*
1 Pretty Blue, Riverside 472, *9472*
1 Portrait of Wes, Riverside 492, *9492*
2 Guitar on the Go, Riverside 949, *9494*

Jack Montrose
3 Arranged/Played/Composed by Jack Montrose (w/ B. Gordon), Atlantic 1223
3 Jack Montrose Sextet (w/B. Gordon, C. Candoli, S. Manne), Pacific Jazz 1208
3 Arranged by Montrose, Pacific Jazz 1214
3 Blues and Vanilla (w/R. Norvo), RCA 1451
3 The Horn's Full (w/R. Norvo), RCA 1572

James Moody
2 James Moody With Strings, Blue Note 5005 (10″)
2 James Moody and his Modernists (w/C. Pozo), Blue Note 5006 (10″)
5 His Saxophone and His Band, Dial 209 (10″).
1 The Moody Story, EmArcy 36031
3 Hi-Fi Party, Prestige 7011
3 Wail, Moody, Wail, Prestige 7036
3 Moody's Moods, Prestige 7056
3 Moody, Prestige 7072
2 James Moody, Vol. 1, Roost 405 (10″)
1 Runnin' the Gamut, Scepter 525, *525*

Moondog (Louis Thomas Hardin)
3 Snaketime Series, Moondog Records 1
3 Caribea, Prestige 7042
3 More Moondog, Prestige 7069
3 The Story of Moondog, Prestige 7099

Joe Mooney, see p. 114.

Ada Moore[133]
3 Jazz Workshop, Vol. 3, Debut 15 (10″)

Brew Moore
3 Brew Moore Quintet, Fantasy 3222
3 Brew Moore, Fantasy, 3264
3 Brew Moore in Europe, Fantasy 6013, *86013*

[132] See also *Cannonball Adderley, Harold Land*.
[133] See also *Buck Clayton*.

Oscar Moore[134]
2 Oscar Moore Quartet, Tampa 10
2 Galivantin' Guitar, Tampa 25

Lee Morgan[135]
3 Lee Morgan Indeed!, Blue Note 1538
4 Lee Morgan Sextet, Blue Note 1541
3 Lee Morgan, Vol. 3, Blue Note 1557
4 City Lights, Blue Note 1575
2 The Cooker, Blue Note 1578
5 Candy, Blue Note 1590
2 Lee-Way, Blue Note 4034
1 Delightfulee, Blue Note 4243, *84243*
3 Take Twelve, Jazzland 80, *980*
2 All the Way, Sunset 5263 (reissue of Blue Note 1590)
1 Here's Lee Morgan, Vee Jay 3007, *3007*
1 Expoobident, Vee Jay 3015, *3015*

Jelly Roll Morton[136]
3 The Saga of Mr. Jelly Lord, Vol. 1, Circle 14001
3 The Saga of Mr. Jelly Lord, Vol. 2, Circle 14002
3 The Saga of Mr. Jelly Lord, Vol. 3, Circle 14003
3 The Saga of Mr. Jelly Lord, Vol. 4, Circle 14004
3 The Saga of Mr. Jelly Lord, Vol. 5, Circle 14005
3 The Saga of Mr. Jelly Lord, Vol. 6, Circle 14006
3 The Saga of Mr. Jelly Lord, Vol. 7, Circle 14007
3 The Saga of Mr. Jelly Lord, Vol. 8, Circle 14008
3 The Saga of Mr. Jelly Lord, Vol. 9, Circle 14009
3 The Saga of Mr. Jelly Lord, Vol. 10, Circle 14010
3 The Saga of Mr. Jelly Lord, Vol. 11, Circle 14011
3 The Saga of Mr. Jelly Lord, Vol. 12, Circle 14012
2 New Orleans Memories, Commodore 30000
2 The King of New Orleans Jazz, RCA 1649
1 Stomps and Joys, RCA Vintage 508
1 Hot Jazz, Pop Jazz, Hokum and Hilarity, RCA Vintage 524
1 Mr. Jelly Lord, RCA Vintage 546
1 I Thought I Heard Buddy Bolden Say, RCA Vintage 559
2 Classic Piano Solos, Riverside 111
2 The Incomparable Jelly Roll Morton, Riverside 128
2 Mr. Jelly Lord, Riverside 132
2 Jelly Roll Morton Plays and Sings, Riverside 133
2 Rags and Blues, Riverside 140
2 Boyhood Memories, Riverside 9001 (reissue of Circle 14001)
2 The Animule Ball, Riverside 9002 (reissue of Circle 14002)
2 Discourse on Jazz, Riverside 9003 (reissue of Circle 14003)
2 Creepy Feeling, Riverside 9004 (reissue of Circle 14004)
2 Georgia Skin Game, Riverside 9005 (reissue of Circle 14005)
2 The Pearls, Riverside 9006 (reissue of Circle 14006)
2 Mamie's Blues, Riverside 9007 (reissue of Circle 14007)
2 The Murder Ballad, Riverside 9008 (reissue of Circle 14008)
2 Jack the Bear, Riverside 9009 (reissue of Circle 14009)
2 Original Jelly Roll Blues, Riverside 9010 (reissue of Circle 14010)

[134] See also *Inez Jones* (p. 111).
[135] See also *Hank Mobley*.
[136] Recorded for the archives of the Library of Congress in 1938 by Alan Lomax. Circle 14001-14012 (Riverside 9001-9012) contain both music and autobiographical reminiscences. They were issued as single volumes only. Estimated value of the complete Circle recordings is $250.
NOTE: All Blue Note LPs with original addresses on label; see p. 128.

2 Buddy Bolden's Blues, Riverside 9011 (reissue of Circle 14011)
2 The Storyville Story, Riverside 9012 (reissue of Circle 14012)

Sam Most
2 I'm Nuts About the Most, Bethlehem 18
1 The Herbie Mann-Sam Most Quintet, Bethlehem 40
3 Sam Most Plays Bird, Bud and Monk, Bethlehem 75
2 Sam Most With Strings, Bethlehem 78, *78*
2 Musically Yours, Bethlehem 6008
3 Sam Most Quartet Plus Two, Debut 11 (10")
1 Doubles in Jazz, Vanguard 8522 (w/D. Elliott, one side each)

Benny Moten
3 Benny Moten's Kansas City Jazz, Vol. 1, "X" 3004 (10")
3 Benny Moten's Kansas City Jazz, Vol. 2, "X" 3005 (10")
3 Benny Moten's Kansas City Jazz, Vol. 3, "X" 3038 (10")

Gerry Mulligan[137]
1 Modern Sounds, Capitol 691 (w/S. Rogers; one side each)
2 Presenting the Gerry Mulligan Sextet, EmArcy 36056
2 Mainstream of Jazz, EmArcy 36101
2 Gerry Mulligan Quartet/Paul Desmond Quintet (one side each), Fantasy 3220
3 Lee Konitz with the Gerry Mulligan Quartet, Pacific Jazz 406
2 California Concerts, Pacific Jazz 1201 or World Pacific 1201
2 Gerry Mulligan Quartet, Pacific Jazz 1207 or World Pacific 1207
2 Paris Concert, Pacific Jazz 1210 or World Pacific 1210
2 Gerry Mulligan Quartet (at Storyville), Pacific Jazz 1228 or World Pacific 1228
2 The Gerry Mulligan Songbook, Vol. 1, Pacific Jazz 1237 or World Pacific 1237, *1001*
2 Reunion with Chet Baker, Pacific Jazz 1241 or World Pacific 1241, *1007*
4 Mulligan Plays Mulligan, Prestige 7006
1 Two of a Mind (w/P. Desmond), RCA 2624, *2624*
3 The Jazz Combo from "I Want to Live" (w/A. Farmer, S. Manne), United Artists 4006, *5006*
2 The Teddy Wilson Trio/Gerry Mulligan Quartet with Bob Brookmeyer at Newport, Verve 8235
3 The Gerry Mulligan–Paul Desmond Quartet, Verve 8246
2 Getz Meets Mulligan in Hi-Fi, Verve 8249, *6003* (*68249*)
3 Gerry Mulligan Meets Ben Webster, Verve 8343, *6104* (*68343*)
2 Gerry Mulligan Meets Johnny Hodges, Verve 8367, *68367*
2 The Concert Jazz Band, Verve 8388, *68388*
2 Gerry Mulligan and the Concert Jazz Band at the Village Vanguard, Verve 8396, *68396*
2 Gerry Mulligan Presents a Concert in Jazz, Verve 8415, *68415*
2 Concert Jazz Band on Tour (w/Z. Sims), Verve 8438, *68438*
1 Gerry Mulligan Quartet, Verve 8466, *68466*
1 Blues in Time, Verve 8478, *68478* (reissue of Verve 8246)
1 Gerry Mulligan '63, Verve 8515, *68515*
1 Gerry Mulligan Meets Ben Webster, Verve 8534, *68534* (reissue of Verve 8343)
1 Lee Konitz–Gerry Mulligan–Chet Baker, World Pacific 1273 (reissue of Pacific Jazz 406)

[137] See also *Thelonious Monk, Annie Ross, Phil Sunkel*.

Lyle (Spud) Murphy
1 Gone With the Woodwinds!, Contemporary 3506
1 New Orbits in Sound, GNP 33

Mark Murphy, see p. 114.

Turk Murphy
1 When the Saints Go Marching In, Columbia 546
1 Barrelhouse Jazz, Columbia 595
1 Dancing Jazz, Columbia 650
1 Live at the New Orleans Jazz Festival, Columbia 793
1 New Orleans Shuffle, Columbia 927
1 Music For Losers, Verve 1013
1 Turk Murphy at Easy Street, Verve 1015
1 George Lewis and Turk Murphy at Newport (one side each), Verve 8232

Vido Musso
2 The Swingin'st, Crown 5007 or Modern 1207
1 Teenage Dance Party, Crown 5029

Boots Mussulli
3 Kenton Presents Boots Mussulli, Capitol 6506 (10")
5 Serge Chaloff and Boots Mussulli, Storyville 310 (10")

Marty Napoleon
2 Rare Musical Vintage (w/T. Napoleon), Heritage 0106

Phil Napoleon[138]
1 Dixieland Classics, Vol. 1, EmArcy 36033

Ted Nash
1 Star Eyes, Columbia 989
1 The Brothers Nash (w/D. Nash), Liberty 6011
1 Made Without Microphones, Repeat 100-5

Fats Navarro
5 The Fabulous Fats Navarro, Vol. 1, Blue Note 1531
5 The Fabulous Fats Navarro, Vol. 2, Blue Note 1532
3 Classics of Modern Jazz, Vol. 1 (w/T. Dameron), Jazzland 50, *950*
1 Fats Navarro Memorial, Savoy 12011

Oliver Nelson[139]
2 Nocturne (w/L. Winchester), Moodsville 13
3 Meet Oliver Nelson, New Jazz 8224
2 Taking Care of Business, New Jazz 8233
3 Screamin' the Blues, New Jazz 8243
3 Straight Ahead (w/E. Dolphy), New Jazz 8255

New Orleans Rhythm Kings
2 N.O.R.K., Riverside 102
2 Tin Roof Blues: N.O.R.K., Vol. 2, Riverside 146

Phineas Newborn, Jr.[140]
3 Here is Phineas, Atlantic 1235, *1235*
3 Phineas' Rainbow, RCA 1421
1 While My Lady Sleeps, RCA 1474
2 Phineas Newborn, Jr. Plays Jamaica, RCA 1589
3 Fabulous Phineas, RCA 1873, *1873*
2 Piano Portraits, Roulette 52031, *52031*
2 I Love a Piano, Roulette 52043, *52043*

[138] See also *Muggsy Spanier*.
[139] See also *Lem Winchester*.
[140] See also *Roy Haynes*.

JAZZ RECORDINGS

David "Fathead" Newman
- 2 Sound of the Wide Open Spaces (w/J. Clay), Riverside 327, *1178*

Joe Newman[141]
- 2 The Happy Cats, Coral 57121
- 1 Soft Swingin' Jazz (w/S. Scott), Coral 57208
- 1 The Count's Men, Jazztone 1220
- 3 Locking Horns (w/Z. Sims), Rama 1003
- 3 All I Want to Do is Swing, RCA 1118
- 3 I'm Still Swinging, RCA 1198
- 3 Salute to Satch, RCA 1324
- 2 Locking Horns (w/Z. Sims), Roulette 52009, *52009*
- 1 Joe Newman with Woodwinds, Roulette 52014, *52014*
- 3 Joe Newman and the Boys in the Band, Storyville 318 (10")
- 3 I Feel Like a Newman, Storyville 905
- 2 Jive at Five (w/F. Wess), Swingville 2011
- 2 Good 'N' Groovy, Swingville 2019
- 2 Joe's Hap'nin's, Swingville 2027
- 3 The Midgets, Vik 1060
- 2 Countin', World Pacific 1288, *1288*

Albert Nicholas
- 2 Creole Reeds, Riverside 216 (w/S. Bechet; one side each)

Herbie Nichols
- 5 Love, Gloom, Cash, Love, Bethlehem 81
- 5 Herbie Nichols Trio, Blue Note 1519
- 5 The Prophetic Herbie Nichols, Vol. 1, Blue Note 5068 (10")
- 5 The Prophetic Herbie Nichols, Vol. 2, Blue Note 5069 (10")

Lennie Niehaus
- 3 Lennie Niehaus, Vol. 3: The Octet, No. 2, Contemporary 3503
- 3 Lennie Niehaus, Vol. 4: The Quintets & Strings, Contemporary 3510
- 3 Lennie Niehaus, Vol. 1: The Quintets, Contemporary 3518
- 3 Lennie Niehaus, Vol. 5: The Sextet, Contemporary 3524
- 3 Zounds! Lennie Niehaus, Vol. 2: The Octet, Contemporary 3540
- 2 I Swing for You, EmArcy 36118 or Mercury 20555, *60123*

Sal Nistico
- 2 Heavyweights, Jazzland 66, *966*
- 2 Comin' On Up, Riverside 457, *9457*

Jimmy Noone
- 2 Apex Club Orchestra, Brunswick 58007 (10")

Ken Nordine, see p. 114.

Red Norvo[142]
- 2 Mainstream Jazz, Continental 16005
- 4 Dancing on the Ceiling, Decca 5501 (10")
- 5 Fabulous Jam Session, Dial 903
- 5 Red Norvo Trio Vol. 1, Discovery 4005
- 1 Windjammer City Style, Dot 3126, *25126*
- 1 Red Norvo and His All Stars, Epic 3128
- 3 The Red Norvo Trio, *Fantasy* 3-19

- 3 Red Norvo with Strings, Fantasy 3218
- 3 Red Norvo Trios, Fantasy 3244
- 5 Collections (w/A. Pepper, J. Morello), Intro 608
- 2 Ad Lib, Liberty 3035
- 2 Vibe-Rations in Hi-Fi, Liberty 6012
- 2 HI-FIve, RCA 1420
- 3 Red Norvo in Hi-Fi/Stereo, RCA 1711, *1711*
- 3 Red Plays the Blues, RCA 1729
- 3 Art Pepper–Red Norvo Sextet, Score 4031 (reissue of Intro 608)
- 1 Norvo Naturally, Tampa 35
- 4 Red's Rose Room, "X" 3034 (10")

Anita O'Day, see p. 114.

Chico O'Farrill
- 2 Jazz North/South of the Border, Clef 699 or Verve 8083

King Oliver
- 2 King Oliver, Brunswick 58020 (10")
- 1 King Oliver, Epic 3208
- 3 Lincoln Gardens, Jazz Panorama 1205
- 1 King Oliver in New York, RCA Vintage 529
- 2 Back o' Town, Riverside 130

Orchestra U.S.A. (John Lewis, musical director)
- 3 Debut, Colpix 448, *448*
- 2 Jazz Journey, Columbia 2247, *9047*
- 2 Sonorities, Columbia 2395, *9195*
- 3 Mack the Knife, RCA 3498, *3498*

Original Dixieland Jazz Band
- 1 The Original Dixieland Jazz Band, RCA Vintage 547
- 2 The Original Dixieland Jazz Band, Riverside 156/157 (2 LPs)
- 2 The Original Dixieland Jazz Band, "X" 3007

Anthony Ortega
- 2 Jazz for Young Moderns, Bethlehem 79
- 5 A Man and His Horns, Herald 0101
- 4 Anthony Ortega Quartet, Vantage 2 (10")

Kid Ory[143]
- 1 The Great New Orleans Trombonist, Columbia 835
- 1 Johnny Dodds and Kid Ory, Epic 3207
- 1 Song of the Wanderer, Verve 1014, *6011*
- 1 The Kid From New Orleans, Verve 1016
- 1 Kid Ory Plays W.C. Handy, Verve 1017, 6061 (*61017*)
- 1 Dance with Kid Ory, Verve 1022, 6125 (*61022*)
- 1 The Original Jazz, Verve 1023, *61023*
- 1 Dixieland Marching Songs, Verve 1026, *61026*
- 2 Kid Ory in Europe, Verve 8251

Mary Osborne
- 4 A Girl and Her Guitar, Warwick 2004

Harold Ousley
- 2 Tenor Sax, Bethlehem 6059, *6059*

Hall Overton
- 3 Dual Piano Jazz (w/D. McKenna), Bethlehem 6049, *6049*
- 5 Jazz Laboratory, Vol. 2, Signal 102

Hot Lips Page
- 2 Hot and Cozy, Continental 16007 (7 titles by Page, 4 titles by C. Cole)

---
[141] See also *Eddie "Lockjaw" Davis.*
[142] See also *Jack Montrose, Mavis Rivers* (p. 116), *Dinah Shore* (p. 116).
[143] See also *Red Allen.*

JAZZ

Marty Paich[145]
- 2 Jazz City Workshop, Bethlehem 44
- 2 Marty Paich Big Band, Cadence 3010
- 1 Revel Without Pause, Interlude 509, *1009* (reissue of Mode 110; see p. 182)
- 2 Marty Paich Trio, Mode 105
- 1 Jazz For Relaxation, Tampa 23
- 3 Marty Paich Quartet (w/A. Pepper), Tampa 28
- 2 The Broadway Bit, Warner Bros. 1296, *1296*
- 2 I Get a Boot Out of You, Warner Bros. 1349, *1349*

Jackie Paris, see p. 115.

Charlie Parker
- 3 A Night at Carnegie Hall (w/D. Gillespie), Birdland 425 (10″)
- 3 Charlie Parker Big Band, Clef 609
- 3 The Magnificent Charlie Parker, Clef 646
- 3 Charlie Parker With Strings, Clef 675
- 3 Night and Day, Clef 5003
- 2 Bird Lives (w/S. Vaughan), Continental 16004
- 5 Jazz at Massey Hall, Vol. 1, Debut 2 (10″)
- 5 Jazz at Massey Hall, Vol. 3, Debut 4 (10″)
- 5 The Quintet, Debut 124 (includes Debut 2 and Debut 4)
- 5 Charlie Parker Quintet/Septet, Dial 201 (10″)
- 5 Charlie Parker Quartet/All Stars, Dial 202 (10″)
- 5 Charlie Parker Quintet/Sextet, Dial 203 (10″)
- 5 Charlie Parker Sextet, Dial 207 (10″)
- 5 Bird Blows the Blues, Dial 901
- 5 Alternate Masters, Vol. 1, Dial 904
- 5 Alternate Masters, Vol. 2, Dial 905
- 5 Bird at St. Nick's, Jazz Workshop 500
- 5 Bird on 52nd Street, Jazz Workshop 501
- 2 Historical Recordings, Vol. 1, Le Jazz Cool 101
- 2 Historical Recordings, Vol. 2, Le Jazz Cool 102
- 2 Historical Recordings, Vol. 3, Le Jazz Cool 103
- 2 Charlie Parker All Star Sextet, Roost 2210
- 2 Diz 'N' Bird In Concert, Roost 2234
- 2 The Charlie Parker Story #1, Verve 8000
- 2 The Charlie Parker Story #2, Verve 8001
- 2 The Charlie Parker Story #3, Verve 8002
- 2 Night and Day, Verve 8003
- 2 April in Paris, Verve 8004
- 2 Now's the Time, Verve 8005
- 2 Bird and Diz, Verve 8006
- 2 Charlie Parker Plays Cole Porter, Verve 8007
- 2 Fiesta, Verve 8008
- 2 Jazz Perennial, Verve 8009
- 2 Swedish Schnapps, Verve 8010
- 3 The Charlie Parker Story, Verve 8100-3 (3 LP boxed set; includes Verve 8000, 8001, and 8002)

Leo Parker[146]
- 3 Let Me Tell You 'Bout It, Blue Note 4087, *84047*

Leroy Parkins
- 1 Leroy Parkins and his Yazoo River Jazz Band (w/ D. Barker), Bethlehem 6047

Horace Parlan
- 3 Movin' & Groovin', Blue Note 4028
- 3 Us Three, Blue Note 4037
- 3 Speakin' My Piece, Blue Note 4043
- 3 Headin' South, Blue Note 4062
- 3 On the Spur of the Moment, Blue Note 4074
- 3 Up & Down, Blue Note 4082, *84082*

Joe Pass
- 3 Catch Me! (w/C. Fischer), Pacific Jazz 73, *73*
- 3 For Django, Pacific Jazz 85, *85*
- 1 12 String Guitar! (Great Motion Picture Themes), World Pacific 1821, *1821*

Les Paul, see p. 115.

Cecil Payne[147]
- 1 Cecil Payne Performing Charlie Parker Music, Charlie Parker 801
- 5 Cecil Payne, Signal 1203
- 5 A Night at the Five Spot, Signal 1204

Duke Pearson
- 1 Honeybuns, Atlantic 3002
- 1 Prairie Dog, Atlantic 3005
- 1 Profile, Blue Note 4022
- 1 Tender Feelin's, Blue Note 4035
- 3 Wahoo!, Blue Note 4191, *84191*
- 2 Sweet Honey Bee, Blue Note 4252, *84252*
- 4 Hush!, Jazzline 33-02, *33-02*

Santo Pecora
- 1 Dixieland Jamboree, Verve 1008 (w/L. Watters; one side each)
- 1 Dixieland Mardi Gras, Vik 1081

Bernard Peiffer
- 1 The Astounding Bernard Peiffer, Decca 8626
- 1 Modern Jazz For People Who Like Original Music, Laurie 1006
- 2 Jazz From Saint Germain Des Pres, Verve 8119 (w/ D. Byas; one side each)

Dave Pell[148]
- 1 The Big Small Bands, Capitol 1309, *1309*
- 1 I Remember John Kirby, Capitol 1687, *1687*
- 1 The Dave Pell Octet Plays Rodgers and Hart, Kapp 1025 (reissue of Trend 1501)
- 1 The Dave Pell Octet Plays Burke and Van Heusen, Kapp 1034
- 1 The Dave Pell Octet Plays Irving Berlin, Kapp 1036 (reissue of Trend 1003)
- 1 A Pell of a Time, RCA 1524
- 2 The Dave Pell Octet Plays Irving Berlin, Trend 1003 (10″)
- 2 The Dave Pell Octet Plays Rodgers and Hart, Trend 1501

Art Pepper[149]
- 1 Pepper-Manne, Charlie Parker 836 (w/S. Manne; one side each)
- 5 Art Pepper Quartet, Discovery 3019 (10″)

---

[145] See also *Russ Garcia, Mel Tormé*, p. 118.
[146] See also *Bill Jennings*.
NOTE: All Verve LP's "Clef Series" with drawing of trumpet player on label.
[147] See also *Randy Weston*.
[148] See also *Lucy Ann Polk*, p. 115.
[149] See also *Red Norvo, Marty Paich, Bill Perkins*.

JAZZ RECORDINGS

5 Art Pepper Quintet, Discovery 3023 (10")
5 Modern Art, Intro 606
5 The Return of Art Pepper, Jazz West 10
2 Picture of Heath (w/C. Baker), Pacific Jazz 18 (reissue of Pacific Jazz 1234)
2 The Artistry of Pepper, Pacific Jazz 60
3 Playboys (w/C. Baker), Pacific Jazz 1234
2 Art Pepper/Sonny Red, Regent 6069
3 Modern Art, Score 4030 (reissue of Intro 606)
3 The Return of Art Pepper, Score 4032 (reissue of Jazz West 10)
3 Art Pepper Quartet, Tampa 20

Bill Perkins[150]
2 Tenors Head On (w/R. Kamuca), Liberty 3051
3 Just Friends (w/A. Pepper, R. Kamuca), Pacific Jazz 401
3 On Stage, Pacific Jazz 1221

Carl Perkins
3 Introducing Carl Perkins, Dooto 211

Charlie Persip
2 Charlie Persip and the Jazz Statesmen, Bethlehem 6046, 6046

Oscar Peterson[151]
3 Oscar Peterson Plays Cole Porter, Clef/Mercury 603
3 Oscar Peterson Plays Irving Berlin, Clef/Mercury 604
3 Oscar Peterson Plays George Gershwin, Clef/Mercury 605
3 Oscar Peterson Plays Duke Ellington, Clef/Mercury 606
3 Oscar Peterson Plays Jerome Kern, Clef 623
3 Oscar Peterson Plays Richard Rodgers, Clef 624
3 Oscar Peterson Plays Vincent Youmans, Clef 625
3 Oscar Peterson Plays Harry Warren, Clef 648
3 Oscar Peterson Plays Harold Arlen, Clef 649
3 Oscar Peterson Plays Jimmy McHugh, Clef 650
3 Oscar Peterson Quartet, Clef 688
2 Recital, Clef 694 or Verve 2044
2 Nostalgic Memories, Clef 695 or Verve 2045
2 Tenderly, Clef 696 or Verve 2046
2 Keyboard, Clef 697 or Verve 2047
2 An Evening With Oscar Peterson, Clef 698 or Verve 2048
2 Oscar Peterson Plays Count Basie, Clef 708 or Verve 8092
2 With Respect to Nat (vocals), Limelight 82029, 86029
3 In a Romantic Mood (vocals), Verve 2002
2 Pastel Moods, Verve 2004
3 Romance (vocals), Verve 2012
3 Soft Sands (vocals), Verve 2079
2 Oscar Peterson Plays the Cole Porter Songbook, Verve 2052, 6083 (62052)
2 Oscar Peterson Plays the Irving Berlin Songbook, Verve 2053, 6084 (62053)
2 Oscar Peterson Plays the George Gershwin Songbook, Verve 2054, 6085 (62054)
2 Oscar Peterson Plays the Duke Ellington Songbook, Verve 2055, 6086 (62055)
2 Oscar Peterson Plays the Jerome Kern Songbook, Verve 2056, 6087 (62056)
2 Oscar Peterson Plays the Richard Rodgers Songbook, Verve 2057, 6088 (62057)
2 Oscar Peterson Plays the Harry Warren Songbook, Verve 2059, 6090 (62059)

2 Oscar Peterson Plays the Harold Arlen Songbook, Verve 2060, 6091 (62060)
2 Oscar Peterson Plays the Jimmy McHugh Songbook, Verve 2061, 6092 (62061)
3 Oscar Peterson Trio at the Stratford Shakespearean Festival, Verve 8024
2 Oscar Peterson Quartet, Verve 8072
2 The Oscar Peterson Trio with Sonny Stitt, Roy Eldridge and Jo Jones at Newport, Verve 8239
3 The Oscar Peterson Trio at the Concertgebouw, Verve 8268
2 The Modern Jazz Quartet and the Oscar Peterson Trio at the Opera House (one side each), Verve 8269
3 On the Town, Verve 8287
3 Jazz Portrait of Frank Sinatra, Verve 8334, 68334
1 The Jazz Soul of Oscar Peterson, Verve 8351, 68351
1 Bursting Out With the All-Star Band, Verve 8476, 68476

Oscar Pettiford[152]
4 The Oscar Pettiford Orchestra in Hi-Fi, ABC-Paramount 135
4 The Oscar Pettiford Orchestra, Vol. 2, ABC-Paramount 227
3 Jazz Mainstream, Bethlehem 2 (w/R. Mitchell; one side each)
3 Bass by Pettiford/Burke (one side each), Bethlehem 6
2 Oscar Pettiford, Vol. 2, Bethlehem 33
5 The New Sextet, Debut 8 (10")
2 My Little Cello, Fantasy 6010, 86010
2 Last Recordings, Jazzland 64
5 New Stars, New Sounds, Vol. 2 (w/S. Chaloff), Mercer 1003 (10")

Flip Phillips
4 Flip Phillips-Buddy Rich Trio, Clef 634
4 Flip Phillips Quintet, Clef 637
4 Flip Wails, Clef 691 or Verve 8075
4 Swingin' With Flip, Clef 692 or Verve 8076
4 Flip, Cleft 693 or Verve 8077
3 Rock With Flip, Clef 740 or Verve 8116 (reissue of Clef 637)

Nat Pierce
2 Kansas City Memories, Coral 57091
3 Chamber Music for Moderns, Coral 57128
3 Charlie Mariano Sextet/Dick Collins-Nat Pierce Nonet (one side each), Fantasy 3224
3 Jazz Romp, Keynote 1101
2 Big Band at the Savoy, RCA 2543, 2543

Dave Pike
4 Pike's Peak, Epic 16025, 17025
2 Oliver!, Moodsville 36
1 Bossa Nova Carnival, New Jazz 8281
2 Limbo Carnival, New Jazz 8284
3 It's Time For Dave Pike, Riverside 360, 9360

King Pleasure (Clarence Beeks)
1 Golden Days, Hi-Fi 425
2 King Pleasure Sings (8 titles)/Annie Ross Sings (4 titles), Prestige 7128
2 Mr. Jazz, United Artists 14012, 15012

---
[150] See also *Bud Shank*.
[151] See also *Louis Armstrong, Benny Carter, Buddy DeFranco, Stan Getz, Bill Henderson* (p. 110), *Sonny Stitt, Ben Webster, Lester Young*.
[152] See also *Lucky Thompson*.

JAZZ

Pony Poindexter
4 Pony's Express, Epic 16035, *17035*

Terry Pollard[153]
1 Young Moderns, Bethlehem 1 (w/B. Scott; one side each)

Herb Pomeroy
4 Life is a Many Splendored Gig, Roulette 52001
5 Jazz in a Stable, Transition 1
4 Band in Boston, United Artists 4015, *5015*
3 The Band and I (w/I. Kral), United Artists 4016, *5016*

Tommy Potter
4 Tommy Potter's Hard Funk, East-West 4001

Bill Potts
2 Bye Bye Birdie, Colpix 451, *451*
3 The Jazz Soul of Porgy and Bess, United Artists 4032, *5032*

Bud Powell[154]
5 The Amazing Bud Powell, Vol. 1, Blue Note 1503
5 The Amazing Bud Powell, Vol. 2, Blue Note 1504
3 Bud!, Blue Note 1571
3 Time Waits, Blue Note 1598
3 The Scene Changes, Blue Note 4009
5 Bud Powell's Moods, Clef/Mercury 610
3 A Portrait of Thelonious, Columbia 2292, *9092*
5 Jazz at Massey Hall, Vol. 2, Debut 3 (10")
5 Jazz Original, Norgran 1017
4 Jazz Giant, Norgran 1063
4 Bud Powell's Moods, Norgran 1064 (different LP than Clef/Mercury 610)
4 Piano Interpretations, Norgran 1077
3 Bud Powell '57, Norgran 1098 or Verve 8185 (reissue of Norgran 1017)
3 Strictly Powell, RCA 1423
3 Swingin' With Bud, RCA 1507
3 Bud Powell in Paris, Reprise 6098, *6098*
4 The Amazing Bud Powell, Roost 412 (10")
4 Bud, Roost 2224
3 Bud Plays Bird, Roulette 52006, *52006*
3 The Return of Bud Powell, Roulette 52115, *52115*
3 The Genius of Bud Powell, Verve 8115 (reissue of Clef/Mercury 610)
3 Jazz Giant, Verve 8153 (reissue of Norgran 1063)
3 Bud Powell's Moods, Verve 8154 (reissue of Norgran 1064)
3 Piano Interpretations, Verve 8167 (reissue of Norgran 1077)
3 Blues in the Closet, Verve 8218
3 The Lonely One, Verve 8301

Mel Powell
2 Jam Session at Carnegie Hall, Columbia 557
2 Borderline, Vanguard 8501
2 Thingamagig, Vanguard 8502
2 Out On a Limb, Vanguard 8506
2 Easy Swing, Vanguard 8519

Seldon Powell[155]
2 We Paid Our Dues, Epic 16018, *17018* (w/C. Rouse; one side each)

2 Seldon Powell Plays, Roost 2205
3 Seldon Powell Sextet (w/J. Cleveland), Roost 2220

Prestige Jazz Quartet (Teddy Charles, Mal Waldron, Addison Farmer, Jerry Segal)
4 Teo with the Prestige Jazz Quartet (w/T. Macero), Prestige 7104
4 Prestige Jazz Quartet, Prestige 7108

André Previn[156]
4 All Star Jazz, Monarch 203 (10")
3 André Previn Plays Duke Ellington, Monarch 204 (10")
2 Collaboration (w/S. Rogers), RCA 1018
1 André Previn Plays Fats Waller, Zenith 1593

Ruth Price, see p. 115.

Julian Priester
2 Spiritsville, Jazzland 25, *925*
1 Keep Swingin', Riverside 316, *1163*

Bob Prince
3 Events and N.Y. Export: Op. Jazz, RCA 2435, *2435*
3 Jazz Ballets From Broadway, Warner Bros. 1240,
1 Charleston 1970, Warner Bros. 1276, *1276*
3 Saxes, Inc., Warner Bros. 1336, *1336*

Russell Procope
2 The Persuasive Sax of Russell Procope, Dot 3010

Joe Puma
2 East Coast Jazz, Bethlehem 1012 (10")
1 Like Tweet, Columbia 1618, *8418*
2 Wild Kitten, Dawn 1118
3 Joe Puma Jazz, Jubilee 1070

Ike Quebec
2 Heavy Soul, Blue Note 4093, *84093*
2 Blue and Sentimental, Blue Note 4098, *84098*
2 It Might as Well Be Spring, Blue Note 4105, *84105*
2 Soul Samba, Blue Note 4114, *84114*

Gene Quill[157]
3 3 Bones and a Quill, Roost 2229

Paul Quinichette[158]
2 The Chase Is On (w/C. Rouse), Bethlehem 6021
3 The Kid From Denver, Dawn 1109
2 Blow Your Horn (w/B. Green; one side each), Decca 8176
2 Moods, EmArcy 36003
1 The Vice Pres, EmArcy 36027
3 On the Sunny Side, Prestige 7103
2 For Basie, Prestige 7127 (1—Swingville 2036)
2 Basie Reunion, Prestige 7147
1 For Basie, Swingville 2036 (reissue of Prestige 7127)
1 Buck Clayton and Paul Quinichette, Swingville 2037 (reissue of Prestige 7147)
2 Like Who?, United Artists 4024, *5024* or United Artists 4054, *5054*
2 Paul Quinichette, United Artists 4077, *5077*

---

[153] See also *Dorothy Ashby*.
[154] See also *Sonny Stitt*.
[155] See also *Tony Aless*.
NOTE: All Blue Note LPs with original addresses on label; see p. 128.
[156] See also *Diahann Carroll* (p. 106), *Dinah Shore* (p. 116).
[157] See also *The Jazz Modes, Phil Woods*.
[158] See also *John Coltrane*.

Boyd Raeburn
- 2 Man With a Horn, Savoy 12025
- 2 Boyd Meets Stravinsky, Savoy 12040

Ma Rainey
- 1 Twelve Classic Selections, Riverside 108
- 1 Broken Hearted Blues, Riverside 137

Jimmy Raney[159]
- 4 Jimmy Raney Featuring Bob Brookmeyer, ABC-Paramount 129
- 4 Jimmy Raney in Three Attitudes, ABC-Paramount 167
- 3 Jimmy Raney Visits Paris, Dawn 1120
- 2 Swingin' in Sweden, EmArcy 36121 (w/G. Wallington; one side each)
- 2 Two Jims and Zoot (w/J. Hall, Z. Sims), Mainstream 56013, *6013*
- 5 Jimmy Raney Ensemble (w/P. Woods), New Jazz 1103 (10") or Prestige 203 (10")
- 4 Jimmy Raney Plays, Prestige 156 (10")
- 5 "A", Prestige 7089
- 4 Two Guitars (w/K. Burrell), Prestige 7119

Sonny Red[160]
- 3 Out of the Blue, Blue Note 4032
- 2 Breezin', Jazzland 32, *932*
- 2 The Mode, Jazzland 59, *959*
- 2 Images (w/B. Mitchell, G. Green), Jazzland 74, *974*
- 2 Art Pepper/Sonny Red, Regent 6069

Freddie Redd
- 3 The Music from "The Connection" (w/J. McLean), Blue Note 4027, *84027*
- 5 Shades of Redd, Blue Note 4045
- 5 Piano East/Piano West, Prestige 7067 (4 titles by Redd, 8 titles by H. Hawes)
- 2 San Francisco Suite, Riverside 250
- 2 Movin', Status 8307 (reissue of Prestige 7067)

Vi Redd
- 1 Lady Soul, Atco *157*
- 2 Bird Call, United Artists 14016, *15016*

Don Redman
- 2 Don Redman's Park Avenue Patter, Golden Crest 3017
- 1 Master of the Big Band, RCA Vintage 520
- 1 Dixieland in High Society, Roulette 25070, *25070*

Dizzy Reece
- 4 Blues in Trinity, Blue Note 4006
- 2 Star Bright, Blue Note 4023
- 3 Soundin' Off, Blue Note 4033
- 3 London Jazz, Imperial 9043
- 2 Asia Minor, New Jazz 8274

Frank Rehak
- 3 Jazzville, Vol. 2 (w/A. Smith; one side each), Dawn 1107

Django Reinhardt
- 5 The Quintet of the Hot Club of France, Dial 214 (10")
- 5 The Quintet of the Hot Club of France, Vol. 2, Dial 218 (10")

[159] See also *Bob Brookmeyer.*
[160] See also *Clifford Jordan.*

- 3 Django Reinhardt, Jay 3008
- 3 Memorial Album, Vol. 1, Period 1201
- 3 Memorial Album, Vol. 2, Period 1202
- 3 Memorial Album, Vol. 3, Period 1203
- 2 The Immortal Django Reinhardt, Reprise 6075
- 2 Jazz From Paris, Verve 8015 (w/D. Gillespie; one side each)

Don Rendell
- 1 Roarin', Jazzland 51, *951*

Tommy Reynolds
- 1 Dixieland All Stars, Audio Lab 1509 (reissue of King 510)
- 1 Jazz For Happy Feet, King 510

Rita Reys, see p. 116.

Mel Rhyne
- 2 Organizing!, Jazzland 16, *916*

Buddy Rich[161]
- 1 Playtime, Argo 676, *676*
- 3 Gene Krupa and Buddy Rich, Clef 684 or Verve 8069
- 2 Richcraft, Mercury 20451, *60136*
- 2 The Voice Is Rich, Mercury 20461, *60144*
- 3 Sing and Swing With Buddy Rich, Norgran 1031
- 3 Buddy Rich and Sweets Edison, Norgran 1038 or Verve 8129
- 4 The Swinging Buddy Rich, Norgran 1052 or Verve 8142
- 4 The Wailing Buddy Rich, Norgran 1078 or Verve 8168
- 3 This One's for Basie, Norgran 1086 or Verve 8176
- 3 Buddy Rich Sings Johnny Mercer, Verve 2009
- 3 Buddy Rich Just Sings, Verve 2075
- 3 Buddy Rich in Miami, Verve 8285
- 2 Blues Caravan, Verve 8425, *68425*

Johnny Richards[162]
- 2 Something Else, Bethlehem 6011
- 2 Wide Range, Capitol 885
- 2 Experiments in Sound, Capitol 981, *981*
- 2 Walk Softly/Run Wild, Coral 57304, *757304*
- 2 Aquí Se Habla Español, Roulette 25351, *25351*
- 2 The Rites of Diablo, Roulette 52008, *52008*

Jerome Richardson[163]
- 3 Midnight Oil, New Jazz 8205
- 2 Roamin' With Richardson, New Jazz 8226

Mavis Rivers, see p. 116.

Sam Rivers
- 1 A New Conception, Blue Note 4249, *84249*

Max Roach[164]
- 1 Max, Argo 623
- 1 The Max Roach Trio featuring the Legendary Hasaan, Atlantic 1435, *1435*
- 5 Max Roach Quintet (3 titles) /Art Blakey and His Band (4 titles), Blue Note 5010 (10")
- 5 We Insist (Freedom Now Suite), Candid 8002, *9002*

[161] See also *Flip Phillips, Art Tatum, Lester Young.*
[162] See also *Hugo Loewenstern, Sonny Stitt.*
[163] See also *Eddie "Lockjaw" Davis.*
[164] See also *Clifford Brown–Max Roach Quintet, Sonny Clark, Duke Ellington, Booker Little.*

JAZZ

- 5 Max Roach Quartet (w/H. Mobley), Debut 13 (10")
- 2 Max Roach + 4, EmArcy 36098
- 2 Jazz in ¾ Time, EmArcy 36108
- 2 The Max Roach 4 Plays Charlie Parker, EmArcy 36127
- 2 On the Chicago Scene, EmArcy 36132
- 2 Max Roach + 4 at Newport 1958, EmArcy 36140
- 1 Max Roach with the Boston Percussion Ensemble, EmArcy 36144 (Mercury *80015*)
- 3 Drummin' the Blues, Liberty 3064 (w/S. Levey; one side each)
- 1 Quiet As It's Kept, Mercury 20491, *60170*
- 2 Moon Faced and Starry Eyed, Mercury 20539, *60215*
- 1 Parisian Sketches, Mercury 20760, *60760*
- 1 The Many Sides of Max, Mercury 20911, *60911*
- 2 Deeds Not Words, Riverside 280, *1122*
- 4 Max Roach, Time *2087* (stereo issue of Time 70003)
- 4 Award Winning Drummer, Time 70003

Howard Roberts
- 2 Mr. Roberts Plays Guitar, Verve 8192
- 2 Good Pickin's, Verve 8305
- 1 The Movin' Man, VSP 29, *29* (reissue of Verve 8305 minus 3 titles)

Luckey Roberts
- 3 Happy Go Lucky, Period 1929

Jim Robinson
- 1 New Orleans Band, Riverside 369, *9369*
- 1 Spirituals, Riverside 393, *9393*

Betty Roche, see p. 116.

Red Rodney
- 3 Red Rodney Returns (w/B. Root), Argo 643
- 3 Modern Music From Chicago, Fantasy 3208
- 5 1957, Signal 1206

Shorty Rogers[165]
- 3 The Swinging Mr. Rogers, Atlantic 1212
- 3 Martians Come Back!, Atlantic 1232, *1232*
- 1 Shorty in Stereo, Atlantic *1232* (same cover as above, but in red rather than green; reissue of various titles from Atlantic 1212 and above.)
- 3 Way Up There, Atlantic 1270
- 1 Modern Sounds, Capitol 691 (w/G. Mulligan; one side each)
- 1 Shorty Rogers Meets Tarzan, MGM 3798, *3798* (movie soundtrack)
- 3 Shorty Rogers Courts the Count, RCA 1004
- 2 Collaboration (w/A. Previn), RCA 1018
- 3 East Coast–West Coast, RCA 1020 (w/A. Cohn; one side each)
- 3 Shorty Rogers and His Giants, RCA 1195
- 3 Wherever the Five Winds Blow, RCA 1326
- 3 Big Shorty Rogers Express, RCA 1350
- 2 Shorty Rogers Plays Richard Rodgers, RCA 1428
- 2 Portrait of Shorty, RCA 1561
- 2 Gigi in Jazz, RCA 1696
- 1 Afro-Cuban Influence, RCA 1763, *1763*
- 2 Chances Are It Swings, RCA 1975, *1975*
- 2 The Wizard of Oz and Other Harold Arlen Songs, RCA 1997, *1997*
- 2 The Swingin' Nutcracker, RCA 2110, *2110*
- 3 Cool & Crazy, RCA 3138

[165] See also *Boots Brown, Teddy Charles, Eartha Kitt* (p. 112), *Mavis Rivers* (p. 116), *Bud Shank.*

Gene Roland
- 3 Swinging Friends, Brunswick 54114
- 2 Jazzville, Vol. 4 (w/H. Serra; one side each), Dawn 1122

Sonny Rollins[166]
- 3 Sonny Rollins, Blue Note 1542
- 3 Sonny Rollins, Vol. 2, Blue Note 1558
- 3 A Night at the Village Vanguard, Blue Note 1581
- 3 Newk's Time, Blue Note 4001
- 3 Sonny Rollins and the Big Brass, Metrojazz 1002, *1002*
- 3 Sonny Rollins at Music Inn, Metrojazz 1011, *1011* (4 titles by Rollins, 2 titles by T. Edwards)
- 5 Sonny Rollins Plays, Period 1204 (w/T. Jones; one side each)
- 5 Worktime, Prestige 7020
- 5 Sonny Rollins With the Modern Jazz Quartet (w/Art Blakey, Kenny Drew), Prestige 7029
- 5 Sonny Rollins Plus 4, Prestige 7038 (original cover)
- 2 Sonny Rollins Plus 4, Prestige 7038 (second cover with abstract design)
- 5 Tenor Madness, Prestige 7047
- 5 Moving Out, Prestige 7058
- 5 Saxophone Colossus, Prestige 7079
- 4 Rollins Plays for Bird, Prestige 7095
- 5 Tour De Force, Prestige 7126
- 4 Sonny Boy, Prestige 7207
- 1 The Bridge, RCA 2527, *2527*
- 1 What's New, RCA 2572, *2572*
- 2 Our Man in Jazz, RCA 2612, *2612*
- 2 Sonny Meets Hawk!, RCA 2712, *2712*
- 2 Now's the Time, RCA 2927, *2927*
- 2 The Standard Sonny Rollins, RCA 3355, *3355*
- 2 The Sound of Sonny, Riverside 241
- 2 Freedom Suite, Riverside 258
- 2 Sonny Rollins Brass/Sonny Rollins Trio, Verve 8430, *68430* (reissue of Metrojazz 1002)

Frank Rosolino
- 2 I Play Trombone, Bethlehem 26
- 4 Kenton Presents Frank Rosolino, Capitol 6507 (10")
- 4 Frankly Speaking, Capitol 6509
- 2 The Legend of Frank Rosolino, Interlude 500, *1000* (reissue of Mode 107)
- 4 Frank Rosolino Quintet, Mode 107
- 2 Turn Me Loose (vocals), Reprise 6016, *96016*

Annie Ross[167]
- 2 Fill My Heart With Song, Decca 4922, *74922*
- 1 Gerry Mulligan and Annie Ross, Kimberly 2018 (reissue of World Pacific 1253 minus 2 titles)
- 2 King Pleasure Sings (8 titles) / Annie Ross Sings (4 titles), Prestige 7128
- 3 Annie Ross Sings a Song With Mulligan!, World Pacific 1253, *1020*
- 2 Gypsy (w/B. Bregman), World Pacific 1276, *1028*
- 3 A Gasser (w/Z. Sims), World Pacific 1285, *1285*

Ronnie Ross
- 2 The Jazz Makers (w/A. Ganley), Atlantic 1333, *1333*

[166] See also *Miles Davis, Kenny Dorham, Dizzy Gillespie, Thelonious Monk, Modern Jazz Quartet.*
[167] See also *Lambert, Hendricks & Ross.*
NOTE: All Blue Note LPs with original addresses on label; see p. 128.

Charlie Rouse[168]
2 The Chase is On (w/P. Quinichette), Bethlehem 6021
1 Bossa Nova Bacchanal, Blue Note 4119, *84119*
1 Yeah!, Epic 16012, *17012*
2 We Paid Our Dues, Epic 16018, *17018* (w/S. Powell; one side each)
2 Takin' Care of Business, Jazzland 19, *919*

Jimmy Rowles
3 Weather in a Jazz Vane, Andex 3007, *3007*
1 Kinda Groovy, Capitol 1831, *1831*
1 Upper Classmen, Interlude 515, *1015* (reissue of Tampa 8)
3 Rare, But Well Done, Liberty 3003
3 Fiorello Uptown/Mary Sunshine Downtown, Signature 6011
1 Let's Get Acquainted With Jazz, Tampa 8, *8*

Ernie Royal
2 Accent on Trumpet, Urania 1203

Howard Rumsey (Lighthouse All Stars)
3 Sunday Jazz a la Lighthouse, Vol. 1, Contemporary 3501
3 Howard Rumsey's Lighthouse All Stars, Vol. 6, Contemporary 3504
3 Howard Rumsey's Lighthouse All Stars, Vol. 3, Contemporary 3508
3 Lighthouse at Laguna, Contemporary 3509
3 In the Solo Spotlight (Vol. 5), Contemporary 3517
3 Oboe/Flute (Vol. 4), Contemporary 3520
3 Music For Lighthousekeeping (Vol. 8), Contemporary 3528, *7008*
3 Double or Nothin' (w/C. Persip), Liberty 3045, *7014*
3 Sunday Night a la Lighthouse, Lighthouse 301
1 Jazz Structure, Philips 200-012, *600-012*

Jimmy Rushing[169]
2 Two Shades of Blue, Audio Lab 1512 (w/J. Dupree; one side each)
1 Five Feet of Soul, Colpix 446, *446*
1 Jazz Odyssey, Columbia 963
2 Little Jimmy and the Big Brass, Columbia 1152, *8060*
1 Rushing Lullabies, Columbia 1401, *8196*
2 Jimmy Rushing and the Smith Girls (Bessie, Clara, Mamie, Trixie), Columbia 1605, *8405*
1 Listen to the Blues, Vanguard 8505
1 If This Ain't the Blues, Vanguard 8513, *2008*
1 Goin' to Chicago, Vanguard 8518

George Russell
3 George Russell Sextet in Kansas City, Decca 4183, *74183*
2 New York, N.Y., Decca 9216, *79216*
2 Jazz in the Space Age (w/B. Evans), Decca 9219, *79219*
3 George Russell Sextet at the Five Spot, Decca 9220, *79220*
5 Octets (Music of Alec Wilder), MGM 3321
4 The Jazz Workshop, RCA 1372 (original black cover)
3 The Jazz Workshop, RCA 2534e ("fake" stereo issue of RCA 1372; brown cover)
3 Stratusphunk, Riverside 341, *9341*
1 Ezz-thetics, Riverside 375, *9375*
3 The Stratus Seekers, Riverside 412, *9412*
2 The Outer View, Riverside 440, *9440*

Pee Wee Russell[170]
2 Jazz Reunion (w/C. Hawkins), Candid 8020, *9020*
1 New Groove (w/M. Brown), Columbia 1985, *8785*
3 A Portrait of Pee Wee, Counterpoint 562, *562*
2 Pee Wee Russell Plays, Dot 3253, *25253*
3 Jack Teagarden's Big Eight/Pee Wee Russell's Rhythmakers (one side each), Riverside 141
2 Pee Wee Russell Plays Pee Wee, Stere-O-craft *105*
4 We're in the Money, Storyville 909
2 Swingin' with Pee Wee, Swingville 2008

Bill Russo
3 World of Alcina, Atlantic 1241
2 School of Rebellion, Roulette 52045, *52045*
2 7 Deadly Sins, Roulette 52063, *52063*

Aaron Sachs
2 We Brought Our Axes, Bethlehem 7 (w/H. D'Amico; one side each)
2 Jazzville Vol. 3, Dawn 1114 (w/C. Smith; one side each)
2 Clarinet and Co., Rama 1004

A.K. Salim
1 Pretty For the People, Savoy 12118
1 Blues Suite, Savoy 12132

Sal Salvador
4 Shades of Sal Salvador, Bethlehem 39
3 Frivolous Sal, Bethlehem 59
3 Tribute to the Greats, Bethlehem 74
3 Sal Salvador Quintet, Blue Note 5035 (10")
3 Kenton Jazz Presents Sal Salvador, Capitol 6505 (10")
2 You Ain't Heard Nothin' Yet, Dauntless 4307, *6307*
2 Beat for this Generation, Decca 4026, *74026*
3 Colors in Sound, Decca 9210, *79210*
1 Sal Salvador Quartet, Jazz Unlimited 1001
1 Music to Stop Smoking By, Roulette 25262, *25262*

Edgar Sampson
1 Swing Softly Sweet Sampson, Coral 57049

Sandole Brothers (Adolphe and Dennis)
2 Modern Music From Philadelphia, Fantasy 3209

Leon Sash
2 Leon Sash Quartet, Storyville 917
2 Toshiko and Leon Sash at Newport (one side each), Verve 8236

Hal Schaefer
2 Just Too Much, RCA 1106
3 The Jazz Workshop, RCA 1199

Lalo Schifrin
1 Lalo = Brilliance, Roulette 52088, *52088*

Bob Scobey[171]
2 Bob Scobey's Band, Down Home 1 or Verve 1001
2 Beauty and the Beat, RCA 1344
1 Swingin' on the Golden Gate (w/C. Hayes), RCA 1443
1 Between 18th & 19th on Any Street (w/C. Hayes), RCA 1567, *1567*

---
168 See also *The Jazz Modes*.
169 See also *Count Basie, Buck Clayton*.
170 See also *Ruby Braff*.
171 See also *Bing Crosby*, p. 107.

1 College Classics (w/C. Hayes), RCA 1700, *1700*
1 Rompin' and Stompin', RCA 2086, *2086*
2 Music From Bourbon St. (w/L. Miles), Verve 1009
1 The San Francisco Jazz of Bob Scobey, Verve 1011

Bobby Scott
1 Young Moderns, Bethlehem 1 (w/T. Pollard; one side each)
2 The Compositions of Bobby Scott, Bethlehem 8

Hazel Scott
2 Relaxed Piano Moods, Debut 16 (10")

Little Jimmy Scott, see p. 116.

Ronnie Scott, see Tubby Hayes.

Tony Scott
2 South Pacific Jazz, ABC-Paramount 235, *235*
3 Tony Scott Quartet in Hi-Fi, Brunswick 54021 (includes 3 titles from Brunswick 58057)
3 Jazz For G.I.'s, Brunswick 58057 (10")
2 Free Blown Jazz (w/J. Knepper), Carlton 113, *113*
3 52nd St. Scene, Coral 57239, *757239*
3 My Kind of Jazz, Perfect 12010, *14010*
3 Scott's Fling, RCA 1022
3 Both Sides of Tony Scott, RCA 1268
3 The Touch of Tony Scott, RCA 1353
3 The Complete Tony Scott, RCA 1452
3 The Modern Art of Jazz, Seeco 425, *4150*
1 Hi-Fi Land of Jazz, Seeco 428 (reissue of Dawn 1106; see *Dick Garcia*)
2 Gypsy, Signature 6001, *6001*

Al Sears
2 Dance Music With a Swing Beat, Audio Lab 1540 (8 titles by Sears, 4 by J. Thomas)
1 Swing's the Thing, Swingville 2018

Hal Serra, see Gene Roland.

Bud Shank[172]
3 Bud Shank Quintet, Nocturne 2 (10")
1 Bud Shank Plays Tenor, Pacific Jazz 4, *4*
1 New Groove (w/C. Jones), Pacific Jazz 21, *21*
2 The Swing's to TV (w/B. Cooper), Pacific Jazz 411 (World Pacific *1002*)
3 Bud Shank Quintet (w/S. Rogers, B. Perkins), Pacific Jazz 1205 (includes Nocturne 2)
3 Strings and Trombones (w/B. Brookmeyer), Pacific Jazz 1213
2 Bud Shank Quartet (w/C. Williamson), Pacific Jazz 1215
2 Jazz at Cal-Tech, Pacific Jazz 1219
2 Flute 'n Oboe (w/B. Cooper), Pacific Jazz 1226
2 Bud Shank Quartet (w/C. Williamson), Pacific Jazz 1230
2 Blowin' Country, World Pacific 1277 (reissue of Pacific Jazz 411)

Ralph Sharon[173]
1 2:38 A.M., Argo 635
3 Mr. and Mrs. Jazz (w/S. Sharon), Bethlehem 13
2 Ralph Sharon Trio, Bethlehem 41
2 Autumn Leaves and Spring Fever, London 1339

3 Easy Jazz, London 1488
3 Jazz Around the World, Rama 1001

Charlie Shavers[174]
1 Gershwin, Shavers and Strings, Bethlehem 27
2 The Complete Charlie Shavers (w/M. Sullvan), Bethlehem 67
1 The Most Intimate, Bethlehem 5002 or Aamco 310
1 Excitement Unlimited, Capitol 1883, *1883*

Artie Shaw
5 Artie Shaw and his Gramercy Five No. 1, Clef 159 (10")
5 Artie Shaw and his Gramercy Five No. 2, Clef 160 (10")
5 Artie Shaw and his Gramercy Five No. 3, Clef 630
5 Artie Shaw and his Gramercy Five No. 4, Clef 645
4 Modern Music For Clarinet, Columbia 4260
3 Dance Program, Decca 5286 (10")
1 Did Someone Say a Party?, Decca 8309
3 Artie Shaw With Strings, Epic 3112
3 Artie Shaw and His Orchestra, Epic 3150
2 Artie Shaw Plays Cole Porter and Irving Berlin (w/M. Torme, K. Kallen), Lion 70058
2 My Concerto, RCA 1020
2 Both Feet in the Groove, RCA 1201
2 Back Bay Shuffle, RCA 1217
2 Artie Shaw and the Gramercy Five, RCA 1241
1 Moonglow, RCA 1244
1 Any Old Time, RCA 1570
4 The Swingin' Mr. Shaw, RCA 6701 (5 LP boxed set w/illustrated booklet; 1938–1945 recordings)
1 One Night Stand, RCA Camden 584
4 Sequence in Music, Verve 2014 (reissue of Clef 159 and Clef 160)
4 I Can't Get Started, Verve 2015

Gene Shaw
1 Breakthrough, Argo 707, *707*
1 Debut in Blues, Argo 726, *726*
1 Carnival Sketches, Argo 743, *743*

Jack Sheldon
2 Out!, Capitol 1851, *1851*
2 Oooo, But It's Good! (comedy LP), Capitol 1963, *1963*
5 The Quartet and the Quintet, Jazz West 6
1 A Jazz Profile of Ray Charles, Reprise 2004, *92004*

Tommy Shepard
2 Shepard's Flock, Coral 57110

Joya Sherrill, see p. 116.

Sahib Shihab
1 Summer Dawn, Argo 742, *742*
2 Jazz Sahib, Savoy 12124

Wayne Shorter
2 Introducing Wayne Shorter, Vee Jay 3006, *3006*
1 Wayning Moments, Vee Jay 3029, *3029*

Eddie Shu
2 Jazz Practitioners, Bethlehem 3 (w/B. Hardaway; one side each)

[172] See also *Herbie Harper*.
[173] See also *Tony Bennett* (p. 105).
[174] See also *Hal Singer*.

JAZZ RECORDINGS

Frank Signorelli
    3 Piano Moods, Davis 103
    2 Ragtime Duo (w/G. Wettling), Kapp 1005

Horace Silver
    3 Horace Silver and the Jazz Messengers, Blue Note 1518
    3 Horace Silver Trio, Blue Note 1520
    3 6 Pieces of Silver, Blue Note 1539
    3 The Stylings of Silver, Blue Note 1562
    2 Further Explorations, Blue Note 1589
    2 Finger Poppin', Blue Note 4008, *84008*
    2 Blowin' the Blues Away, Blue Note 4017, *84017*
    2 Horace-Scope, Blue Note 4042, *84042*
    2 Silver's Blue, Epic 3326

Omer Simeon, see Sidney Bechet.

Nina Simone, see p. 117.

Zoot Sims[175]
    4 Zoot Sims Plays Alto, Tenor and Baritone, ABC-Paramount 155
    4 Zoot Sims Plays Four Altos, ABC-Paramount 198
    1 Zoot, Argo 608 (color cover)
    2 Down Home, Bethlehem 6051, *6051*
    2 New Beat Bossa Nova, Colpix 435, *435*
    2 New Beat Bossa Nova, Vol. 2, Colpix 437, *437*
    4 The Modern Art of Jazz, Dawn 1102
    4 Zoot Sims Goes to Jazzville, Dawn 1115
    4 Zoot Sims Quartet, Discovery 3015 (10")
    5 Starring Zoot Sims, Ducretet-Thompson 93099 (10") (English pressing)
    1 Zoot!, Jazzland 2 (reissue of Riverside 228)
    2 Good Old Zoot, New Jazz 8280
    3 Choice, Pacific Jazz 20
    5 Zoot Sims Quartets, Prestige 7026
    2 Zoot!, Riverside 228
    2 The Modern Art of Jazz, Seco 452 (reissue of Dawn 1102)
    3 Koo Koo (w/P. Woods), Status 8309 (reissue of Prestige 7033; see *Jon Eardley*)
    3 Stretching Out, United Artists 4023, *5023*
    3 A Night at the Half-Note (w/A. Cohn, P. Woods), United Artists 4040, *5040*
    4 Zoot Sims in Paris, United Artists 14013, *15013*

Hal Singer
    2 Blue Stompin' (w/C. Shavers), Prestige 7153
    1 Blue Stompin', Swingville 2023 (reissue of Prestige 7153)

The Six (B. Wilber, J. Glasel, others)
    2 The Six, Bethlehem 28
    2 The View From Jazzbo's Head, Bethlehem 57
    3 An Evening of Jazz, Norgran 1065 or Verve 8155 (one side The Six, other side S. Criss) [4 titles]/T. Turk [4 titles])

Don Sleet
    1 All Members, Jazzland 45, *945*

Carol Sloane, see p. 117.

Alex Smith, see Frank Rehak.

Buster Smith
    4 The Legendary Buster Smith, Atlantic 1323, *1323*

Charlie Smith, see Aaron Sachs.

Jimmy Smith
    2 A New Star, Vol. 1, Blue Note 1512
    2 A New Star, Vol. 2, Blue Note 1514
    2 A New Star, Vol. 3, Blue Note 1525
    2 A Date With Jimmy Smith, Vol. 1, Blue Note 1547
    2 A Date With Jimmy Smith, Vol. 2, Blue Note 1548
    2 Jimmy Smith at the Organ, Vol. 1, Blue Note 1551
    2 Jimmy Smith at the Organ, Vol. 2, Blue Note 1552
    2 Jimmy Smith's House Party, Blue Note 4002
    2 The Sermon, Blue Note 4011, *84011*

Johnny Smith[176]
    2 Johnny Smith Plays Jimmy Van Heusen, Roost 2201
    2 Johnny Smith Quartet, Roost 2203
    2 Moonlight in Vermont (w/S. Getz), Roost 2211
    2 Moods, Roost 2215
    2 The New Johnny Smith Quartet, Roost 2216
    2 The Johnny Smith Foursome, Roost 2223
    2 The Johnny Smith Foursome, Vol. 2, Roost 2228, *2228*
    2 Flower Drum Song, Roost 2231, *2231*
    2 Easy Listening, Roost 2233, *2233*
    2 Johnny Smith Favorites, Roost 2237, *2237*
    2 Designed For You, Roost 2238, *2238*
    2 Johnny Smith Plus the Trio, Roost 2243, *2243*
    2 Sound of the Johnny Smith Guitar, Roost 2246, *2246*
    2 Man With the Blue Guitar, Roost 2248, *2248*

Louis Smith
    3 Here Comes Louis Smith, Blue Note 1584
    4 Smithville, Blue Note 1594

Stuff Smith
    1 Swingin' Stuff, EmArcy 26008, *66068*
    2 Together (w/H. Ellis), Epic 16039, *17039*
    3 Stuff Smith, Verve 2041 or Verve 8206
    4 Dizzy Gillespie and Stuff Smith, Verve 8214
    3 Have Violin, Will Swing, Verve 8282
    3 Cat on a Hot Fiddle, Verve 8339, *6097 (68339)*

Willie Smith
    2 Relaxin' After Hours, EmArcy 26000 (10")

Willie "The Lion" Smith
    2 Lion of the Piano, Commodore 30004
    4 Harlem Memories, Dial 305 (10")
    3 The Lion Roars (talking and music), Dot 3094
    1 The Legend of Willie "The Lion" Smith, Grand Award 368
    2 Accent on Piano, Urania 1207

Elmer Snowden
    1 Harlem Banjo!, Riverside 348, *9348*

Frank Socolow
    2 Sounds by Socolow, Bethlehem 70

---

[175] See also *Bob Brookmeyer, Clifford Brown, Teddy Charles, Al Cohn–Zoot Sims, Jutta Hipp, Joe Newman, Jimmy Raney.*
NOTE: All Blue Note LPs with original addresses on label; see p. 128.

[176] See also *Beverly Kenney* (p. 112), *Ruth Price* (p. 115), *Jeri Southern* (p. 117).
NOTE: All Blue Note LPs with original addresses on label; see p. 128.

Martial Solal[177]
  3 Martial Solal, Capitol 10261, *10261*
  3 Modern Sounds: France/Piano, Contemporary 2512 (10")
  3 Martial Solal in Concert, Liberty 3335, *7335*
  3 Martial Solal at Newport '63, RCA 2777, *2777*

Eddie South
  2 The Distinguished Violin of Eddie South, Mercury 20401, *60070*

Muggsy Spanier
  3 Duets (w/S. Bechet), Atlantic 1206
  1 Chicago Jazz, Commodore 30016
  2 Jazz Greats Vol. VII: Dixieland, EmArcy 36055 (8 titles by Spanier from Mercury 20171, 4 titles by P. Napoleon)
  2 Muggsy Spanier and his Dixieland Band, Mercury 20171
  2 The Great 16, RCA 1295
  2 Classic Early Chicago Recordings, Riverside 107
  2 Chicago Jazz, RKO-Unique 130
  5 Muggsy Spanier, Weathers 5401

Les Spann
  2 Gemini, Jazzland 35, *935*

Jess Stacy
  3 Jess Stacy, Brunswick 54017
  3 Tribute to Benny Goodman, Atlantic 1225
  2 The Return of Jess Stacy, Hanover 8010

Jo Stafford, see p. 117.

Jeremy Steig
  3 Flute Fever (w/D. Zeitlin), Columbia 2136, *8936*

Hal Stein
  5 Hal Stein–Warren Fitzgerald, Progressive 1002

Herbie Steward
  2 So Pretty, Ava/Choreo 9, *9*

Rex Stewart[178]
  3 Big Jazz (w/J. Teagarden; one side each), Atlantic 1209
  4 Ellingtonia, Dial 215 (10")
  2 Rendezvous With Rex, Felsted 7001, *2001*
  2 Rex Stewart Plays Duke Ellington, Grand Award 315 (w/I. Jacquet; one side each)
  1 Just For Kicks, Grand Award 414
  2 Dixieland Free-For-All, Jazztone 1202
  2 The Big Reunion, Jazztone 1285
  1 Things Ain't What They Used to Be (w/J. Hodges), RCA Vintage 533
  2 Rex Stewart and the Ellingtonians, Riverside 144
  2 The Happy Jazz of Rex Stewart, Swingville 2006
  2 Henderson Homecoming, United Artists 4009, *5009*
  1 Cool Fever, Urania 2012 ("Fake" Stereo reissue of Jazztone 1285)
  1 Porgy and Bess Revisited, Warner Bros. 1260

Slam Stewart[179]
  2 Bowin' Singin' Sam, Savoy 12067

Tom Stewart
  3 Sextette/Quintette, ABC-Paramount 117

Sonny Stitt[180]
  1 Burnin'!, Argo 629
  1 Sonny Stitt & the Top Brass, Atlantic 1395, *1395*
  1 Stitt Plays Bird, Atlantic 1418, *1418*
  1 Low Flame, Jazzland 71, *971*
  5 Sonny Stitt with Bud Powell and Jay Jay Johnson, Prestige 7024
  4 Kaleidoscope, Prestige 7077
  3 Stitt's Bits, Prestige 7133
  3 Plays Arrangements From the Pen of Johnny Richards, Roost 415 (10")
  3 Jazz at the Hi-Hat, Roost 418 (10")
  2 Battle of Birdland (w/E. Davis), Roost 1203
  3 Sonny Stitt Plays Arrangements of Quincy Jones, Roost 2204
  2 Sonny Stitt, Roost 2208
  2 37 Minutes and 48 Seconds, Roost 2219
  2 Sonny Stitt With the New Yorkers, Roost 2226
  1 The Saxophones of Sonny Stitt, Roost 2230
  1 A Little Bit of Stitt, Roost 2235
  1 The Sonny Side of Stitt, Roost 2240
  3 New York Jazz, Verve 8219
  3 Only the Blues, Verve 8250
  3 The Hard Swing, Verve 8306, *6038* (*68306*)
  3 Sonny Stitt Plays Jimmy Giuffre Arrangements, Verve 8309, *6041* (*68309*)
  3 Personal Appearance, Verve 8324
  2 Sonny Stitt Sits in With the Oscar Peterson Trio, Verve 8344, *6108* (*68344*)
  2 Sonny Stitt Blows the Blues, Verve 8374, *6149* (*68374*)
  3 Saxophone Supremacy, Verve 8377 *68377*
  2 Sonny Stitt Swings the Most, Verve 8380, *68380*
  1 Sensual Sound, Verve 8451, *68451*

Don Stratton
  2 Modern Jazz With Dixieland Roots, ABC-Paramount 118

Billy Strayhorn[181]
  2 Billy Strayhorn Septet, Felsted 7008, *2008*
  5 Billy Strayhorn Trio (w/D. Ellington), Mercer 1001 (10")
  1 Duets (w/D. Ellington), Riverside 475
  1 The Peaceful Side of Billy Strayhorn, United Artists 14010, *15010*

Frank Strozier[182]
  3 Long Night, Jazzland 56, *956*
  3 March of the Siamese Children, Jazzland 70, *970*
  1 Fantastic Frank Strozier, Vee Jay 1007, *3005*

Ira Sullivan[183]
  2 Billy Taylor Introduces Ira Sullivan, ABC-Paramount 162
  2 Bird Lives!, Vee Jay 3033, *3033*

[177] See also *Sidney Bechet, Lucky Thompson*.
[178] See also *Jack Teagarden, Cootie Williams*.
[179] See also *Rose Murphy* (p. 114).
[180] See also *Dizzy Gillespie, Oscar Peterson, Kai Winding*.
[181] See also *Johnny Hodges*.
[182] See also *Roy Haynes*.
[183] See also *Roland Kirk*.

Joe Sullivan
2 Mr. Piano Man, Down Home 2 or Verve 1002
2 Little Rock Getaway, Riverside 158
3 New Solos by an Old Master, Riverside 202

Maxine Sullivan, see p. 118.

Sun Ra
5 Jazz by Sun Ra, Transition 10

Phil Sunkel
3 Phil Sunkel's Jazz Band, ABC-Paramount 136
3 Jazz Concerto Grosso (w/B. Brookmeyer, G. Mulligan), ABC-Paramount 225

Ralph Sutton
2 Piano Solos, Commodore 30001
2 Backroom Piano, Down Home 4 or Verve 1004
1 A Salute to Fats, Harmony 7019
1 Jazz at the Olympics, Omega 51
2 Piano in the Classic Jazz Tradition, Riverside 212
1 Ragtime U.S.A., Roulette 25232, 25232

Buddy Tate[184]
3 Swinging Like Tate, Felsted 7004, 2004
2 Tate's Date, Swingville 2003
1 Buck and Buddy (w/B. Clayton), Swingville 2017
2 Groovin' With Tate, Swingville 2029
1 Buck and Buddy Blow the Blues, Swingville 2030, 2030

Duane Tatro
1 Jazz For Moderns, Contemporary 3514

Art Tatum
2 Here's Art Tatum, Brunswick 54004
2 Art Tatum, Capitol 216
3 The Genius of Art Tatum No. 1, Clef 612 or Verve 8036
3 The Genius of Art Tatum No. 2, Clef 613 or Verve 8037
3 The Genius of Art Tatum No. 3, Clef 614 or Verve 8038
3 The Genius of Art Tatum No. 4, Clef 615 or Verve 8039
3 The Genius of Art Tatum No. 5, Clef 618 or Verve 8040
3 The Tatum, Carter, Bellson Trio, Clef 643
3 The Genius of Art Tatum No. 6, Clef 657 or Verve 8055
3 The Genius of Art Tatum No. 7, Clef 658 or Verve 8056
3 The Genius of Art Tatum No. 8, Clef 659 or Verve 8057
3 The Genius of Art Tatum No. 9, Clef 660 or Verve 8058
3 The Genius of Art Tatum No. 10, Clef 661 or Verve 8059
3 The Art Tatum-Roy Eldridge-Alvin Stoller-John Simmons Quartet, Clef 679 or Verve 8064
3 Hampton-Tatum-Rich Trio, Clef 709 or Verve 8093
3 The Genius of Art Tatum No. 11, Clef 712 or Verve 8095
1 The Art of Tatum, Decca 8715
4 Art Tatum Trio, Dial 206 (10")
1 Gene Norman Presents an Art Tatum Concert, Harmony 7006
1 Giants of the Piano, Roost 2213 (w/E. Garner; one side each)
2 Piano Discoveries, 20th Century Fox 3029, 3029
2 Piano Discoveries, Vol. 2, 20th Century Fox 3033, 3033
3 Piano Discoveries, 20th Century Fox 102-2 (2 LP issue of 20th Century Fox 3029 and 3033)
3 The Three Giants, Verve 8013 (reissue of Clef 643)
3 Presenting the Art Tatum Trio, Verve 8118
3 The Art Tatum-Ben Webster Quartet, Verve 8220

3 Makin' Whoopee (w/B. Carter, L. Bellson), Verve 8227
3 The Art Tatum-Buddy DeFranco Quartet, Verve 8229
3 The Greatest Piano of Them All, Verve 8323
3 The Incomparable Art Tatum, Verve 8332
3 More of the Greatest Piano, Verve 8347
3 Still More of the Greatest Piano, Verve 8360

Art Taylor
3 A.T.'s Delight, Blue Note 4047
3 Taylor's Tenors, New Jazz 8219
4 Taylor's Wailers, Prestige 7117

Billy Taylor[185]
1 Evergreens, ABC-Paramount 112
1 Billy Taylor at the London House, ABC-Paramount 134
2 My Fair Lady Loves Jazz, ABC-Paramount 177
1 The New Billy Taylor Trio, ABC-Paramount 226, 226
2 Taylor Made Jazz, Argo 650, 650
1 The Billy Taylor Touch, Atlantic 1277
1 One For Fun, Atlantic 1329, 1329
2 Jazz Score of "Kwamina," Mercury 20654, 60654
1 Impromptu, Mercury 20722, 60722
1 Interlude, Moodsville 16
5 A Touch of Taylor, Prestige 7001
3 Billy Taylor Trio, Vol. 1, Prestige 7015
3 Billy Taylor Trio, Vol. 2, Prestige 7016
3 Billy Taylor Trio with Candido, Prestige 7051
3 Cross Section, Prestige 7071
3 Billy Taylor Trio at Town Hall, Prestige 7093
2 Billy Taylor with Four Flutes, Riverside 306, 1151
2 Billy Taylor Trio Uptown (Live at the Prelude), Riverside 319, 1168
2 Warming Up, Riverside 339, 1195
2 Jazz at Storyville, Vol. 2, Roost 406 (10")
3 Taylor Made Jazz, Roost 2222 (includes 3 titles from Roost 406, 6 from Roost 409)
2 Custom Taylored, Sesac 3301/02

Cecil Taylor
5 World of Cecil Taylor, Candid 8006, 9006
5 Jazz Advance, Transition 19
5 Hard Driving Jazz, United Artists 4014
5 Stereo Drive, United Artists 5014 (stereo issue of United Artists 4014)
5 Love For Sale, United Artists 4046, 5046
3 The Gigi Gryce, Donald Byrd Jazz Laboratory/... Quintet at Newport (one side each), Verve 8238

Sam "the Man" Taylor[186]
3 Jazz For Commuters, Metrojazz 1008, 1008
1 The Bad and the Beautiful, Moodsville 24

Jack Teagarden[187]
3 Big Jazz (w/R. Stewart; one side each), Atlantic 1209
2 Jazz Great, Bethlehem 32
1 Dixieland, Bethlehem 6042 (partial reissue of Bethlehem 32)
2 This is Teagarden, Capitol 721
3 Swing Low Sweet Spiritual, Capitol 820 (backed on 3 titles by the *Five Keys*)
2 Big T's Dixieland Band, Capitol 1095

---
[184] See also *Frank "Floorshow" Culley*, p. 53.
[185] See also *Ira Sullivan*.
[186] See also p. 74.
[187] See also *Red Allen*.

2 Shades of Night, Capitol 1143, *1143*
2 Big T's Jazz, Decca 8304
1 Jack Teagarden, RCA Vintage 528
3 Jack Teagarden's Big Eight/Pee Wee Russell's Rhythmakers (one side each), Riverside 141
1 The Blues and Dixie, Rondolette 18
2 Jack Teagarden at the Roundtable, Roulette 25091, *25091*
1 Jazz Maverick, Roulette 25119, *25119*
1 Dixie Sound, Roulette 25177, *25177*
1 Portrait of Mr. T., Roulette 25243, *25243*
3 Accent on Trombone, Urania 1205
2 Mis'ry and the Blues, Verve 8416, *68416*
2 Think Well of Me, Verve 8465, *68465*
2 Jack Teagarden, Verve 8495, *68495*

Clark Terry
1 Out on a Limb, Argo 620
1 More (w/B. Webster), Cameo 1064
1 Tread Ye Lightly, Cameo 1071, *1071*
4 Color Changes (w/Y. Lateef), Candid 8009, *9009*
3 Eddie Costa Memorial, Colpix 450, *450* (w/2 titles by C. Hawkins)
2 Clark Terry, EmArcy 36007
1 Everything's Mellow, Moodsville 20
2 All-American, Moodsville 26
3 Serenade to a Bus Seat, Riverside 237
3 Duke With a Difference, Riverside 246, *1108*
3 In Orbit (w/T. Monk), Riverside 271
3 Top and Bottom Brass, Riverside 295, *1137*
2 What Makes Sammy Swing!, 20th Century Fox 3137, *4137*

Toots Thielemans[188]
1 The Whistler and his Guitar, ABC-Paramount 482, *482*
3 Time Out for Toots, Decca 9204
2 The Soul of Toots Thielemans, Signature 6006, *6006*
3 Man Bites Harmonica!, Riverside 257

Joe Thomas (trumpet), see Vic Dickenson.

Joe Thomas (tenor sax), see Al Sears.

Rene Thomas
4 Guitar Groove (w/J. P. Monterose), Jazzland 27, *927*

Sir Charles Thompson
5 Sir Charles Thompson and his All-Stars, Apollo 103 (10")
1 Sir Charles Thompson and the Swing Organ, Columbia 1364, *8205*
1 Rockin' Rhythm, Columbia 1663, *8463*
2 Sir Charles Thompson Sextet, Vanguard 8003 (10")
2 Sir Charles Thompson Quartet, Vanguard 8006 (10")
2 Sir Charles Thompson and His Band, Vanguard 8009 (10")
2 Sir Charles Thompson Trio, Vanguard 8018 (10")

Les Thompson
2 Just Jazz, RCA 3102 (10")

Lucky Thompson[189]
3 Lucky Thompson Featuring Oscar Pettiford, Vol. 1, ABC-Paramount 111

3 Lucky Thompson Featuring Oscar Pettiford, Vol. 2, ABC-Paramount 171
3 Lucky Thompson (w/G. Pochonet, M. Solal), Dawn 1113
4 Lucky Thompson Plays Jerome Kern and No More, Moodsville 39
3 Lucky Strikes, Prestige 7365
2 Happy Days Are Here Again, Prestige 7394
3 Lucky is Back! (then, so is love), Rivoli 40, *40*
3 Kinfolks Corner, Rivoli 44, *44*
5 Lucky Strikes, Transition 21 (different LP than Prestige 7365)
3 Accent on Tenor, Urania 1206

Fran Thorne
2 Piano Reflections, Transition 27

Claude Thornhill
2 Dancing After Midnight, Columbia 709
2 Piano Reflections, Columbia 6035 (10")
1 Claude On a Cloud, Decca 8722, *78722*
1 Dance to the Sound, Decca 8878, *78878*
2 The Thornhill Sound, Harmony 7088
2 Two Sides of Claude Thornhill, Kapp 1058
2 Dinner For Two, RCA Camden 307
3 Claude Thornhill and His Orchestra Play Gerry Mulligan Arrangements, Trend 1002 (10")

Bobby Timmons[190]
1 Soul Man, Prestige 7465
1 This Here is Bobby Timmons, Riverside 317, *1164*
2 Soul Time, Riverside 334, *9334*
2 Easy Does It, Riverside 363, *9363*
1 Bobby Timmons Trio in Person, Riverside 391, *9391*
2 Sweet and Soulful Sounds, Riverside 422, *9422*
2 Born to Be Blue, Riverside 468, *9468*

Cal Tjader[191]
2 Tjader Plays Tjazz, Fantasy 3211 or Fantasy 3278
1 The Cal Tjader–Stan Getz Sextet, Fantasy 3266, *8005*

Mel Torme, see p. 118.

Toshiko, see Toshiko Akiyoshi.

Cy Touff
1 Doorway to Dixie, Argo 606 (w/ M. Mole; one side each)
1 Touff Assignment, Argo 641, *641*
2 Keester Parade, Pacific Jazz 42 (reissue of Pacific Jazz 410)
2 Havin' a Ball (w/R. Kamuca, H. Edison), Pacific Jazz 410
2 His Octet and Quintet, Pacific Jazz 1211 (reissue of Pacific Jazz 410)

Nick Travis
3 The Panic is On, RCA 1010

Lennie Tristano
2 Lee Wiley Sings/Lennie Tristano Plays (one side each), Allegro-Elite 4049 (10")
4 Lennie Tristano, Atlantic 1224
4 The New Tristano, Atlantic 1357
3 Holiday in Piano (w/A. Ross; one side each), EmArcy 26029 (10")

---
[188] See also *Harry Arnold*.
[189] See also *Harry Arnold*.
[190] See also *John Jenkins*.
[191] See also *Anita O'Day*.

JAZZ RECORDINGS

Bobby Troup, see p. 118.

Joe Turner, see p. 74.

Stanley Turrentine
- 3 Look Out!, Blue Note 4039
- 2 Blue Hour (w/Three Sounds), Blue Note 4057, *84057*
- 2 Up at Minton's Vol. 1, Blue Note 4069, *84069*
- 2 Up at Minton's Vol. 2, Blue Note 4070, 84070
- 1 That's Where It's At, Blue Note 4096, *84096*
- 1 The Soul of Stanley Turrentine, Sunset 5255 (reissue of Blue Note 4039)
- 4 Stan the Man, Time 52086, *2086*

Tommy Turrentine
- 4 Tommy Turrentine, Time 70008

Richard Twardzik
- 4 The Last Set, Pacific Jazz 37 (includes Twardzik side of Pacific Jazz 1212 plus 2 additional titles)
- 4 Russ Freeman/Richard Twardzik Trio (one side each), Pacific Jazz 1212

Phil Urso
- 1 The Philosophy of Urso, Savoy 12056

George Van Eps
- 3 Mellow Guitar, Columbia 929

Sarah Vaughan[192]
- 2 After Hours, Columbia 660
- 2 Sarah Vaughan in Hi-Fi, Columbia 745
- 2 Linger Awhile, Columbia 914
- 2 Sarah Vaughan, EmArcy 36004
- 2 Sarah Vaughan in the Land of Hi-Fi, EmArcy 36058
- 2 Sassy, EmArcy 36089
- 2 Swingin' Easy, EmArcy 36109
- 1 Sarah Vaughan, Lion 70052
- 3 Great Songs From Hit Shows, Mercury 2-100 (2 LPs)
- 3 Sarah Vaughan Sings George Gershwin, Mercury 2-101 (2 LPs)
- 2 Sarah Vaughan at the Blue Note, Mercury 20094, *60020*
- 2 Wonderful Sarah, Mercury 20219
- 2 In a Romantic Mood, Mercury 20223
- 3 Sarah Vaughan and Billy Eckstine Sing the Best of Irving Berlin, Mercury *20316*, *60002*
- 3 Sarah Vaughan at Mr. Kelly's, Mercury 20326
- 2 Sarah Vaughan at the London House, Mercury 20383, *60020*
- 3 Sassy Swings the Tivoli, Mercury 20831, *60831*
- 5 Sarah Vaughan Sings, MGM 544 (10")
- 5 My Kinda Love, MGM 3274
- 2 After Hours, Roulette 52070, *52070*
- 3 Sarah + 2, Roulette 52118, *52118*

Al Vega
- 1 Al Vega Trio, Prestige 156 (10")

Charlie Ventura
- 3 The New Charlie Ventura in Hi-Fi, Baton 1202
- 3 Here's Charlie, Brunswick 54025
- 2 Open House, Coral 56067 (10")
- 3 Stomping With the Sax, Crystalette 5000 (10")
- 3 A Charlie Ventura Concert, Decca 8046

- 1 Jumping With Ventura, EmArcy 36015
- 3 Charlie Ventura Septet, Imperial 3002 (10")
- 3 Adventure With Charlie, King 543
- 3 An Evening with Charlie Ventura and Mary Ann McCall, Norgran 20 (10")
- 3 Charlie Ventura and His Orchestra, Norgran 1013
- 3 Carnegie Hall Concert, Norgran 1041 or Verve 8132)
- 3 An Evening With Mary Ann McCall and Charlie Ventura, Norgran 1053 or Verve 8143 (partial reissue of Norgran 1013 and Norgran 20)
- 3 In a Jazz Mood, Norgran 1073 or Verve 8163
- 3 Blue Saxophone, Norgran 1075 or Verve 8165
- 3 High on an Open Mike, RCA 1135
- 1 The Crazy Rhythms of Charlie Kennedy and Charlie Ventura (one side each), Regent 6047
- 2 East of Suez, Regent 6064
- 1 Charlie Ventura Plays Hi-Fi Jazz, Tops 1528

Joe Venuti
- 1 Joe Venuti Plays Gershwin, Golden Crest 3100
- 1 Joe Venuti Plays Jerome Kern, Golden Crest 3101
- 3 Fiddle on Fire, Grand Award 351

Millie Vernon, see p. 118.

Leroy Vinnegar
- 2 Leroy Walks!, Contemporary 3542, *7003*
- 2 Leroy Walks Again!, Contemporary 3608, *7608*

Eddie "Cleanhead" Vinson
- 2 Cleanhead's Back in Town, Aamco 312 (reissue of Bethlehem 5005)
- 3 Cleanhead's Back in Town, Bethlehem 5005
- 3 Battle of the Blues, Vol. 3 (w/J. Witherspoon; one side each), King 634
- 3 Back Door Blues, Riverside 3502, *93502*

Al Viola
- 2 Solo Guitar, Mode 121

Mal Waldron[193]
- 2 Left Alone, Bethlehem 6045
- 5 Impressions, New Jazz 8242
- 3 The Quest (w/E. Dolphy), New Jazz 8269
- 3 Reflections in Modern Jazz, Powertree 1003
- 5 Mal 1, Prestige 7090
- 5 Mal 2, Prestige 7111
- 5 Mal 3, Prestige/New Jazz 8201
- 5 Mal 4, Prestige/New Jazz 8208
- 3 The Dealers (w/J. Coltrane), Status 8316

T-Bone Walker, see p. 75.

Fats Waller
- 2 Fats Waller Plays and Sings, RCA 1001
- 3 Fats Waller Favorites, RCA 14 (10")
- 3 Swingin' the Organ, RCA 3040 (10")
- 4 "Fats", RCA 6001 (2 LP boxed set)
- 2 The Real Fats Waller, RCA Camden 473
- 1 '34/'35, RCA Vintage 516
- 1 Valentine Stomp, RCA Vintage 525
- 1 Smashing Thirds, RCA Vintage 550
- 1 African Ripples, RCA Vintage 562
- 2 Young Fats Waller, Riverside 103

---

[192] See also *Charlie Parker*.

[193] See also *Dizzy Gillespie*.

2 The Amazing Mr. Waller, Riverside 109
4 Young Fats Waller, "X" 3035 (10")

George Wallington
3 Knight Music, Atlantic 1275, *1275*
5 George Wallington Showcase, Blue Note 5045 (10")
5 The Prestidigitator, East-West 4004
2 Swingin' in Sweden, EmArcy 36121 (w/G. Wallington; one side each)
5 The New York Scene, New Jazz 8207
5 Workshop of the George Wallington Trio, Norgran 24 (10")
4 George Wallington With Strings, Norgran 1010
4 George Wallington Trio, Prestige 136 (10")
4 George Wallington Trio, Vol. 2, Prestige 158 (10")
5 Jazz For the Carriage Trade, Prestige 7032
5 George Wallington Quintet at the Bohemia, Progressive 1001
5 George Wallington Trio, Progressive 3001 (10")
2 George Wallington, Savoy, 12081
3 Jazz at Hotchkiss, Savoy 12122
4 Variations, Verve 2017 (reissue of Norgran 1010)

Wilbur Ware
1 The Chicago Cookers, Jazzland 12 (reissue of Riverside 252)
2 The Chicago Sound (w/J. Griffin), Riverside 252

Dinah Washington
2 Dinah Jams, EmArcy 36000
2 For Those in Love, EmArcy 36011
2 After Hours With Miss D, EmArcy 36028
2 Dinah, EmArcy 36065
2 Dinah Washington in the Land of Hi-Fi, EmArcy 36073
2 The Swingin' Miss "D," EmArcy 36104
2 Dinah Washington Sings Fats Waller, EmArcy 36119
2 Dinah Washington Sings Bessie Smith, EmArcy 36130
3 Dinah Washington Sings the Blues (w/E. Hines, B. Roche), Grand Award 318
1 Dinah Washington Sings the Blues, Grand Award *264* ("fake" stereo reissue of Grand Award 318)
1 Music for a First Love, Mercury 20119
1 Music for Late Hours, Mercury 20120
2 The Best in Blues, Mercury 20247
1 The Queen, Mercury 20439
1 Dinah '62, Roulette 25170, *25170*
1 Dinah Washington in Love, Roulette 25180, *25180*
1 Drinking Again, Roulette 25183, *25183*
1 Back to the Blues, Roulette 25189, *25189*

Doug Watkins
3 Soulnik (w/Y. Lateef), New Jazz 8238
5 Watkins at Large, Transition 20

Julius Watkins[194]
5 Julius Watkins Sextet, Blue Note 5053 (10")
5 Julius Watkins Sextet, Vol. 2, Blue Note 5064 (10")

Lu Watters
2 Lu Watters and his Yerba Buena Jass Band, Down Home 5 or Verve 1005
2 San Francisco Style Jazz, Riverside 213 (w/B. Helm; one side each)
1 Dixieland Jamboree, Verve 1008 (w/S. Pecora; one side each)

[194] See also *The Jazz Modes.*

Chuck Wayne[195]
2 Tapestry, Focus 333, *333*
1 Morning Mist, Prestige 7367, *7367*
4 Chuck Wayne Quintet, Progressive 3003 (10")
1 The Jazz Guitarist, Savoy 12077 (includes Progressive 3003)
3 String Fever, Vik 1098

Ben Webster[196]
4 The Kid and the Brute (w/I. Jacquet), Clef 680 or Verve 8065
2 Ben Webster-Sweets Edison, Columbia 1891, *8691*
4 The Big Tenor, EmArcy 26006 (10")
4 The Consummate Artistry of Ben Webster, Norgran 1001
4 Music For Loving, Norgran 1018
4 Music with Feeling, Norgran 1039A
3 The Warm Moods, Reprise 2001, *9200I*
4 Soulmates (w/J. Zawinul), Riverside 476, *9476*
3 Sophisticated Lady, Verve 2026 (reissue of Norgran 1018)
3 King of the Tenors, Verve 8020 (reissue of Norgran 1001)
3 Music with Feeling, Verve 8130 (reissue of Norgran 1039)
4 Soulville, Verve 8274
4 Ben Webster and Associates, Verve 8318, *6056 (68318)*
4 Coleman Hawkins Encounters Ben Webster, Verve 8327, *6066 (68327)*
3 Gerry Mulligan Meets Ben Webster, Verve 8343, *6104 (68343)*
3 Ben Webster Meets Oscar Peterson, Verve 8349, *6114 (68349)*
4 The Soul of Ben Webster, Verve 8359, *68359*
1 Gerry Mulligan Meets Ben Webster, Verve 8534, *68534* (reissue of Verve 8343)

George Wein
1 Wein, Women & Song (vocals), Atlantic 1221
2 Jazz at the Modern, Bethlehem 6050, *6050*
2 The Magic Horn (w/R. Braff), RCA 1332

Dickie Wells[197]
3 Bones for the King, Felsted 7006, *2006*
3 Trombone Four in Hand, Felsted 7009, *2009*

Dick Wellstood
2 The Stride Piano of Dick Wellstood, Riverside 2506 (10")
1 Uptown and Lowdown, Swingville 2026 (w/Cliff Jackson; one side each)

Frank Wess[198]
2 Frank Wess Quartet, Moodsville 8
1 Southern Comfort, Prestige 7231
1 Yo Ho, Poor You, Little Me, Prestige 7266, *7266*
1 North, South, East, Wess, Savoy 12072
1 No Count, Savoy 12078
1 Opus in Swing (w/K. Burrell) Savoy 12085
1 Trombones and Flute, Savoy 12086
1 Jazz For Playboys (k/K. Burrell), Savoy 12095
1 Opus the Blues, Savoy 12142

[195] See also *Tony Bennett,* p. 105.
[196] See also *Benny Carter, Coleman Hawkins, Richard "Groove" Holmes, Art Tatum, Jimmy Witherspoon.*
[197] See also *Tommy Gwaltney.*
[198] See also *Dorothy Ashby, Thad Jones.*

JAZZ RECORDINGS

Randy Weston
5 Randy, Bakton 1001, *1001*[199]
3 Highlife, Colpix 456, *456*
4 The Modern Art of Jazz, Dawn 1116
1 Zulu!, Jazzland 4 (reissue of Riverside 227)
2 Greenwich Village Jazz, Jazzland 13 (reissue of Riverside 232)
3 Piano A-La-Mode, Jubilee 1060
3 New Faces at Newport (w/L. Winchester; one side each) Metrojazz 1005, *1005*
3 Get Happy, Riverside 203
4 With These Hands (w/C. Payne), Riverside 214
2 Trio and Solo (w/A. Blakey), Riverside 227
3 Jazz a la Bohemia, Riverside 232
5 Cole Porter in a Modern Mood, Riverside 2508 (10")
3 Uhuru Afrika, Roulette 65001, *65001*
2 Little Niles, United Artists 4011, *5011*
2 Destry Rides Again, United Artists 4045, *5045*
3 Live at the Five Spot, United Artists 4066, *5066*

George Wettling
1 Dixieland in Hi-Fi, Harmony 7080
2 Jazz Duo (w/F. Signorelli), Kapp 1005
2 Jazz Trios, Kapp 1028
5 High Fidelity Rhythms, Weathers 5501

Paul Whiteman
2 Fiftieth Anniversary Album, Grand Award 901 (2 LPs)

Gerald Wiggins
1 The King and I, Challenge 604
3 Gerald Wiggins Trio, Dig 102
2 Gerald Wiggins Trio, Discovery 2003 (10")
2 Wiggin Out, Hi Fi 618
2 Reminiscin' With Wig, Motif 504
3 Around the World in 80 Days, Specialty 2101, *2101*
1 The Loveliness of You, Tampa 1
1 Gerald Wiggins Trio, Tampa 33 (reissue of Dig 102)

Bob Wilber[200]
3 Young Men with Horns, Riverside 2501 (10")

Joe Wilder
2 Joe Wilder, Columbia 1319, *8121*
2 The Pretty Sound, Columbia 1372, *8173*
2 Wilder 'N Wilder, Savoy 12063

Don Wilkerson
2 Preach Brother!, Blue Note 4107, *84107*
1 The Texas Twister, Riverside 332, *1186*

Ernie Wilkins[201]
1 Here Comes the Swingin' Mr. Wilkins, Everest 5077, *1007*
1 The Big New Band of the '60's, Everest 5104, *1104*
1 Wilkins-Clarke Septet, Savoy 12007
1 Flutes & Reeds, Savoy 12022

Cootie Williams
3 Around Midnight (w/W. Brown), Jaro 5001
1 The Big Challenge (w/R. Stewart), Jazztone 1268
2 The Solid Trumpet of Cootie Williams, Moodsville 27
3 Cootie Williams in Hi-Fi, RCA 1718, *1718*
3 Do Nothing Till You Hear From Me, Warwick 2027, *2027*

Joe Williams[202]
1 Jump For Joy, RCA 2713, *2713*
2 Joe Williams at Newport '63, RCA 2762, *2762*
1 Me and the Blues, RCA 2879, *2879*
2 Joe Williams Sings Everyday, Regent 6002
1 Together (w/H. Edison), Roulette 52069, *52069*
1 A Swingin' Night at Birdland, Roulette 52085, *52085*

John Williams
2 The John Williams Trio, EmArcy 36061

Mary Lou Williams[203]
3 Ladies in Jazz, Atlantic 1271 (w/B. Carroll; one side each)
3 Piano Contempo, Circle 412 (10")
2 Mary Lou Williams, Contemporary 2507 (10")
2 Mary Lou, EmArcy 26033 (10")
2 A Keyboard History, Jazztone 1206
4 Her Progressive Piano Stylings, King 295-85 (10")

Richard Williams
2 New Horn in Town, Candid 8003, *9003*

Tony Williams
2 Life Time, Blue Note 4180, *84180*
2 Spring, Blue Note 4216, *84216*
2 Emergency!, Polydor 25-3001 (2 LPs)

Claude Williamson[204]
2 Claude Williamson, Bethlehem 54
2 Round Midnight, Bethlehem 69
3 Kenton Presents Claude Williamson, Capitol 6502 (10")
3 Keys West, Capitol 6511
1 The Fabulous Trio, Contract 15001
1 Theatre Party, Contract 15003
1 Williamson Mulls the Mulligan Scene, Criterion 601

Stu Williamson
3 Stu Williamson Plays, Bethlehem 31
3 Stu Williamson, Bethlehem 55

Gerald Wilson
4 Big Band Modern, Audio Lab 1538
1 You Better Believe It (w/R. Holmes), Pacific Jazz 34, *34*
1 Moment of Truth, Pacific Jazz 61, *61*
1 Portraits, Pacific Jazz 80, *80*

Jack Wilson
3 Easterly Winds, Blue Note *84270*

Teddy Wilson[205]
2 Mr. Wilson, Columbia 748
1 Mr. Wilson and Mr. Gershwin, Columbia 1318, *8120*

[199] Weston produced and released a limited number of copies of this LP on his own Bakton label; it was later released as *African Cookbook* (Atlantic 1609).
[200] See also *Jim Chapin, The Six*.
[201] See also *Manny Albam*.
[202] See also *Count Basie*.
[203] See also *Dizzy Gillespie*.
[204] See also *Bob Cooper, Bud Shank*.
[205] See also *Gene Krupa, Lester Young*.

1 Gypsy, Columbia 1352, *8160*
1 And Then They Wrote, Columbia 1442, *8238*
3 Keyboard Kings, MGM 100 (10")
4 Running Wild, MGM 129 (10")
3 Pianorama, MGM 3093 (includes MGM 100 plus 4 titles by E. Heywood)
3 For Quiet Lovers, Norgran 1019 or Verve 2029
3 Intimate Listening, Verve 2011
3 I Got Rhythm, Verve 2073
2 The Teddy Wilson Trio/Gerry Mulligan Quartet with Bob Brookmeyer at Newport, Verve 8235
3 The Impeccable Mr. Wilson, Verve 8272
2 These Tunes Remind Me of You, Verve 8299
2 The Touch of Teddy Wilson, Verve 8330

Lem Winchester[206]
3 New Faces at Newport (w/R. Weston; one side each), Metrojazz 1005, *1005*
3 With Feeling, Moodsville 11
3 Winchester Special (w/B. Golson), New Jazz 8223
2 Lem's Beat (w/O. Nelson), New Jazz 8239
3 Another Opus, New Jazz 8244

Johnny Windhurst[207]
3 Jazz on Columbus Avenue, Transition 2

Kai Winding[208]
2 The Trombone Sound, Columbia 936
3 Trombone Panorama, Columbia 999
1 The Swingin' States, Columbia 1264, *8062*
1 Dance to the City Beat, Columbia 1329, *8136*
1 Modern Jazz Spectacular, Jazztone 1231 (reissue of Roost 408 plus 4 titles by S. Stitt)
3 Kai Winding All Stars, Roost 408 (10")

Jimmy Witherspoon
1 New Orleans Blues (w/W. DeParis), Atlantic 1266
2 Jimmy Witherspoon, Crown 5156
2 Jimmy Witherspoon at the Monterey Jazz Festival, Hi-Fi 421, *421*
2 Jimmy Witherspoon at the Renaissance, Hi-Fi 426, *426*
3 Battle of the Blues (w/E. Vinson; one side each), King 634
3 Goin' to Kansas City Blues, RCA 1639
1 Spoon, Reprise 2008, *92008*
1 Hey, Mrs. Jones, Reprise 6012, *96012*
3 Roots (w/B. Webster), Reprise 6057, *96057*
2 Singin' the Blues, World Pacific 1267

Phil Woods[209]
3 Rights of Swing, Candid 8016, *9016*
4 Warm Woods, Epic 3436
5 Phil Talks With Quill, Epic 3521, *554*
1 Phil Woods at the Montreux Jazz Festival, MGM *4695*
4 Pot Pie (w/J. Eardley), New Jazz 8291
5 Woodlore, Prestige 7018
5 Pairing Off, Prestige 7046
5 Youngbloods (w/D. Byrd), Prestige 7080
5 Phil and Quill With Prestige, Prestige 7115
3 Phil and Quill, RCA 1284
4 Sugan (w/R. Garland), Status 8304

[206] See also *Oliver Nelson.*
[207] See also *Barbara Lea*, p. 112.
[208] See also *J.J. Johnson–Kai Winding.*
[209] See also *Jim Chapin, Jimmy Raney, Z. Sims.*

Dempsey Wright
1 The Wright Approach, Andex 3006, *3006*

Leo Wright
2 Blues Shout, Atlantic 1358, *1358*
1 Suddenly the Blues, Atlantic 1393, *1393*

Nat Wright
3 The Biggest Voice in Jazz, Warwick 2040

Sol Yaged
1 It Might As Well Be Swing, Herald 0103
1 Jazz at the Metropole (w/C. Hawkins), Philips 200–002, 600–002

Jimmy Yancey
2 Pure Blues (w/Mama Yancey), Atlantic 1283
3 Yancey's Getaway, Riverside 124
3 Blues and Boogie, "X" 3000 (10")

Larry Young
3 Into Somethin', Blue Note 4187, *84187*
3 Unity, Blue Note 4221, *84221*
1 Testifying, New Jazz 8249
1 Young Blues, New Jazz 8264

Lester Young[210]
5 Battle of the Saxes (w/I. Jacquet; one side each), Aladdin 701 (10")
5 Lester Young Trio, Aladdin 705 (10")
5 Lester Young and his Tenor Sax, Aladdin 706 (10")
5 Lester Young and his Tenor Sax, Vol. 1, Aladdin 801
5 Lester Young and his Tenor Sax, Vol. 2, Aladdin 802
2 Lester Young and the Kansas City 5, Commodore 30014
3 Lester Leaps in (w/C. Basie), Epic 3107
3 Let's Go to Prez (w/ C. Basie), Epic 3168
2 The Immortal Lester Young, Vol. 1, Imperial 9181
2 The Immortal Lester Young, Vol. 2, Imperial 9187
4 Swinging, Intro 602
4 The Greatest, Intro 603
4 The President, Norgran 1005
4 Lester Young, Norgran 1022
4 Pres and Sweets (w/H. Edison), Norgran 1043
4 The President Plays With the Oscar Peterson Trio, Norgran 1054
4 Lester's Here, Nogran 1071
4 Pres, Norgran 1072
4 The Lester Young-Buddy Rich Trio, Norgran 1074
3 Lester Swings Again, Norgran 1093 or Verve 8181 (reissue of Norgran 1005)
1 Blue Lester, Savoy 12068
1 The Master's Touch, Savoy 12071
1 Jazz Immortal, Savoy 12155
3 Pres and Sweets (w/H. Edison), Verve 8134 (reissue of Norgran 1043)
3 The President Plays With the Oscar Peterson Trio, Verve 8144 (reissue of Norgran 1054)
3 Lester's Here, Verve 8161 (reissue of Norgran 1071)
3 Pres, Verve 8162 (reissue of Norgran 1072)
3 The Lester Young-Buddy Rich Trio, Verve 8164 (reissue of Norgran 1074)
3 It Don't Mean a Thing, Verve 8187 (reissue of Norgran 1022)
4 Pres and Teddy (Wilson), Verve 8205

[210] See also *Count Basie, Coleman Hawkins.*

4 Going For Myself (w/H. Edison), Verve 8298
3 The Lester Young Story, Verve 8308
4 Laughin' to Keep From Cryin' (w/R. Eldridge, H. Edison), Verve 8316, *6054 (68316)*
4 Lester Young in Paris, Verve 8378 (his last recording session)

Webster Young
4 For Lady, Prestige 7106

Joe Zawinul[211]
1 The Rise and Fall of the Third Stream, Vortex 2002

Denny Zeitlin[212]
3 Cathexis, Columbia 2182, *8982*
3 Carnival, Columbia 2340, *9140*
2 Shining Hour (Live at the Trident), Columbia 2463, *9263*
1 Zeitgeist, Columbia 2748, *9548*

Atilla Zoller
1 The Horizon Beyond, EmArcy 26013, *66013*

Bob Zurke
2 The Tom Cat of the Keys, RCA 1013

[211] See also *Ben Webster*.

[212] See also *Jeremy Steig*.

14. ANTHOLOGIES, VARIOUS ARTISTS

ABC-Paramount
3 The Fourmost Guitars (J. Raney, C. Wayne, J. Puma, D. Garcia), ABC-Paramount 109
4 Swingin' On the Vibories (S. Clark, K. Drew, L. Feather), ABC-Paramount 110
2 Know Your Jazz, ABC-Paramount 115

Andex
3 Mucho Calor (A. Pepper, B. Perkins, C. Candoli), Andex 3002

Atlantic
2 Dixieland at Jazz, Ltd. (S. Bechet, M. Spanier, M. Mole), Atlantic 1261
2 Jazz Piano International (D. Smith, R. Urtreger, D. Katz), Atlantic 1287
2 Historic Jazz Concert at Music Inn (J. Giuffre, T. Charles, P. Russell), Atlantic 1298
1 Newport Jazz Festival All Stars (P. Russell, B. Freeman, V. Dickenson), Atlantic 1331, *1331*
1 Jazz at Jazz, Ltd. (M. Marsala, D. Remington), Atlantic 1338

Bethlehem
2 Jazz at the Metropole (C. Shavers, R. Allen), Bethlehem 21
3 Jazz City Presents (C. Mariano, F. Rosolino, H. Geller), Bethlehem 80
3 Winner's Circle (J. Coltrane, A. Cohn, E. Costa, A. Farmer), Bethlehem 6024, *6024*
3 Trombone Bandstand (J.J. Johnson, K. Winding, J. Teagarden, U. Green, F. Rosolino), Bethlehem 6036

Blue Note
2 Mellow the Mood (B. Webster, B. Clayton), Blue Note 5001 (10″)
1 The Cool Britons (D. Rendell, H. Klein), Blue Note 5052 (10″)
4 Best From the West, Vol. 1 (C. Candoli, C. Mariano, H. Geller, S. Levey), Blue Note 5059 (10″)
4 Best From the West, Vol. 2 (same as above), Blue Note 5060 (10″)

Brunswick
3 Jazztime U.S.A., Vol. I (T. Gibbs, M. L. Williams, H. Silver, H. McGhee, A. Eager), Brunswick 54000
3 Jazztime U.S.A., Vol. II (T. Scott, S. Smith), Brunswick 54001
3 Jazztime U.S.A., Vol. III (T. Gibbs, J. Paris, Hot Lips Page), Brunswick 54002
3 Piano Jazz, Vol. 1 (M. Taylor, R. Nelson, Speckled Red), Brunswick 54014
3 Piano Jazz, Vol. 2 (Jelly Roll Morton, F. Melrose), Brunswick 54015
3 Concert Jazz (C. Hawkins, T. Scott, T. Gibbs)

Candid
3 The Jazz Life (C. Mingus, M. Roach, B. Little), Candid 8019, *9019*
3 Newport Rebels (C. Mingus, M. Roach, E. Dolphy, R. Eldridge), Candid 8022, *9022*

Capitol
2 Cool and Quiet (L. Tristano, B. DeFranco, B. Harris), Capitol 371
1 The History of Jazz, Vol. 1 (N'Orleans Origins), Capitol 793
1 The History of Jazz, Vol. 2 (The Turbulent Twenties), Capitol 794
1 The History of Jazz, Vol. 3 (Everybody Swings), Capitol 795
1 The History of Jazz, Vol. 4 (Enter the Cool), Capitol 796
2 Kansas City in the 30's (J. Lee, J. McShann, B. Webster), Capitol 1057

Clef
4 The Jazz Scene (C. Parker, C. Hawkins, L. Young, D. Ellington, B. Powell), Clef 674 or Verve 8060
3 Metronome All Stars 1956 (E. Fitzgerald, C. Basie, T. Farlow, C. Mingus, S. Chaloff), Clef 743 or Verve 8030

Colpix
2 Jazz Mission to Moscow (Z. Sims, P. Woods, E. Costa), Colpix 433, *433*
3 Eddie Costa Memorial Concert (C. Terry, C. Hawkins), Colpix 450, *450*

Columbia
4 Modern Jazz Concert (G. Schuller, G. Russell, B. Evans, C. Mingus), Columbia 127
3 Outstanding Jazz Compositions of the 20th Century (includes material from Columbia 127 and Columbia 941), Columbia C2L 31, *C2S 831* (2 LPs)
3 One World Jazz (B. Webster, M. Solal, J.J. Johnson), Columbia 162, *314*
1 Chicago Style Jazz (E. Condon, B. Freeman, M. Mole), Columbia 632
2 Upright and Lowdown (P. Johnson, A. Ammons, J. Turner), Columbia 685
3 What's New (T. Macero, B. Prince), Columbia 842

180

ANTHOLOGIES, VARIOUS ARTISTS

3 Music For Brass (G. Schuller, J.J. Johnson, J. Lewis), Columbia 941
3 Something New, Something Blue (M. Albam, T. Macero, T. Charles, B. Russo), Columbia 1388, *8183*
2 New Jazz Sound of Showboat (B. Brookmeyer, P. Woods, Guitar Choir), Columbia 1419, *8216*
2 Swinging Guys and Dolls (Manhattan Jazz Stars: T. Charles, P. Woods, Z. Sims), Columbia 1426, *8223*

Coral
4 East Coast Jazz Scene (C. Hawkins, T. Fruscella), Coral 57035

Counterpoint
4 Saturday Night Swing Session (F. Navarro, B. Harris, R. Eldridge), Counterpoint 549 (reissue of Esoteric 2 and Esoteric 3

Dawn
1 Critics' Choice (sampler), Dawn 1123
4 Tenors Anyone? (W. Gray, S. Getz, A. Haig), Dawn 1126

Debut
5 Jazz at Massey Hall, Vol. 1 (C. Parker, D. Gillespie, B. Powell, M. Roach, C. Mingus), Debut 2 (10")
5 Jazz at Massey Hall, Vol. 3 (same as above), Debut 4 (10")
5 Jazz Workshop—Trombone Rapport, Vol. 1 (J.J. Johnson, K. Winding, B. Green, W. Dennis), Debut 5 (10")
5 Jazz Workshop—Trombone Rapport, Vol. 2 (same as Debut 5), Debut 14 (10")
5 The Quintet, Debut 124 (includes Debut 2 and Debut 4)
4 4 Trombones (same as above), Debut 126
3 Autobiography in Jazz (sampler), Debut 198

Decca
3 The Encyclopedia of Jazz on Records, Decca DXF 140 (4 LP boxed set)
1 Gems of Jazz (A. Hodes, J. McPartland), Decca 8043
3 Kansas City Jazz (C. Basie, A. Kirk, E. Durham), Decca 8044
3 Jazz Studio One (J. Newman, B. Green, F. Foster, P. Quinichette), Decca 8058
1 New Orleans Jazz (L. Armstrong, J. Dodds, R. Allen), Decca 8283
1 Jazz of the Twenties, Decca 8398
1 Jazz of the Thirties, Decca 8399
1 Jazz of the Forties, Decca 8400
1 Jazz of the Fifties, Decca 8401
1 Kansas City Piano (C. Basie, J. McShann, M. L. Williams, P. Johnson), Decca 9226

Dial
5 Mr. Saxophone (C. Parker, J. Moody, S. Chaloff, D. Gordon), Dial 211 (10")
5 Night Music (H. McGhee, D. Marmarosa, H. Jones), Dial 217 (10")

Elektra
3 4 French Horns (J. Watkins, D. Amram), Elektra 134

EmArcy
1 Jazz of Two Decades (sampler), EmArcy DEM-2

NOTE: Decca 8398-8401 are single volume issues of Decca DXF 140

2 Jam Session (C. Brown, M. Roach, M. Ferguson, H. Geller, D. Washington), EmArcy 36002
3 The Advance Guard of the '40's, EmArcy 36016
2 Alto Altitude, EmArcy 36018
2 Battle of the Saxes, EmArcy 36023
2 Boning Up On Bones, EmArcy 36038
2 Best Coast Jazz (C. Brown, H. Geller, M. Roach), EmArcy 36039
2 The Jazz Greats, Vol. 1, EmArcy 36048
2 The Jazz Greats, Vol. 2 (The Piano Players), EmArcy 36049
2 The Jazz Greats, Vol. 3 (Reeds, Part 1), EmArcy 36050.
2 The Jazz Greats, Vol. 3 (Reeds, Part 2), EmArcy 36051
2 The Jazz Greats, Vol. 4 (Folk Blues), EmArcy 36052
2 The Jazz Greats, Vol. 5 (Brass), EmArcy 36053
2 The Jazz Greats, Vol. 6 (Modern Swedes), EmArcy 36054
2 The Jazz Greats, Vol. 7 (Dixieland), EmArcy 36055
2 The Jazz Greats, Vol. 8 (Drum Role), EmArcy 36071
1 The Young Ones of Jazz (sampler), EmArcy 36085
2 The Jazz School (C. Terry, P. Gonsalves, J. Gordon), EmArcy 36093

Epic
1 The Duke's Men (J. Hodges, R. Stewart, C. Williams, B. Bigard), Epic 3108
1 Ellington Sidekicks (same as Epic 3108), Epic 3237
2 Trumpeters Holiday (R. Eldridge, F. Newton, W. Manone, R. Allen), Epic 3252
3 The Rhythm Section (H. Jones, B. Galbraith, M. Hinton), Epic 3271
3 The Sax Section (A. Cohn, Z. Sims, B. Richman), Epic 3278
2 The Art of Jazz Piano (A. Tatum, J.P. Johnson, J. Sullivan, E. Hines), Epic 3295
3 Rhythm + 1 (C. Candoli, G. Quill, S. Powell, J. Cleveland), Epic 3297
1 Swedes From Jazzville (A. Persson, A. Domnerus), Epic 3309
3 After Hours Jazz (S. Shihab, T. Flannagan), Epic 3339

Esoteric
4 Jazz Off the Air, Vol. 1 (R. Eldridge, F. Phillips), Esoteric 2 (10")
4 Jazz Off the Air, Vol. 2 (F. Navarro, B. Harris), Esoteric 3 (10")

Fantasy
3 Modern Music From San Francisco (J. Dodgian, S. Clark, V. Guaraldi), Fantasy 3213

Grand Award
4 Jazz Concert (C. Hawkins, B. Webster, G. Auld), Grand Award 316

Groove
2 The Cool Gabriels (N. Travis, C. Candoli, D. Sherman, B. Glow, E. Lawrence), Groove 1003
3 Trombone Scene (J. Knepper, J. Cleveland, F. Rehak, U. Green), Groove 1087

Harmony
2 Metronome All Stars (L. Tristano, L. Konitz, S. Chaloff, D. Gillespie, S. Getz), Harmony 7044

Jazztone
3 Combo Jazz (S. Chaloff, B. Harris, S. Berman, C. Hawkins, B. Clayton), Jazztone 1221

Kapp
4 Modern Jazz Gallery (W. Marsh (4 titles), M. Flory, M. Paich, R. Garcia), Kapp 5001 (2 LPs)

Liberty
2 Escapade Reviews the Jazz Scene (interviews w/B. Troup, J. Otis, J. Teagarden, others), Liberty 9005

Metrojazz
3 Keeping Up With the Joneses (Thad, Hank, Elvin, Eddie), Metrojazz 1003
3 The Seven Ages of Jazz (C. Hawkins, B. Holiday, D. Hyman, B. Clayton), Metrojazz 2-1009 (2 LPs)

MGM
1 Strictly From Dixie (B. Haggart, L. McGarity), MGM 3262
3 Hot vs. Cool (D. Gillespie, J. McPartland), MGM 3286
2 West Coast vs. East Coast (B. Collette, D. Fagerquist, T. Jones, F. Wess), MGM 3390
3 Cool Canaries (G. Shearing, B. Eckstine, T. King), MGM 3393
3 Cats vs. Chicks (Men: C. Terry, U. Green, L. Thompson, H. Silver, T. Farlow; Women: N. Carson, C. Hale, T. Pollard, M. Osborne), MGM 3614

Mode
2 A Jazz Band Ball, 1st Set (M. Paich, J. Sheldon, S. Williamson), Mode 110
2 A Jazz Band Ball, 2nd Set (T. Gibbs, V. Feldman, L. Levy), Mode 123
4 Leonard Feather Presents Bop (P. Woods, G. Wallington, T. Jones), Mode 127

New Jazz[213]
4 Coolin' (T. Charles, M. Waldron, J. Jenkins, I. Sulieman), New Jazz 8216
3 The Cats (T. Flanagan, J. Coltrane, I. Sulieman, K. Burrell), New Jazz 8217
3 Trumpet Giants (F. Navarro, M. Davis, D. Gillespie), New Jazz 8296

Norgran
4 Swing Guitars (T. Farlow, O. Moore, B. Kessel), Norgran 1033 or Verve 8124
3 Tenor Saxes, Norgran 1034 or Verve 8125
3 Alto Sax, Norgran 1035 or Verve 8126
3 Piano Interpretations, Norgran 1036 or Verve 8127
4 The Modern Jazz Society Presents a Concert of Contemporary Music (G. Schuller, J. Lewis, J.J. Johnson, L. Thompson, S. Getz), Norgran 1040 or Verve 8131
4 The Jazz Giants '56 (L. Young, R. Eldridge, V. Dickenson, T. Wilson), Norgran 1056 or Verve 8146
4 Midnight Jazz at Carnegie Hall, Norgran 3501 or Verve 8189-2 (2 LPs)

Pacific Jazz[214]
2 Jazz Swings Broadway (C. Hamilton, S. Williamson, B. Shank, B. Cooper), Pacific Jazz 404

[213] See also *Prestige*.
[214] Many of these LPs were also issued with World Pacific label.

1 Jazz West Coast, Vol. 1, Pacific Jazz 500
1 Jazz West Coast, Vol. 2, Pacific Jazz 501
1 The Blues, Vol. 1, Pacific Jazz 502
1 Solo Flight, Pacific Jazz 505
1 Pianists Galore!, Pacific Jazz 506
1 Jazz West Coast, Vol. 3, Pacific Jazz 507
1 The Hard Swing, Pacific Jazz 508
1 The Blues, Vol. 2 (Have Blues Will Travel), Pacific Jazz 509
1 Jazz West Coast, Vol. 4, Pacific Jazz 510 (World Pacific *1009*)
1 Jazz West Coast, Vol. 5, Pacific Jazz 511
1 The Blues, Vol. 3 (Blowin' the Blues), Pacific Jazz 512 (World Pacific *1029*)
2 Grand Encounter: 2° East/3° West (J. Lewis, C. Hamilton, J. Hall, B. Perkins, P. Heath), Pacific Jazz 1217

Period
4 The Jones Boys (Quincy, Thad, Reunald, Eddie, Jimmy, Jo), Period 1210
4 The Birdlanders, Vol. 1 (O. Pettiford, T. Farlow, A. Cohn), Period 1211
4 The Birdlanders, Vol. 2 (same as Period 1211), Period 1212
4 The Birdlanders, Vol. 3 (M. Jackson, J.J. Johnson, D. Jordan), Period 1213

Playboy
2 The Playboy Jazz All Stars (1957), Playboy 1957 (2 LPs)
2 The Playboy Jazz All Stars (1958), Playboy 1958 (2 LPs)
5 The Playboy Jazz All Stars, Playboy 3, 3 (3 LPs boxed set)

Prestige
4 Conception (M. Davis, L. Konitz, S. Rollins, S. Getz), Prestige 7013
4 The Brothers (S. Getz, A. Cohn, Z. Sims, A. Eager, B. Moore), Prestige 7022
4 Trombone By 3 (J.J. Johnson, K. Winding, B. Green), Prestige 7023
5 3 Trumpets (D. Byrd, A. Farmer, I. Sulieman), Prestige 7029
4 J.J. Johnson-Kai Winding (8 titles)/Bennie Green (4 titles), Prestige 7030
4 All Night Long (D. Byrd, H. Mobley, M. Waldron), Prestige 7073
4 Tenor Conclave (H. Mobley, A. Cohn, J. Coltrane, Z. Sims), Prestige 7074
4 All Day Long (D. Byrd, F. Foster, K. Burrell), Prestige 7081
5 Olio (T. Jones, F. Wess, T. Charles, M, Waldron), Prestige 7084
5 Earthy (A. Farmer, H. McKusick, A. Cohn, M. Waldron, K. Burrell), Prestige 7102
4 Interplay For Two Trumpets and Two Saxophones (I. Sulieman, W. Young, J. Coltrane, B. Jaspar), Prestige 7112
5 4 Altos (P. Woods, G. Quill, S. Shihab, H. Stein), Prestige 7116
4 After Hours (T. Jones, K. Burrell, F. Wess, M. Waldron), Prestige 7118
4 Wheelin' and Dealin' (F. Wess, J. Coltrane, P. Quinichette), Prestige 7131
3 Outskirts of Town (Prestige Blues Swingers: A. Farmer, J. Richardson, J. Forrest, P. Adams, R. Bryant, T. Grimes), Prestige 7145

ANTHOLOGIES, VARIOUS ARTISTS

3 Very Saxy (C. Hawkins, A. Cobb, E. Davis, B. Tate), Prestige 7167
2 Soul Battle (O. Nelson, K. Curtis, J. Forrest), Prestige 7223
5 Roots (I. Sulieman, B. Evans, F. Rehak, C. Payne, J. Cleveland, P. Adams), Prestige/New Jazz 8202
5 Bird Feathers (P. Woods, J. McLean, H. McKusick), Prestige/New Jazz 8204

RCA

3 Basses Loaded (M. Hinton, W. Marshall, B. Ruther), RCA 1107
3 The Brothers (A. Cohn, B. Perkins, R. Kamuca), RCA 1162
3 Birdland Stars on Tour, Vol. 1 (P. Woods, K. Dorham, A. Cohn), RCA 1327
3 Birdland Stars on Tour, Vol. 2 (same as Vol. 1), RCA 1328
2 Mellow Moods of Jazz (B. Butterfield, U. Green, P. Hucko, H. McKusick), RCA 1365
1 String of Swingin' Pearls (B. Berigan, B. Goodman, E. Condon), RCA 1373
2 Son of Drum Suite (D. Lamond, C. Persip, A. Cohn), RCA 2312, 2312
2 Live at Newport Jazz Festival (B. Freeman, J.C. Higginbotham), RCA 3369, 3369
2 The Jazz Piano (live from Pittsburgh Jazz Festival w/D. Ellington, E. Hines, W. Smith, B. Taylor), RCA 3499, 3499
3 Tribute to Charlie Parker (J. McLean, J.J. Johnson, S. Stitt, H. McGhee), RCA 3783, 3783

RCA Camden

1 Great Jazz Pianists, RCA Camden 328
1 Great Jazz Reeds, RCA Camden 339
1 Great Jazz Brass, RCA Camden 383
2 Modern Jazz Piano: Four Views (L. Tristano, M. L. Williams, A. Tatum, E. Garner), RCA Camden 384
2 Metronome All Stars, RCA Camden 426
1 Dixieland and New Orleans Jazz, RCA Camden 446
2 Singin' the Blues, RCA Camden 588

RCA Vintage

2 The Be-Bop Era, RCA Vintage 519
1 The Panassie Sessions, RCA Vintage 542
1 Classic Jazz Piano Styles, RCA Vintage 543
2 Esquire's All-American Hot Jazz, RCA Vintage 544

Riverside

3 History of Classic Jazz, Riverside SDP 11 (5 LP set w/introductory essay by C.E. Smith)
2 Giants of Boogie-Woogie (A. Ammons, M.L. Lewis, P. Johnson), Riverside 106
1 The Golden Age of Ragtime, Riverside 110
1 Classic Jazz (Backgrounds and Ragtime), Riverside 112
1 Classic Jazz (Blues and New Orleans Style), Riverside 113
1 Classic Jazz (Boogie-Woogie and South Side Chicago), Riverside 114
1 Classic Jazz (Chicago Style and Harlem), Riverside 115
1 Classic Jazz (New York Style and New Orleans Revival), Riverside 116
1 New Orleans Legends (K. Ory, B. Johnson, K. Rena), Riverside 119
1 Great Blues Singers (B. Smith, M. Rainey, C. Hill, I. Cox, T. Smith), Riverside 121

NOTE: All yellow label original issues; see p. 128.

1 Classics of Ragtime (S. Joplin, J. Scott, T. Turpin), Riverside 126
1 On the Road Jazz (B. Beiderbecke, W. Manone), Riverside 127
2 The Birth of Big Band Jazz (F. Henderson, D. Ellington), Riverside 129
1 Kings of Classic Jazz, Riverside 131
1 Early and Rare, Riverside 134
2 Giants of Small Band Swing, Vol. 1 (T. Young, B. Bailey, B. Rich), Riverside 143
2 Giants of Small Band Swing, Vol. 2 (J.C. Higginbotham, J. Hodges, D. Wells), Riverside 145
2 Gospel, Blues and Street Songs (Rev. G. Davis, P. Anderson), Riverside 148
1 Gut Bucket Trombone (R. Palmer, I. Rodgers), Riverside 150
2 Blues For Tomorrow (S. Rollins, C. Hawkins, M. Lowe, B. Jaspar), Riverside 243
2 Jazz For Lovers (C. Hawkins, K. Dorham, E. Henry, K. Drew), Riverside 244
2 Riverside Drive (T. Monk, S. Rollins, C. Terry, K. Dorham), Riverside 267
2 8 Ways to Cole Porter (S. Rollins, Z. Sims), Riverside 272
2 Saxophone Revolt (J. Hodges, J. Griffin, B. Golson), Riverside 284
3 New Blue Horns (C. Baker, K. Dorham, C. Terry, B. Mitchell, N. Adderley), Riverside 294, 1134
1 New Orleans: The Living Legends, Riverside 356/357, 9356/9357 (2 LPs)
1 Chicago: The Living Legends, Riverside 389/390, 9389/9390 (2 LPs)
3 Jazz Version of "Kean" (B. Mitchell, C. Terry, J. Heath), Riverside 397, 9397
1 Jazz of the Roaring Twenties (R. Nichols, Dorsey Bros), Riverside 801
1 This Could Lead to Love (B. Lea, M. Lowe, B. Taylor), Riverside 808
1 The Compositions of Thelonious Monk, Riverside 3503, 93503
1 The Compositions of Miles Davis, Riverside 3504, 93504
1 The Compositions of Benny Golson, Riverside 3505, 93505
1 The Compositions of Charlie Parker, Riverside 3506, 93506
1 The Compositions of Duke Ellington, Vol. 1, Riverside 3507, 93507
1 The Compositions of Dizzy Gillespie, Riverside 3508, 93508
1 The Compositions of Horace Silver, Riverside 3509, 93509
1 The Compositions of Duke Ellington, Vol. 2, Riverside 3510, 93510
1 The Compositions of Tadd Dameron, Riverside 3511, 93511
1 The Compositions of Bobby Timmons, Riverside 3512, 93512
1 Great Jazz Artists Play Richard Rodgers, Riverside 3514, 93514
1 Great Jazz Artists Play Cole Porter, Riverside 3515, 93515
1 Great Jazz Artists Play Jerome Kern, Riverside 3516, 93516
1 Great Jazz Artists Play George Gershwin, Riverside 3517, 93517
1 Great Jazz Artists Play Harold Arlen, Riverside 3518, 93518
1 Great Jazz Artists Play Irving Berlin, Riverside 3519, 93519

Roulette

1 Dixiecats (R. Allen, T. Glenn, W. Smith, B. Richman, Z. Singleton), Roulette 25015
3 Monday Night at Birdland (L. Morgan, C. Fuller, B. Root, H. Mobley, R. Bryant), Roulette 52015, *52015*
3 Another Monday Night at Birdland (same as above), Roulette, 52022, *52022*

Savoy

1 Bohemia After Dark (C. Adderley, K. Clarke, D. Byrd, H. Silver), Savoy 12017
2 Montage (E. Bert, J. R. Monterose, D. Byrd, J. Mehegan), Savoy 12029
1 Jazz at Storyville (P. Russell, R. Braff), Savoy 12034
1 Jazz at Storyville (B. Davison, E. Hubble, F. Chase), Savoy 12035
1 Jazz at Storyville (P. Russell, R. Braff), Savoy 12041
2 The Jazz Keyboards (L. Tristano, M. McPartland, B. Scott, J. Bushkin), Savoy 12043
2 Top Brass (D. Byrd, R. Copeland, E. Royal, I. Sulieman, J. Wilder), Savoy 12044
1 Ringside at Condon's (B. Davison, E. Hall, E. Condon), Savoy 12055
1 The Jazz Message (H. Mobley, D. Byrd, J. LaPorta), Savoy 12064
2 Night People (S. Shihab, K. Clarke, R. Ball), Savoy 12073
1 Jazz Men Detroit (K. Burrell, P. Adams, T. Flanagan), Savoy 12083
1 Jazz Message #2 (H. Mobley, D. Byrd, B. Harris), Savoy 12092
2 Trumpets All Out (A. Farmer, C. Shavers, E. Berry, E. Royal, H. Baker), Savoy 12096
3 I Just Love Jazz Piano (H. Nichols, H. Hawes, J. Mehegan, P. Smith), Savoy 12100
2 The Things We Did Last Summer (S. Shihab, J. Jenkins, C. Jordan, P. Woods, B. Golson), Savoy 12112
2 Jazz For Playgirls (B. Harris, P. Woods, E. Costa), Savoy 12121
1 4 French Horns, Savoy 12173 (reissue of Elektra 134; see *Elektra*)
2 The Angry Tenors (B. Webster, I. Jacquet, I. Quebec), Savoy 14009

Specialty

5 Dizzy Atmosphere (L. Morgan, A. Grey, B. Mitchell, B. Root, W. Kelly), Specialty 5001

Storyville

4 Messin' Round in Montmartre (M.L. Williams, D. Byas, A. Combelle), Storyville 906
4 The Women in Jazz (L. Wiley, T. King, T. Akiyoshi, J. Cain), Storyville 916

Swingville

2 Rockin' In Rhythm (A. Sears, H. Jefferson, T. Jordan), Swingville 2010
1 At the Jazz Band Ball (D. Cheatham, E. Hall, V. Dickenson), Swingville 2031, *2031*
1 Darktown Strutters Ball (H. Autrey, D. Wells, B. Freeman), Swingville 2033, *2033*
1 Dixieland Hits (B. Morton, S. DeParis, K. Davern), Swingville 2040, *2040*

Transition

5 Jazz in Transition (C. Taylor, J. Coltrane, H. Silver), Transition 30

United Artists

4 Young Men From Memphis (B. Little, F. Strozier, P. Newborn, G. Coleman, L. Smith), United Artists 4029, *5029*

Verve[215]

1 A Potpourri of Jazz, Verve 2032
2 Here Come the Girls! (E. Fitzgerald, A. O'Day, T. Harper), Verve 2036
1 Verve Compendium of Jazz #1, Verve 8194
1 Verve Compendium of Jazz #2, Verve 8195
2 Here Come the Swinging Bands (C. Basie, L. Hampton, G. Krupa, W. Herman, D. Gillespie), Verve 8207
3 Tour De Force (D. Gillespie, R. Eldridge, H. Edison, O. Peterson), Verve 8212
3 Jazz at the Hollywood Bowl (L. Armstrong, E. Fitzgerald, A. Tatum, O. Peterson), Verve 8231-2 (2 LPs)
3 The Coleman Hawkins, Roy Eldridge, Pete Brown, Jo Jones All Stars at Newport, Verve 8240
3 Jazz Giants '58 (S. Getz, G. Mulligan, H. Edison, C. Peterson), Verve 8248

Vik

3 Trombone Scene (J. Knepper, J. Cleveland, F. Rehak, U. Green), Vik 1087
4 The Four Brothers Together Again (Z. Sims, S. Chaloff, A. Cohn, H. Steward), Vik 1096
3 Jazz Goes Broadway (A. Cohn, G. Quill, A. Farmer, Z. Sims, H. McKusick), Vik 1113

Warwick

4 The Soul of Jazz Percussion (B. Little, B. Evans, C. Fuller, P. Adams), Warwick 5003, *5003*

World Pacific, see Pacific Jazz.

[215] See also *Clef, Norgran.*